CHAPTER 1 A ROYAL SUMMONS

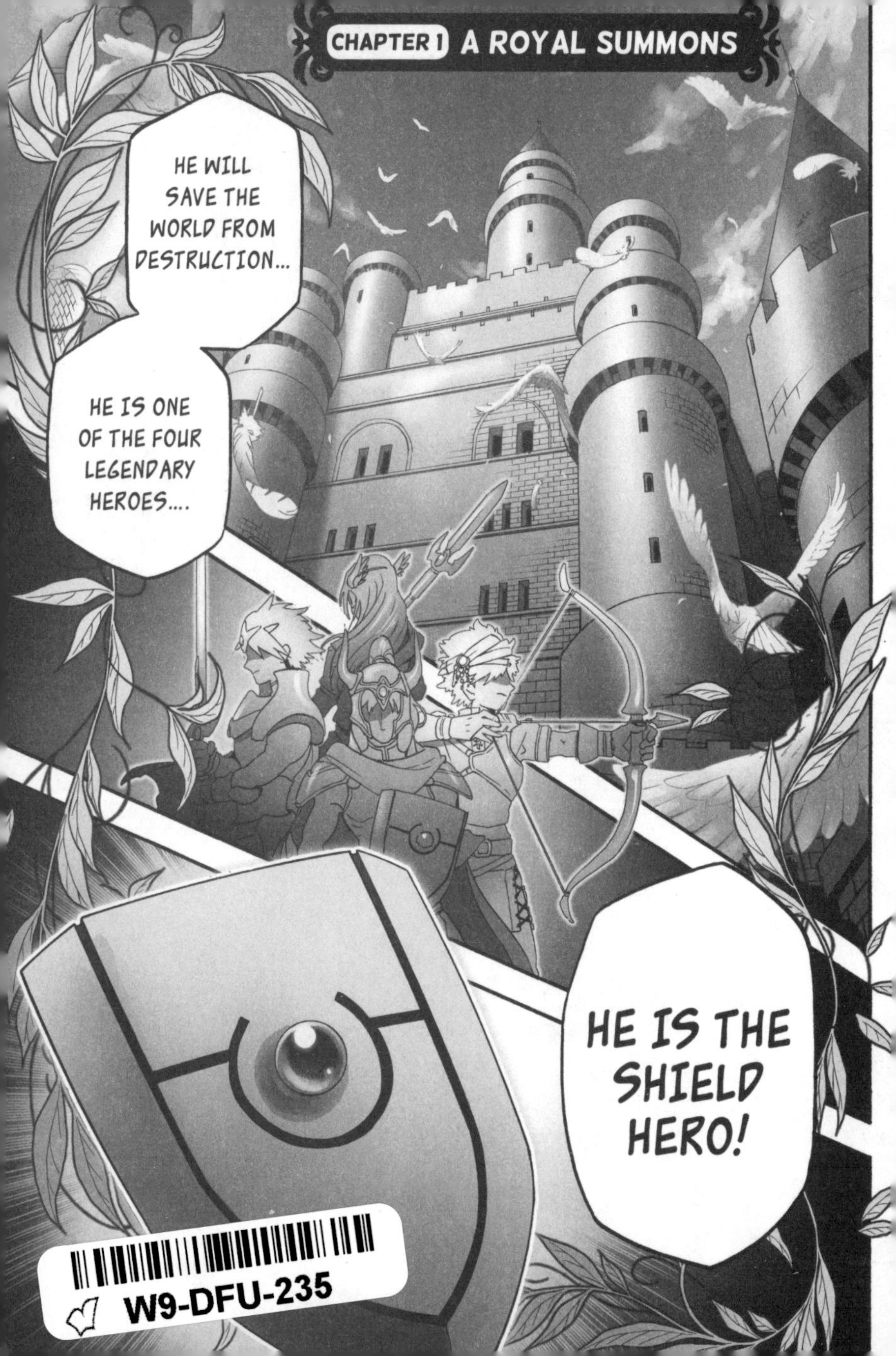
HE WILL SAVE THE WORLD FROM DESTRUCTION...
HE IS ONE OF THE FOUR LEGENDARY HEROES....
HE IS THE SHIELD HERO!

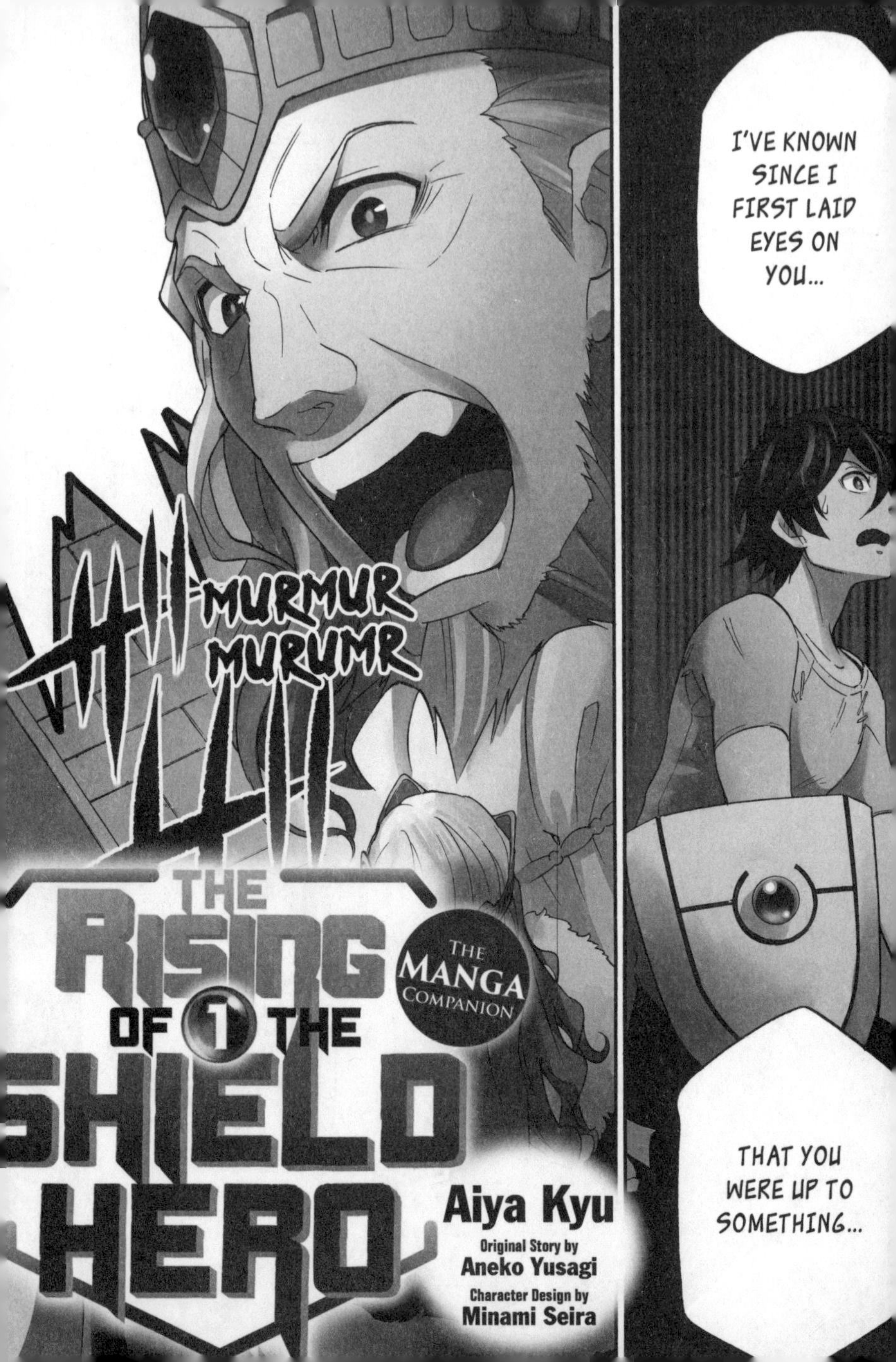
I'VE KNOWN SINCE I FIRST LAID EYES ON YOU...
THAT YOU WERE UP TO SOMETHING...
MURMUR MURUMR
THE RISING OF THE SHIELD HERO
1
THE MANGA COMPANION
Aiya Kyu
Original Story by
Aneko Yusagi
Character Design by
Minami Seira

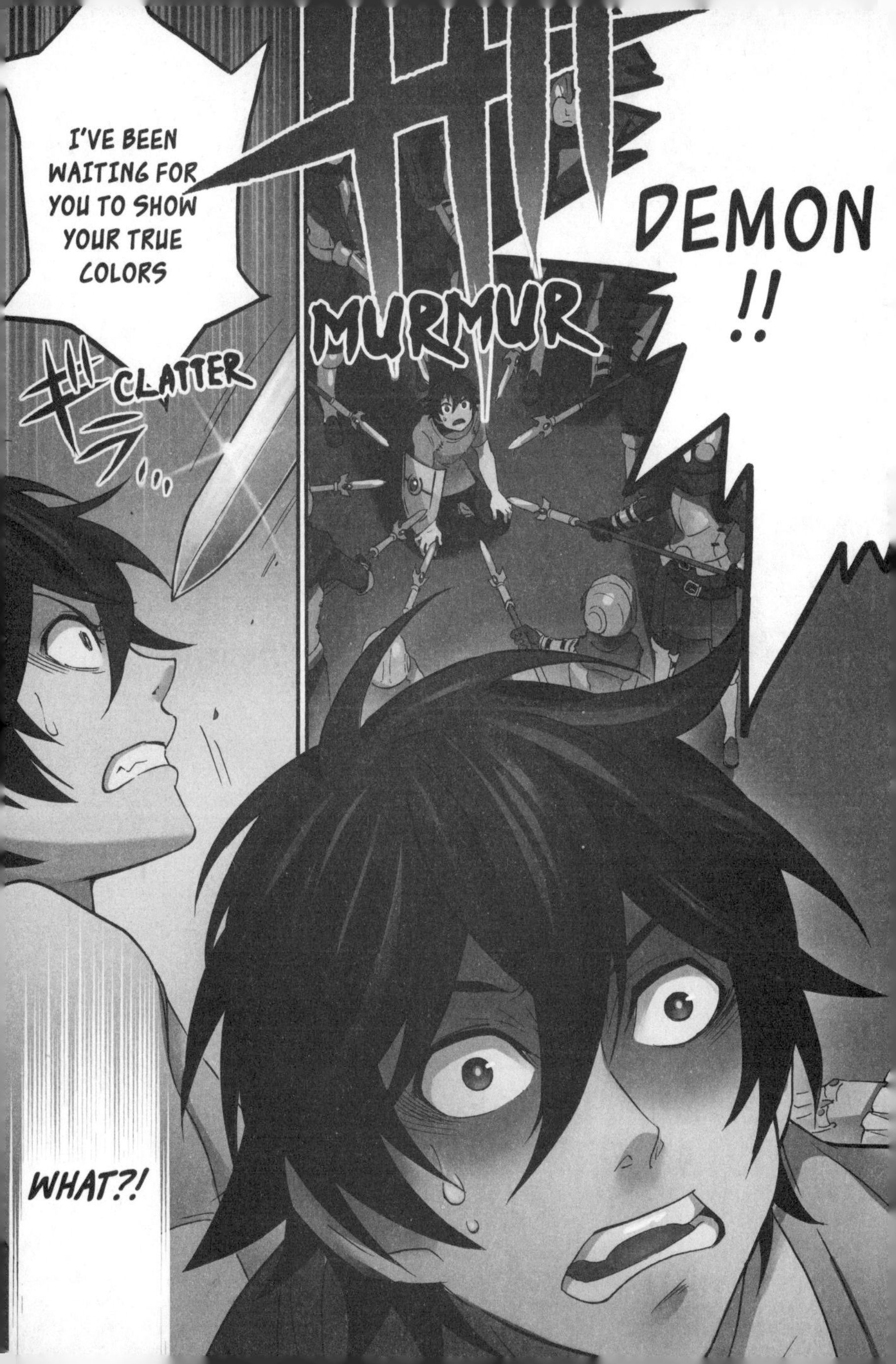
DEMON!!
MURMUR
I'VE BEEN WAITING FOR YOU TO SHOW YOUR TRUE COLORS
キラ…
CLATTER
WHAT?!

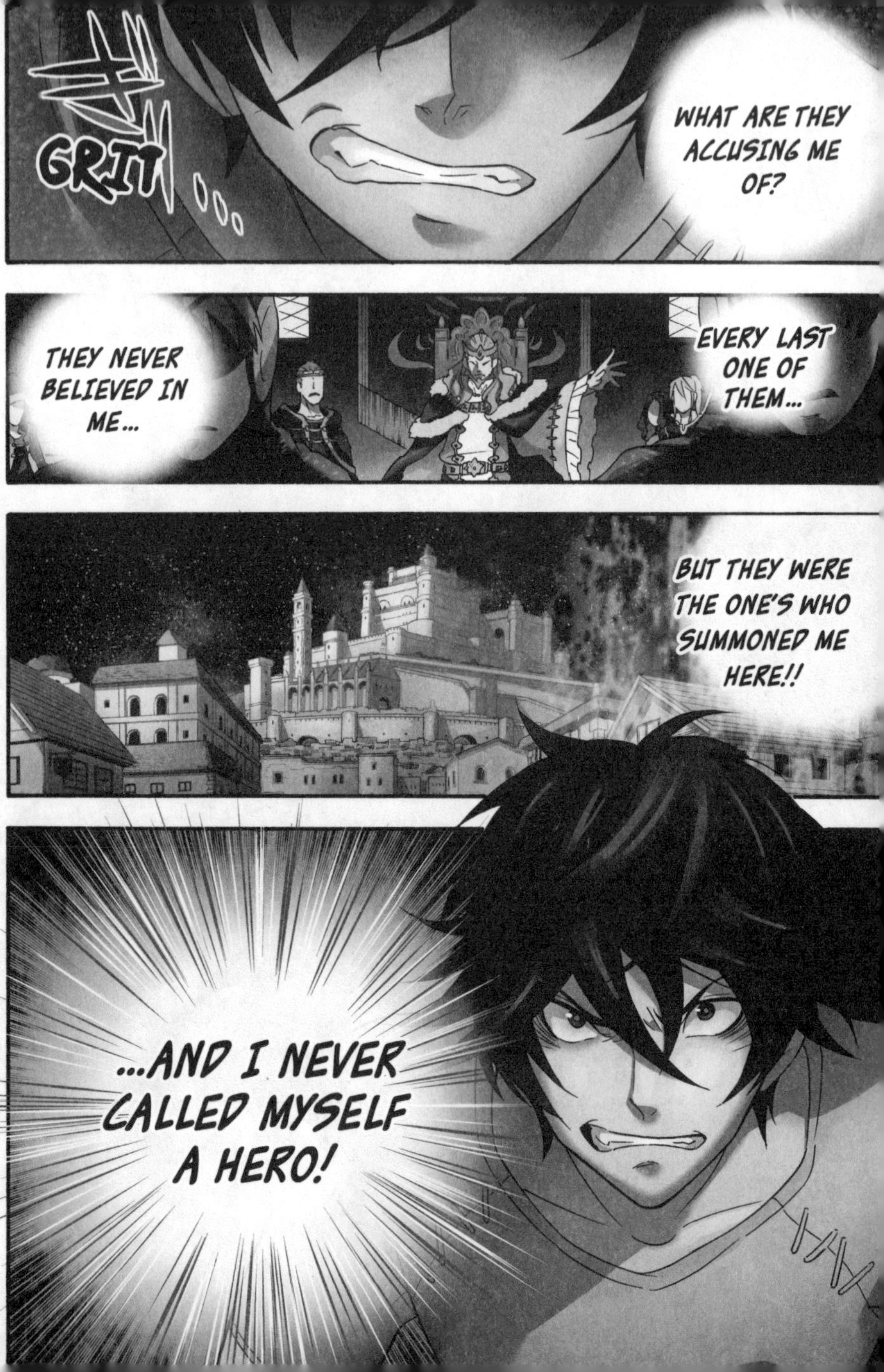
WHAT ARE THEY ACCUSING ME OF?
GRIT
EVERY LAST ONE OF THEM...
THEY NEVER BELIEVED IN ME...
BUT THEY WERE THE ONE'S WHO SUMMONED ME HERE!!
...AND I NEVER CALLED MYSELF A HERO!

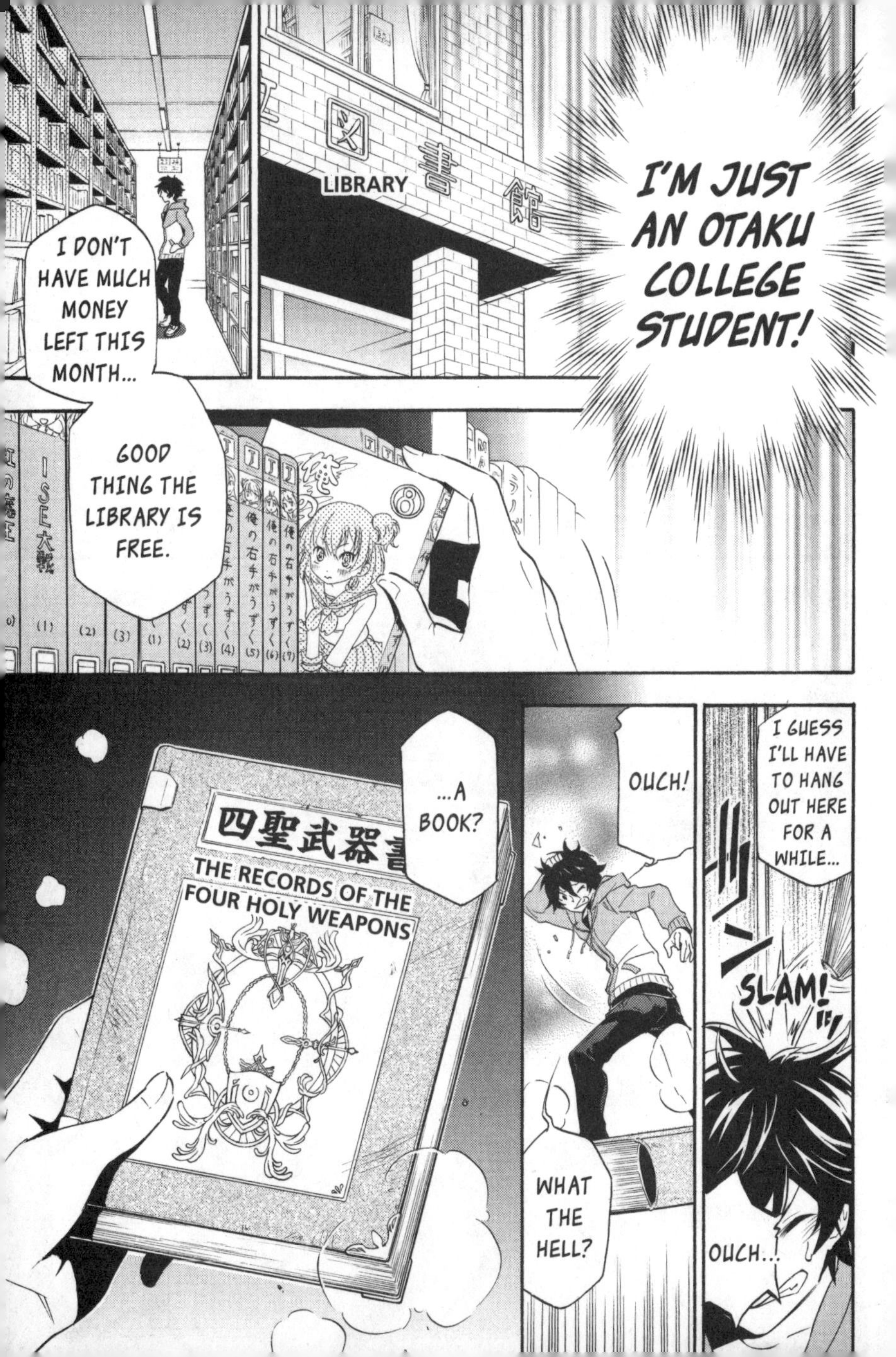
I'M JUST AN OTAKU COLLEGE STUDENT!
図書館
LIBRARY
I DON'T HAVE MUCH MONEY LEFT THIS MONTH...
GOOD THING THE LIBRARY IS FREE.
I GUESS I'LL HAVE TO HANG OUT HERE FOR A WHILE...
SLAM!
OUCH..!
OUCH!
WHAT THE HELL?
...A BOOK?
四聖武器書
THE RECORDS OF THE FOUR HOLY WEAPONS

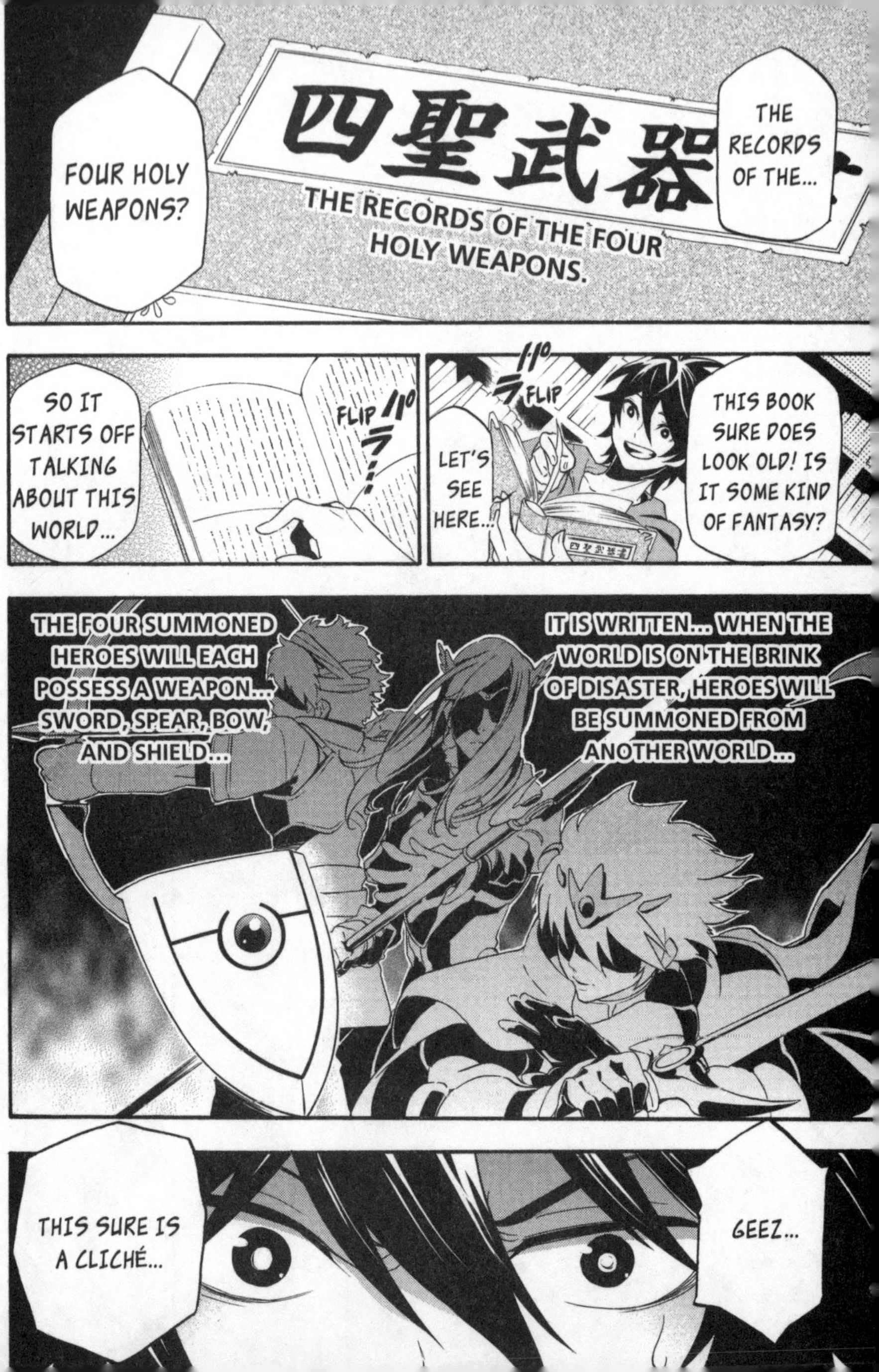
THE RECORDS OF THE...
四聖武器
THE RECORDS OF THE FOUR HOLY WEAPONS.
FOUR HOLY WEAPONS?
パラ FLIP
THIS BOOK SURE DOES LOOK OLD! IS IT SOME KIND OF FANTASY?
LET'S SEE HERE...
FLIP パラ...
SO IT STARTS OFF TALKING ABOUT THIS WORLD...
IT IS WRITTEN... WHEN THE WORLD IS ON THE BRINK OF DISASTER, HEROES WILL BE SUMMONED FROM ANOTHER WORLD...
THE FOUR SUMMONED HEROES WILL EACH POSSESS A WEAPON... SWORD, SPEAR, BOW, AND SHIELD...
GEEZ...
THIS SURE IS A CLICHÉ...

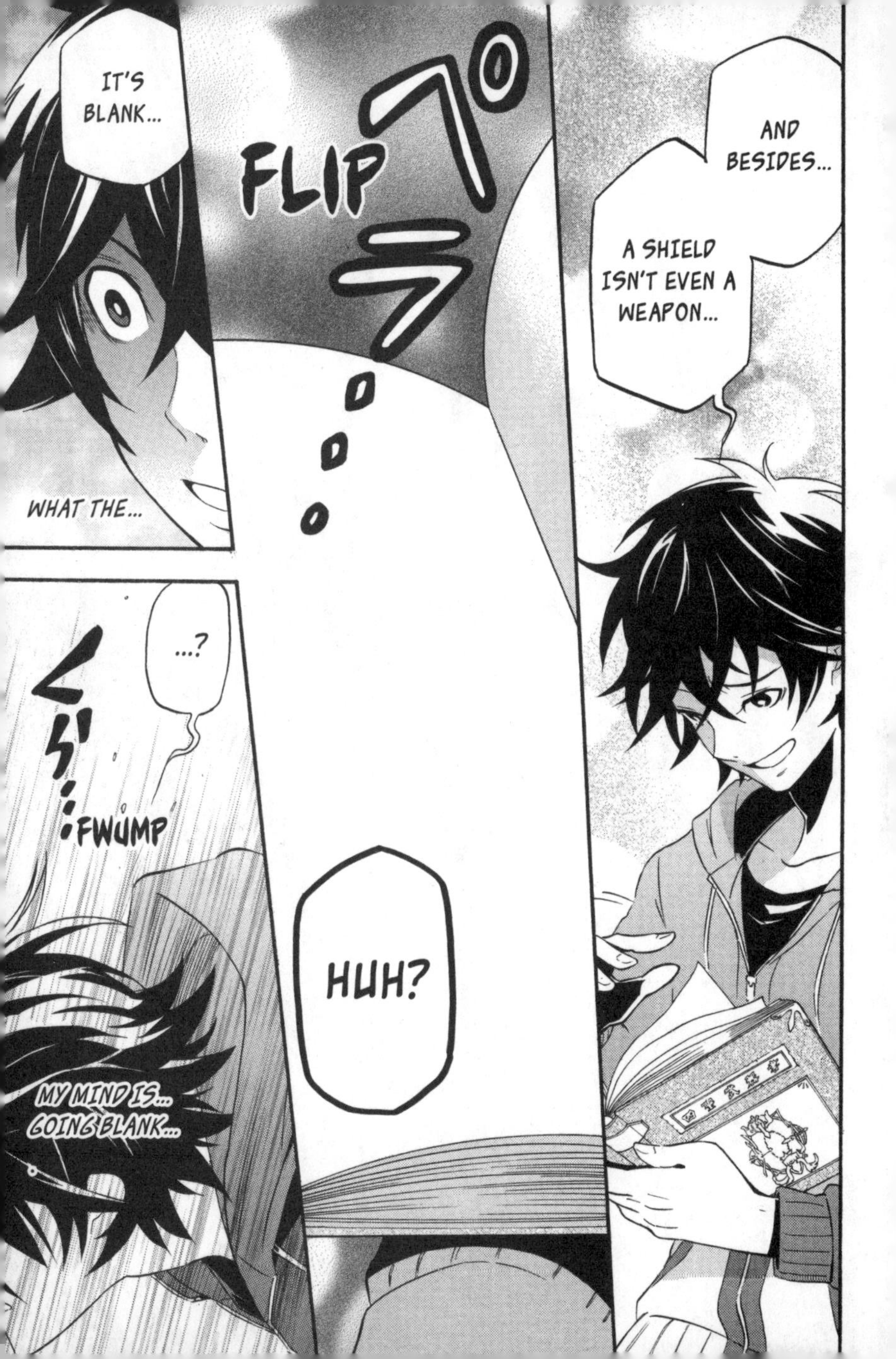
AND BESIDES...
A SHIELD ISN'T EVEN A WEAPON...
FLIP
HUH?
IT'S BLANK...
WHAT THE...
...?
FWUMP
MY MIND IS... GOING BLANK...

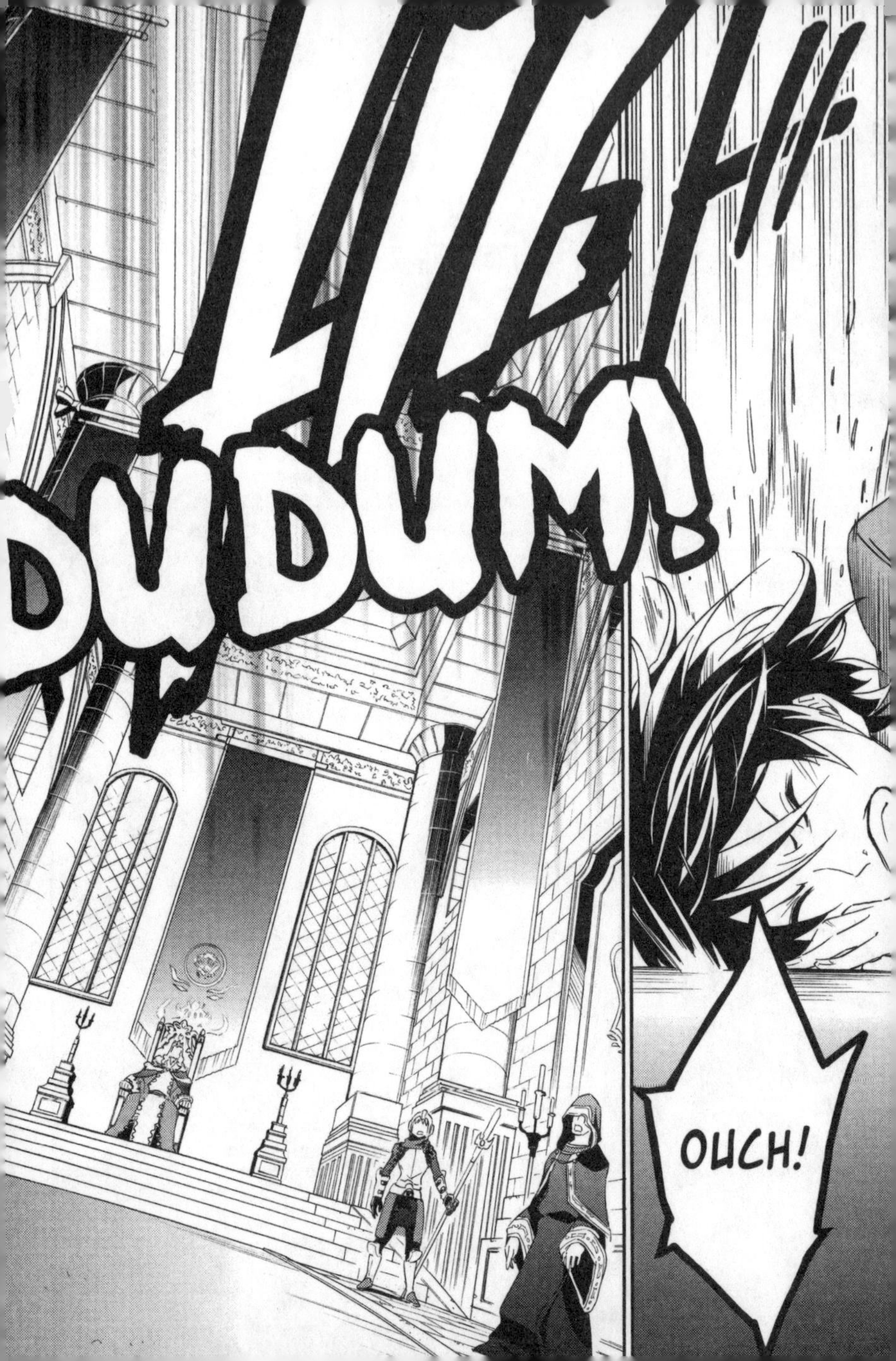
OUCH!
DUDUM!

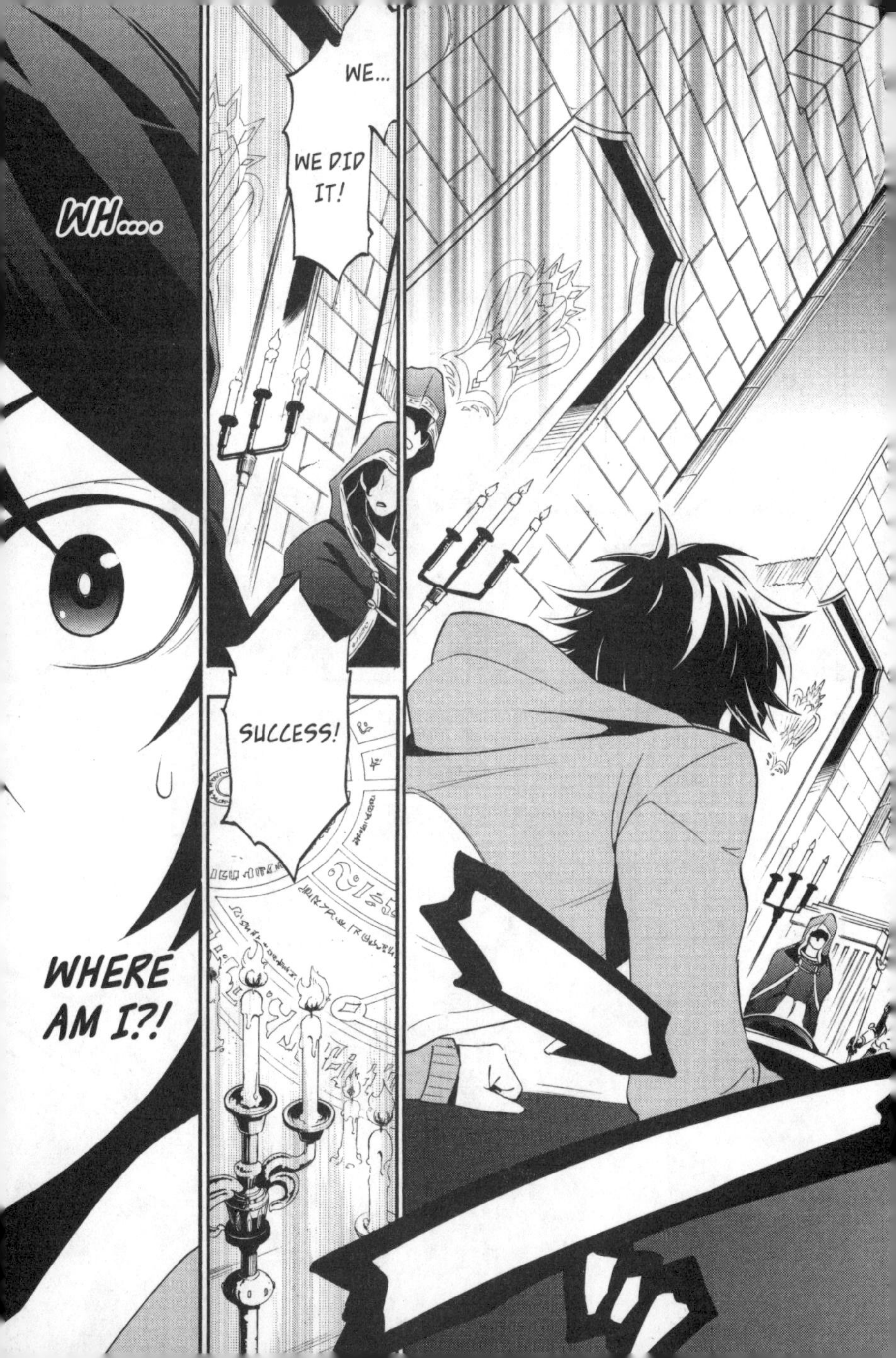
WE...
WE DID IT!
SUCCESS!
WH....
WHERE AM I?!

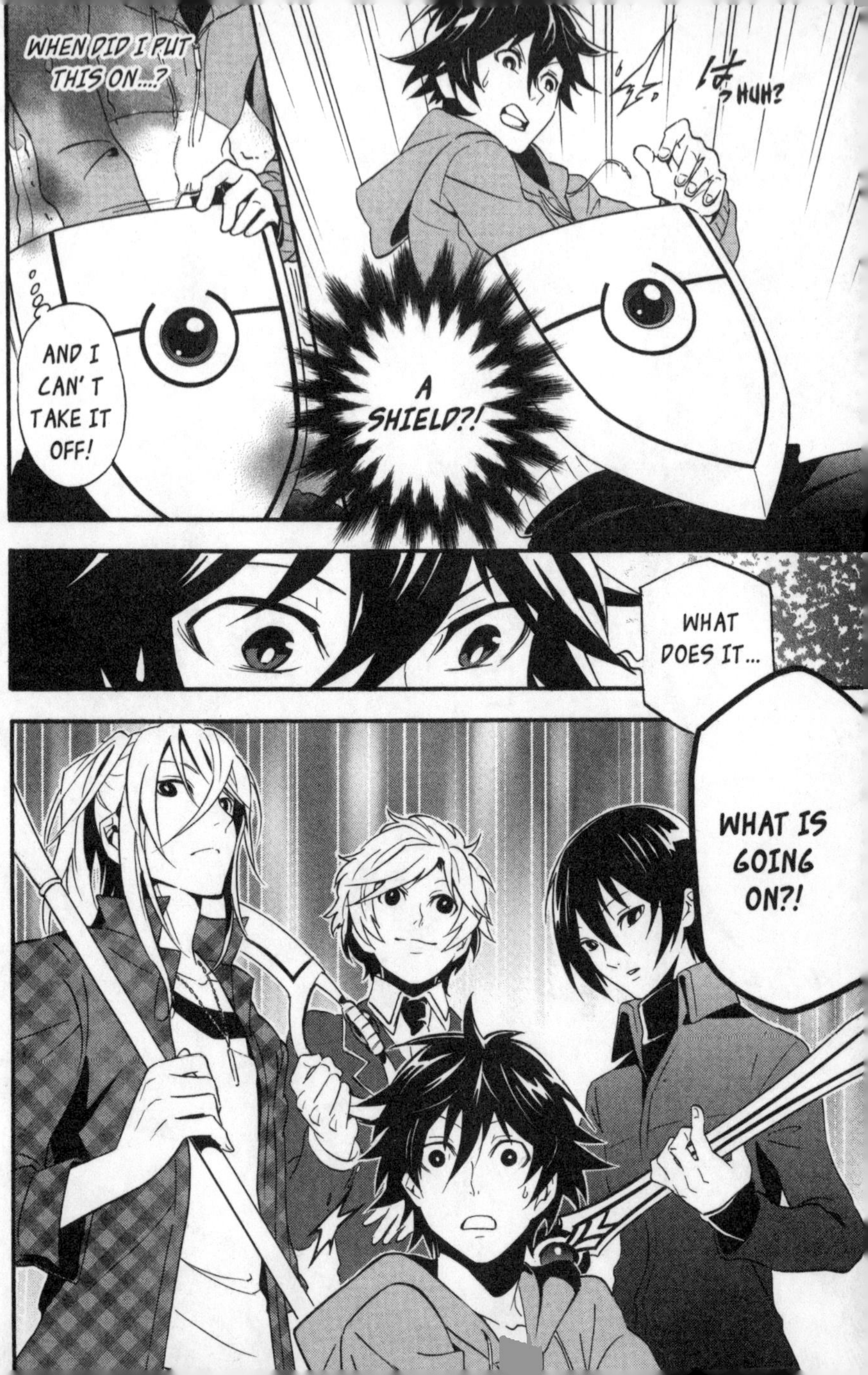

はっ HUH?
WHEN DID I PUT THIS ON...?
A SHIELD?!
AND I CAN'T TAKE IT OFF!
WHAT DOES IT...
WHAT IS GOING ON?!

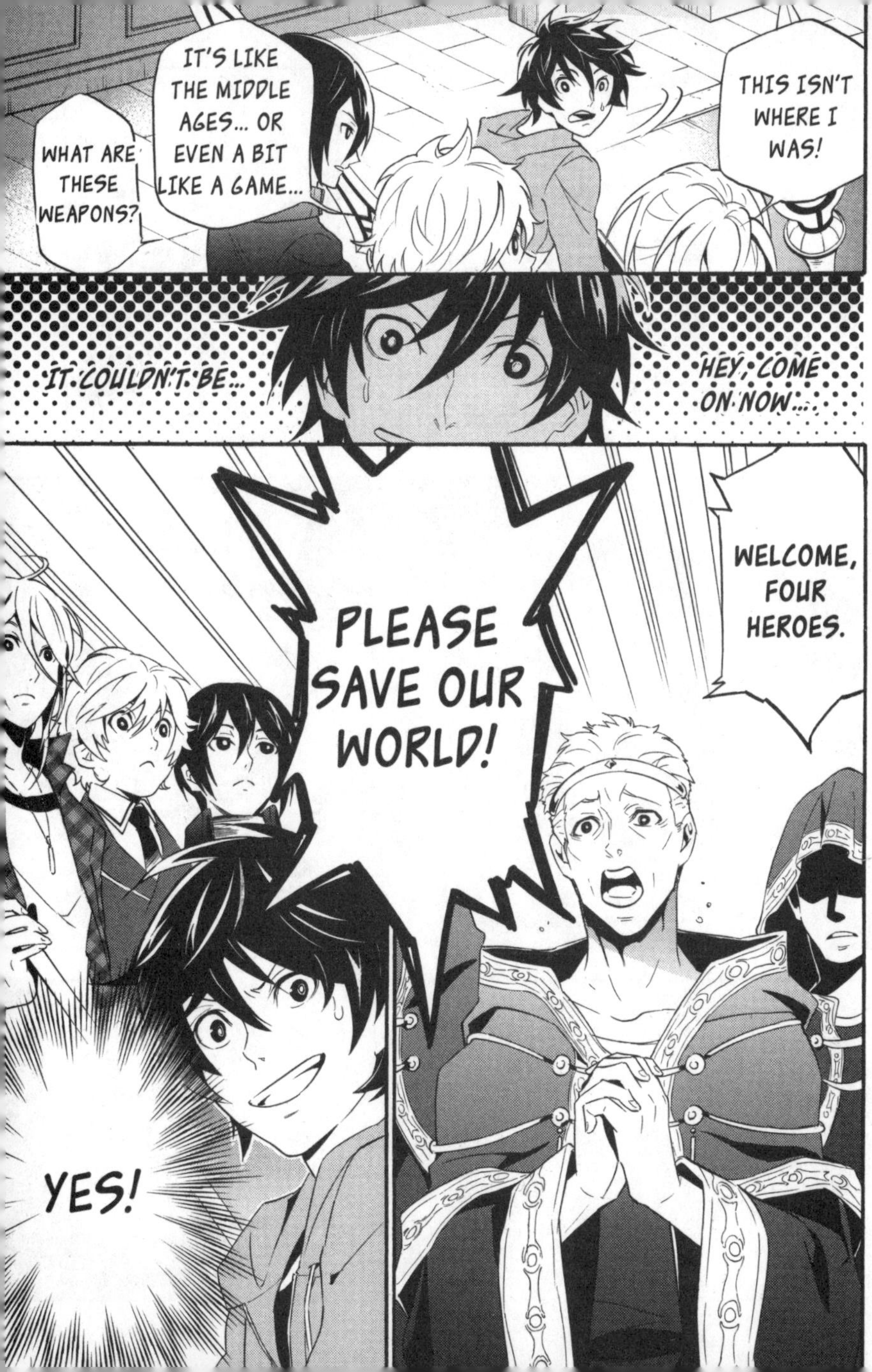
THIS ISN'T WHERE I WAS!
IT'S LIKE THE MIDDLE AGES... OR EVEN A BIT LIKE A GAME...
WHAT ARE THESE WEAPONS?
HEY, COME ON NOW...
IT COULDN'T BE...
WELCOME, FOUR HEROES.
PLEASE SAVE OUR WORLD!
YES!

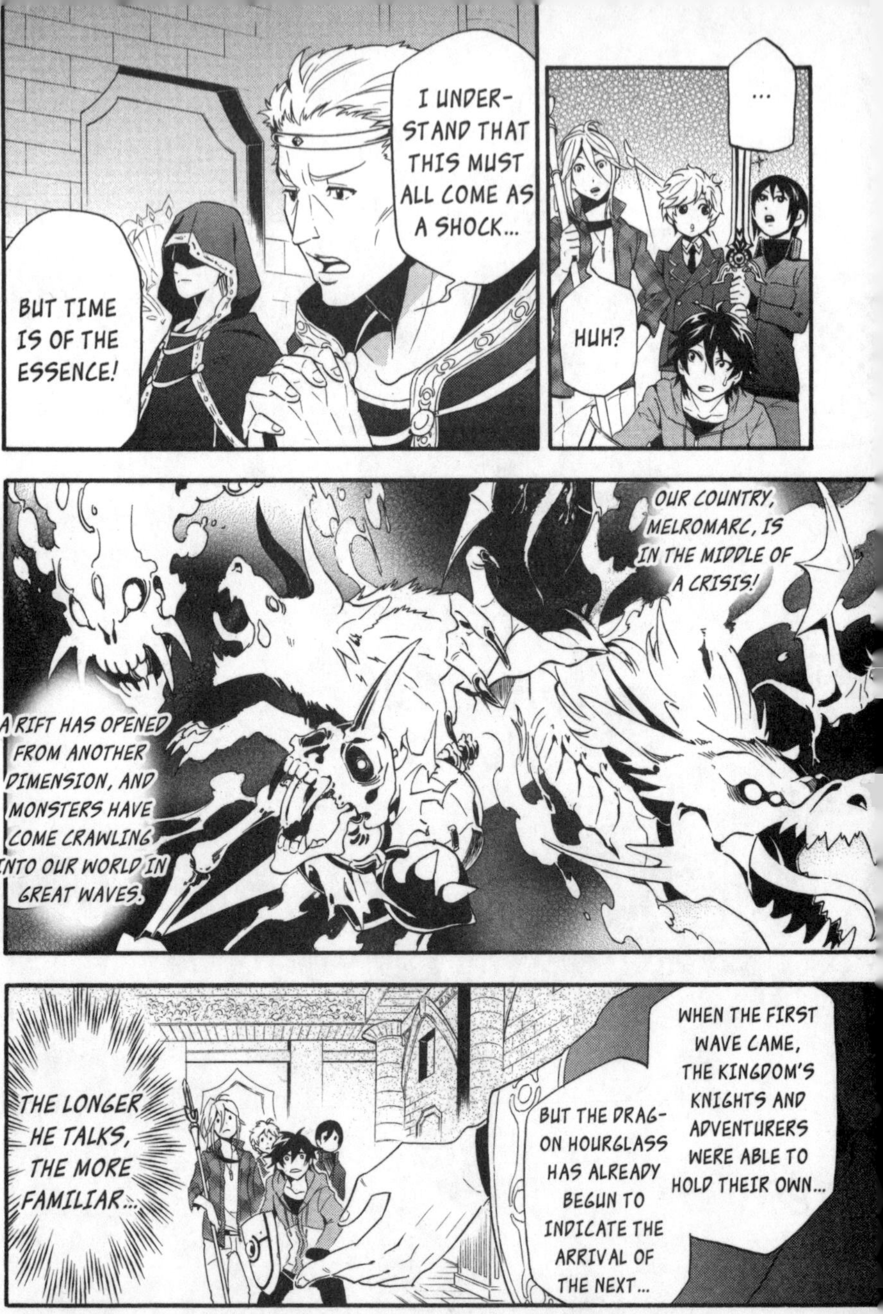
...
HUH?
I UNDER-STAND THAT THIS MUST ALL COME AS A SHOCK...
BUT TIME IS OF THE ESSENCE!
OUR COUNTRY, MELROMARC, IS IN THE MIDDLE OF A CRISIS!
A RIFT HAS OPENED FROM ANOTHER DIMENSION, AND MONSTERS HAVE COME CRAWLING INTO OUR WORLD IN GREAT WAVES.
WHEN THE FIRST WAVE CAME, THE KINGDOM'S KNIGHTS AND ADVENTURERS WERE ABLE TO HOLD THEIR OWN...
BUT THE DRAG-ON HOURGLASS HAS ALREADY BEGUN TO INDICATE THE ARRIVAL OF THE NEXT...
THE LONGER HE TALKS, THE MORE FAMILIAR...

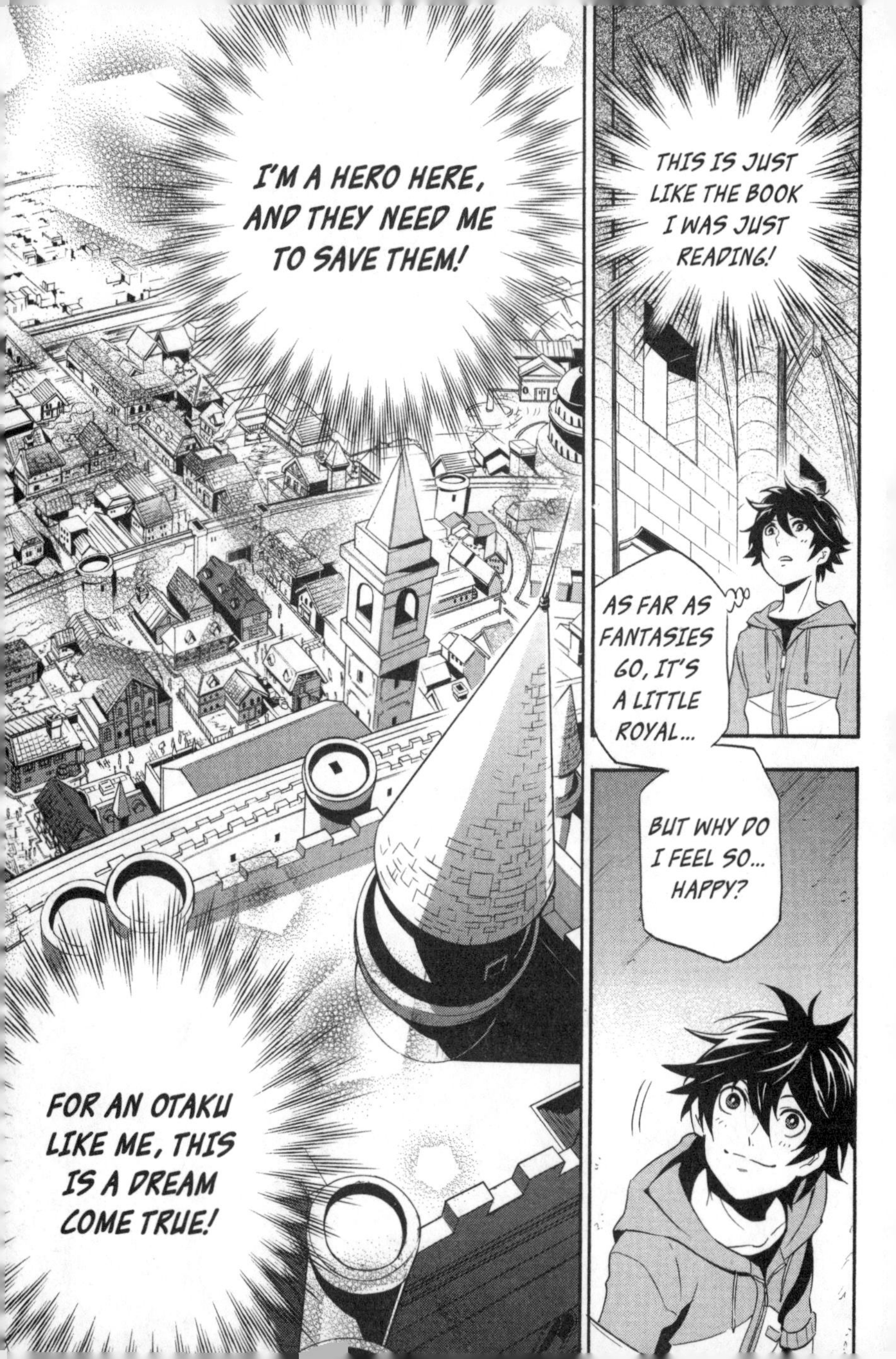
THIS IS JUST LIKE THE BOOK I WAS JUST READING!
AS FAR AS FANTASIES GO, IT'S A LITTLE ROYAL...
BUT WHY DO I FEEL SO... HAPPY?
I'M A HERO HERE, AND THEY NEED ME TO SAVE THEM!
FOR AN OTAKU LIKE ME, THIS IS A DREAM COME TRUE!

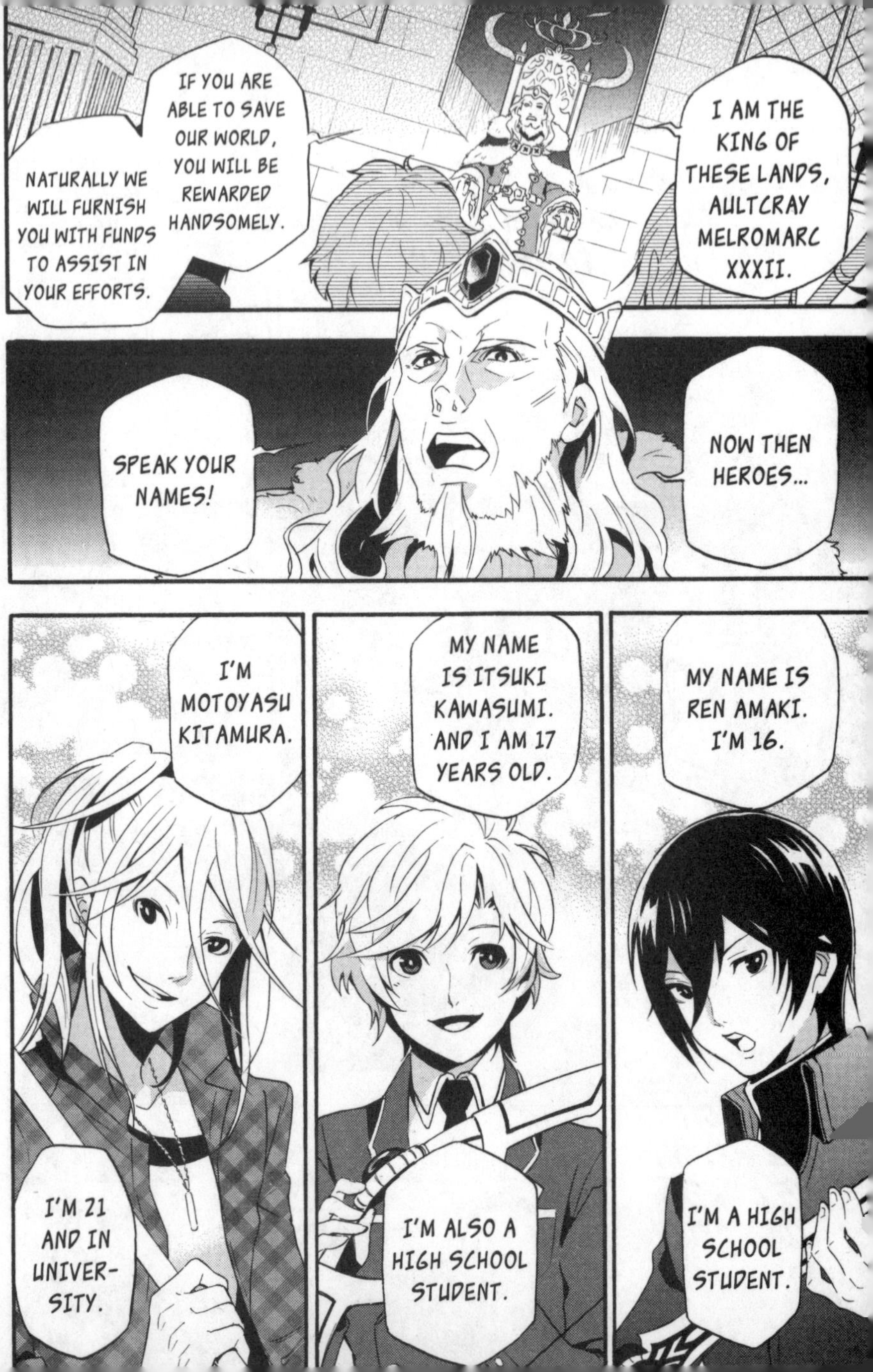
I AM THE KING OF THESE LANDS, AULTCRAY MELROMARC XXXII.
IF YOU ARE ABLE TO SAVE OUR WORLD, YOU WILL BE REWARDED HANDSOMELY.
NATURALLY WE WILL FURNISH YOU WITH FUNDS TO ASSIST IN YOUR EFFORTS.
NOW THEN HEROES...
SPEAK YOUR NAMES!
MY NAME IS REN AMAKI. I'M 16.
I'M A HIGH SCHOOL STUDENT.
MY NAME IS ITSUKI KAWASUMI. AND I AM 17 YEARS OLD.
I'M ALSO A HIGH SCHOOL STUDENT.
I'M MOTOYASU KITAMURA.
I'M 21 AND IN UNIVER-SITY.

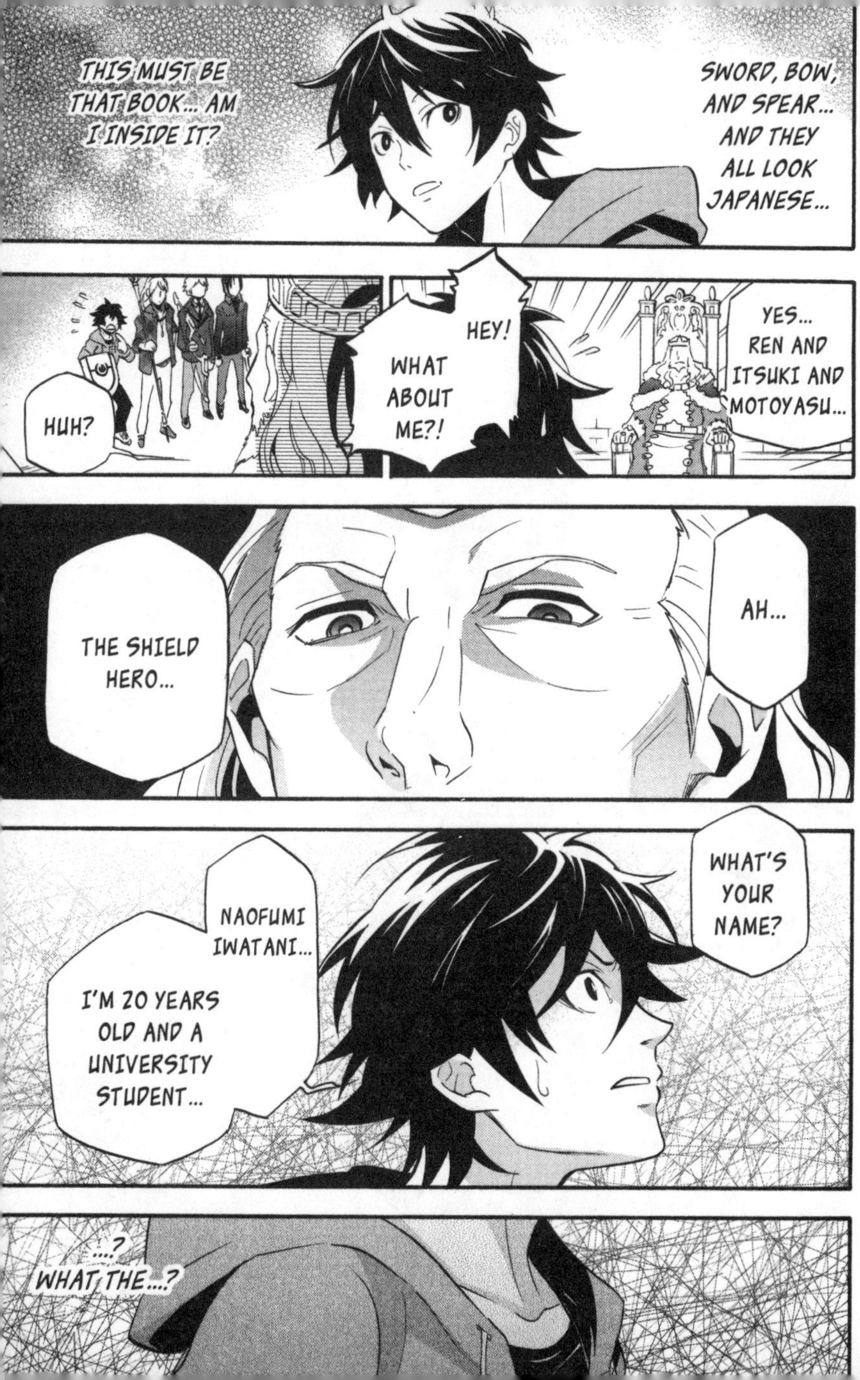
SWORD, BOW, AND SPEAR... AND THEY ALL LOOK JAPANESE...
THIS MUST BE THAT BOOK... AM I INSIDE IT?
YES... REN AND ITSUKI AND MOTOYASU...
HEY! WHAT ABOUT ME?!
HUH?
AH...
THE SHIELD HERO...
WHAT'S YOUR NAME?
NAOFUMI IWATANI...
I'M 20 YEARS OLD AND A UNIVERSITY STUDENT...
...? WHAT THE...?

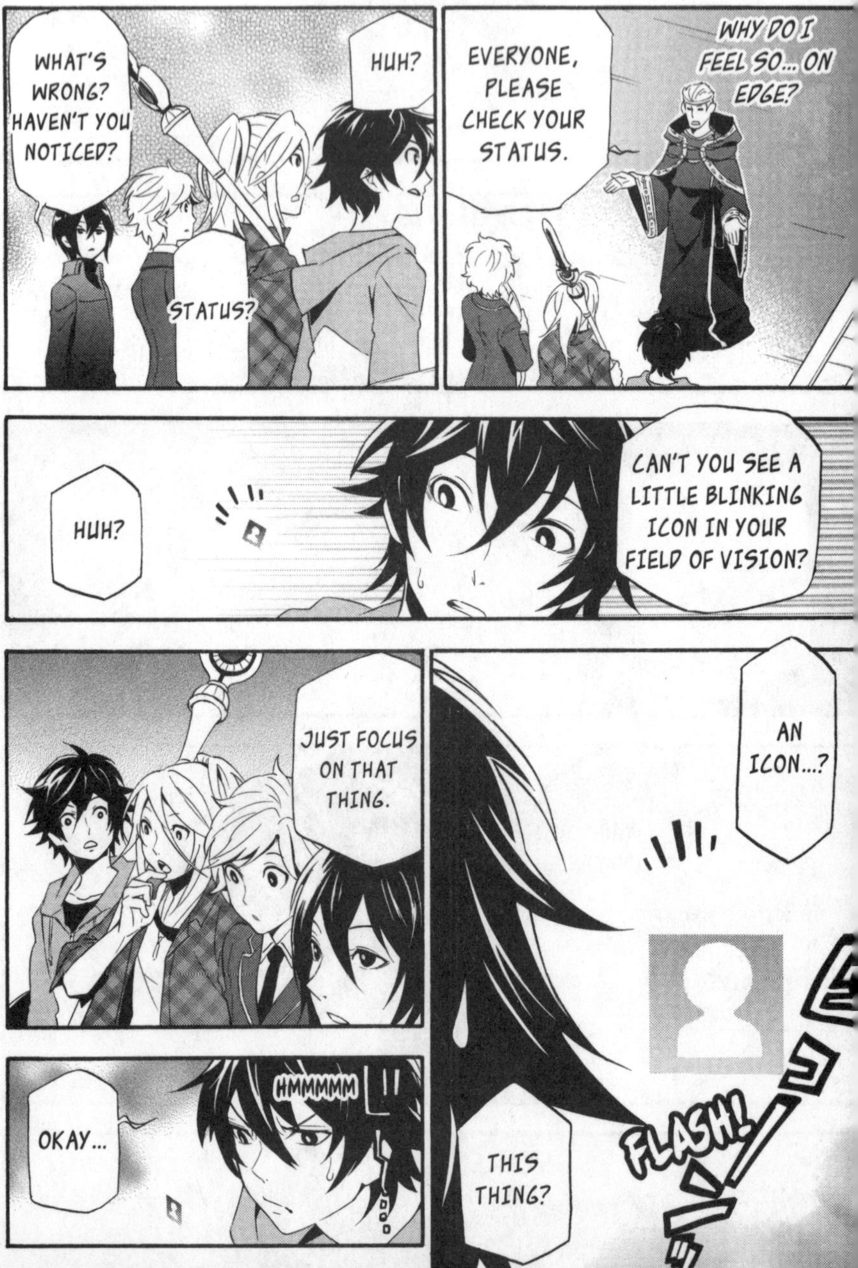
WHY DO I FEEL SO... ON EDGE?
EVERYONE, PLEASE CHECK YOUR STATUS.
HUH?
WHAT'S WRONG? HAVEN'T YOU NOTICED?
STATUS?
CAN'T YOU SEE A LITTLE BLINKING ICON IN YOUR FIELD OF VISION?
HUH?
AN ICON...?
FLASH!
THIS THING?
JUST FOCUS ON THAT THING.
HMMMMM
OKAY...

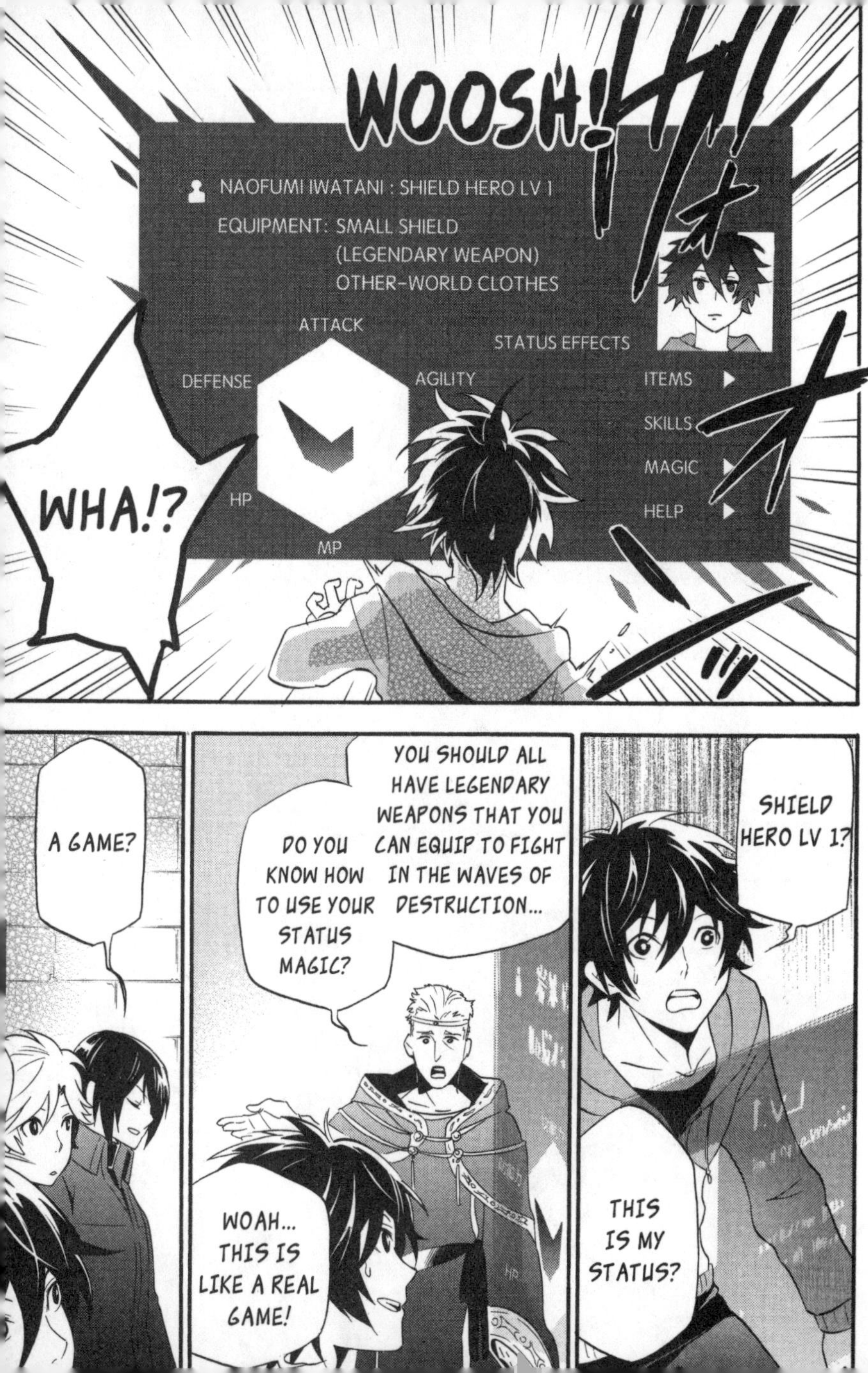
WOOSH!
NAOFUMI IWATANI : SHIELD HERO LV 1
EQUIPMENT: SMALL SHIELD
(LEGENDARY WEAPON)
OTHER-WORLD CLOTHES
STATUS EFFECTS
ATTACK
AGILITY
DEFENSE
HP
MP
ITEMS
SKILLS
MAGIC
HELP
WHA!?
SHIELD HERO LV 1?
THIS IS MY STATUS?
YOU SHOULD ALL HAVE LEGENDARY WEAPONS THAT YOU CAN EQUIP TO FIGHT IN THE WAVES OF DESTRUCTION...
DO YOU KNOW HOW TO USE YOUR STATUS MAGIC?
WOAH... THIS IS LIKE A REAL GAME!
A GAME?

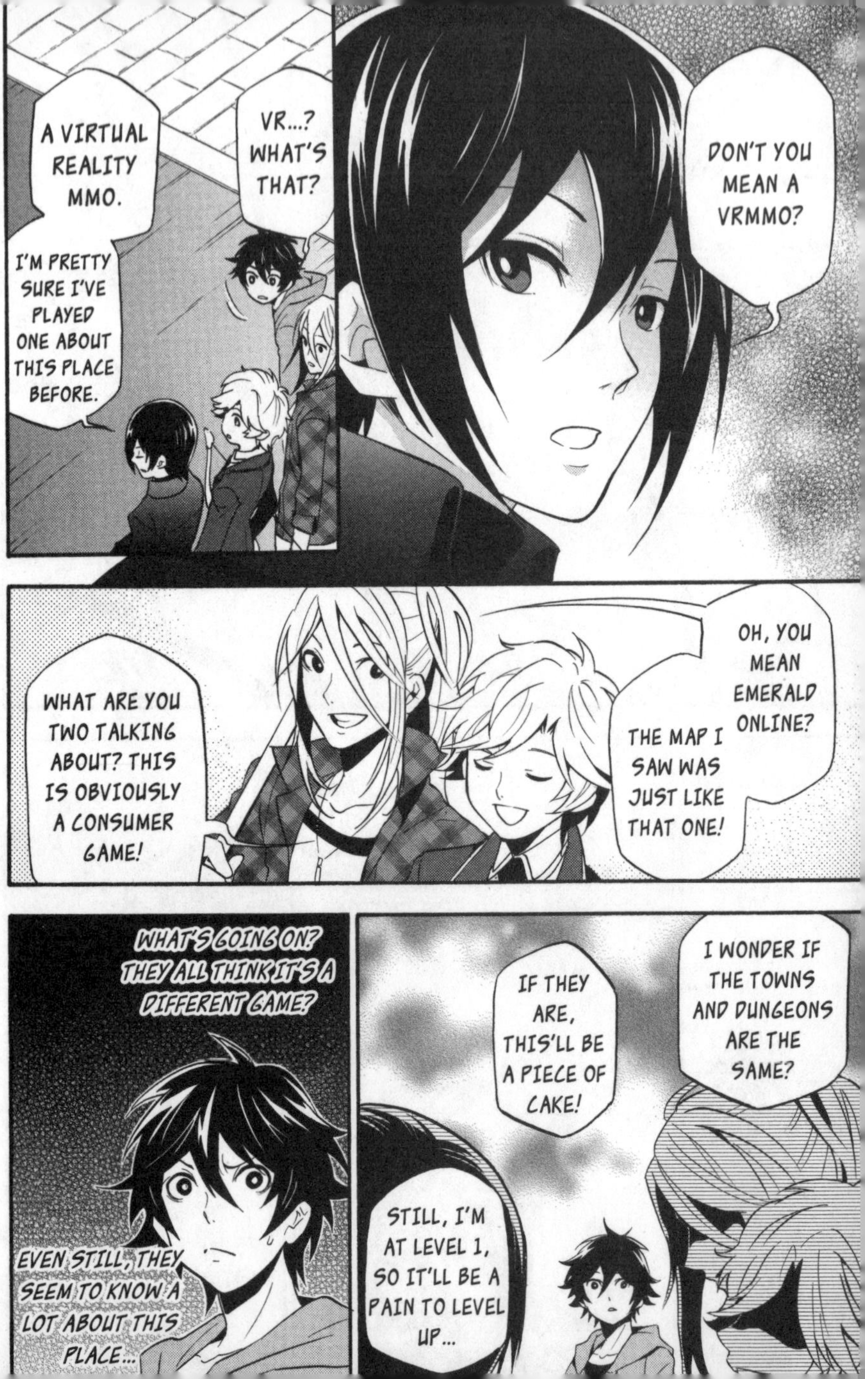
DON'T YOU MEAN A VRMMO?
VR...? WHAT'S THAT?
A VIRTUAL REALITY MMO.
I'M PRETTY SURE I'VE PLAYED ONE ABOUT THIS PLACE BEFORE.
OH, YOU MEAN EMERALD ONLINE?
THE MAP I SAW WAS JUST LIKE THAT ONE!
WHAT ARE YOU TWO TALKING ABOUT? THIS IS OBVIOUSLY A CONSUMER GAME!
I WONDER IF THE TOWNS AND DUNGEONS ARE THE SAME?
IF THEY ARE, THIS'LL BE A PIECE OF CAKE!
STILL, I'M AT LEVEL 1, SO IT'LL BE A PAIN TO LEVEL UP...
WHAT'S GOING ON? THEY ALL THINK IT'S A DIFFERENT GAME?
EVEN STILL, THEY SEEM TO KNOW A LOT ABOUT THIS PLACE...

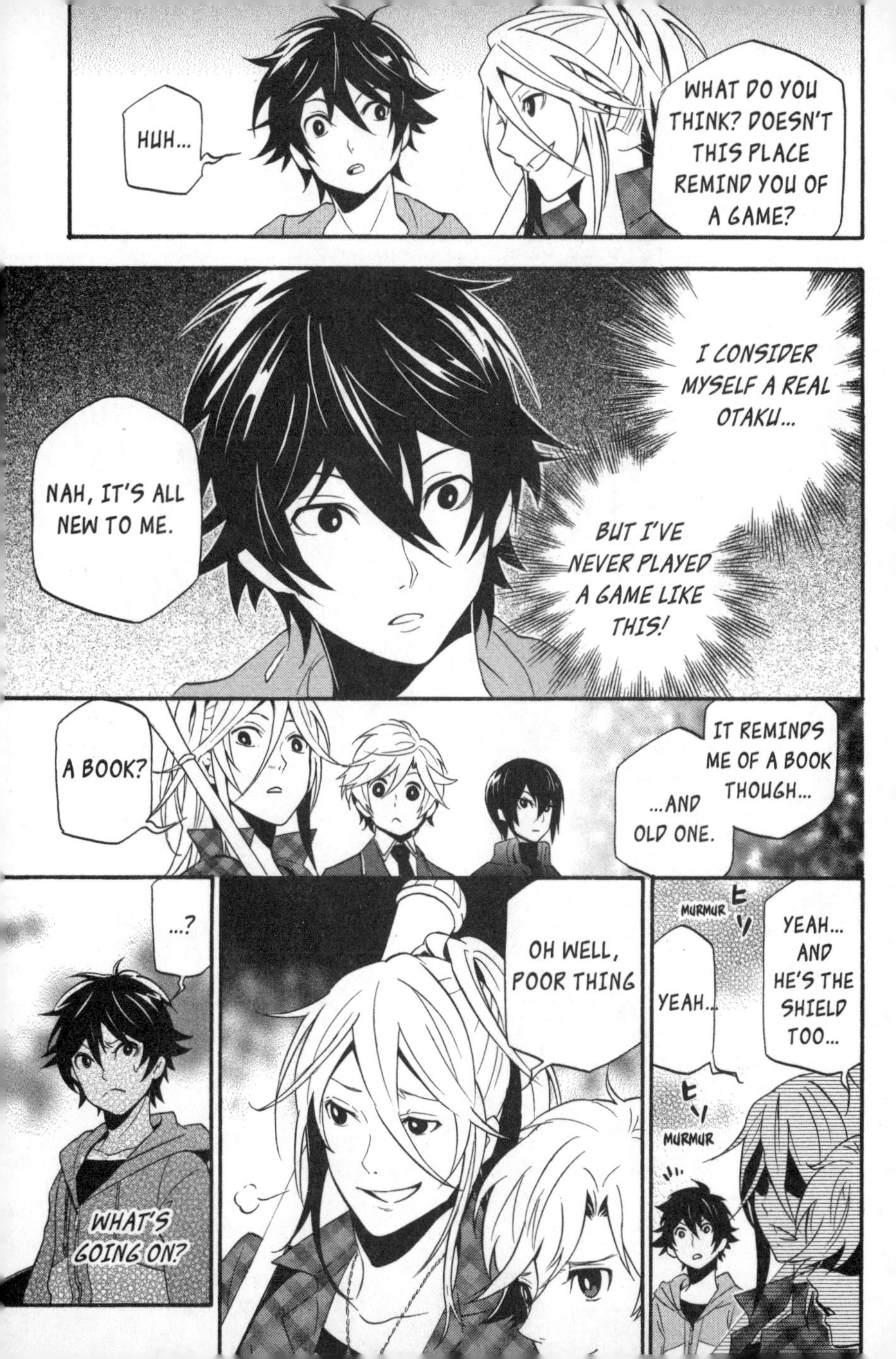
WHAT DO YOU THINK? DOESN'T THIS PLACE REMIND YOU OF A GAME?
HUH...
I CONSIDER MYSELF A REAL OTAKU...
NAH, IT'S ALL NEW TO ME.
BUT I'VE NEVER PLAYED A GAME LIKE THIS!
IT REMINDS ME OF A BOOK THOUGH...
...AND OLD ONE.
A BOOK?
YEAH... AND HE'S THE SHIELD TOO...
ヒソ
MURMUR
YEAH...
ヒソ
MURMUR
OH WELL, POOR THING
...?
WHAT'S GOING ON?

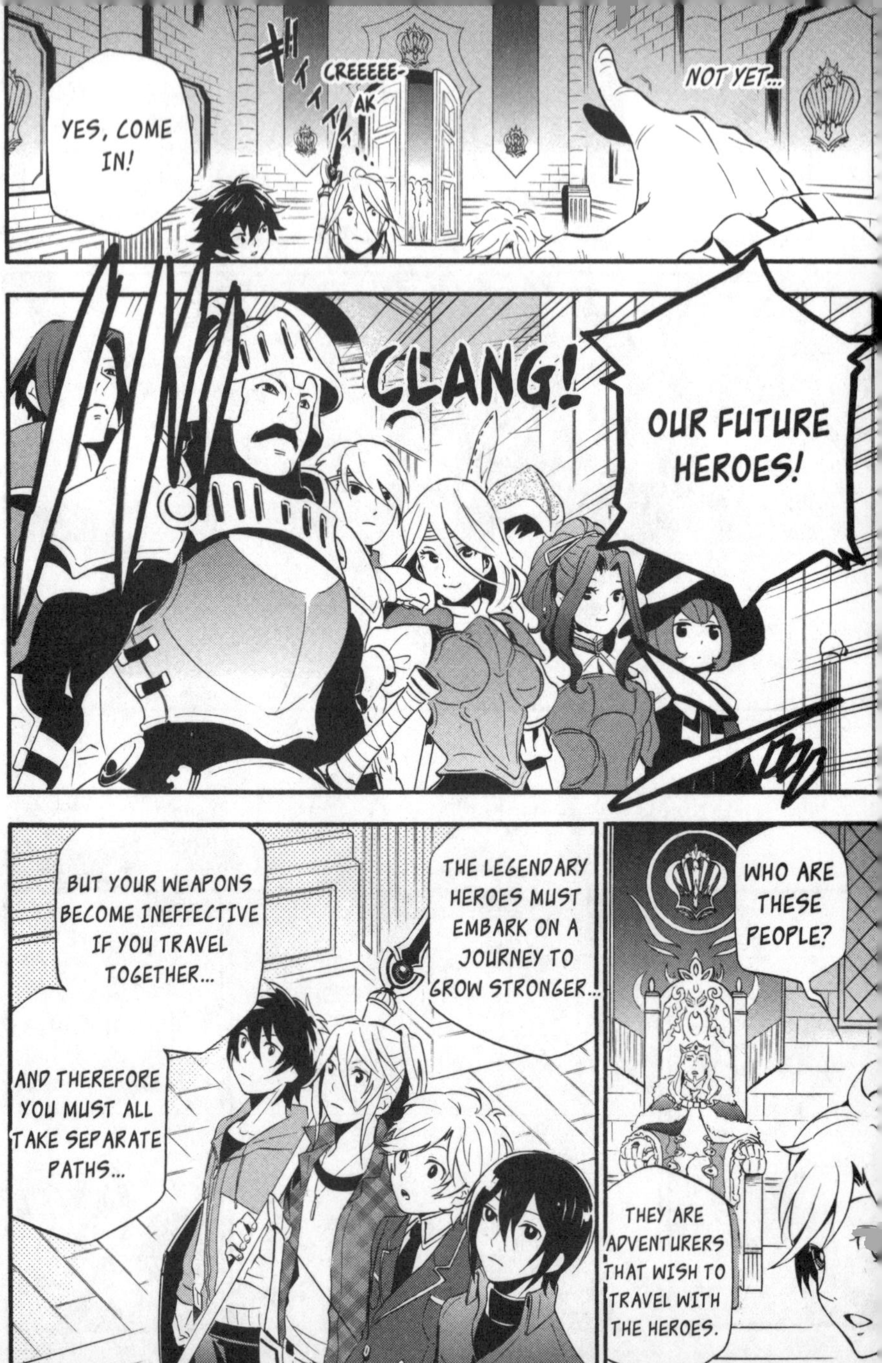
NOT YET...
CREEEEEE-AK
YES, COME IN!
OUR FUTURE HEROES!
CLANG!
WHO ARE THESE PEOPLE?
THEY ARE ADVENTURERS THAT WISH TO TRAVEL WITH THE HEROES.
THE LEGENDARY HEROES MUST EMBARK ON A JOURNEY TO GROW STRONGER...
BUT YOUR WEAPONS BECOME INEFFECTIVE IF YOU TRAVEL TOGETHER...
AND THEREFORE YOU MUST ALL TAKE SEPARATE PATHS...

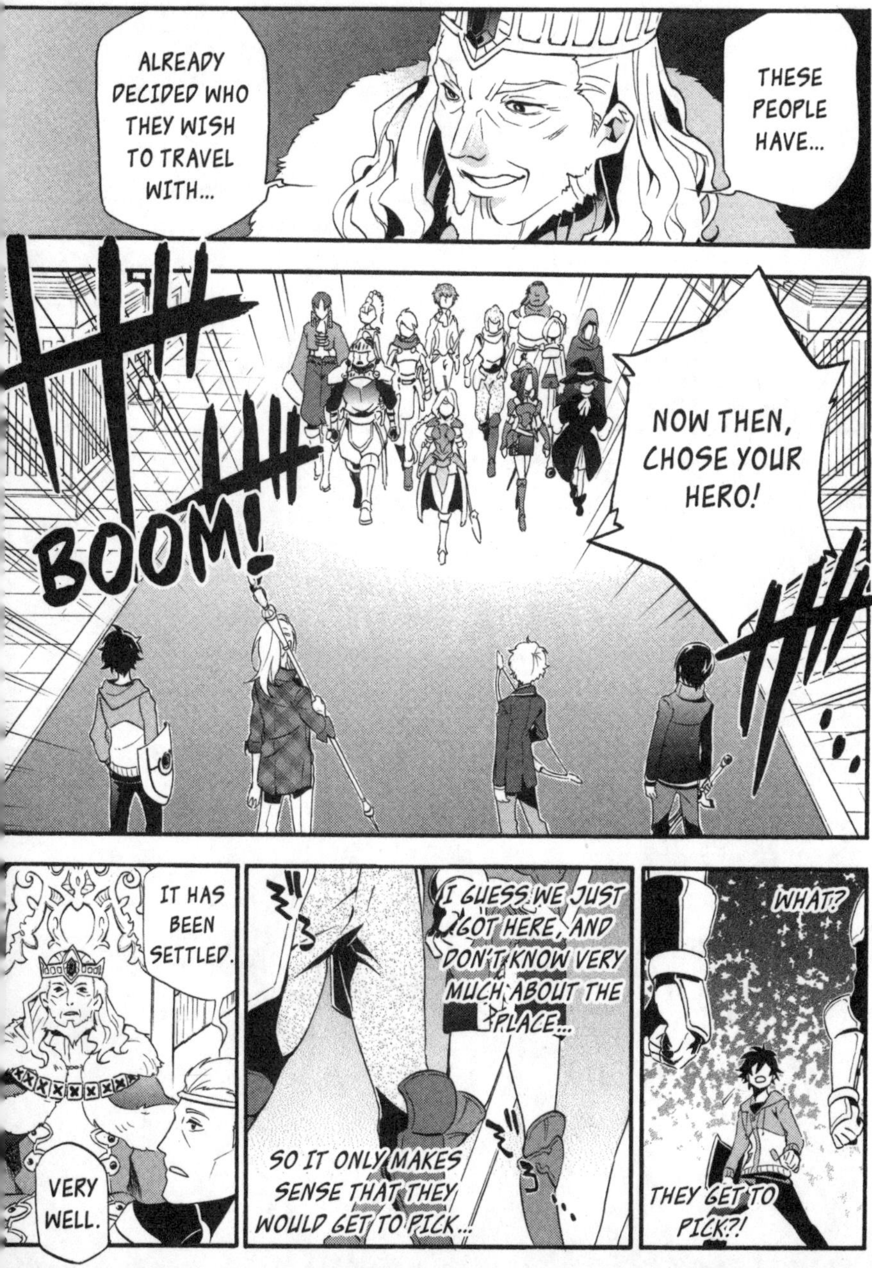
THESE PEOPLE HAVE...
ALREADY DECIDED WHO THEY WISH TO TRAVEL WITH...
NOW THEN, CHOSE YOUR HERO!
BOOM!
...
WHAT?
THEY GET TO PICK?!
I GUESS WE JUST GOT HERE, AND DON'T KNOW VERY MUCH ABOUT THE PLACE...
SO IT ONLY MAKES SENSE THAT THEY WOULD GET TO PICK...
IT HAS BEEN SETTLED.
VERY WELL.

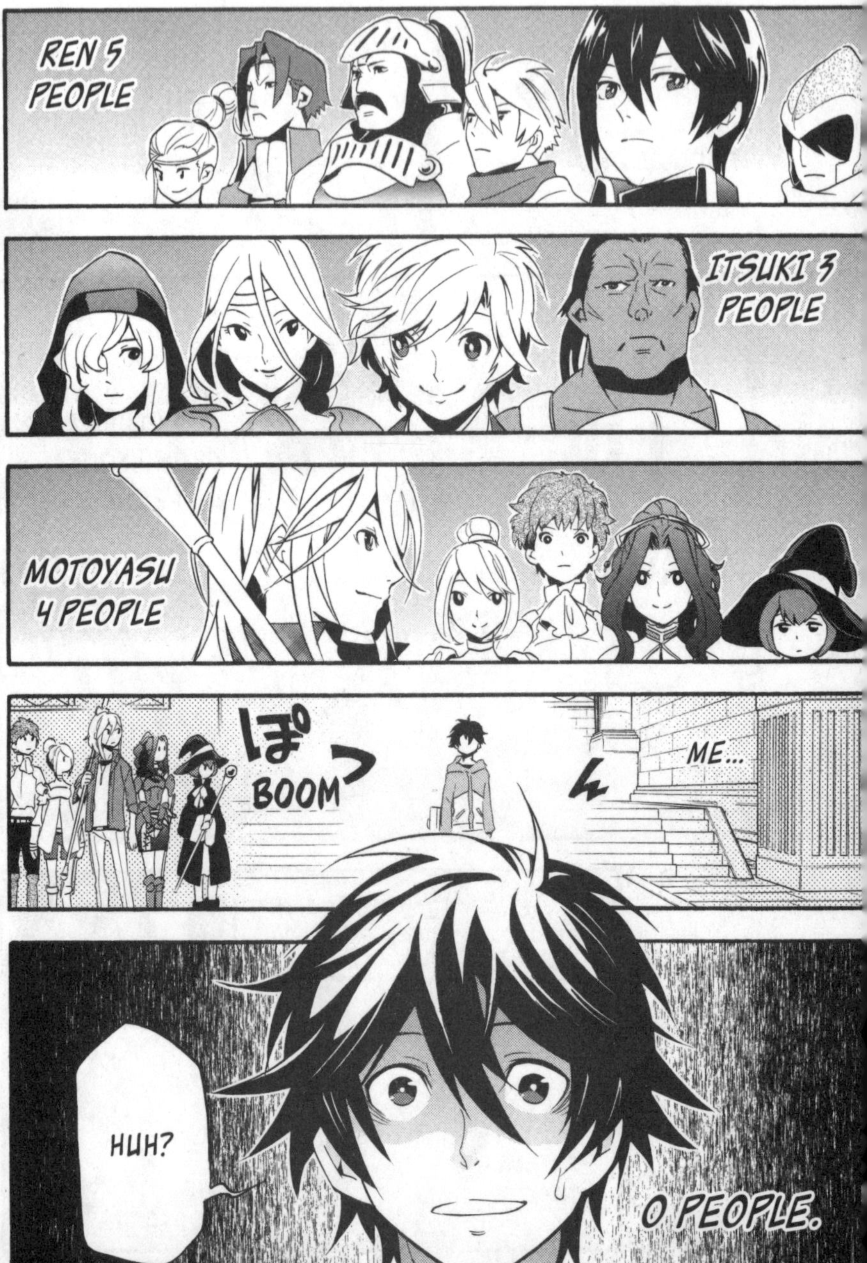
REN 5 PEOPLE
ITSUKI 3 PEOPLE
MOTOYASU 4 PEOPLE
ME...
ぽ
BOOM
0 PEOPLE.
HUH?

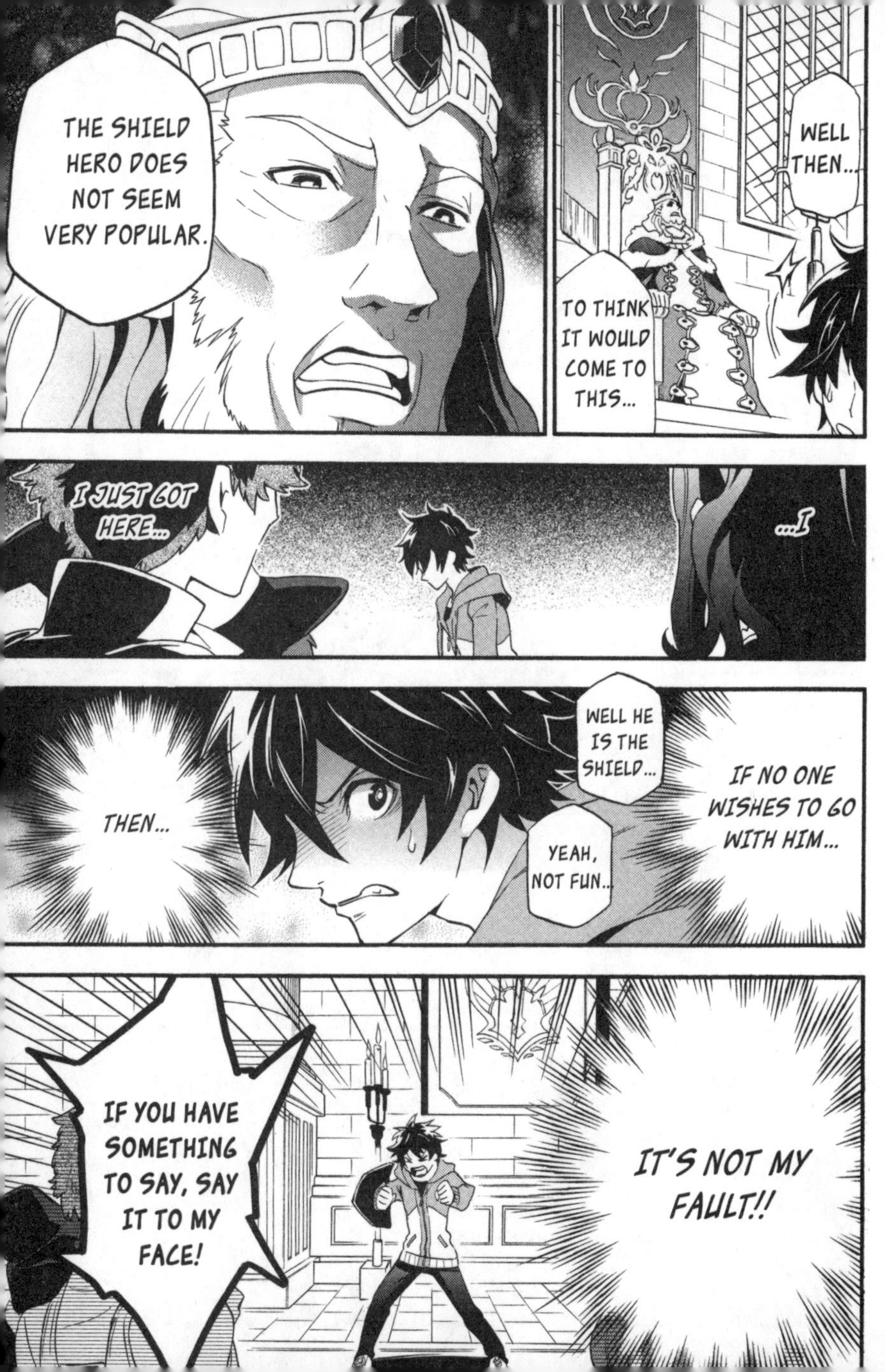
WELL THEN...
TO THINK IT WOULD COME TO THIS...
THE SHIELD HERO DOES NOT SEEM VERY POPULAR.
...I
I JUST GOT HERE...
IF NO ONE WISHES TO GO WITH HIM...
WELL HE IS THE SHIELD...
YEAH, NOT FUN...
THEN...
IT'S NOT MY FAULT!!
IF YOU HAVE SOMETHING TO SAY, SAY IT TO MY FACE!

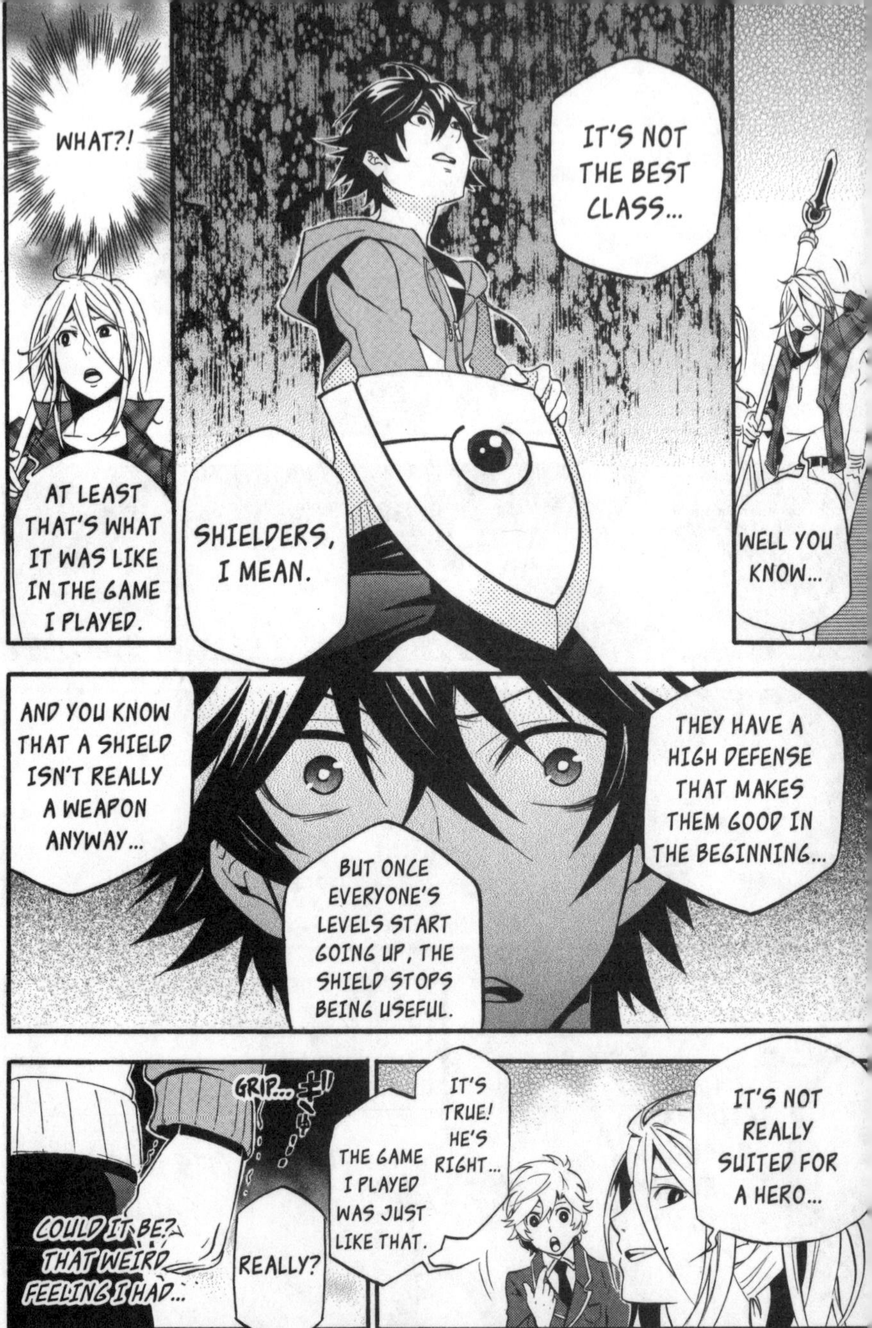
WELL YOU KNOW...
IT'S NOT THE BEST CLASS...
SHIELDERS, I MEAN.
WHAT?!
AT LEAST THAT'S WHAT IT WAS LIKE IN THE GAME I PLAYED.
THEY HAVE A HIGH DEFENSE THAT MAKES THEM GOOD IN THE BEGINNING...
BUT ONCE EVERYONE'S LEVELS START GOING UP, THE SHIELD STOPS BEING USEFUL.
AND YOU KNOW THAT A SHIELD ISN'T REALLY A WEAPON ANYWAY...
IT'S NOT REALLY SUITED FOR A HERO...
IT'S TRUE! HE'S RIGHT...
THE GAME I PLAYED WAS JUST LIKE THAT.
REALLY?
GRIP...
COULD IT BE? THAT WEIRD FEELING I HAD...

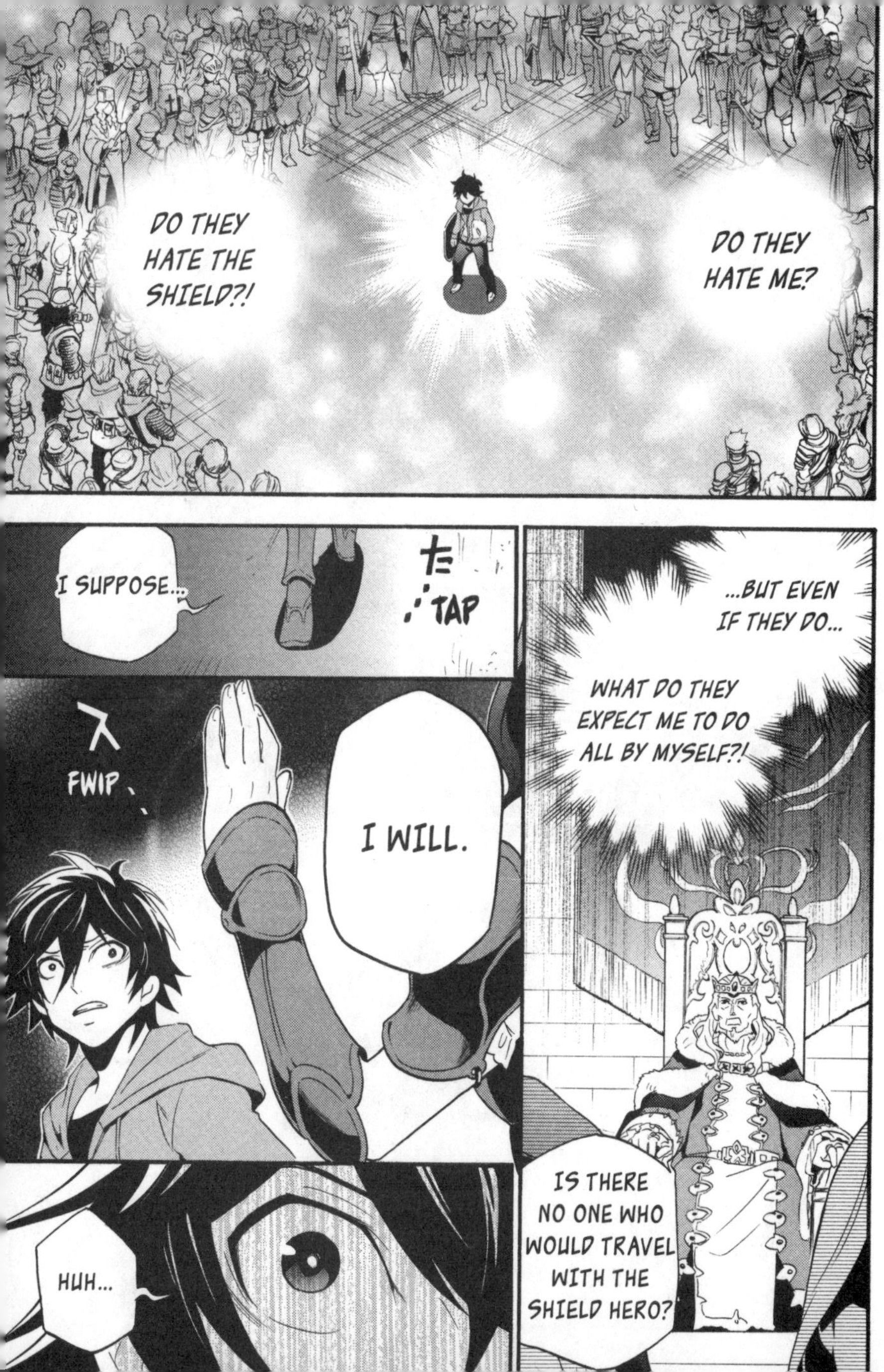
DO THEY HATE ME?
DO THEY HATE THE SHIELD?!
...BUT EVEN IF THEY DO...
WHAT DO THEY EXPECT ME TO DO ALL BY MYSELF?!
IS THERE NO ONE WHO WOULD TRAVEL WITH THE SHIELD HERO?
TAP
I SUPPOSE...
I WILL.
FWIP
HUH...

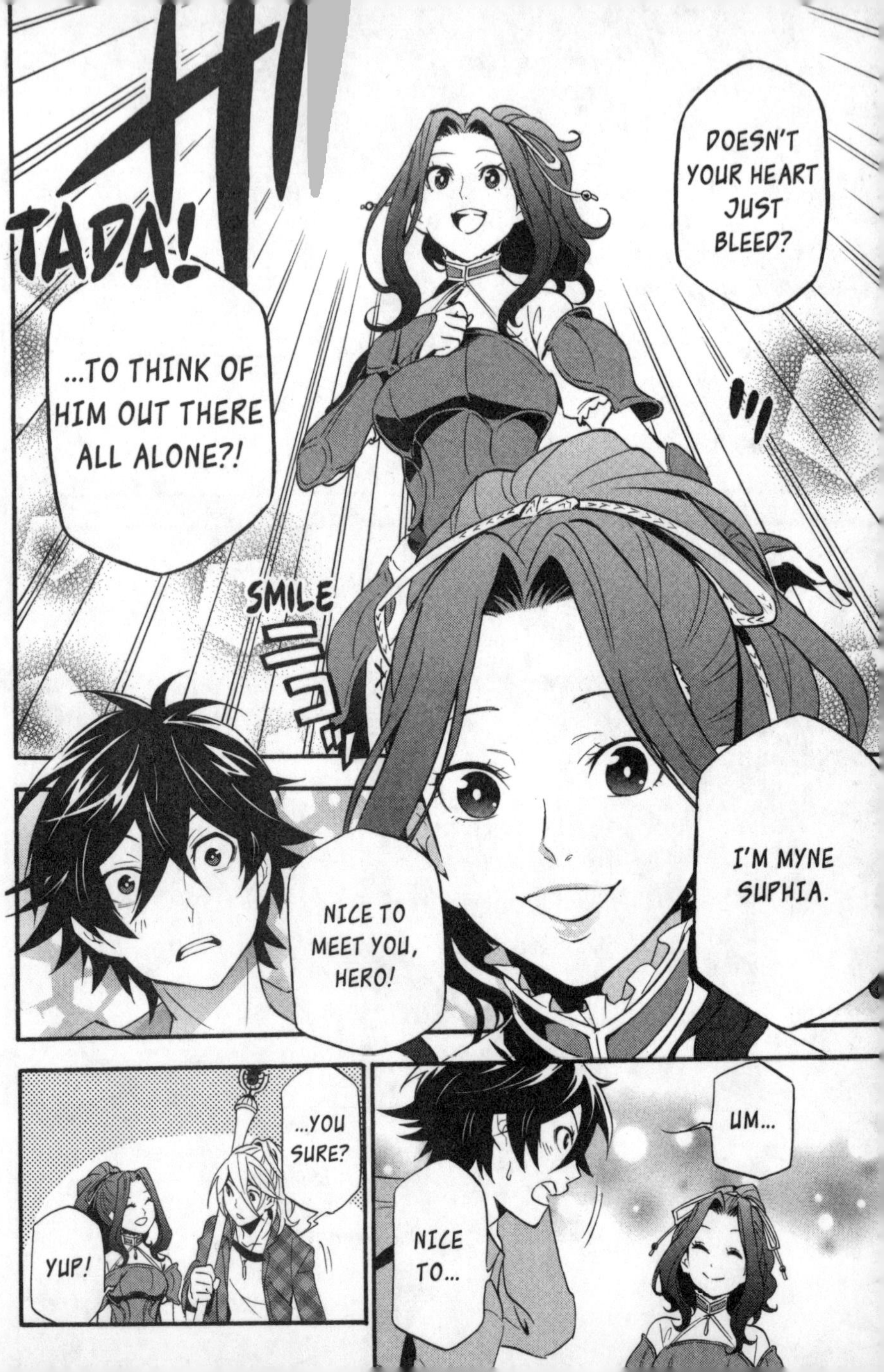
DOESN'T YOUR HEART JUST BLEED?
TADA!
...TO THINK OF HIM OUT THERE ALL ALONE?!
SMILE
I'M MYNE SUPHIA.
NICE TO MEET YOU, HERO!
UM...
NICE TO...
...YOU SURE?
YUP!

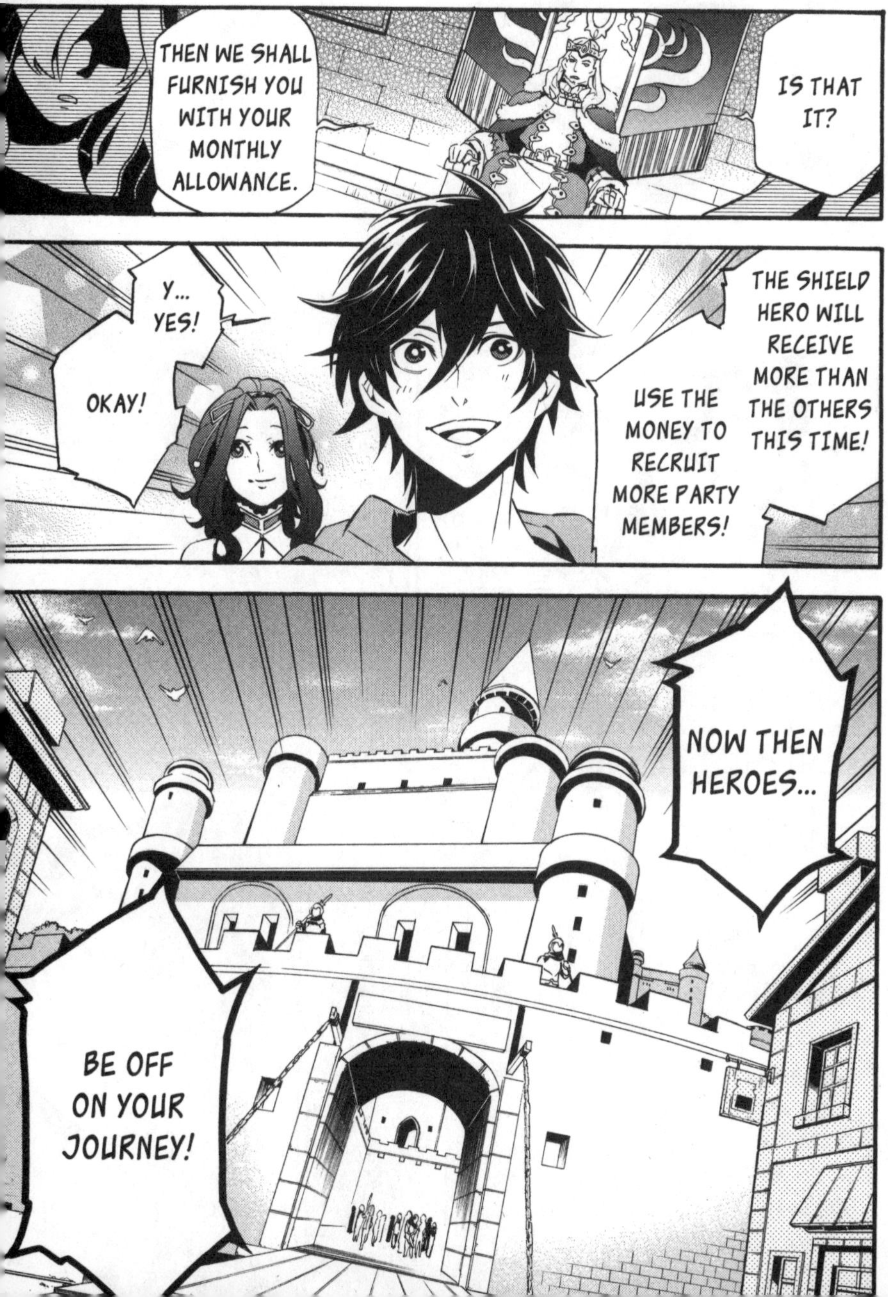
IS THAT IT?
THEN WE SHALL FURNISH YOU WITH YOUR MONTHLY ALLOWANCE.
THE SHIELD HERO WILL RECEIVE MORE THAN THE OTHERS THIS TIME!
USE THE MONEY TO RECRUIT MORE PARTY MEMBERS!
Y... YES!
OKAY!
NOW THEN HEROES...
BE OFF ON YOUR JOURNEY!

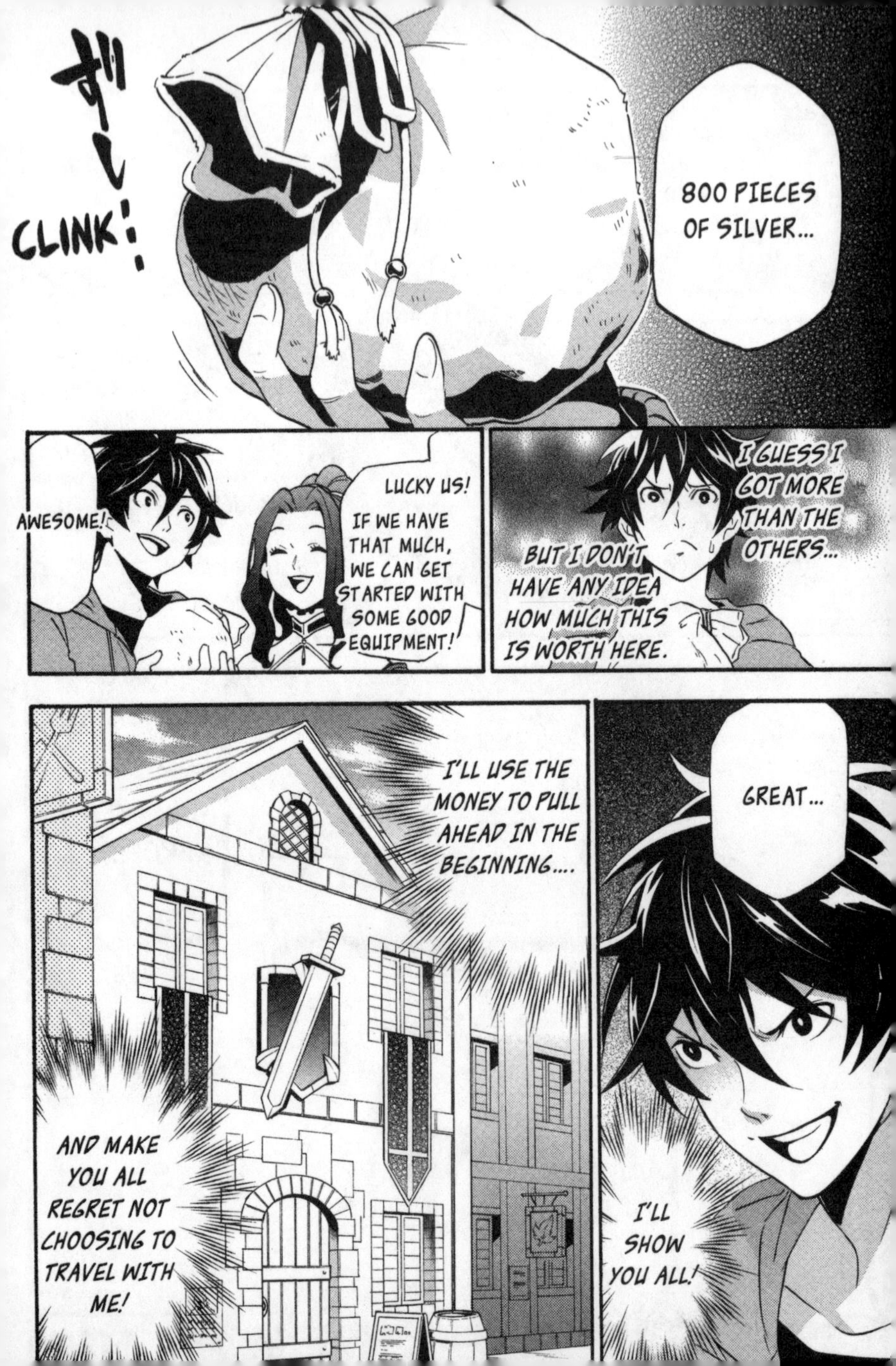
CLINK!
800 PIECES OF SILVER...
I GUESS I GOT MORE THAN THE OTHERS...
BUT I DON'T HAVE ANY IDEA HOW MUCH THIS IS WORTH HERE.
LUCKY US!
IF WE HAVE THAT MUCH, WE CAN GET STARTED WITH SOME GOOD EQUIPMENT!
AWESOME!
GREAT...
I'LL SHOW YOU ALL!
I'LL USE THE MONEY TO PULL AHEAD IN THE BEGINNING....
AND MAKE YOU ALL REGRET NOT CHOOSING TO TRAVEL WITH ME!

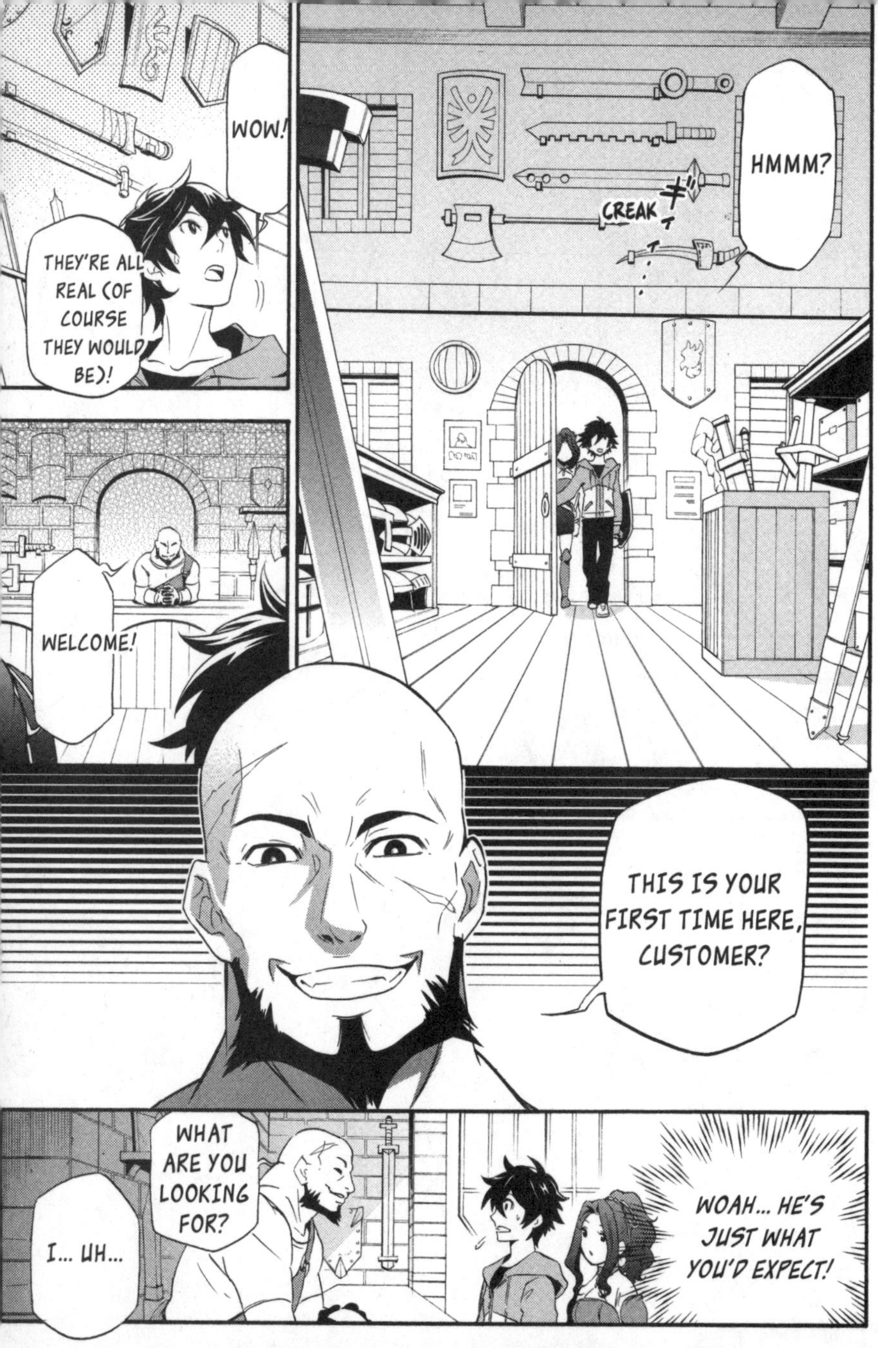
HMMM?
CREAK
WOW!
THEY'RE ALL REAL (OF COURSE THEY WOULD BE)!
WELCOME!
THIS IS YOUR FIRST TIME HERE, CUSTOMER?
WOAH... HE'S JUST WHAT YOU'D EXPECT!
WHAT ARE YOU LOOKING FOR?
I... UH...

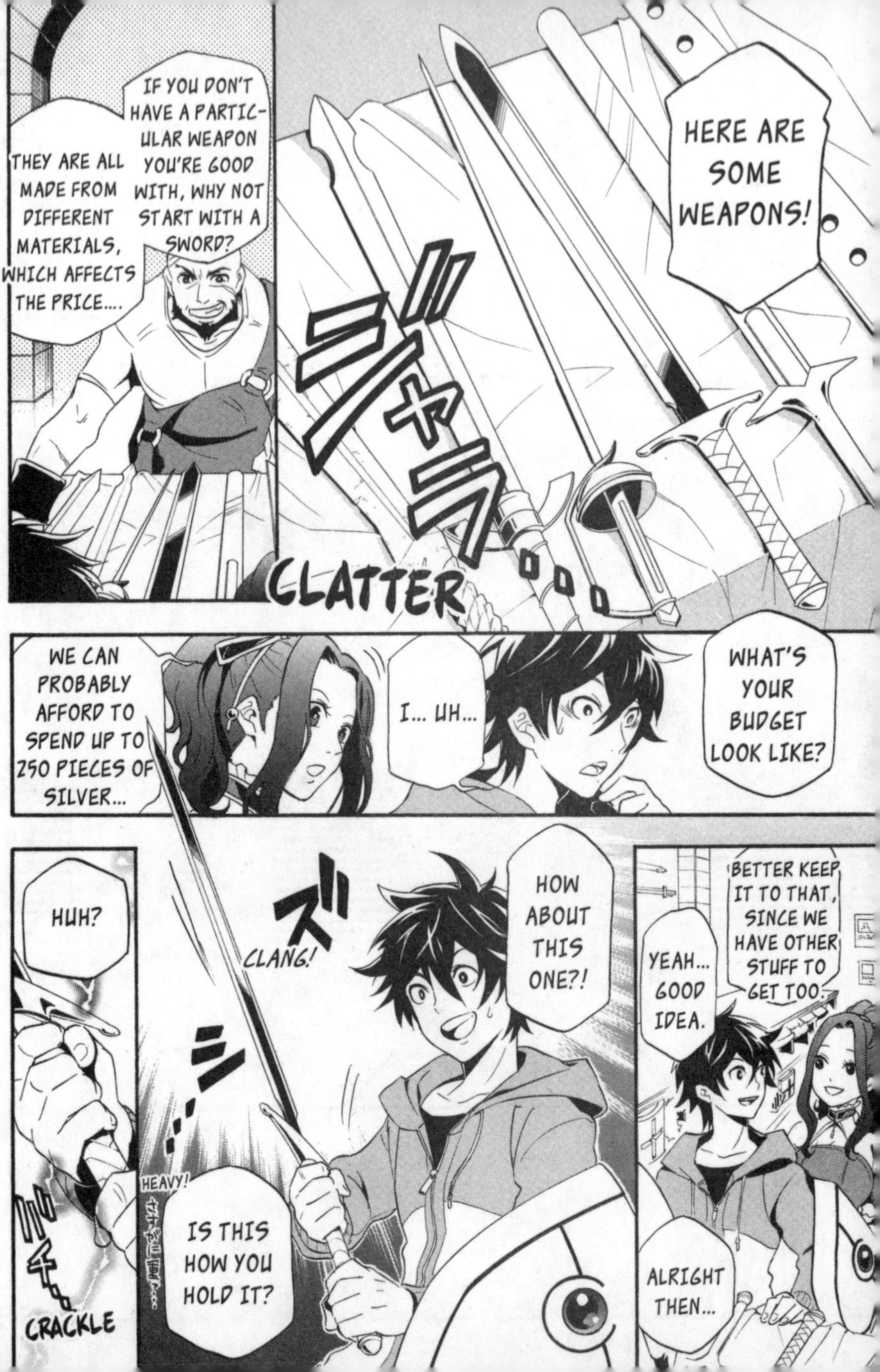
HERE ARE SOME WEAPONS!
ジャラ…
CLATTER
IF YOU DON'T HAVE A PARTICULAR WEAPON YOU'RE GOOD WITH, WHY NOT START WITH A SWORD?
THEY ARE ALL MADE FROM DIFFERENT MATERIALS, WHICH AFFECTS THE PRICE....
WHAT'S YOUR BUDGET LOOK LIKE?
I... UH...
WE CAN PROBABLY AFFORD TO SPEND UP TO 250 PIECES OF SILVER...
BETTER KEEP IT TO THAT, SINCE WE HAVE OTHER STUFF TO GET TOO.
YEAH... GOOD IDEA.
ALRIGHT THEN...
HOW ABOUT THIS ONE?!
ズ
CLANG!
シ…
HEAVY!
さすがに重っ…
IS THIS HOW YOU HOLD IT?
HUH?
ミシ…
CRACKLE

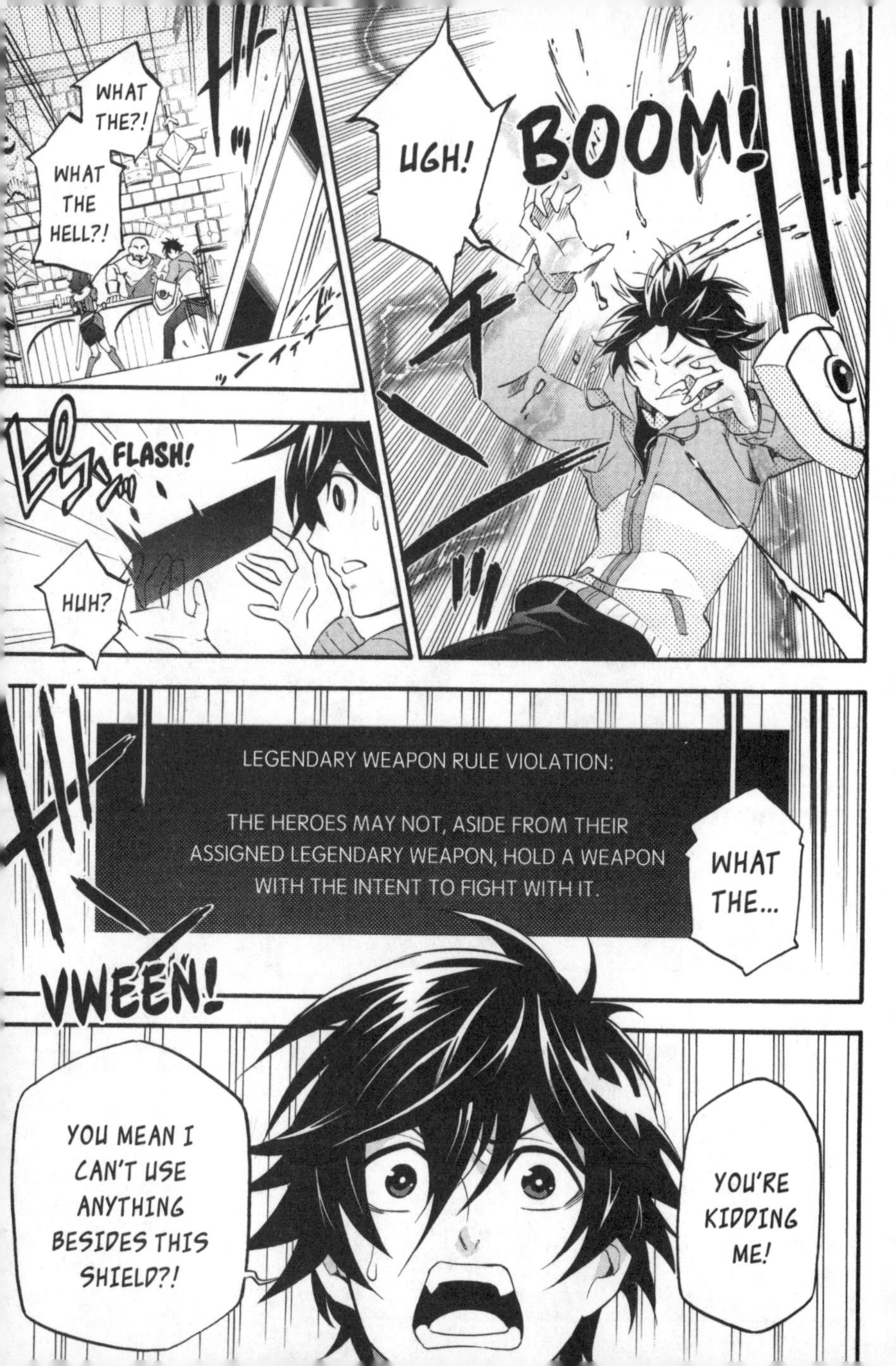
BOOM!
UGH!
WHAT THE?!
WHAT THE HELL?!
FLASH!
HUH?
WHAT THE...
LEGENDARY WEAPON RULE VIOLATION:
THE HEROES MAY NOT, ASIDE FROM THEIR ASSIGNED LEGENDARY WEAPON, HOLD A WEAPON WITH THE INTENT TO FIGHT WITH IT.
VWEEN!
YOU'RE KIDDING ME!
YOU MEAN I CAN'T USE ANYTHING BESIDES THIS SHIELD?!

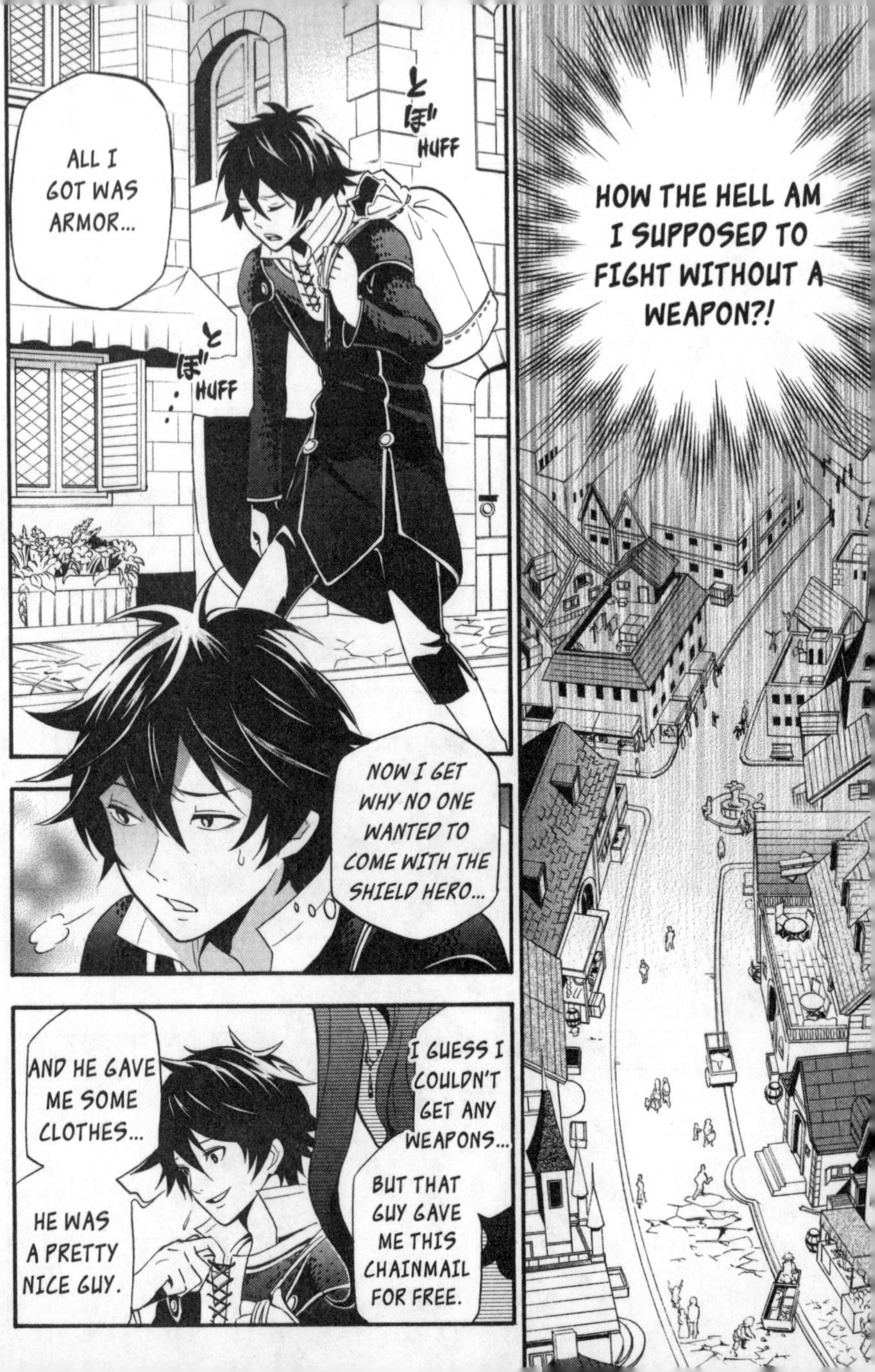
HOW THE HELL AM I SUPPOSED TO FIGHT WITHOUT A WEAPON?!
とぼ
HUFF
とぼ
HUFF
ALL I GOT WAS ARMOR...
NOW I GET WHY NO ONE WANTED TO COME WITH THE SHIELD HERO...
I GUESS I COULDN'T GET ANY WEAPONS...
BUT THAT GUY GAVE ME THIS CHAINMAIL FOR FREE.
AND HE GAVE ME SOME CLOTHES...
HE WAS A PRETTY NICE GUY.

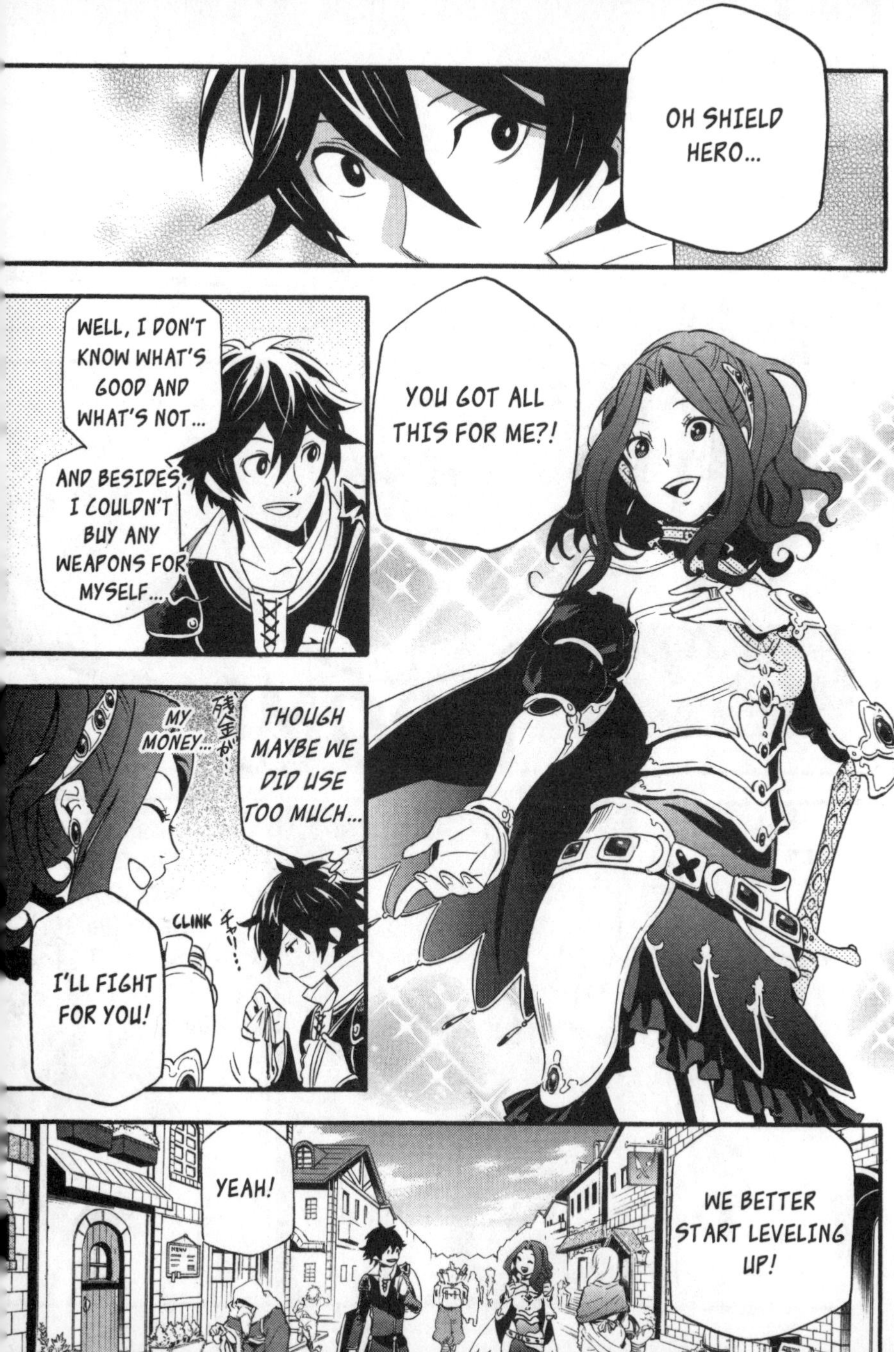
OH SHIELD HERO...
YOU GOT ALL THIS FOR ME?!
WELL, I DON'T KNOW WHAT'S GOOD AND WHAT'S NOT...
AND BESIDES, I COULDN'T BUY ANY WEAPONS FOR MYSELF...
THOUGH MAYBE WE DID USE TOO MUCH...
MY MONEY...
残金が…
CLINK
チャリ…
I'LL FIGHT FOR YOU!
WE BETTER START LEVELING UP!
YEAH!

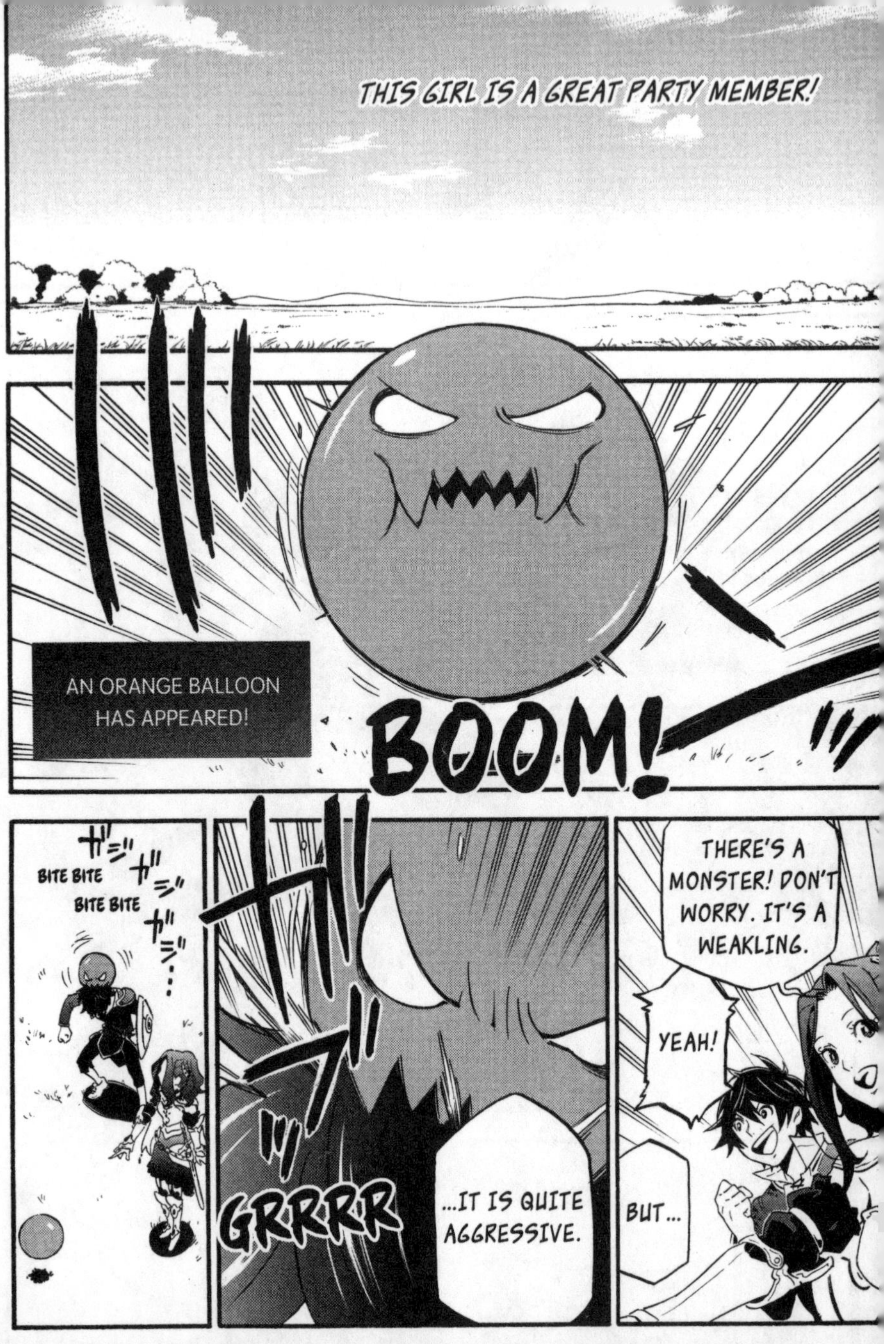
THIS GIRL IS A GREAT PARTY MEMBER!
AN ORANGE BALLOON HAS APPEARED!
BOOM!
THERE'S A MONSTER! DON'T WORRY. IT'S A WEAKLING.
YEAH!
BUT...
...IT IS QUITE AGGRESSIVE.
GRRRR
BITE BITE
BITE BITE

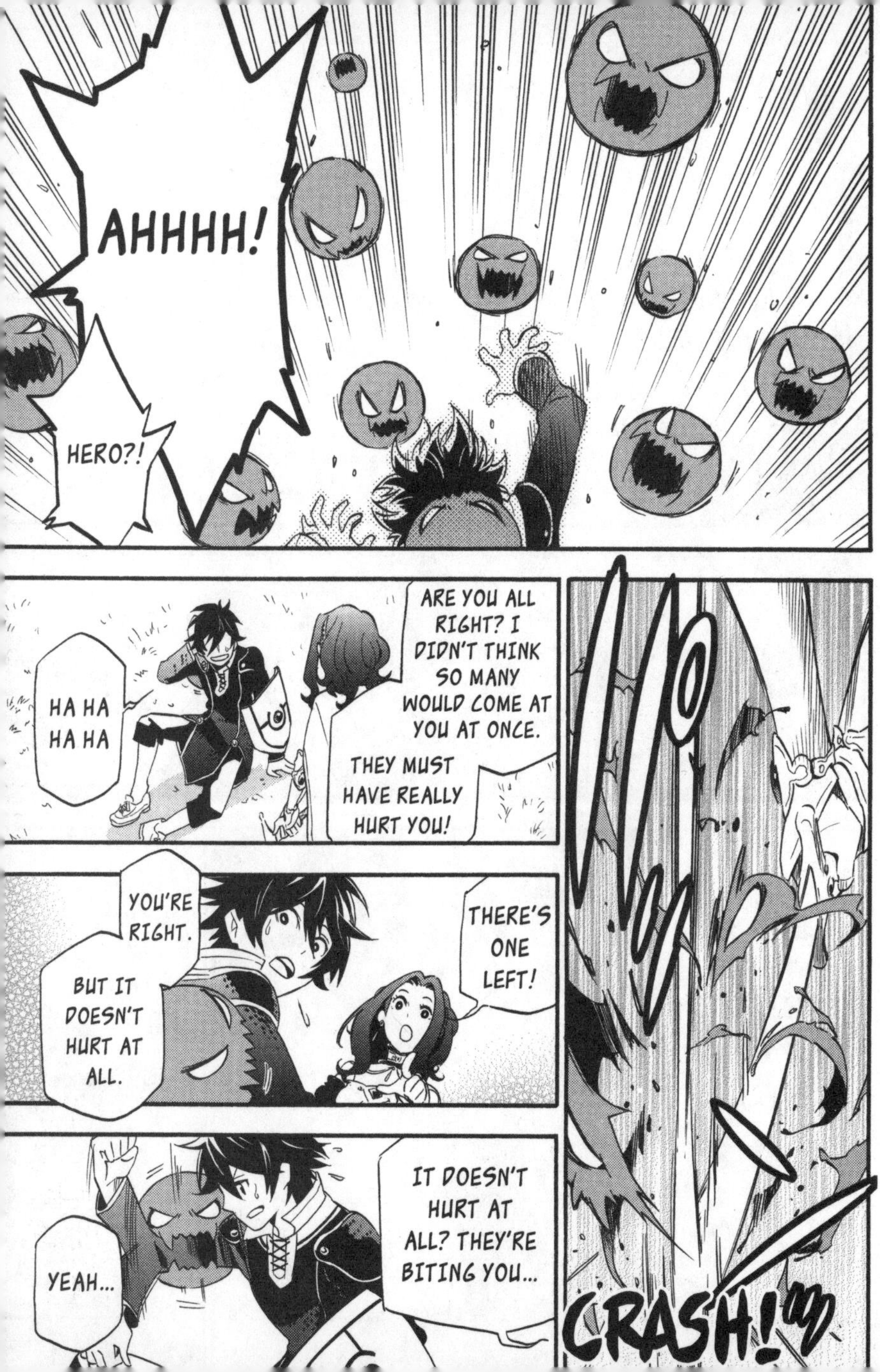
AHHHH!
HERO?!
CRASH!
ARE YOU ALL RIGHT? I DIDN'T THINK SO MANY WOULD COME AT YOU AT ONCE.
THEY MUST HAVE REALLY HURT YOU!
HA HA HA HA
THERE'S ONE LEFT!
YOU'RE RIGHT.
BUT IT DOESN'T HURT AT ALL.
IT DOESN'T HURT AT ALL? THEY'RE BITING YOU...
YEAH...

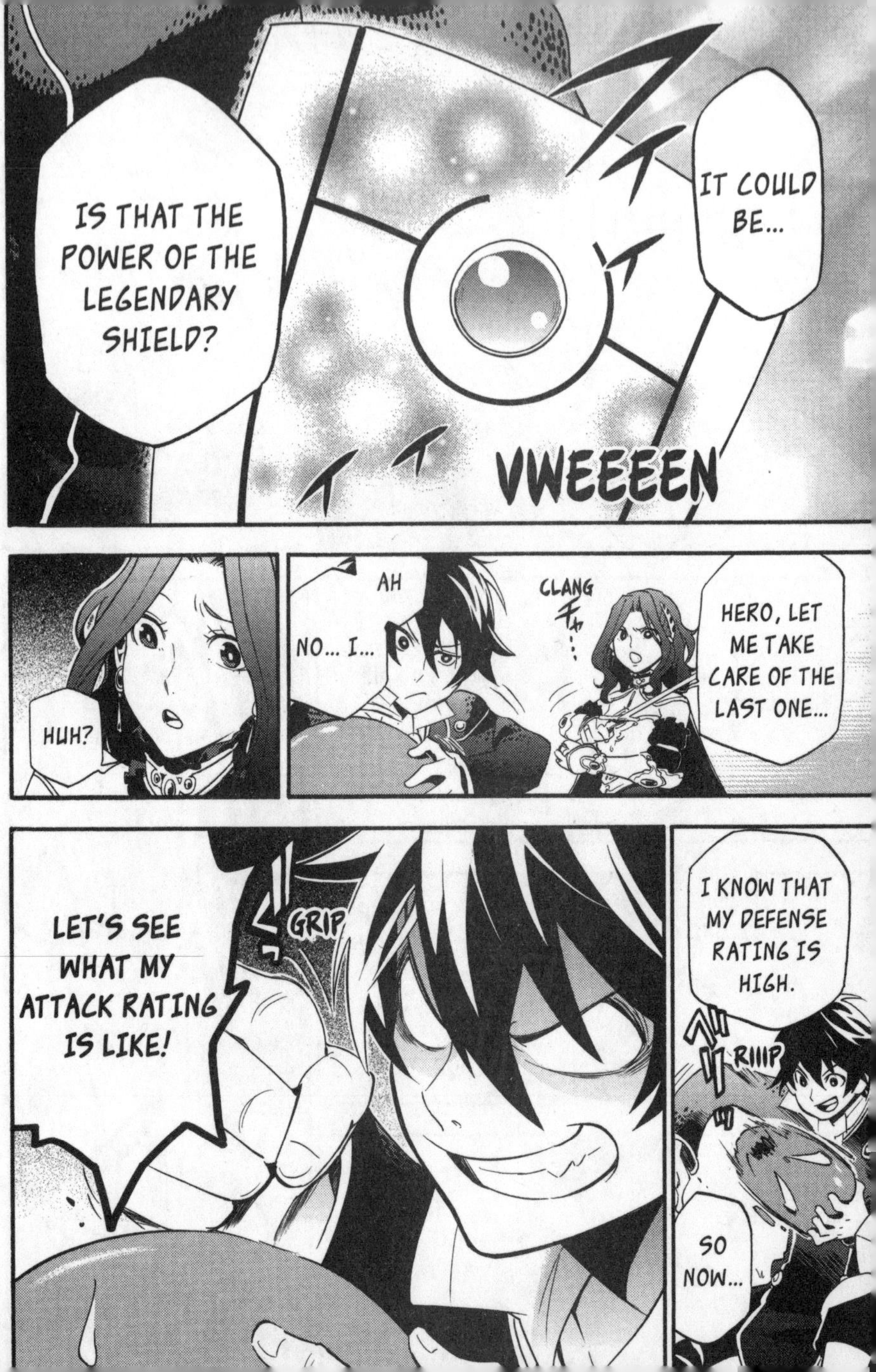
IT COULD BE...
IS THAT THE POWER OF THE LEGENDARY SHIELD?
VWEEEEN
HERO, LET ME TAKE CARE OF THE LAST ONE...
CLANG
AH
NO... I...
HUH?
I KNOW THAT MY DEFENSE RATING IS HIGH.
RIIIP
SO NOW...
GRIP
LET'S SEE WHAT MY ATTACK RATING IS LIKE!

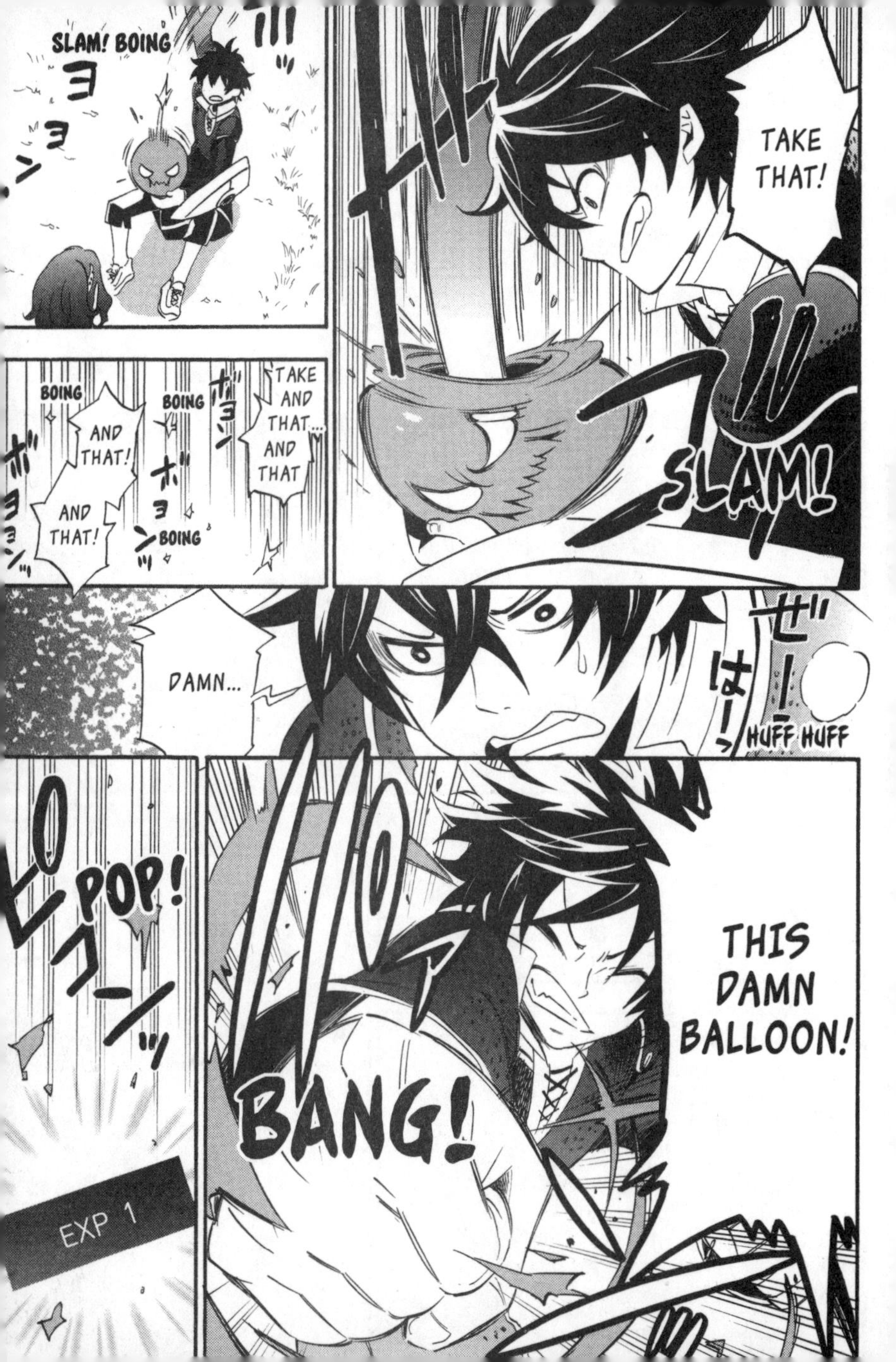

TAKE THAT!
SLAM!
SLAM! BOING
TAKE AND THAT... AND THAT
BOING
AND THAT!
BOING
AND THAT!
BOING
HUFF HUFF
DAMN...
THIS DAMN BALLOON!
BANG!
POP!
EXP 1

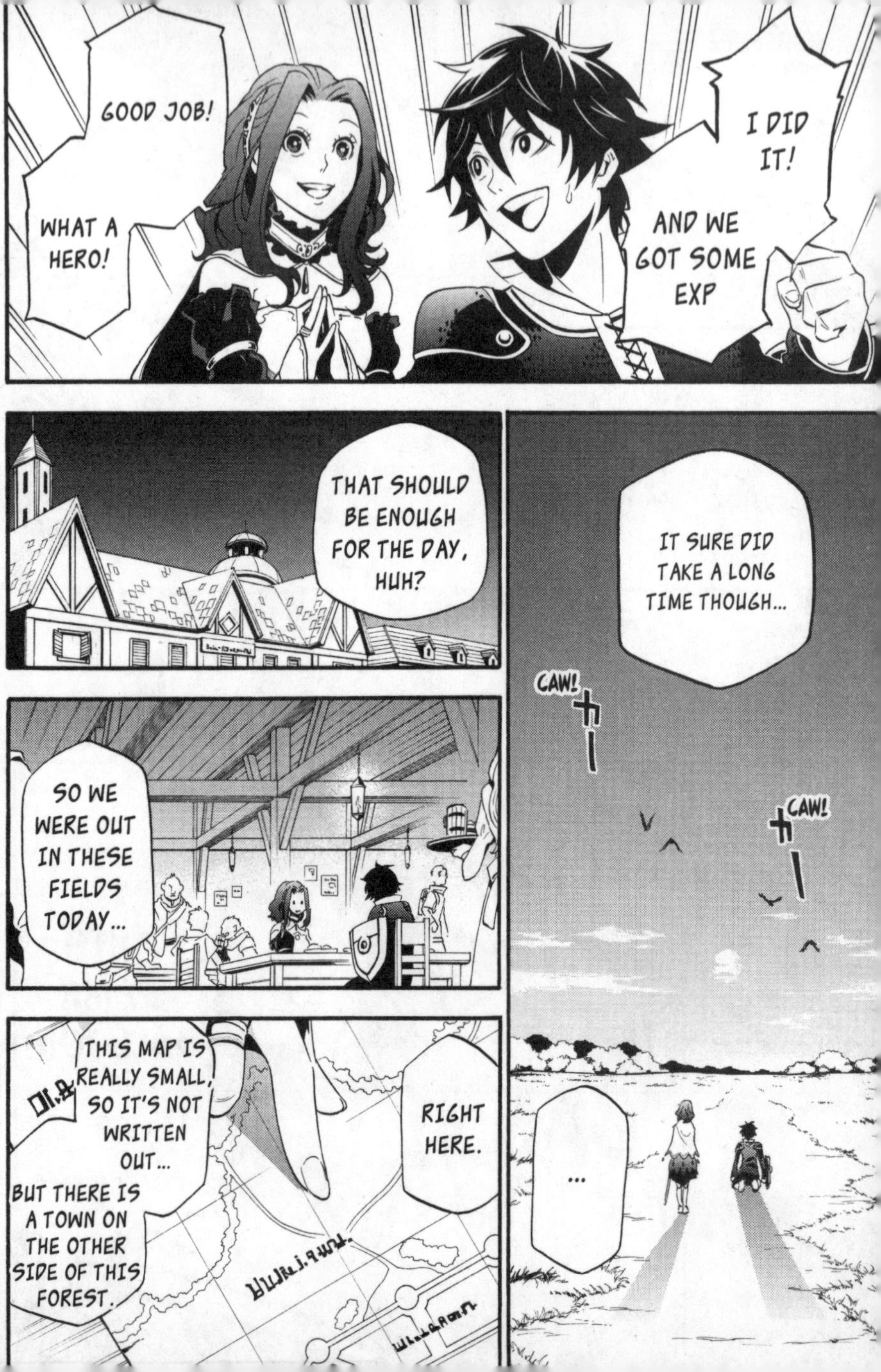
I DID IT!
AND WE GOT SOME EXP
GOOD JOB!
WHAT A HERO!
IT SURE DID TAKE A LONG TIME THOUGH...
CAW!
CAW!
...
THAT SHOULD BE ENOUGH FOR THE DAY, HUH?
SO WE WERE OUT IN THESE FIELDS TODAY...
RIGHT HERE.
THIS MAP IS REALLY SMALL, SO IT'S NOT WRITTEN OUT...
BUT THERE IS A TOWN ON THE OTHER SIDE OF THIS FOREST.

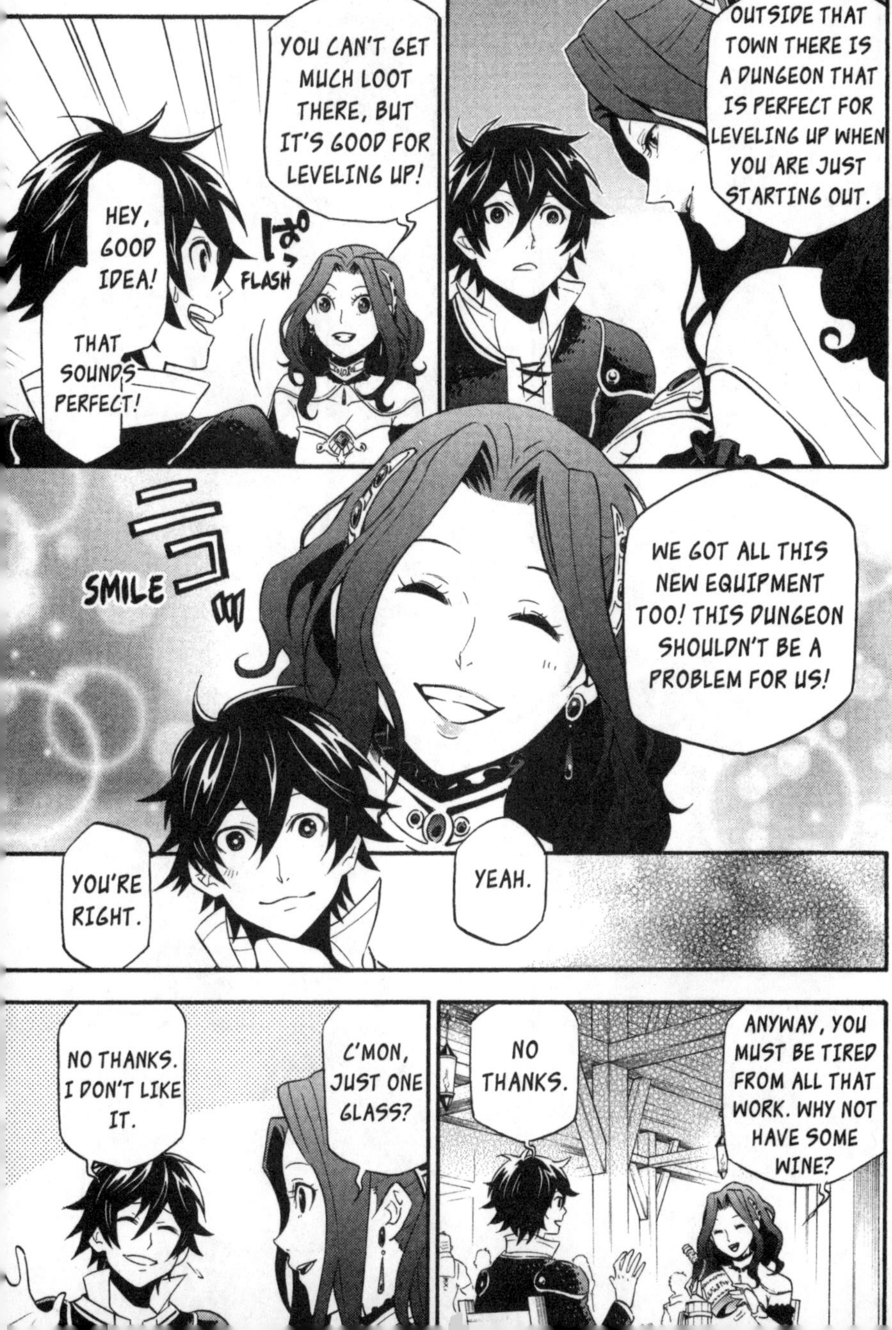

OUTSIDE THAT TOWN THERE IS A DUNGEON THAT IS PERFECT FOR LEVELING UP WHEN YOU ARE JUST STARTING OUT.
YOU CAN'T GET MUCH LOOT THERE, BUT IT'S GOOD FOR LEVELING UP!
ぽっ
FLASH
HEY, GOOD IDEA!
THAT SOUNDS PERFECT!
WE GOT ALL THIS NEW EQUIPMENT TOO! THIS DUNGEON SHOULDN'T BE A PROBLEM FOR US!
ニコ
SMILE
YEAH.
YOU'RE RIGHT.
ANYWAY, YOU MUST BE TIRED FROM ALL THAT WORK. WHY NOT HAVE SOME WINE?
NO THANKS.
C'MON, JUST ONE GLASS?
NO THANKS. I DON'T LIKE IT.

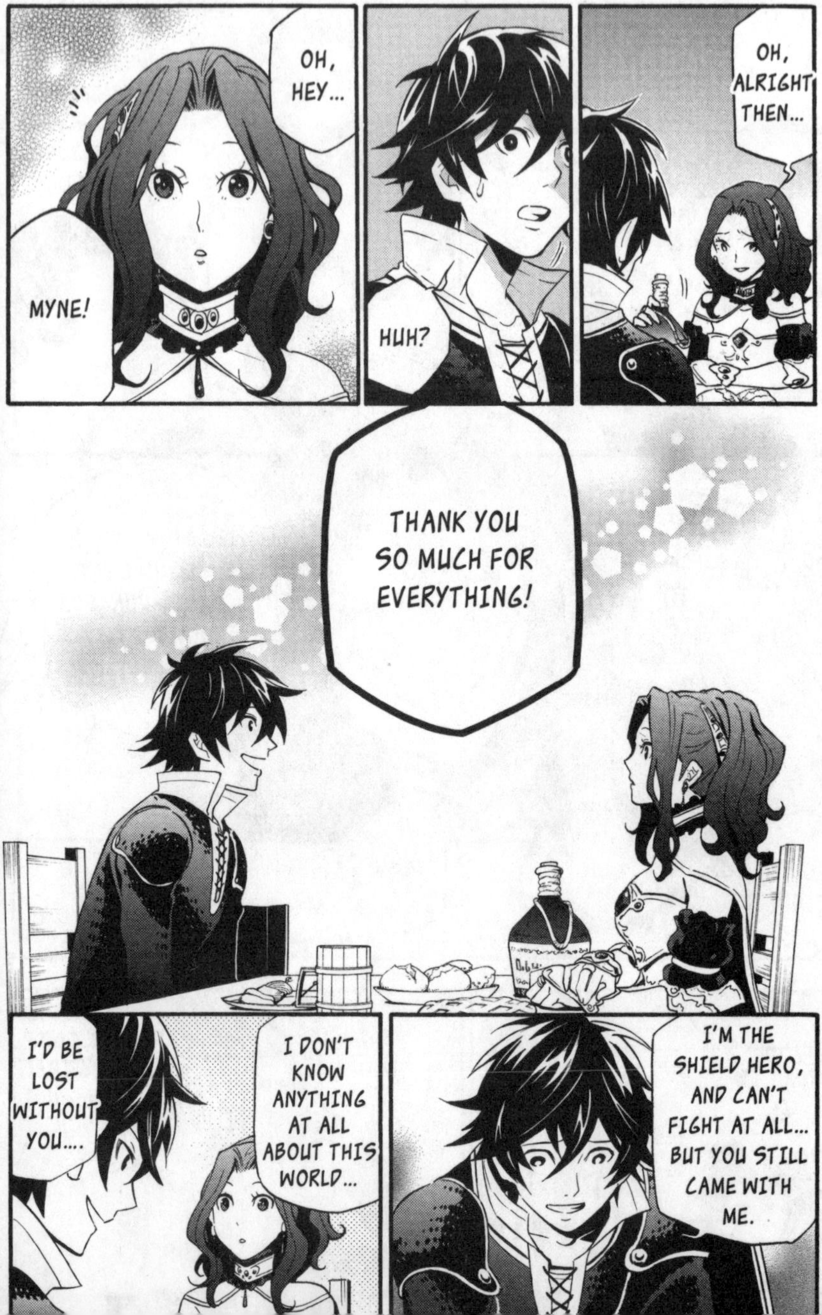

OH, ALRIGHT THEN...
HUH?
OH, HEY...
MYNE!
THANK YOU SO MUCH FOR EVERYTHING!
I'M THE SHIELD HERO, AND CAN'T FIGHT AT ALL... BUT YOU STILL CAME WITH ME.
I DON'T KNOW ANYTHING AT ALL ABOUT THIS WORLD...
I'D BE LOST WITHOUT YOU....

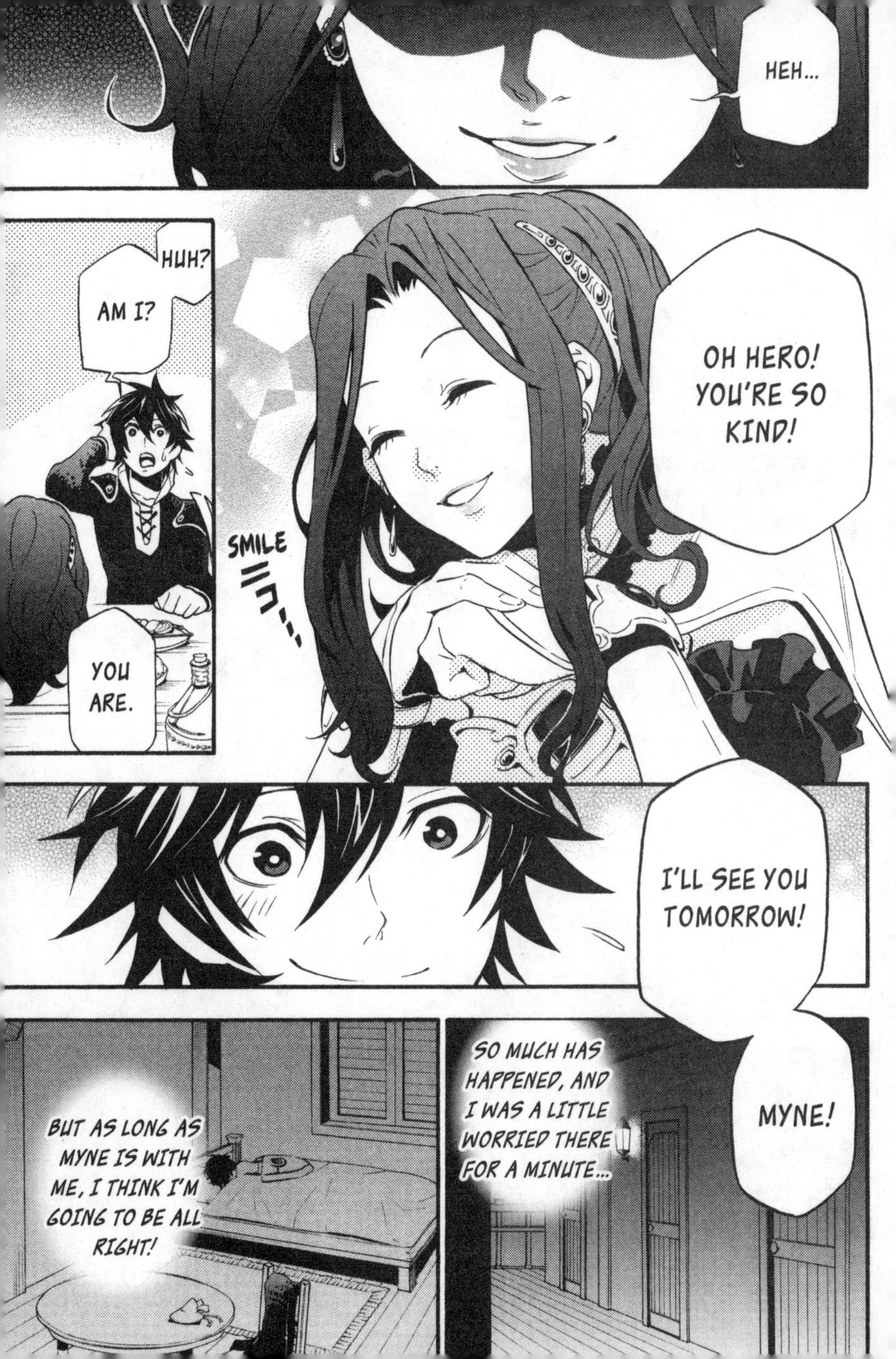
HEH...
OH HERO! YOU'RE SO KIND!
SMILE
HUH?
AM I?
YOU ARE.
I'LL SEE YOU TOMORROW!
MYNE!
SO MUCH HAS HAPPENED, AND I WAS A LITTLE WORRIED THERE FOR A MINUTE...
BUT AS LONG AS MYNE IS WITH ME, I THINK I'M GOING TO BE ALL RIGHT!

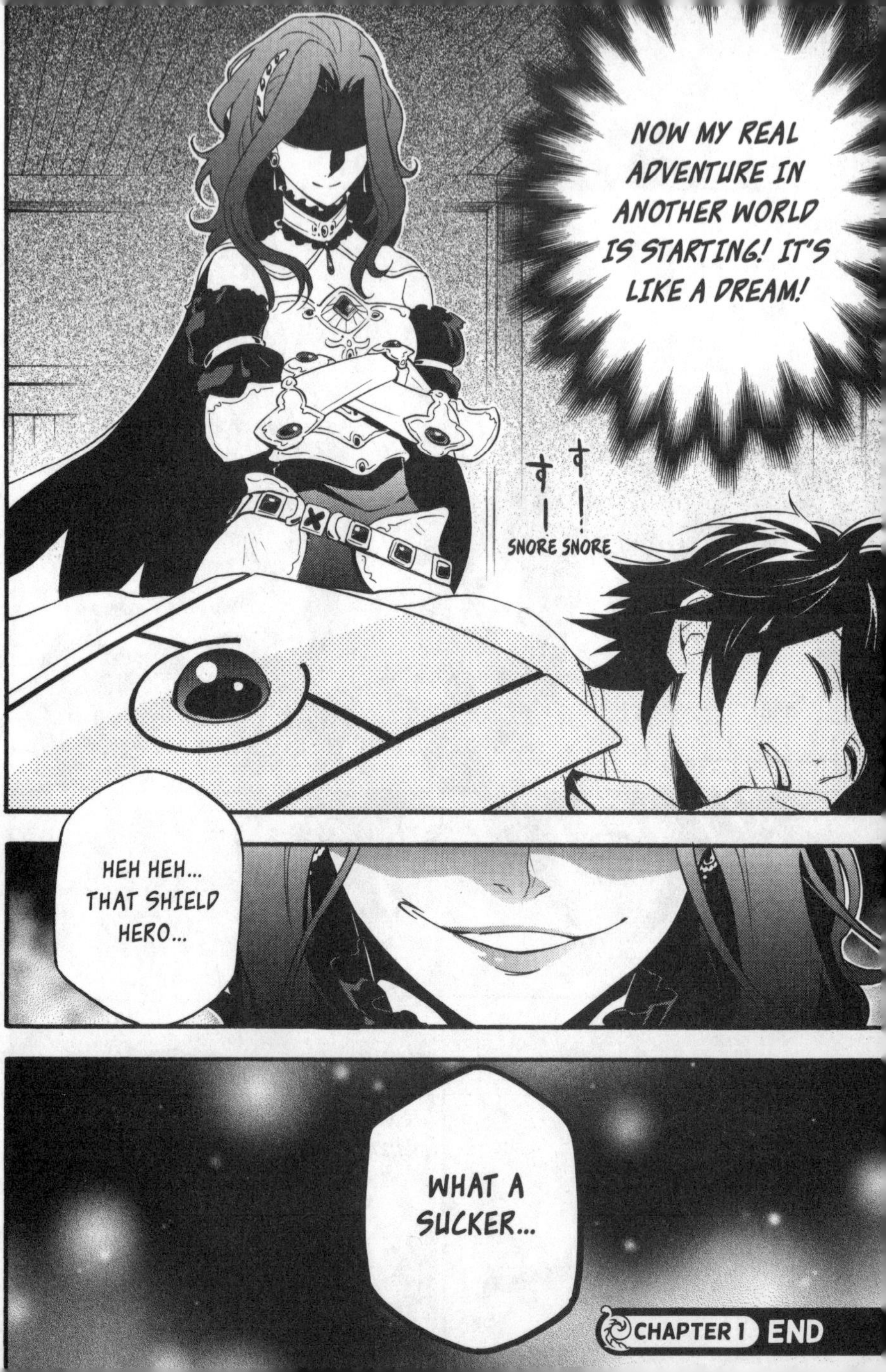
NOW MY REAL ADVENTURE IN ANOTHER WORLD IS STARTING! IT'S LIKE A DREAM!
すー すー
SNORE SNORE
HEH HEH... THAT SHIELD HERO...
WHAT A SUCKER...
CHAPTER 1 END

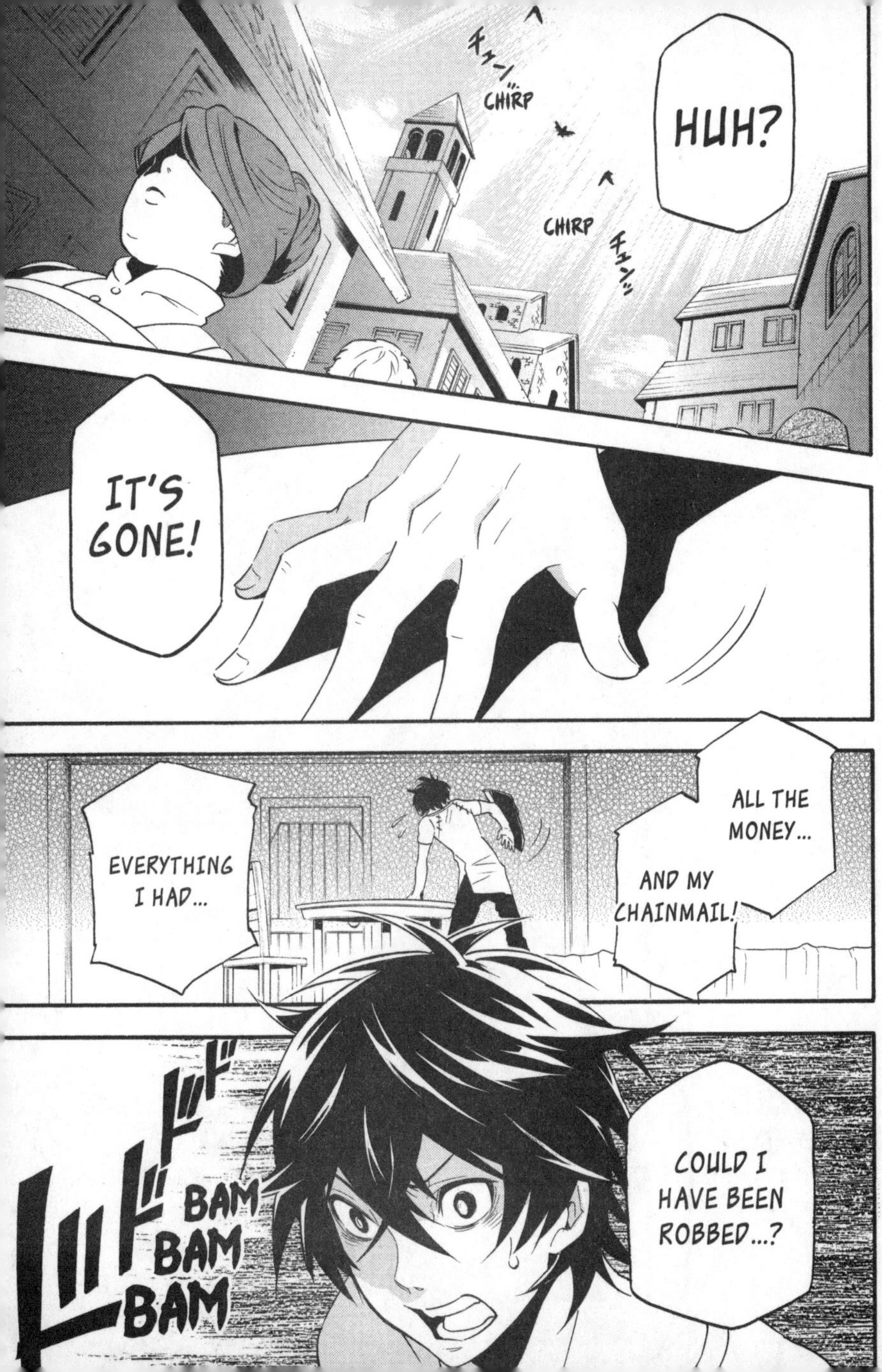
HUH?
チュン
CHIRP
CHIRP
チュンッ
IT'S GONE!
ALL THE MONEY...
AND MY CHAINMAIL!
EVERYTHING I HAD...
COULD I HAVE BEEN ROBBED...?
BAM BAM BAM

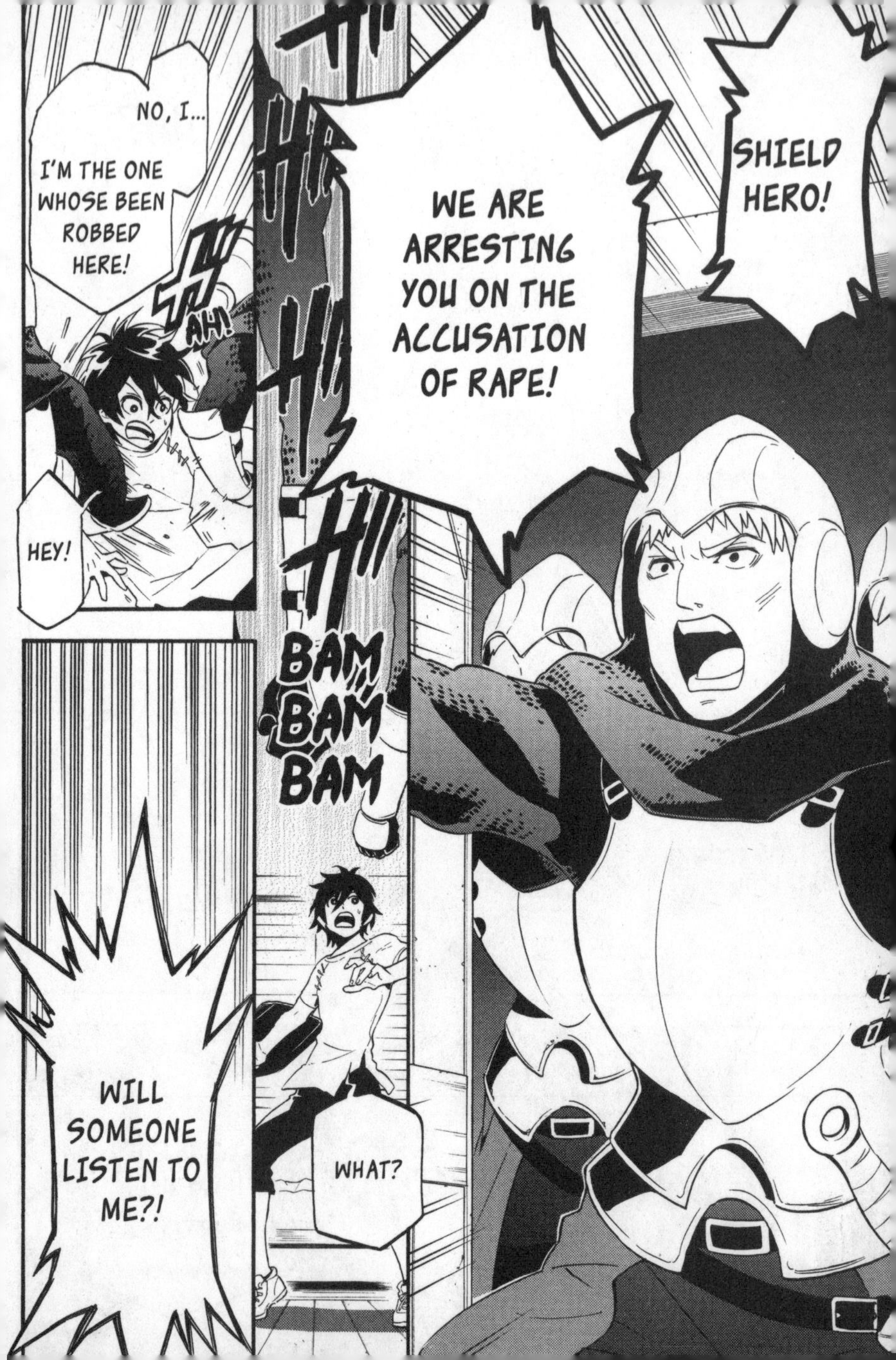
SHIELD HERO!
WE ARE ARRESTING YOU ON THE ACCUSATION OF RAPE!
BAM BAM BAM
WHAT?
NO, I...
I'M THE ONE WHOSE BEEN ROBBED HERE!
AH!
HEY!
WILL SOMEONE LISTEN TO ME?!

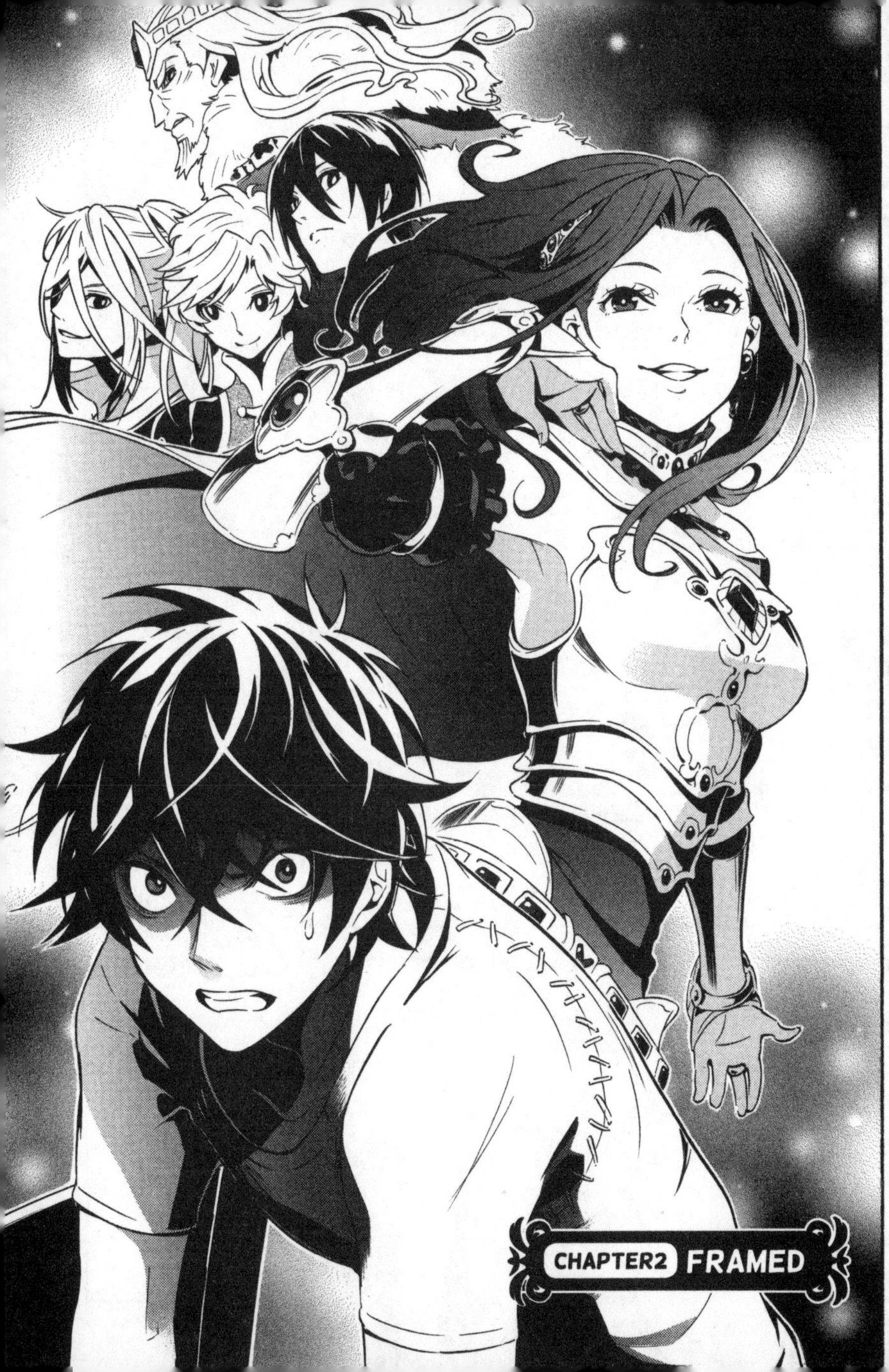
CHAPTER2 FRAMED

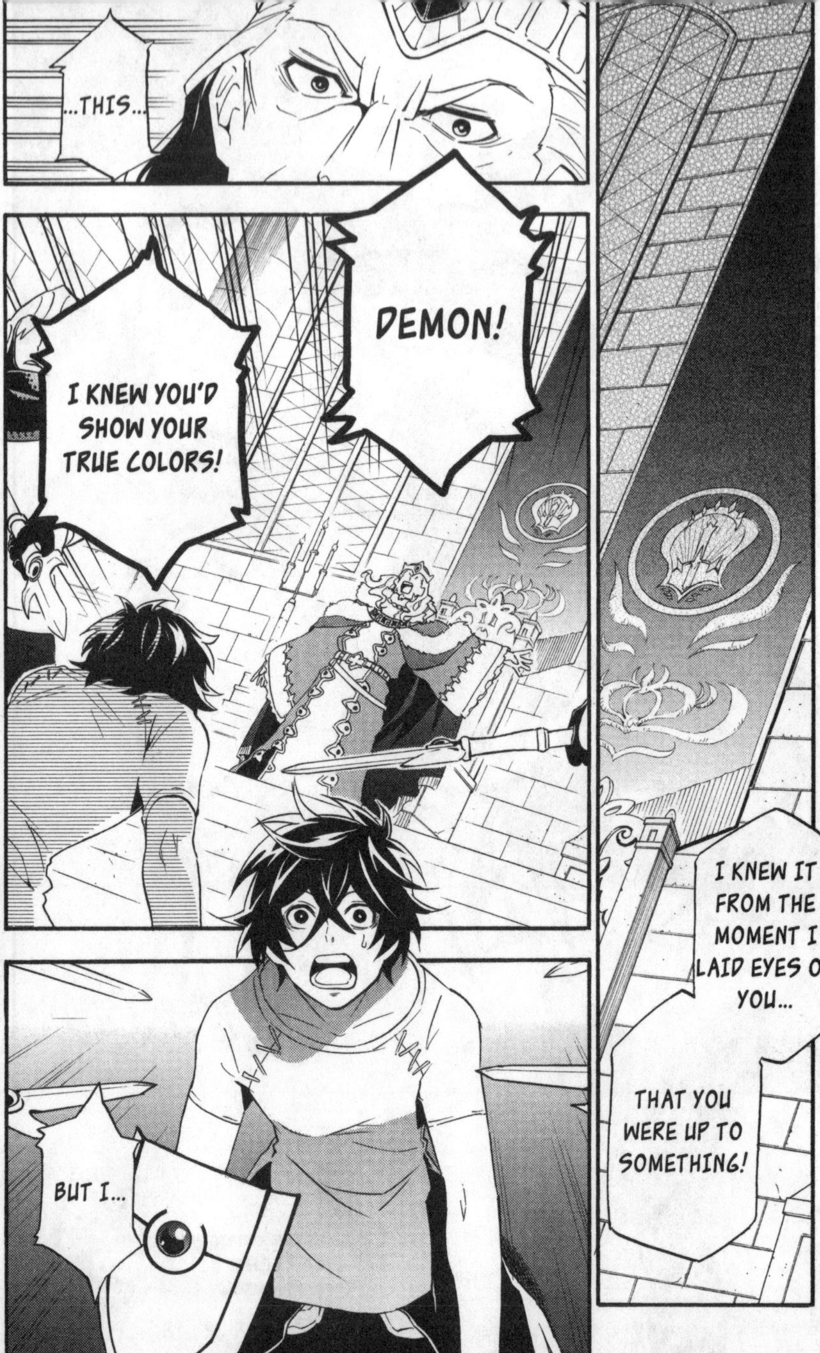
I KNEW IT FROM THE MOMENT I LAID EYES ON YOU...
THAT YOU WERE UP TO SOMETHING!
...THIS...
DEMON!
I KNEW YOU'D SHOW YOUR TRUE COLORS!
BUT I...

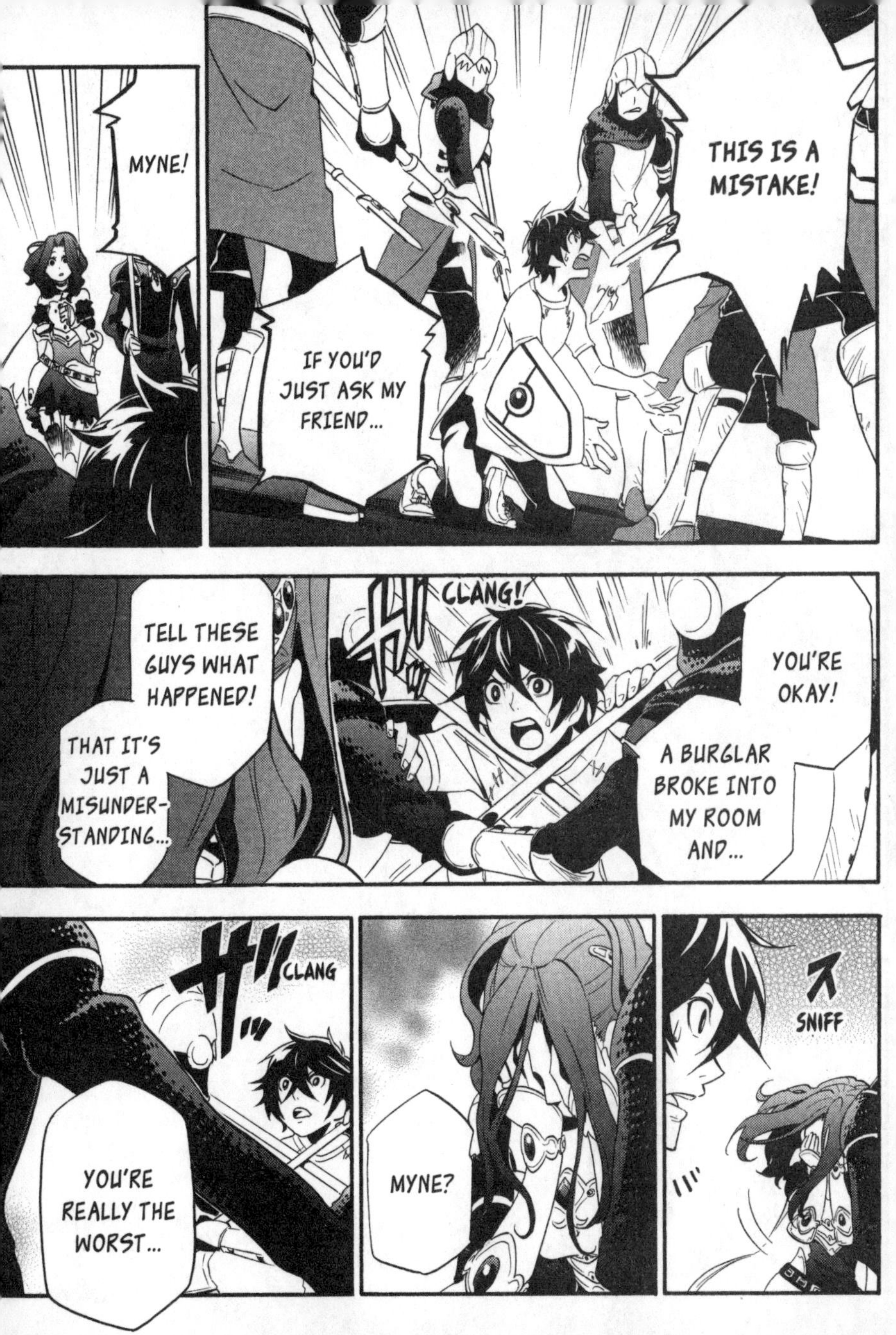
THIS IS A MISTAKE!
IF YOU'D JUST ASK MY FRIEND...
MYNE!
CLANG!
YOU'RE OKAY!
A BURGLAR BROKE INTO MY ROOM AND...
TELL THESE GUYS WHAT HAPPENED!
THAT IT'S JUST A MISUNDER-STANDING...
SNIFF
MYNE?
CLANG
YOU'RE REALLY THE WORST...

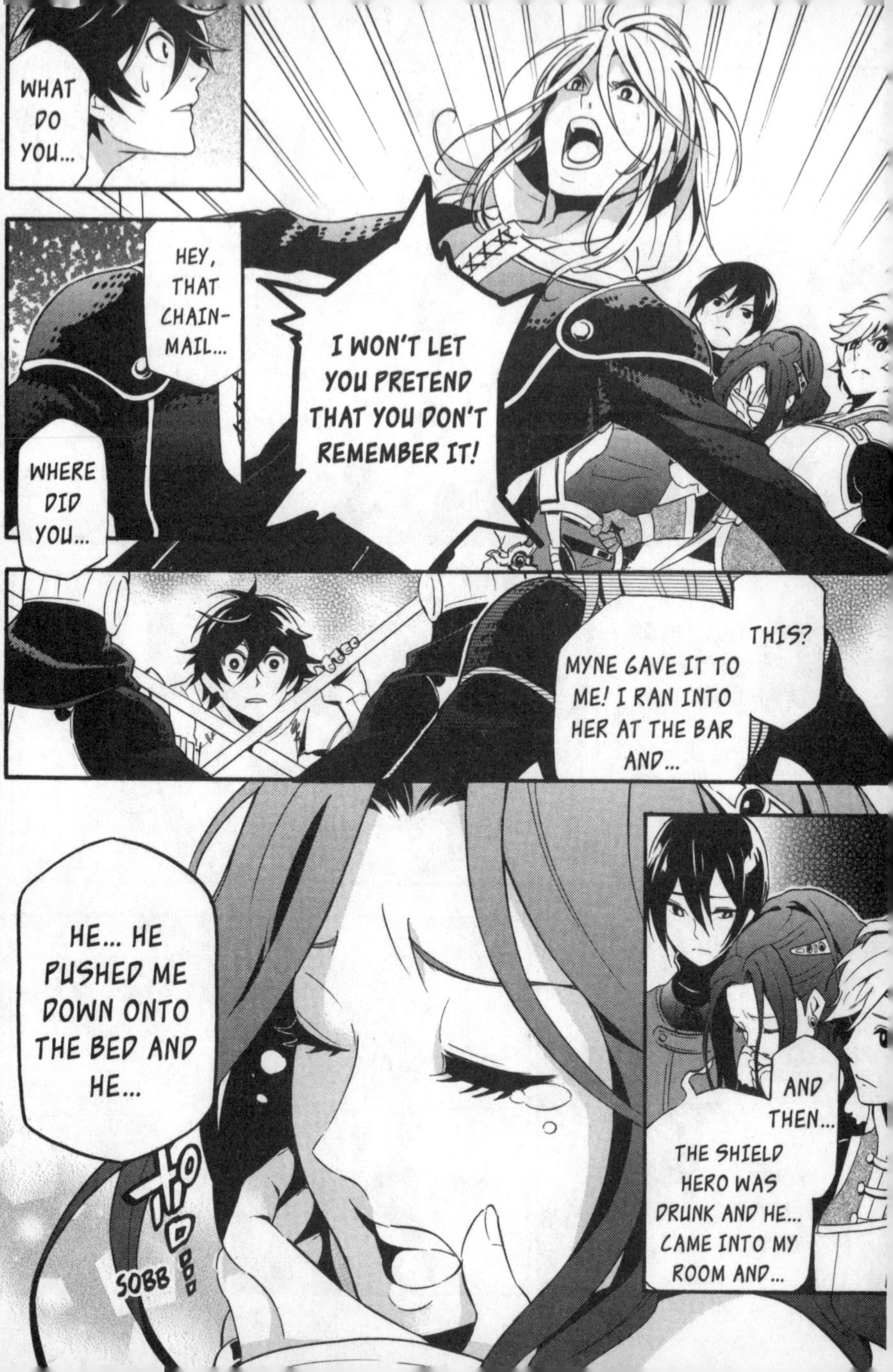
I WON'T LET YOU PRETEND THAT YOU DON'T REMEMBER IT!
WHAT DO YOU...
HEY, THAT CHAIN-MAIL...
WHERE DID YOU...
THIS?
MYNE GAVE IT TO ME! I RAN INTO HER AT THE BAR AND...
AND THEN...
THE SHIELD HERO WAS DRUNK AND HE... CAME INTO MY ROOM AND...
HE... HE PUSHED ME DOWN ONTO THE BED AND HE...
SOBB

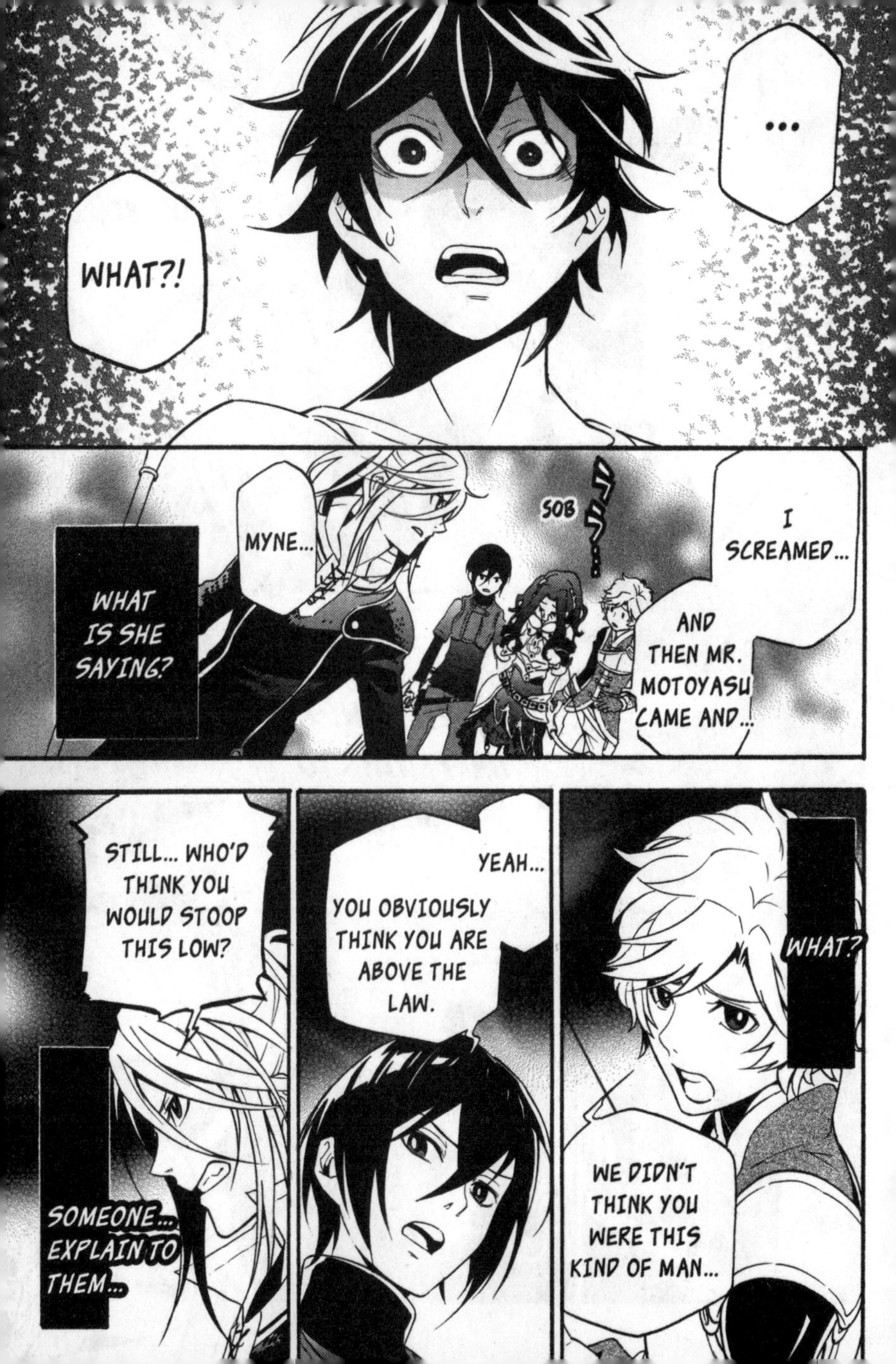
...
WHAT?!
I SCREAMED... AND THEN MR. MOTOYASU CAME AND...
SOB
MYNE...
WHAT IS SHE SAYING?
WHAT?
WE DIDN'T THINK YOU WERE THIS KIND OF MAN...
YEAH...
YOU OBVIOUSLY THINK YOU ARE ABOVE THE LAW.
STILL... WHO'D THINK YOU WOULD STOOP THIS LOW?
SOMEONE... EXPLAIN TO THEM...

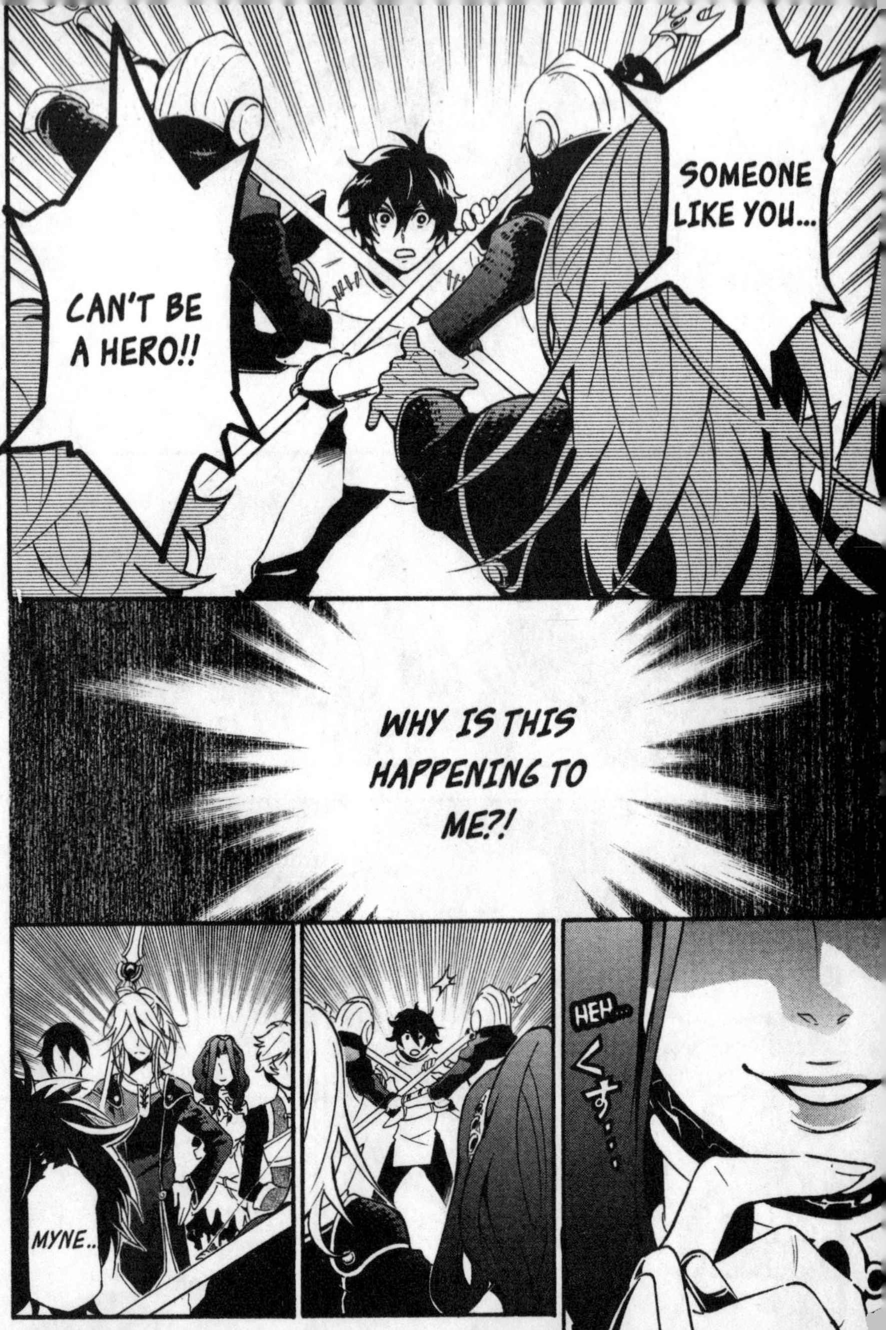
SOMEONE LIKE YOU...
CAN'T BE A HERO!!
WHY IS THIS HAPPENING TO ME?!
HEH...
くす...
MYNE..

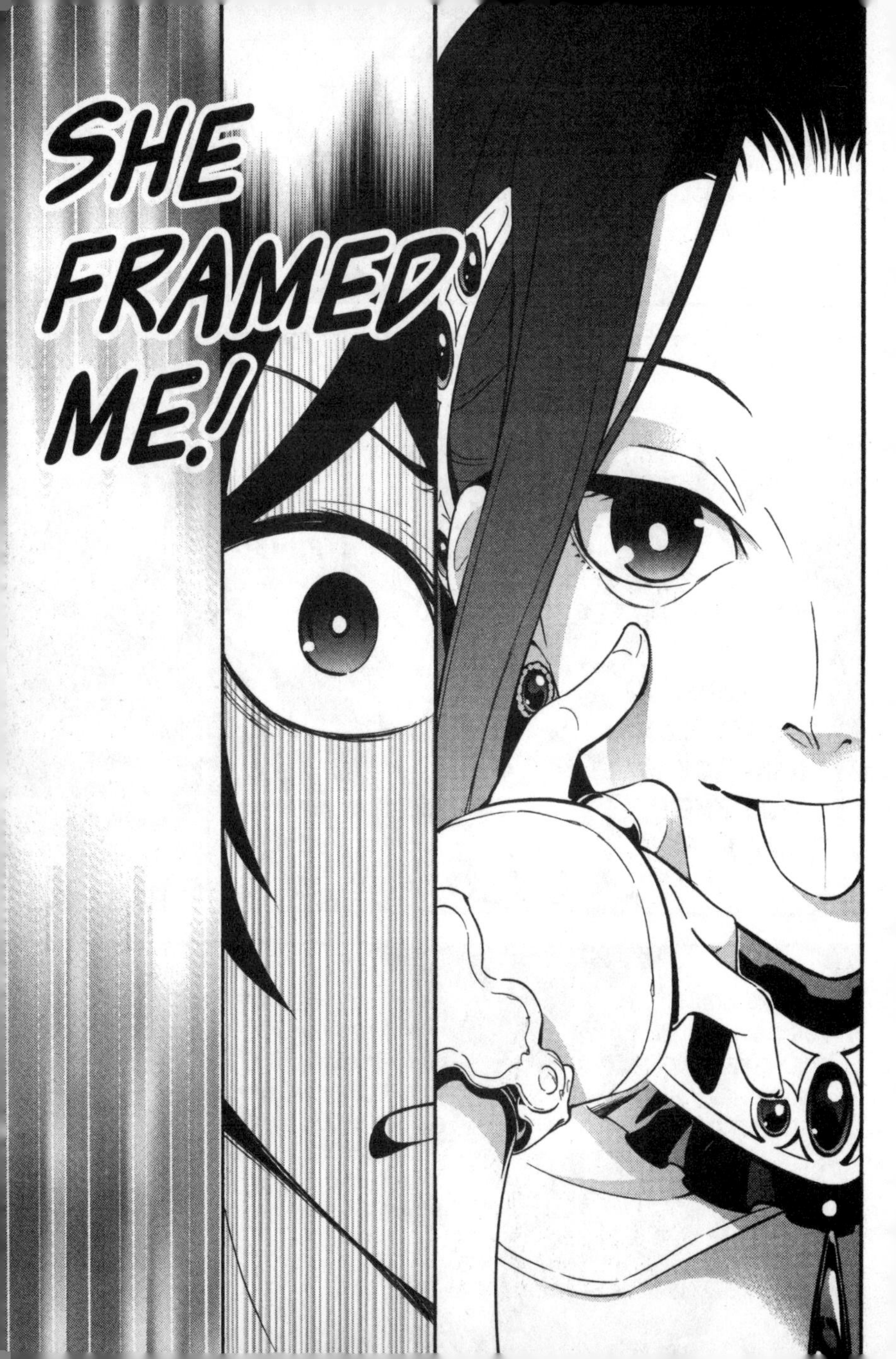
SHE FRAMED ME!

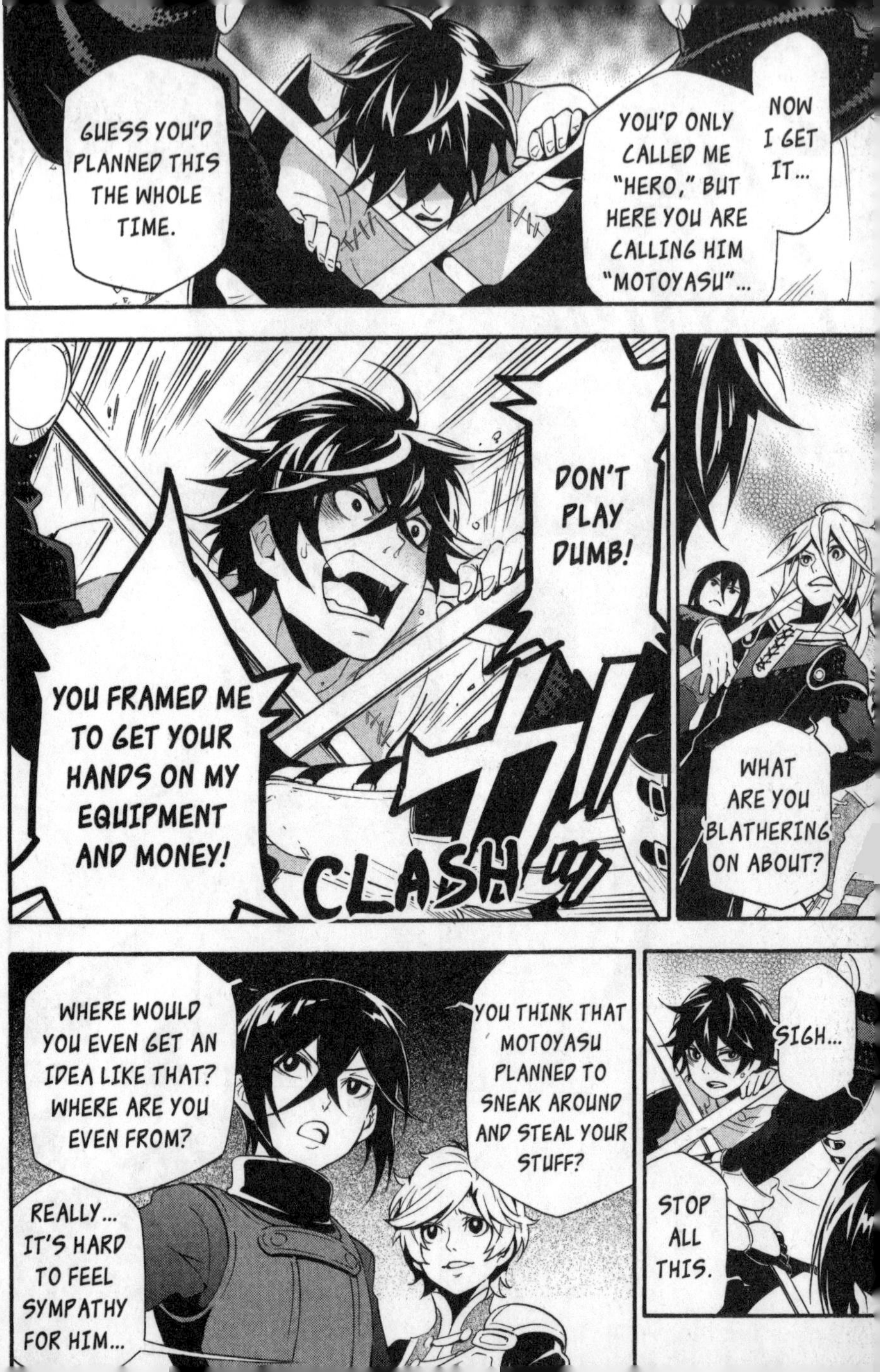
NOW I GET IT...
YOU'D ONLY CALLED ME "HERO," BUT HERE YOU ARE CALLING HIM "MOTOYASU"...
GUESS YOU'D PLANNED THIS THE WHOLE TIME.
WHAT ARE YOU BLATHERING ON ABOUT?
DON'T PLAY DUMB!
YOU FRAMED ME TO GET YOUR HANDS ON MY EQUIPMENT AND MONEY!
CLASH
SIGH...
STOP ALL THIS.
YOU THINK THAT MOTOYASU PLANNED TO SNEAK AROUND AND STEAL YOUR STUFF?
WHERE WOULD YOU EVEN GET AN IDEA LIKE THAT? WHERE ARE YOU EVEN FROM?
REALLY... IT'S HARD TO FEEL SYMPATHY FOR HIM...

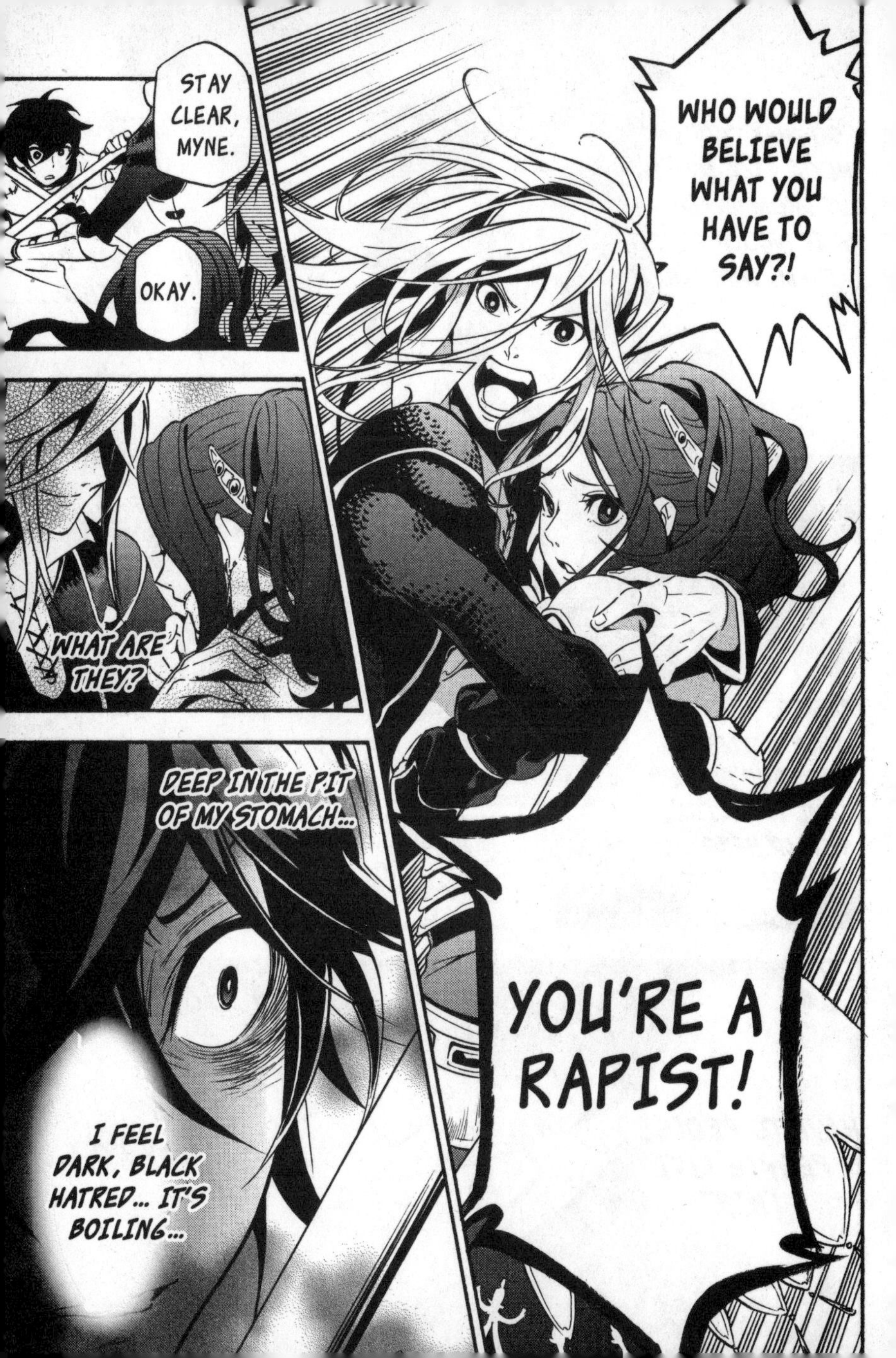
WHO WOULD BELIEVE WHAT YOU HAVE TO SAY?!
YOU'RE A RAPIST!
STAY CLEAR, MYNE.
OKAY.
WHAT ARE THEY?
DEEP IN THE PIT OF MY STOMACH...
I FEEL DARK, BLACK HATRED... IT'S BOILING...

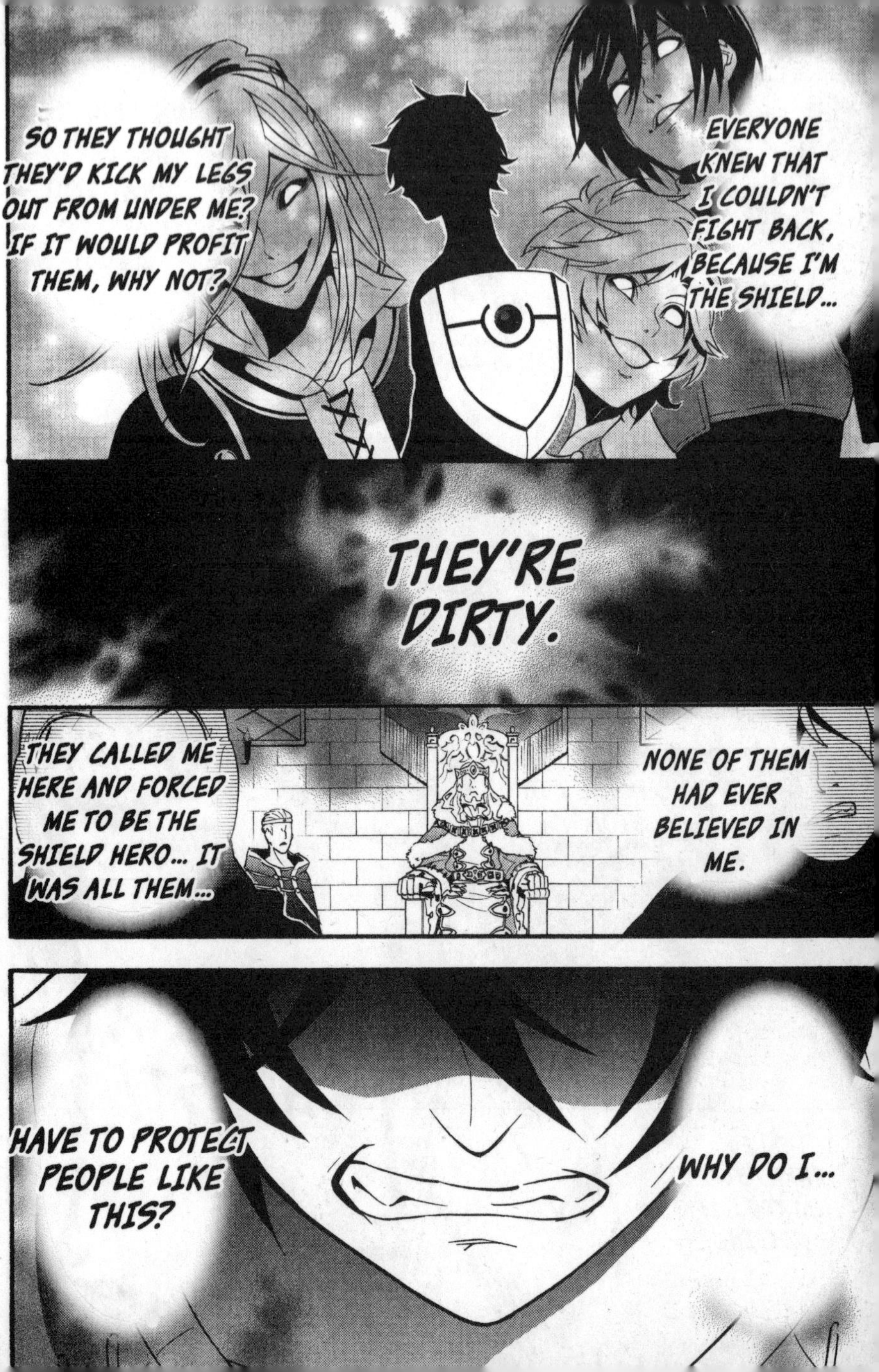
EVERYONE KNEW THAT I COULDN'T FIGHT BACK, BECAUSE I'M THE SHIELD...
SO THEY THOUGHT THEY'D KICK MY LEGS OUT FROM UNDER ME? IF IT WOULD PROFIT THEM, WHY NOT?
THEY'RE DIRTY.
NONE OF THEM HAD EVER BELIEVED IN ME.
THEY CALLED ME HERE AND FORCED ME TO BE THE SHIELD HERO... IT WAS ALL THEM...
WHY DO I...
HAVE TO PROTECT PEOPLE LIKE THIS?

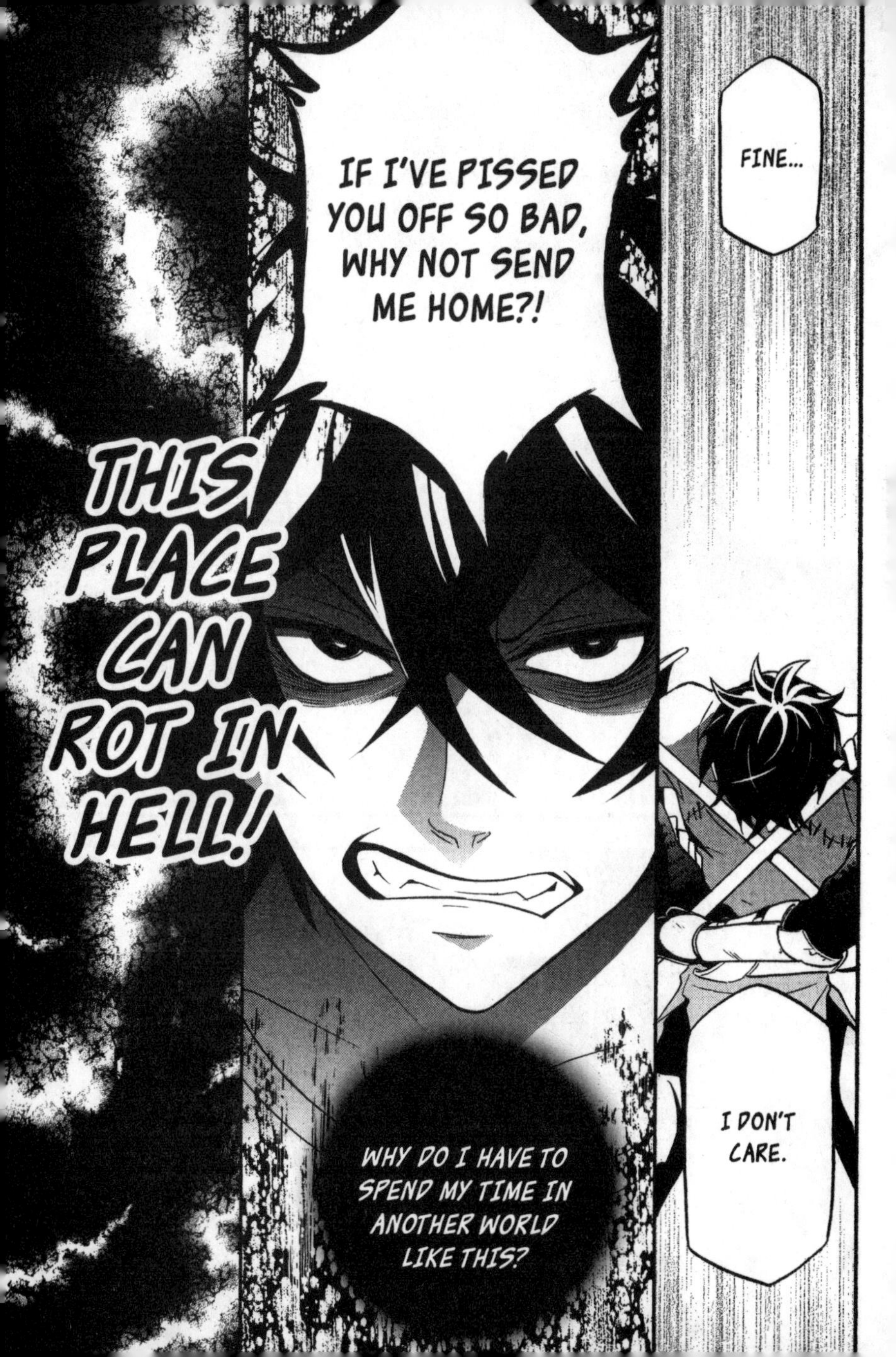
FINE...
I DON'T CARE.
IF I'VE PISSED YOU OFF SO BAD, WHY NOT SEND ME HOME?!
THIS PLACE CAN ROT IN HELL!
WHY DO I HAVE TO SPEND MY TIME IN ANOTHER WORLD LIKE THIS?

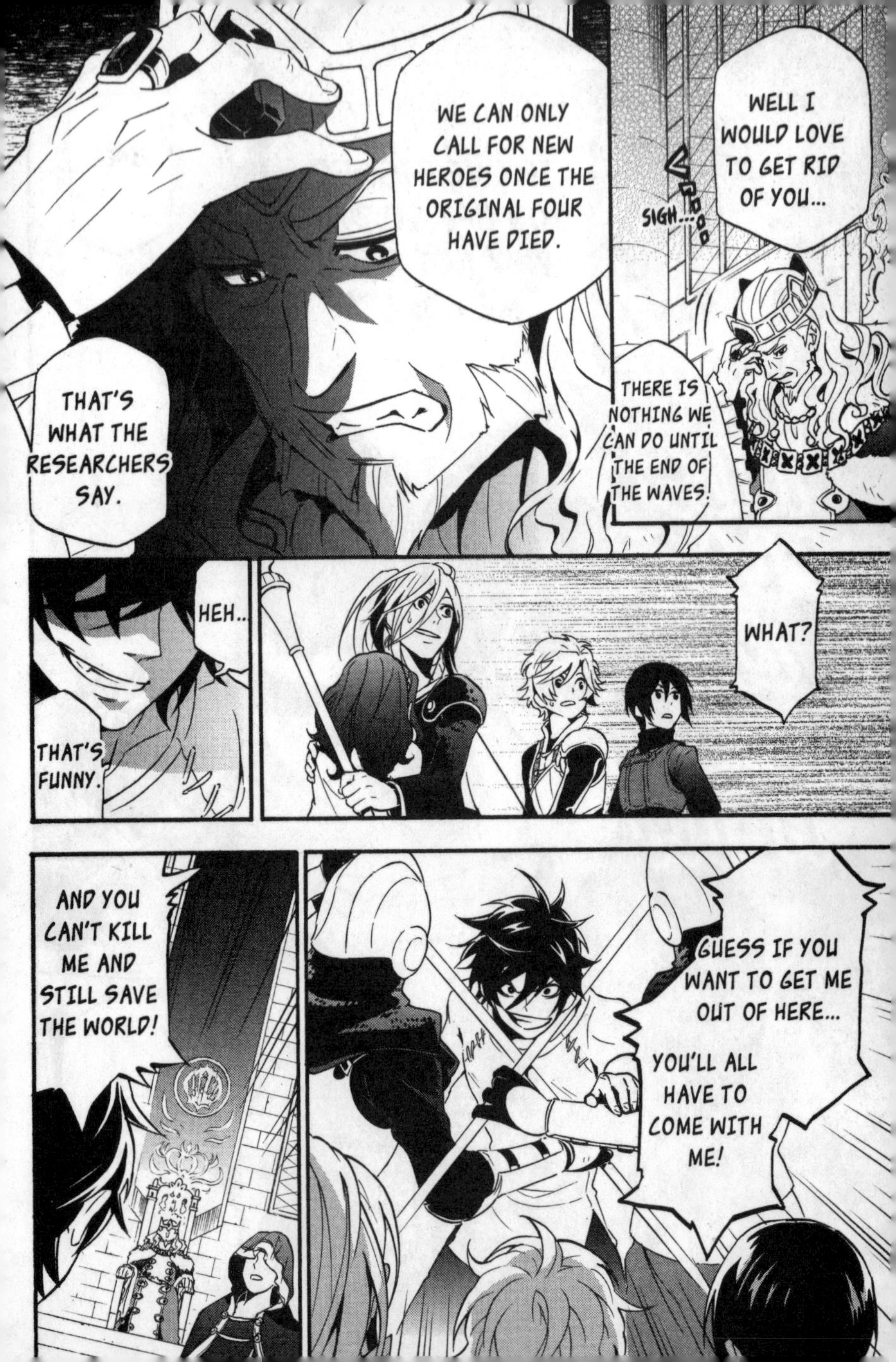
WELL I WOULD LOVE TO GET RID OF YOU...
SIGH...
THERE IS NOTHING WE CAN DO UNTIL THE END OF THE WAVES.
WE CAN ONLY CALL FOR NEW HEROES ONCE THE ORIGINAL FOUR HAVE DIED.
THAT'S WHAT THE RESEARCHERS SAY.
WHAT?
HEH...
THAT'S FUNNY.
GUESS IF YOU WANT TO GET ME OUT OF HERE...
YOU'LL ALL HAVE TO COME WITH ME!
AND YOU CAN'T KILL ME AND STILL SAVE THE WORLD!

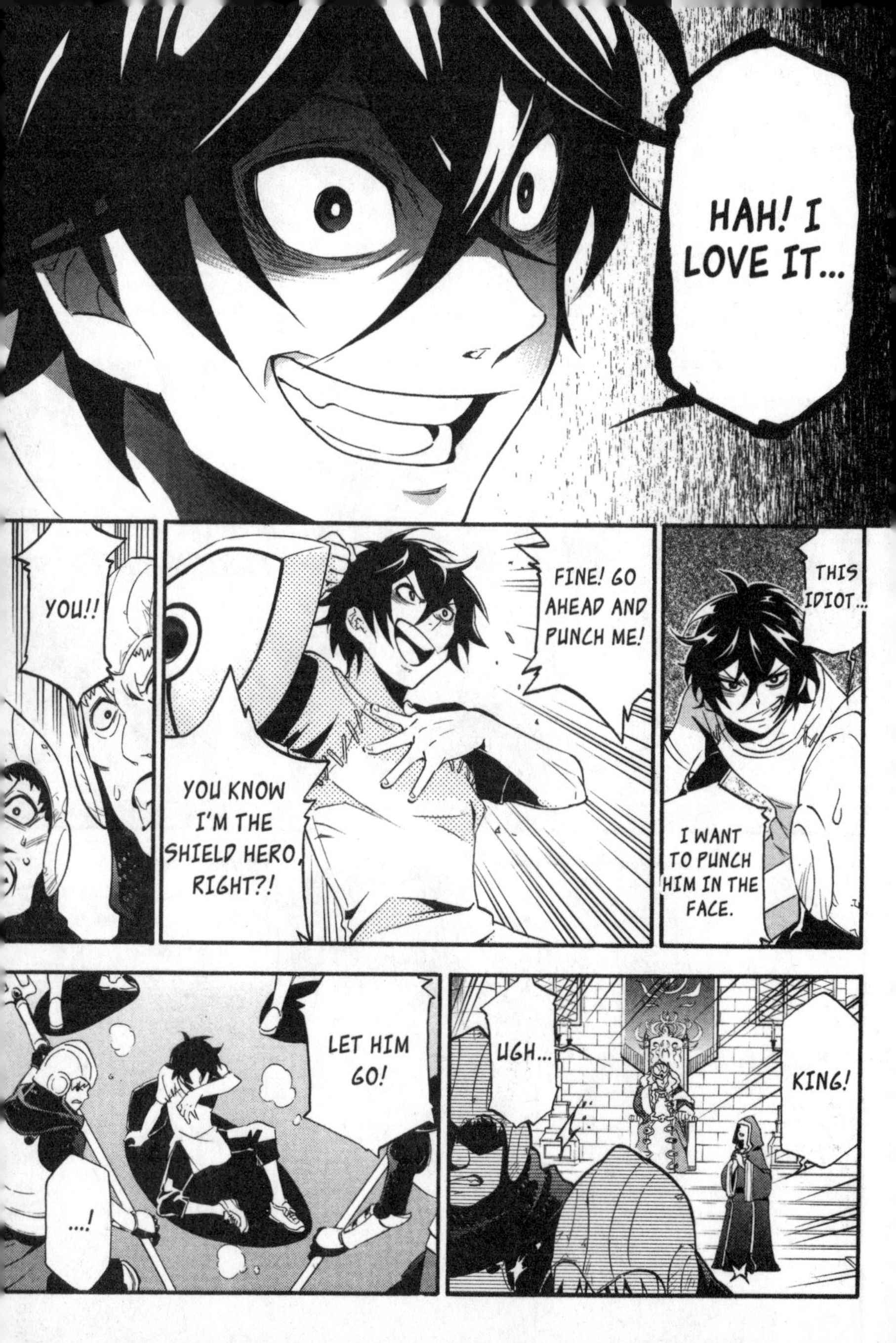
HAH! I LOVE IT...
THIS IDIOT...
I WANT TO PUNCH HIM IN THE FACE.
FINE! GO AHEAD AND PUNCH ME!
YOU KNOW I'M THE SHIELD HERO, RIGHT?!
YOU!!
KING!
UGH...
LET HIM GO!
...!

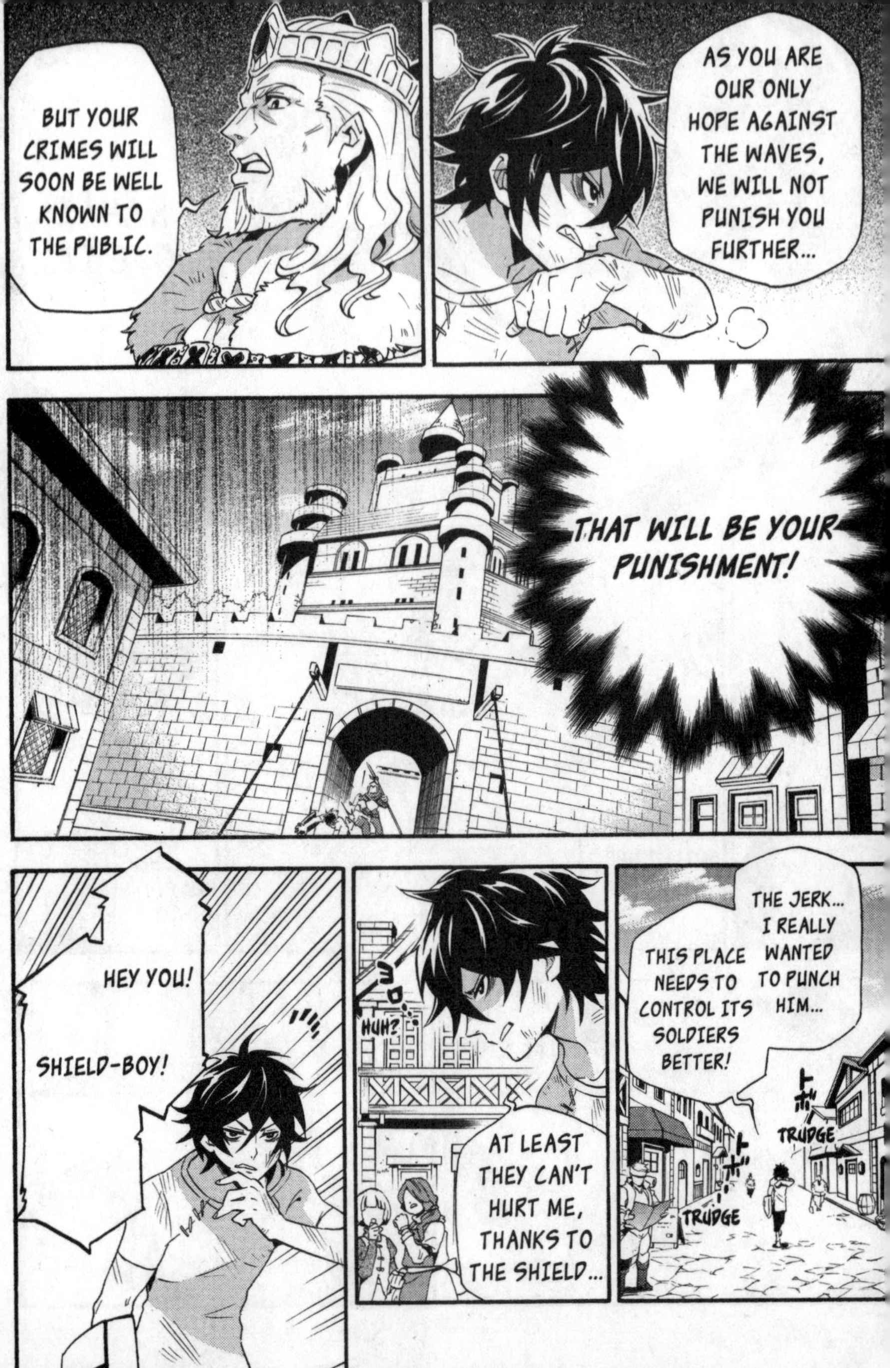
AS YOU ARE OUR ONLY HOPE AGAINST THE WAVES, WE WILL NOT PUNISH YOU FURTHER...
BUT YOUR CRIMES WILL SOON BE WELL KNOWN TO THE PUBLIC.
THAT WILL BE YOUR PUNISHMENT!
THE JERK... I REALLY WANTED TO PUNCH HIM...
THIS PLACE NEEDS TO CONTROL ITS SOLDIERS BETTER!
TRUDGE
TRUDGE
HUH?
AT LEAST THEY CAN'T HURT ME, THANKS TO THE SHIELD...
HEY YOU!
SHIELD-BOY!

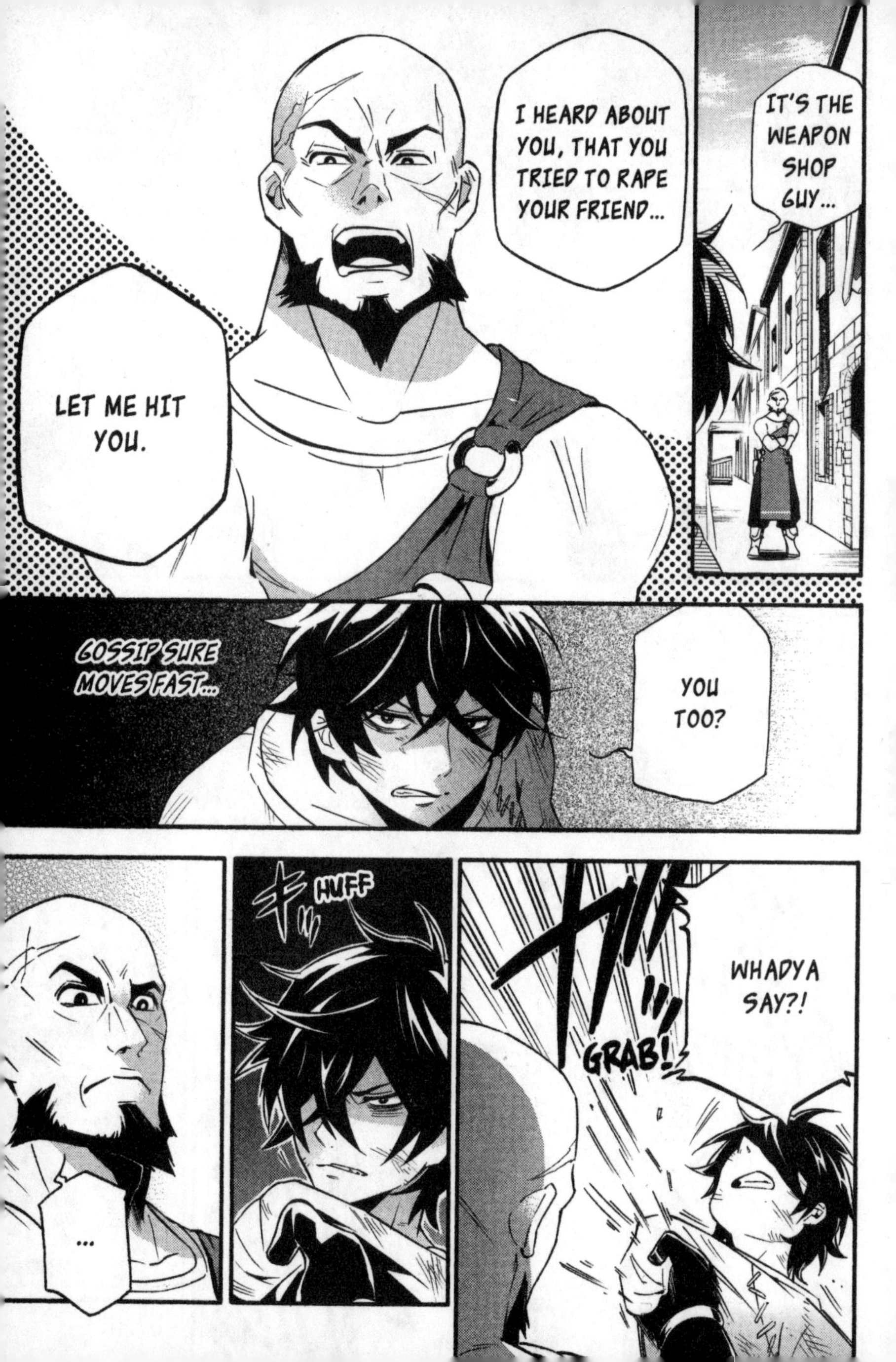
IT'S THE WEAPON SHOP GUY...
I HEARD ABOUT YOU, THAT YOU TRIED TO RAPE YOUR FRIEND...
LET ME HIT YOU.
YOU TOO?
GOSSIP SURE MOVES FAST...
WHADYA SAY?!
GRAB!
HUFF
...

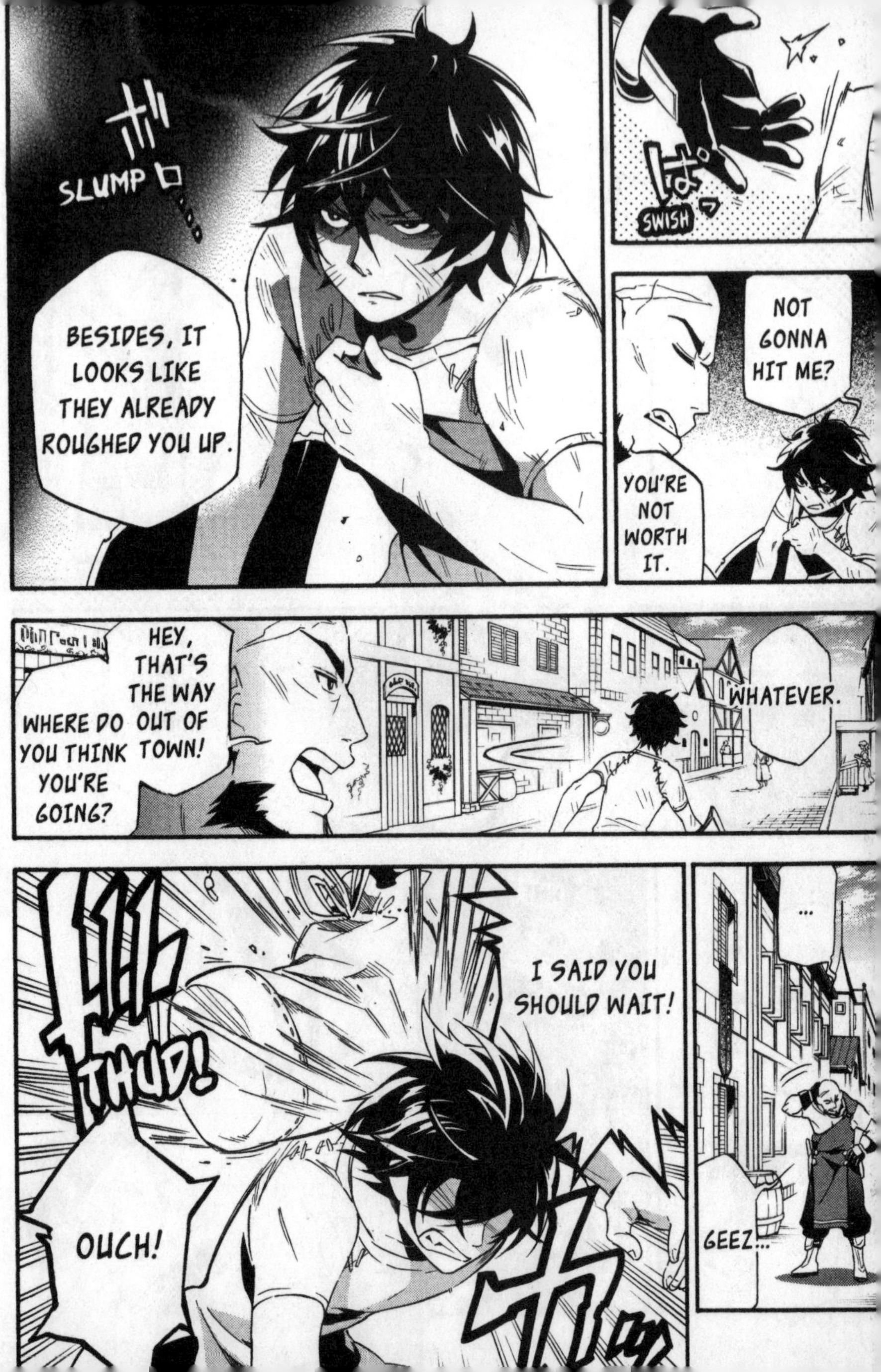
SWISH
NOT GONNA HIT ME?
YOU'RE NOT WORTH IT.
SLUMP
BESIDES, IT LOOKS LIKE THEY ALREADY ROUGHED YOU UP.
WHATEVER.
HEY, THAT'S THE WAY OUT OF TOWN!
WHERE DO YOU THINK YOU'RE GOING?
...
GEEZ...
I SAID YOU SHOULD WAIT!
THUD!
OUCH!

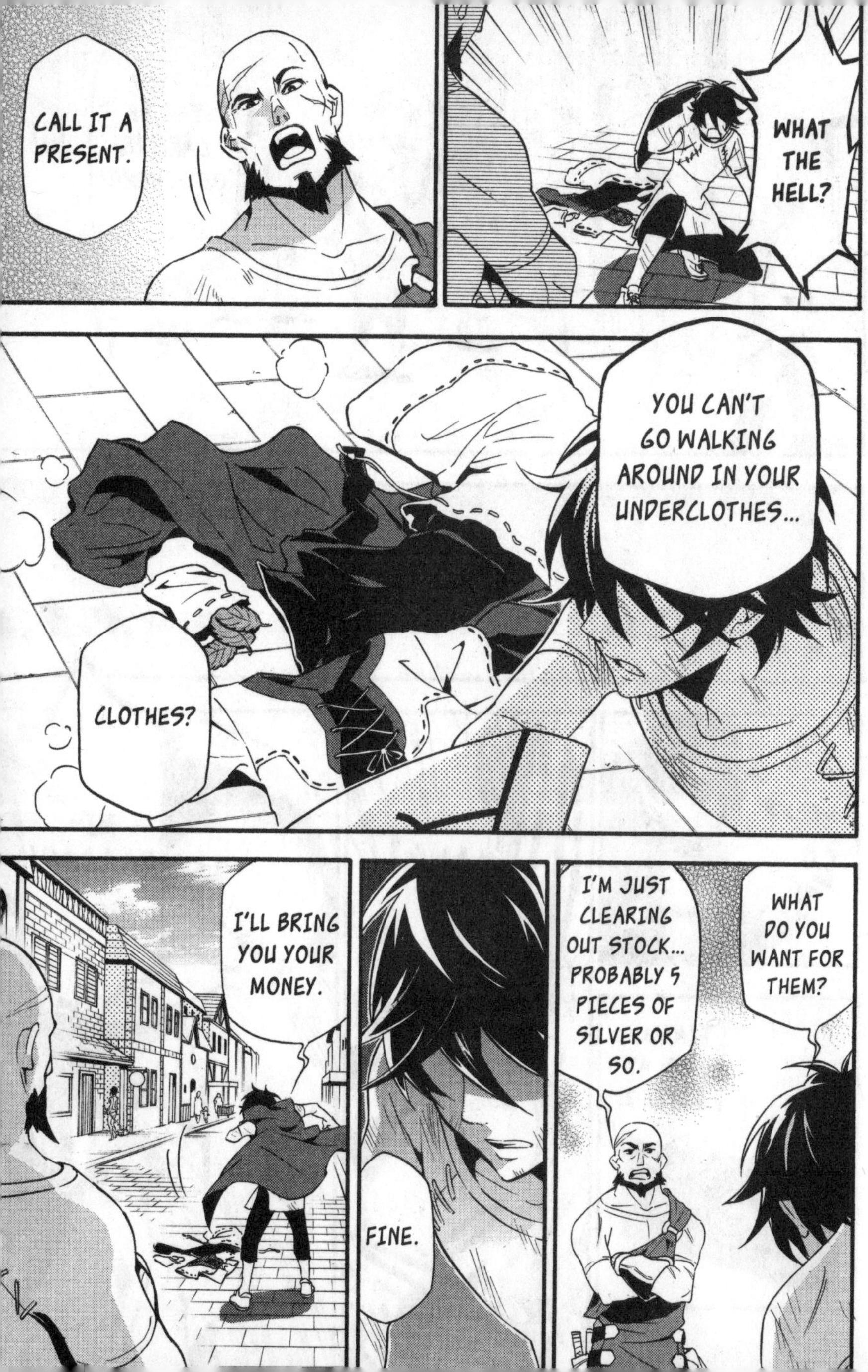
WHAT THE HELL?
CALL IT A PRESENT.
YOU CAN'T GO WALKING AROUND IN YOUR UNDERCLOTHES...
CLOTHES?
WHAT DO YOU WANT FOR THEM?
I'M JUST CLEARING OUT STOCK... PROBABLY 5 PIECES OF SILVER OR SO.
FINE.
I'LL BRING YOU YOUR MONEY.

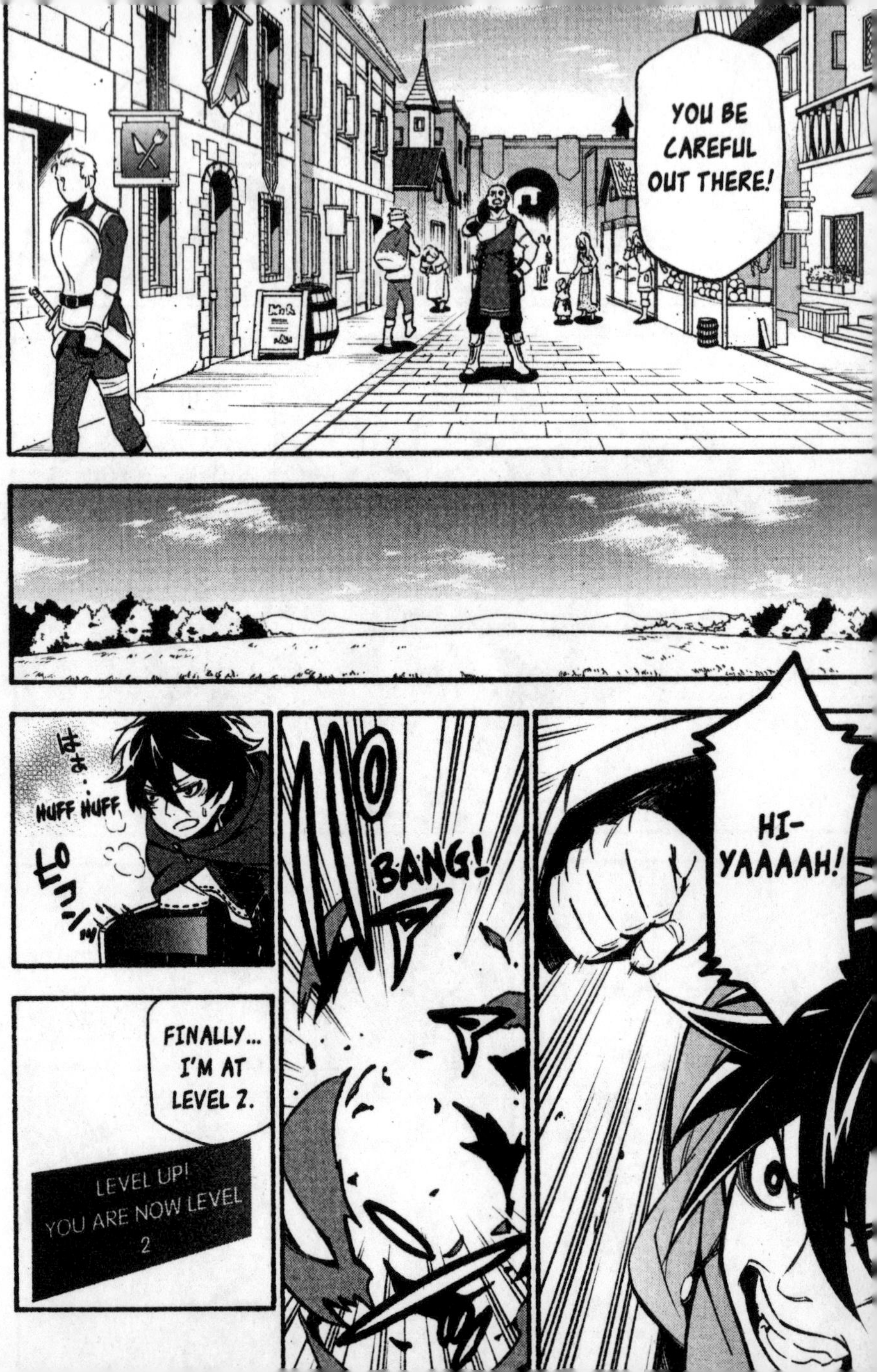
YOU BE CAREFUL OUT THERE!
HI-YAAAAH!
BANG!
HUFF HUFF
FINALLY... I'M AT LEVEL 2.
LEVEL UP! YOU ARE NOW LEVEL 2

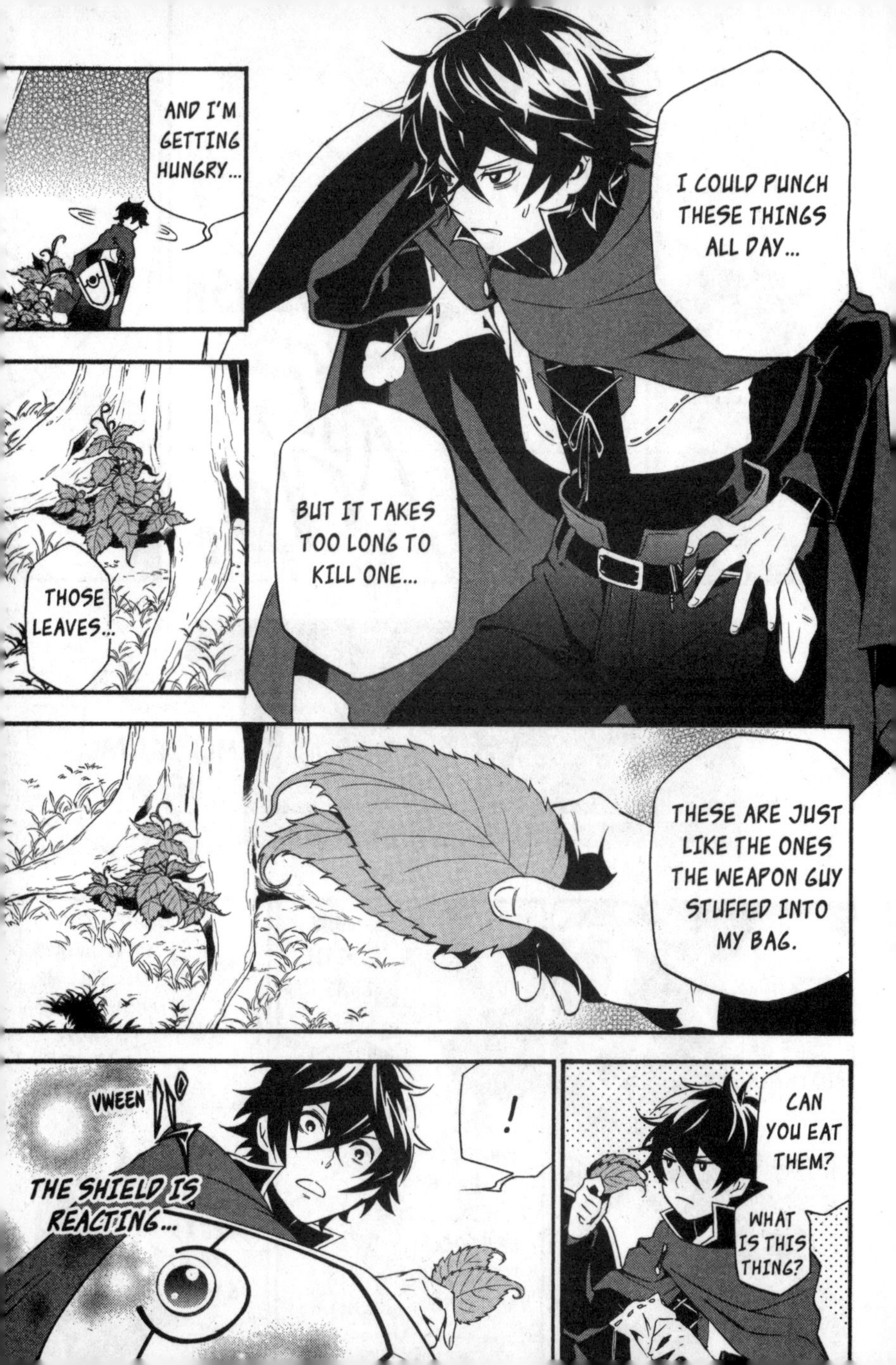
I COULD PUNCH THESE THINGS ALL DAY...
BUT IT TAKES TOO LONG TO KILL ONE...
AND I'M GETTING HUNGRY...
THOSE LEAVES...
THESE ARE JUST LIKE THE ONES THE WEAPON GUY STUFFED INTO MY BAG.
CAN YOU EAT THEM?
WHAT IS THIS THING?
!
VWEEN
THE SHIELD IS REACTING...

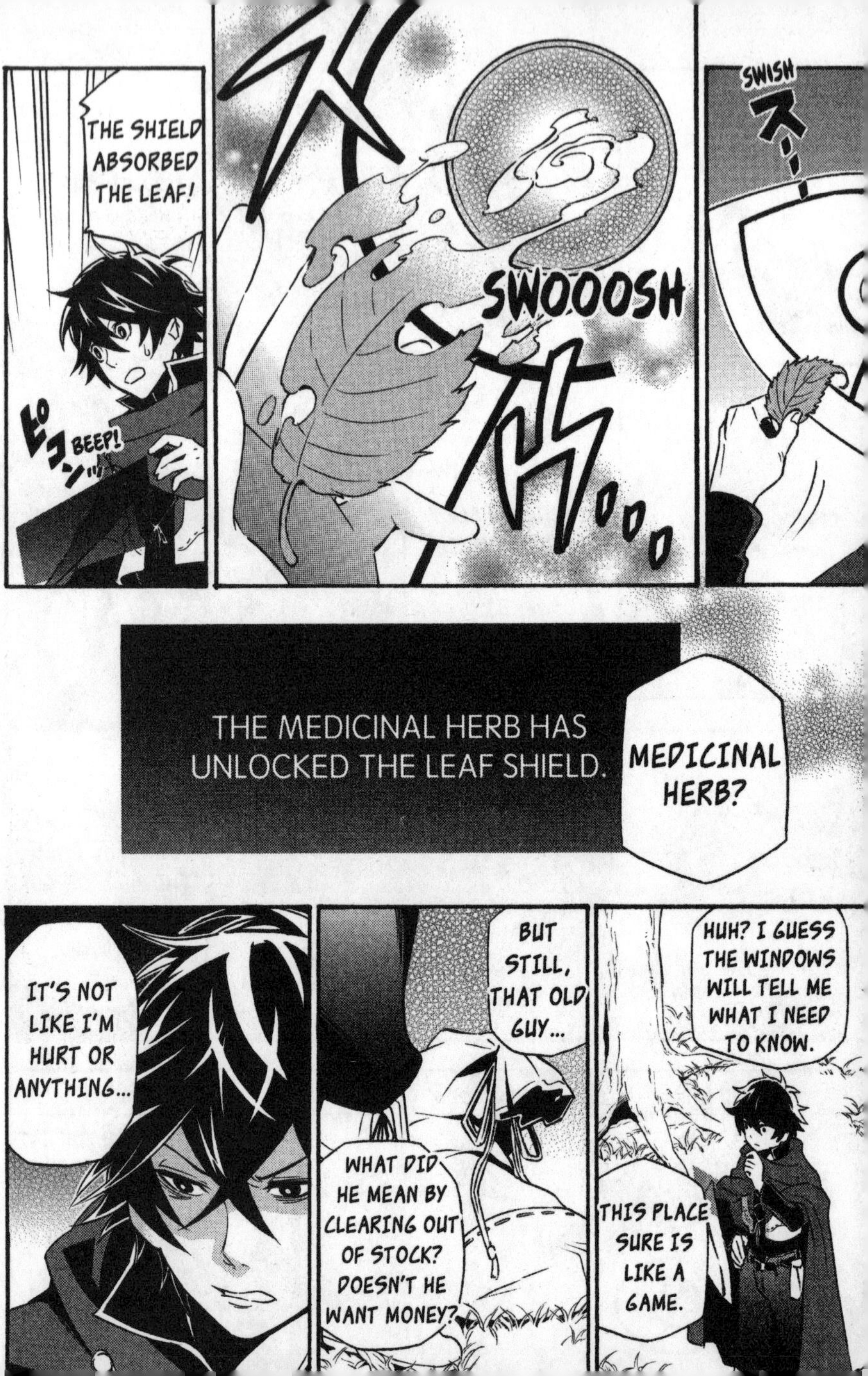
SWISH
SWOOOSH
THE SHIELD ABSORBED THE LEAF!
BEEP!
THE MEDICINAL HERB HAS UNLOCKED THE LEAF SHIELD.
MEDICINAL HERB?
HUH? I GUESS THE WINDOWS WILL TELL ME WHAT I NEED TO KNOW.
THIS PLACE SURE IS LIKE A GAME.
BUT STILL, THAT OLD GUY...
WHAT DID HE MEAN BY CLEARING OUT OF STOCK? DOESN'T HE WANT MONEY?
IT'S NOT LIKE I'M HURT OR ANYTHING...

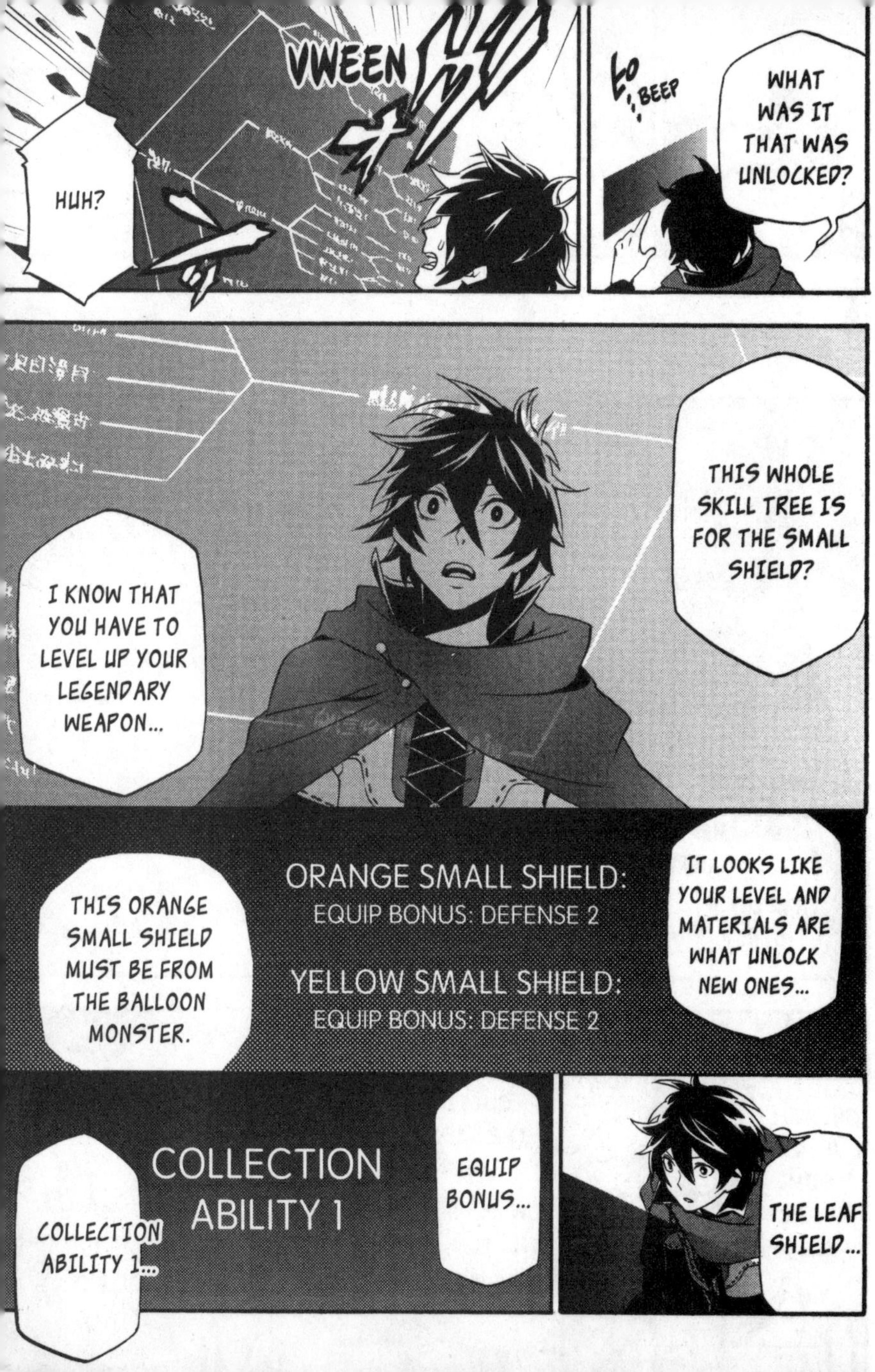
BEEP
WHAT WAS IT THAT WAS UNLOCKED?
VWEEN
HUH?
THIS WHOLE SKILL TREE IS FOR THE SMALL SHIELD?
I KNOW THAT YOU HAVE TO LEVEL UP YOUR LEGENDARY WEAPON...
IT LOOKS LIKE YOUR LEVEL AND MATERIALS ARE WHAT UNLOCK NEW ONES...
ORANGE SMALL SHIELD:
EQUIP BONUS: DEFENSE 2
YELLOW SMALL SHIELD:
EQUIP BONUS: DEFENSE 2
THIS ORANGE SMALL SHIELD MUST BE FROM THE BALLOON MONSTER.
THE LEAF SHIELD...
EQUIP BONUS...
COLLECTION ABILITY 1
COLLECTION ABILITY 1...

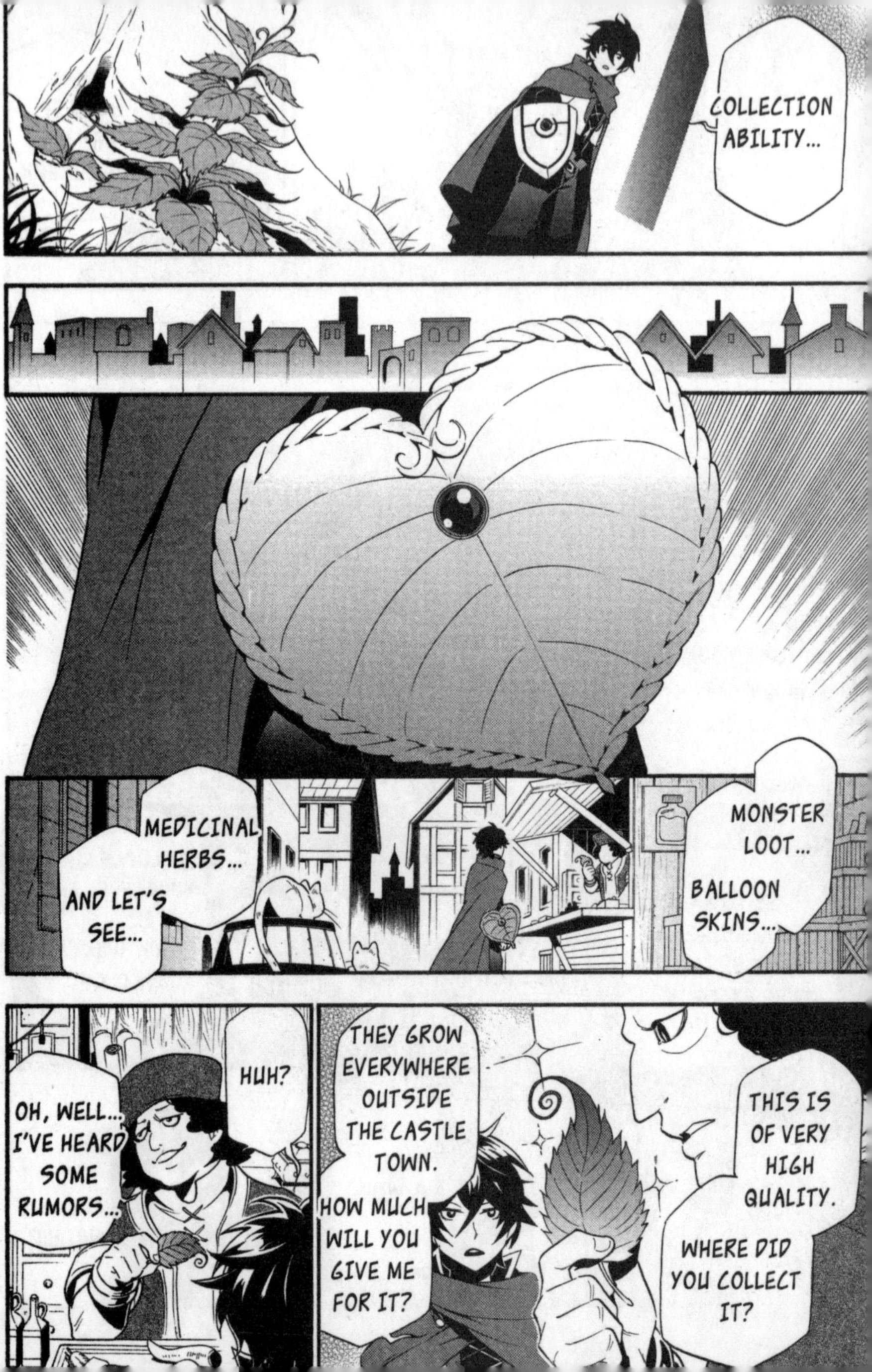
COLLECTION ABILITY...
MONSTER LOOT...
BALLOON SKINS...
MEDICINAL HERBS...
AND LET'S SEE...
THIS IS OF VERY HIGH QUALITY.
WHERE DID YOU COLLECT IT?
THEY GROW EVERYWHERE OUTSIDE THE CASTLE TOWN.
HOW MUCH WILL YOU GIVE ME FOR IT?
HUH?
OH, WELL... I'VE HEARD SOME RUMORS...

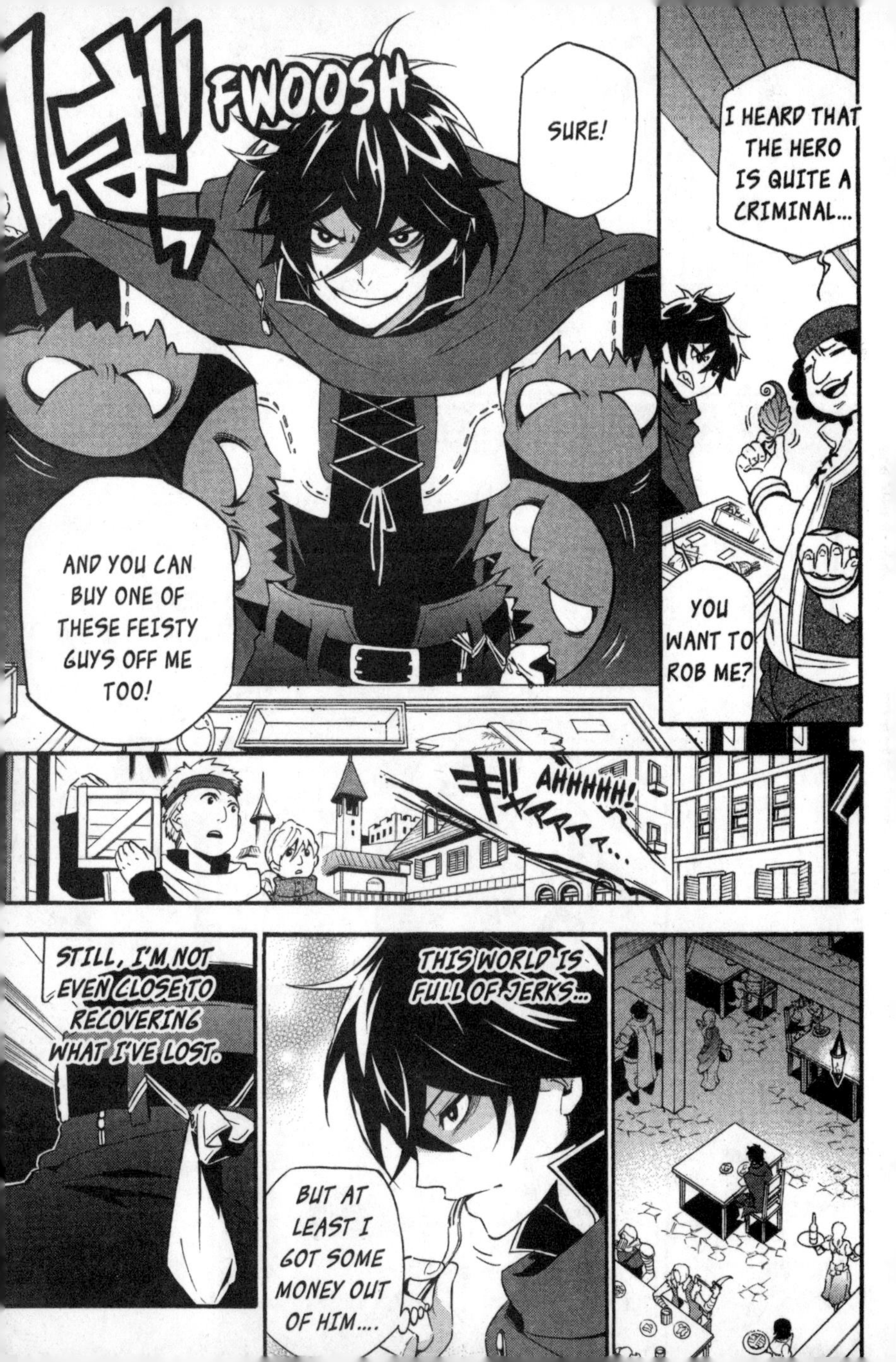
I HEARD THAT THE HERO IS QUITE A CRIMINAL...
YOU WANT TO ROB ME?
FWOOSH
SURE!
AND YOU CAN BUY ONE OF THESE FEISTY GUYS OFF ME TOO!
AHHHHH!
THIS WORLD IS FULL OF JERKS...
BUT AT LEAST I GOT SOME MONEY OUT OF HIM....
STILL, I'M NOT EVEN CLOSE TO RECOVERING WHAT I'VE LOST.

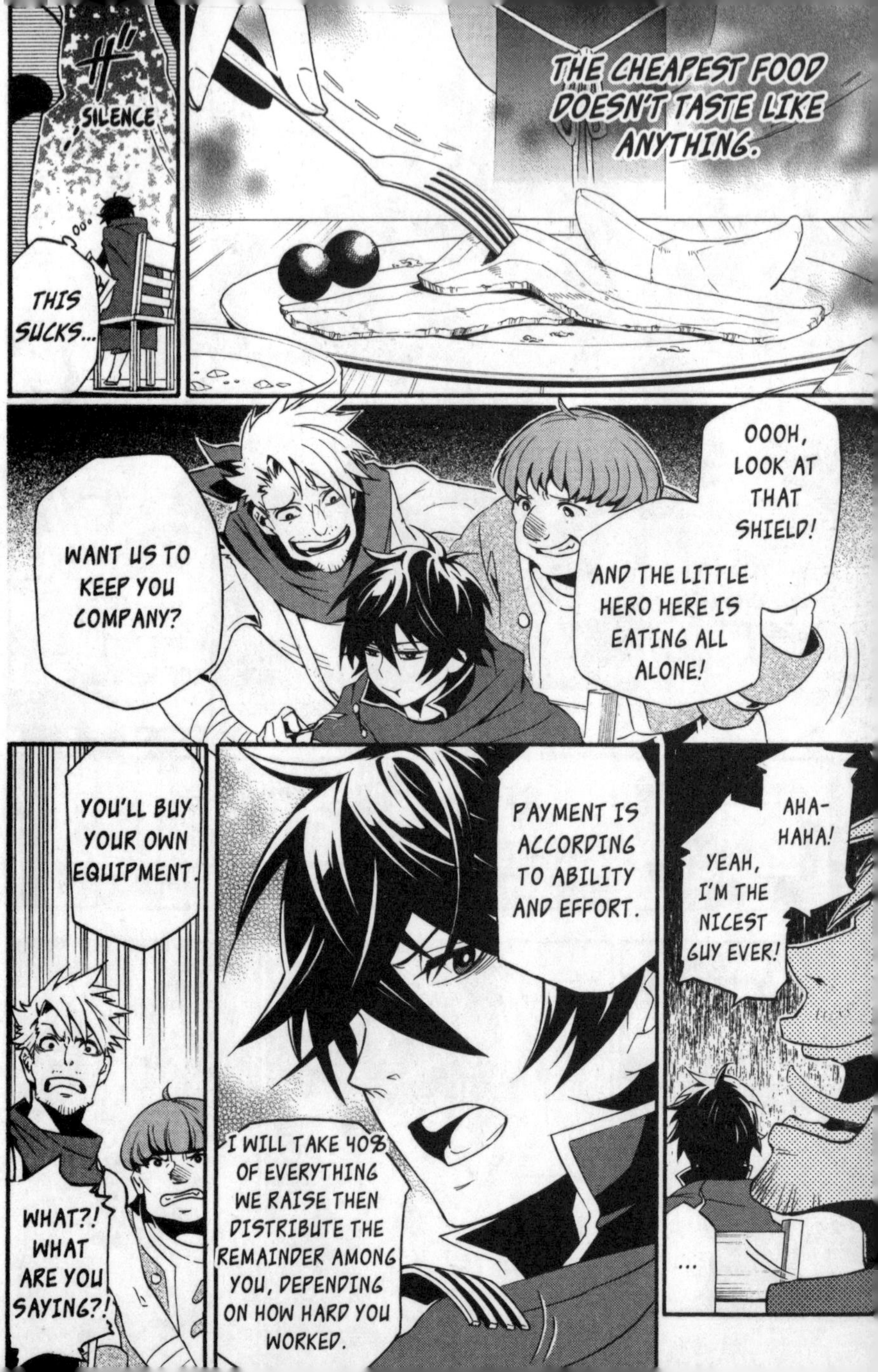
THE CHEAPEST FOOD DOESN'T TASTE LIKE ANYTHING.
SILENCE
THIS SUCKS...
OOOH, LOOK AT THAT SHIELD!
AND THE LITTLE HERO HERE IS EATING ALL ALONE!
WANT US TO KEEP YOU COMPANY?
AHA-HAHA!
YEAH, I'M THE NICEST GUY EVER!
...
PAYMENT IS ACCORDING TO ABILITY AND EFFORT.
I WILL TAKE 40% OF EVERYTHING WE RAISE THEN DISTRIBUTE THE REMAINDER AMONG YOU, DEPENDING ON HOW HARD YOU WORKED.
YOU'LL BUY YOUR OWN EQUIPMENT.
WHAT?! WHAT ARE YOU SAYING?!

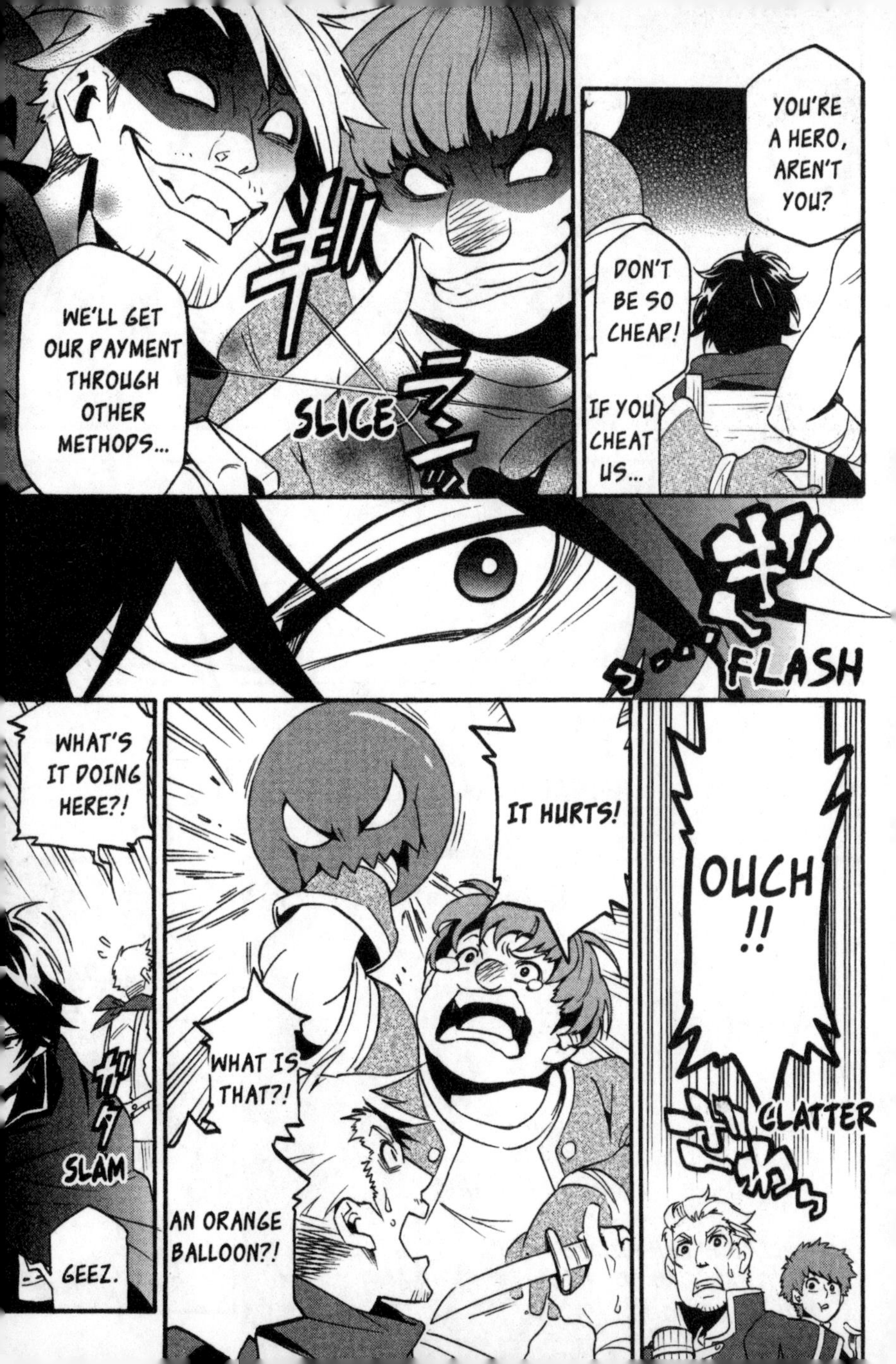
YOU'RE A HERO, AREN'T YOU?
DON'T BE SO CHEAP!
IF YOU CHEAT US...
SLICE
WE'LL GET OUR PAYMENT THROUGH OTHER METHODS...
FLASH
OUCH!!
CLATTER
IT HURTS!
WHAT IS THAT?!
AN ORANGE BALLOON?!
WHAT'S IT DOING HERE?!
SLAM
GEEZ.

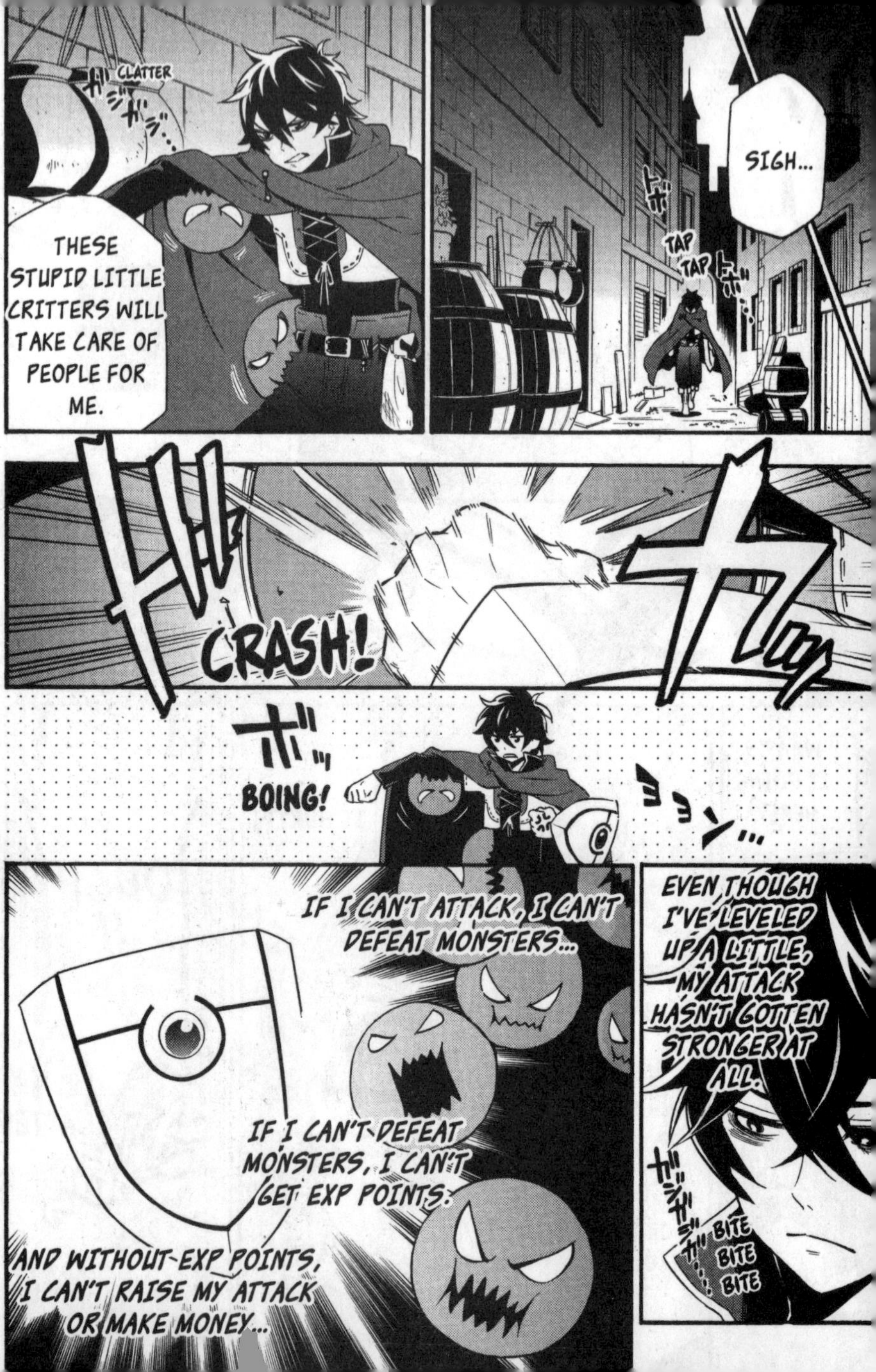
SIGH...
TAP TAP
CLATTER
THESE STUPID LITTLE CRITTERS WILL TAKE CARE OF PEOPLE FOR ME.
CRASH!
BOING!
EVEN THOUGH I'VE LEVELED UP A LITTLE, MY ATTACK HASN'T GOTTEN STRONGER AT ALL.
BITE BITE BITE
IF I CAN'T ATTACK, I CAN'T DEFEAT MONSTERS...
IF I CAN'T DEFEAT MONSTERS, I CAN'T GET EXP POINTS.
AND WITHOUT EXP POINTS, I CAN'T RAISE MY ATTACK OR MAKE MONEY...

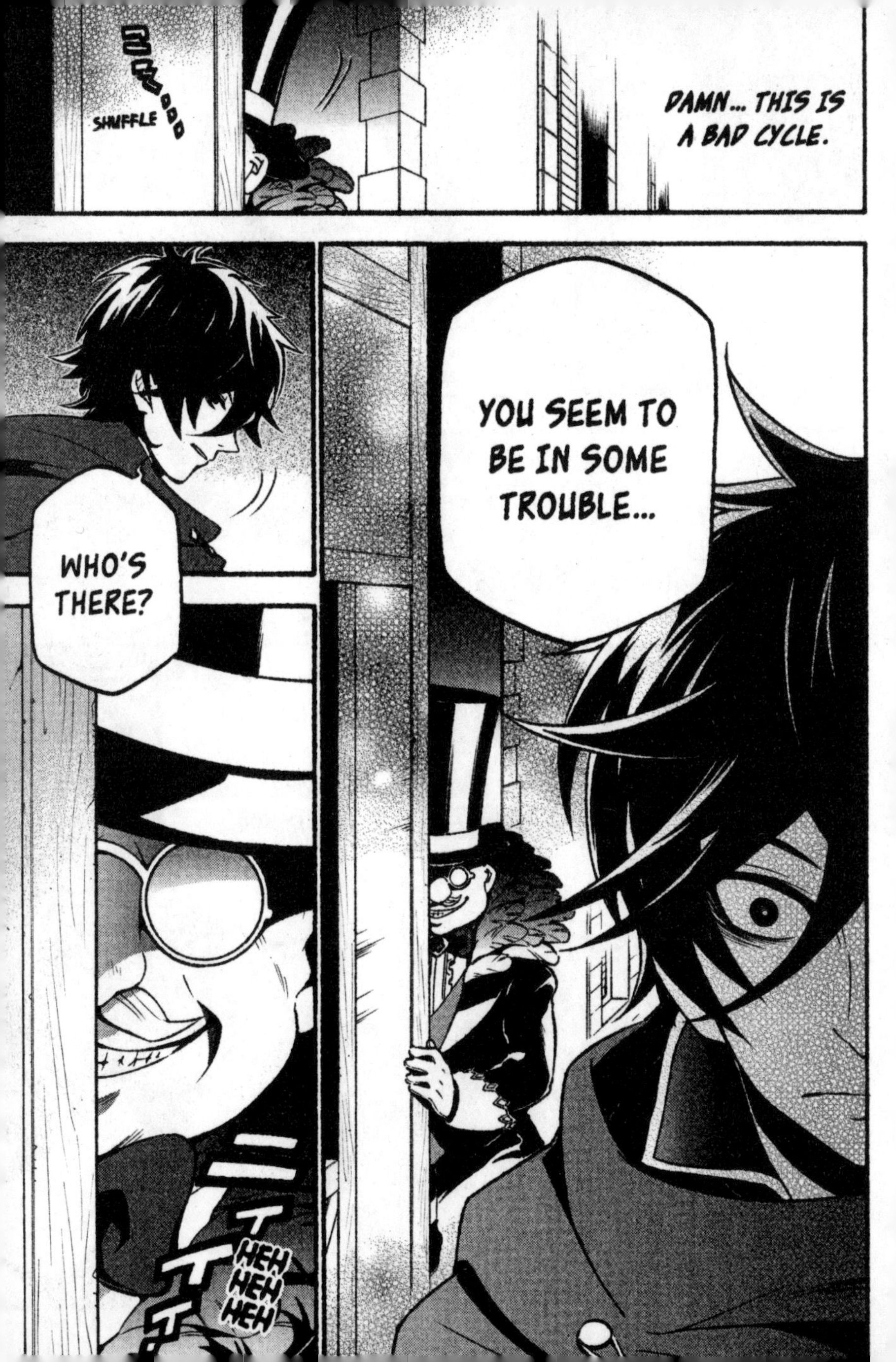
DAMN... THIS IS A BAD CYCLE.
SHUFFLE
YOU SEEM TO BE IN SOME TROUBLE...
WHO'S THERE?
HEH HEH HEH

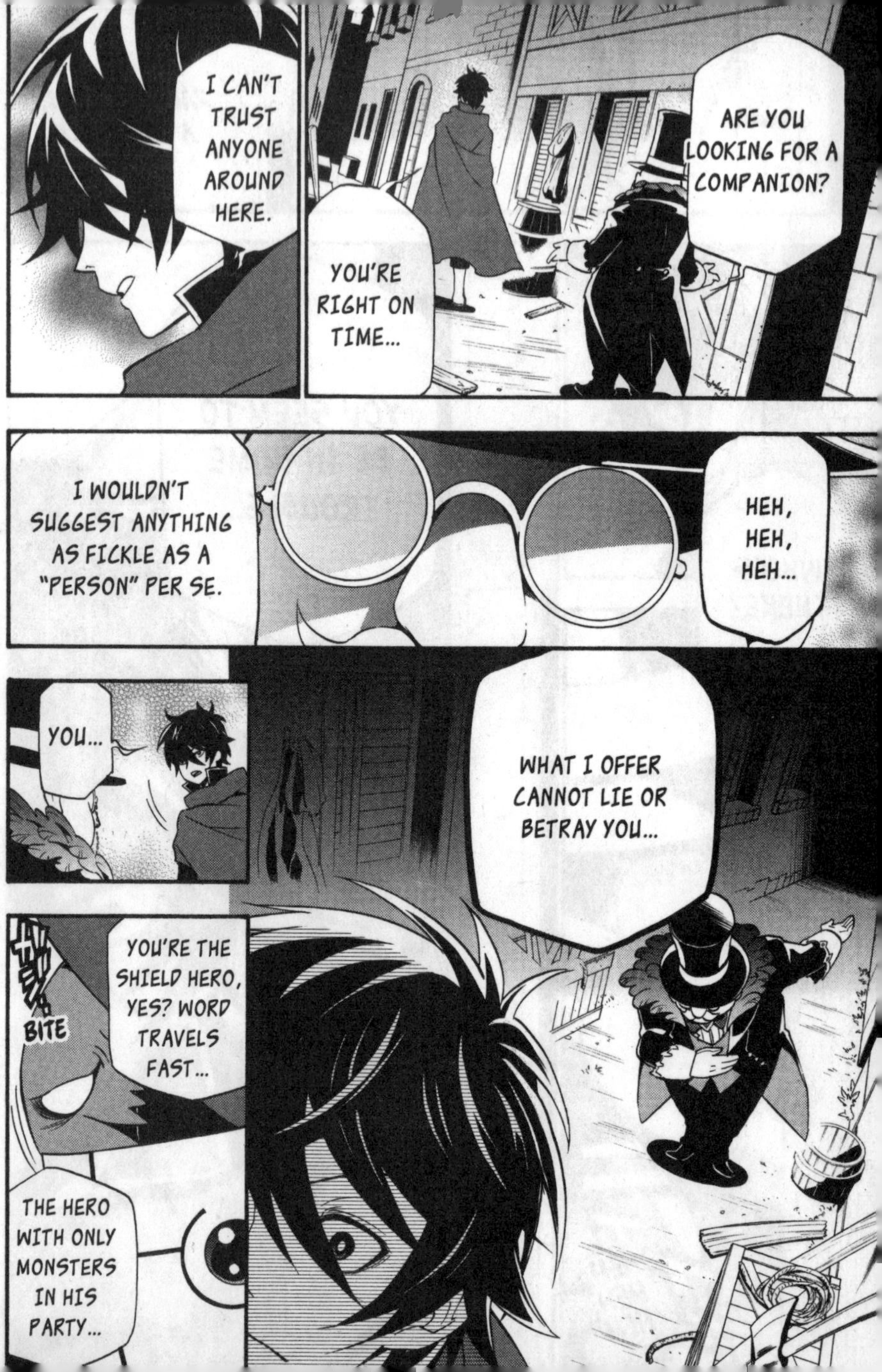
ARE YOU LOOKING FOR A COMPANION?
YOU'RE RIGHT ON TIME...
I CAN'T TRUST ANYONE AROUND HERE.
HEH, HEH, HEH...
I WOULDN'T SUGGEST ANYTHING AS FICKLE AS A "PERSON" PER SE.
WHAT I OFFER CANNOT LIE OR BETRAY YOU...
YOU...
BITE
YOU'RE THE SHIELD HERO, YES? WORD TRAVELS FAST...
THE HERO WITH ONLY MONSTERS IN HIS PARTY...

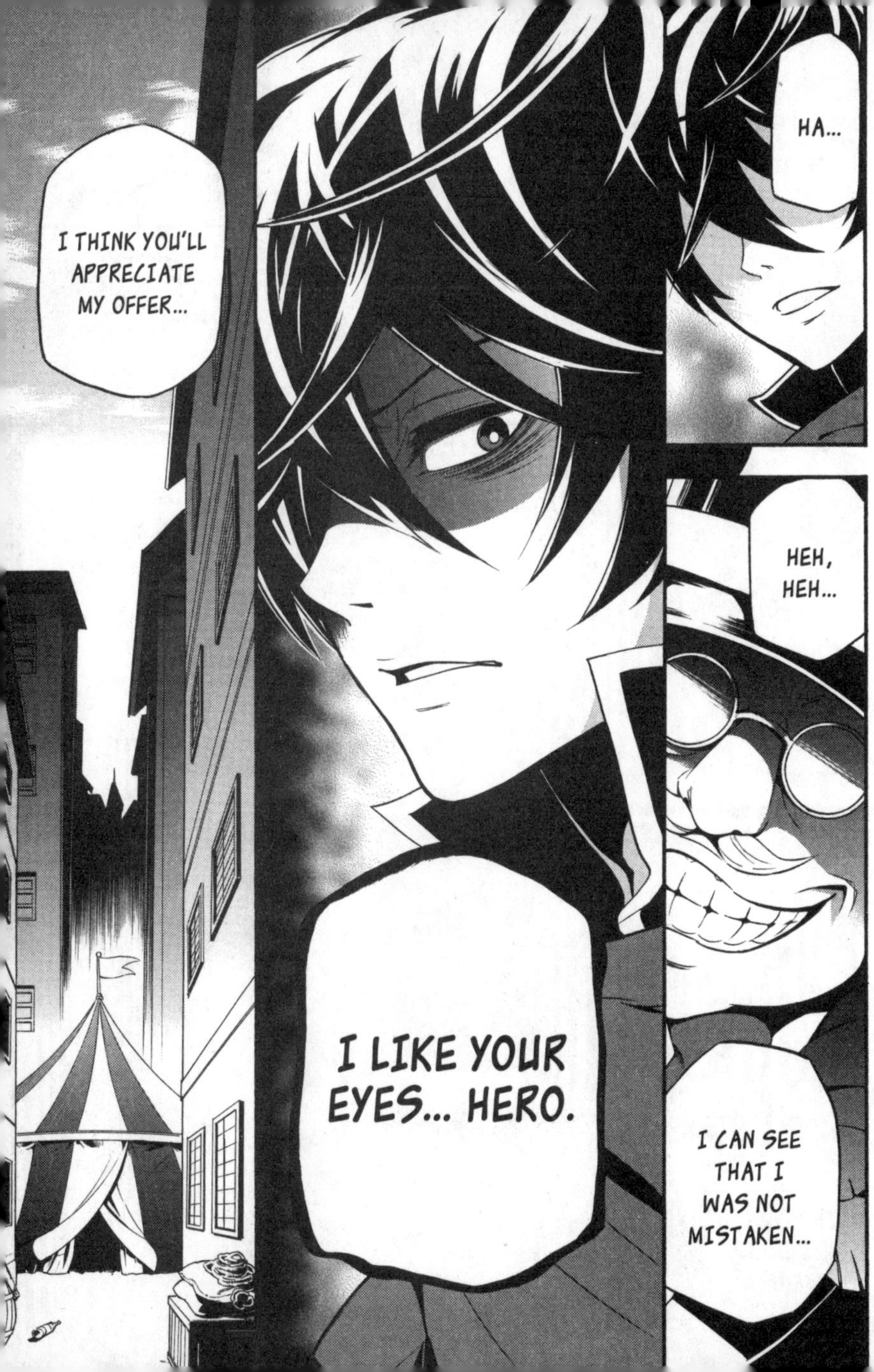
HA...
HEH, HEH...
I CAN SEE THAT I WAS NOT MISTAKEN...
I LIKE YOUR EYES... HERO.
I THINK YOU'LL APPRECIATE MY OFFER...

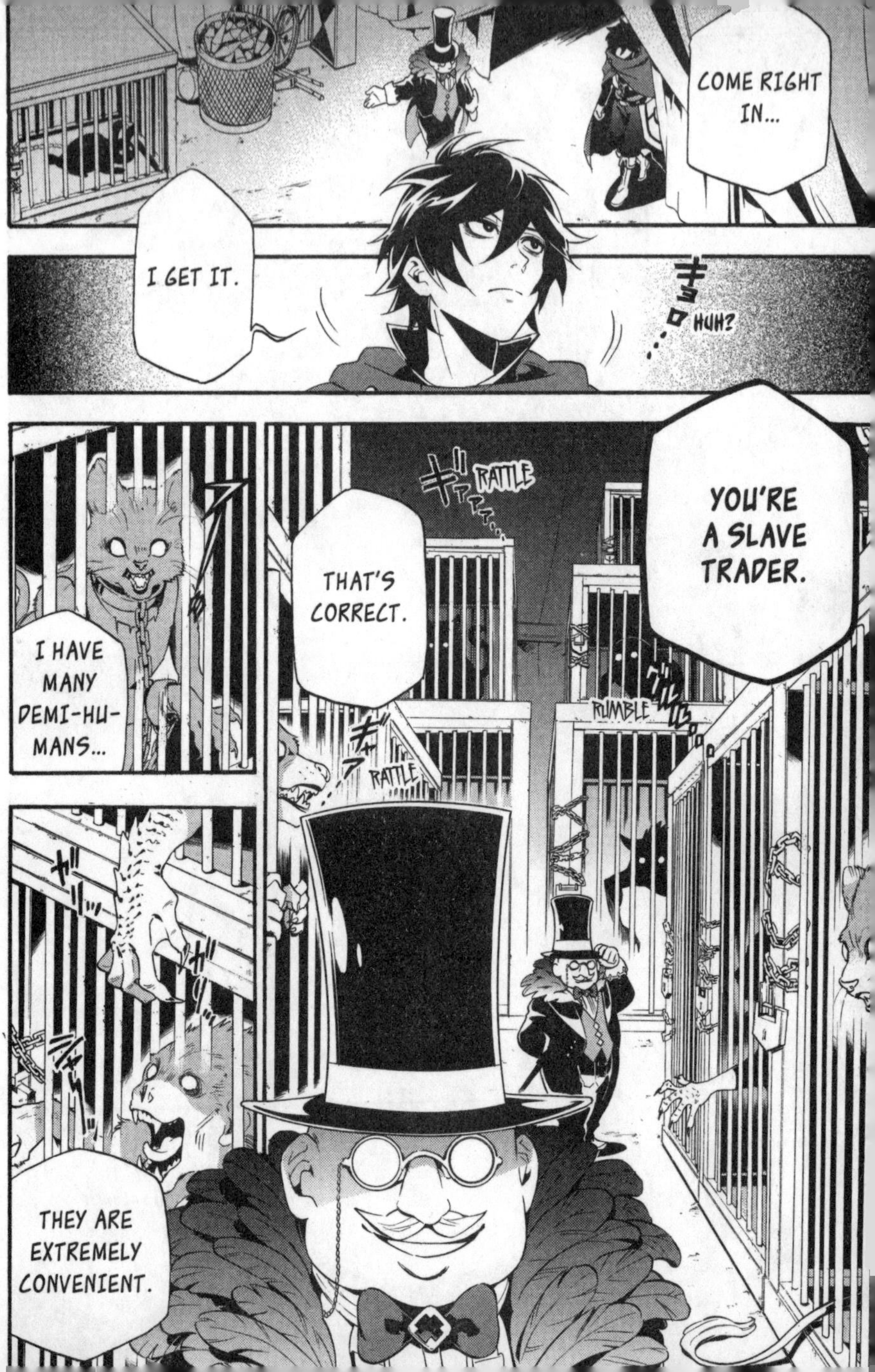
COME RIGHT IN...
HUH?
I GET IT.
YOU'RE A SLAVE TRADER.
RATTLE
THAT'S CORRECT.
RUMBLE
RATTLE
I HAVE MANY DEMI-HUMANS...
THEY ARE EXTREMELY CONVENIENT.

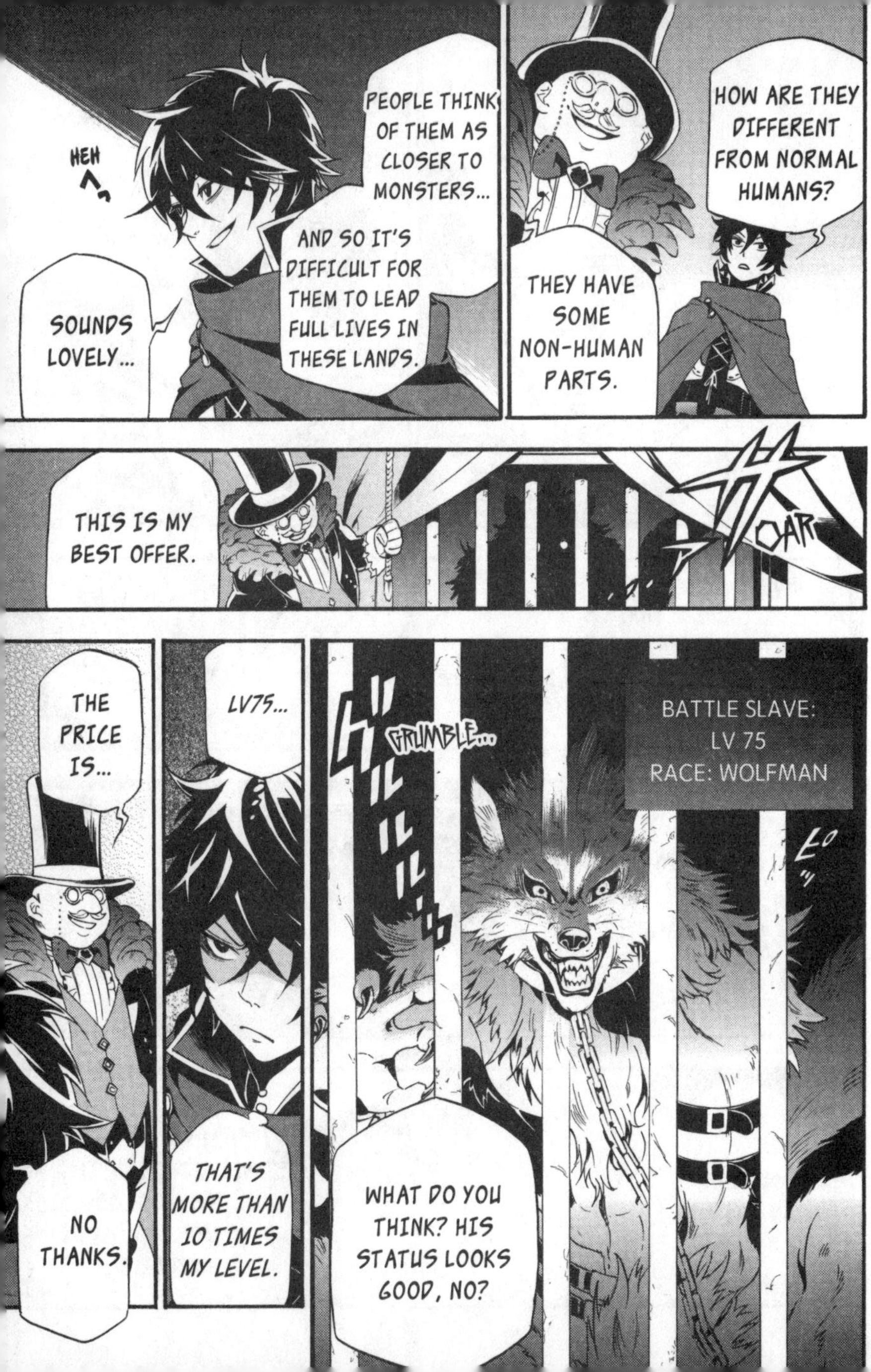
HOW ARE THEY DIFFERENT FROM NORMAL HUMANS?
THEY HAVE SOME NON-HUMAN PARTS.
PEOPLE THINK OF THEM AS CLOSER TO MONSTERS...
AND SO IT'S DIFFICULT FOR THEM TO LEAD FULL LIVES IN THESE LANDS.
HEH
SOUNDS LOVELY...
OAR
THIS IS MY BEST OFFER.
BATTLE SLAVE: LV 75 RACE: WOLFMAN
GRUMBLE...
WHAT DO YOU THINK? HIS STATUS LOOKS GOOD, NO?
LV75...
THAT'S MORE THAN 10 TIMES MY LEVEL.
THE PRICE IS...
NO THANKS.

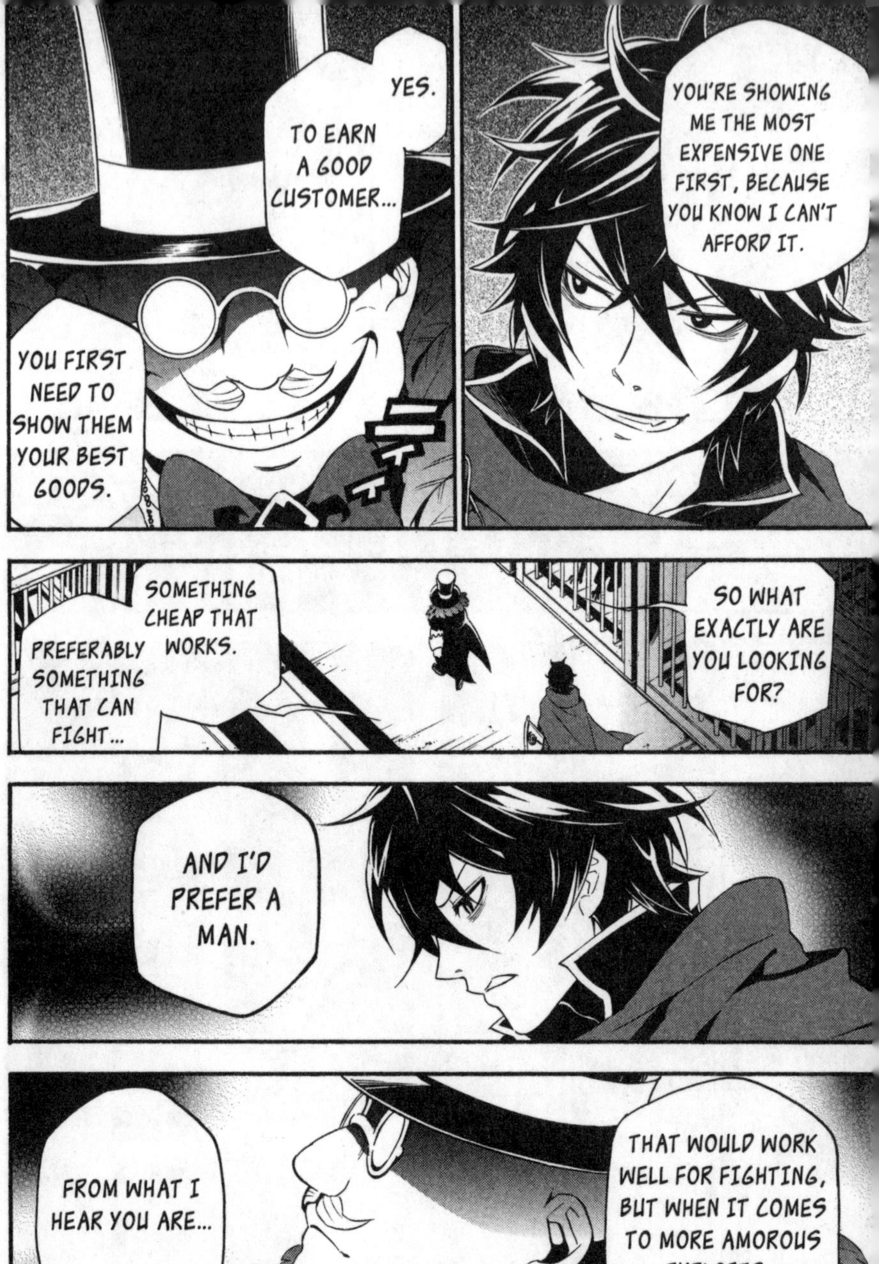
YOU'RE SHOWING ME THE MOST EXPENSIVE ONE FIRST, BECAUSE YOU KNOW I CAN'T AFFORD IT.
YES.
TO EARN A GOOD CUSTOMER...
YOU FIRST NEED TO SHOW THEM YOUR BEST GOODS.
SO WHAT EXACTLY ARE YOU LOOKING FOR?
SOMETHING CHEAP THAT WORKS.
PREFERABLY SOMETHING THAT CAN FIGHT...
AND I'D PREFER A MAN.
THAT WOULD WORK WELL FOR FIGHTING, BUT WHEN IT COMES TO MORE AMOROUS EXPLOITS...
FROM WHAT I HEAR YOU ARE...

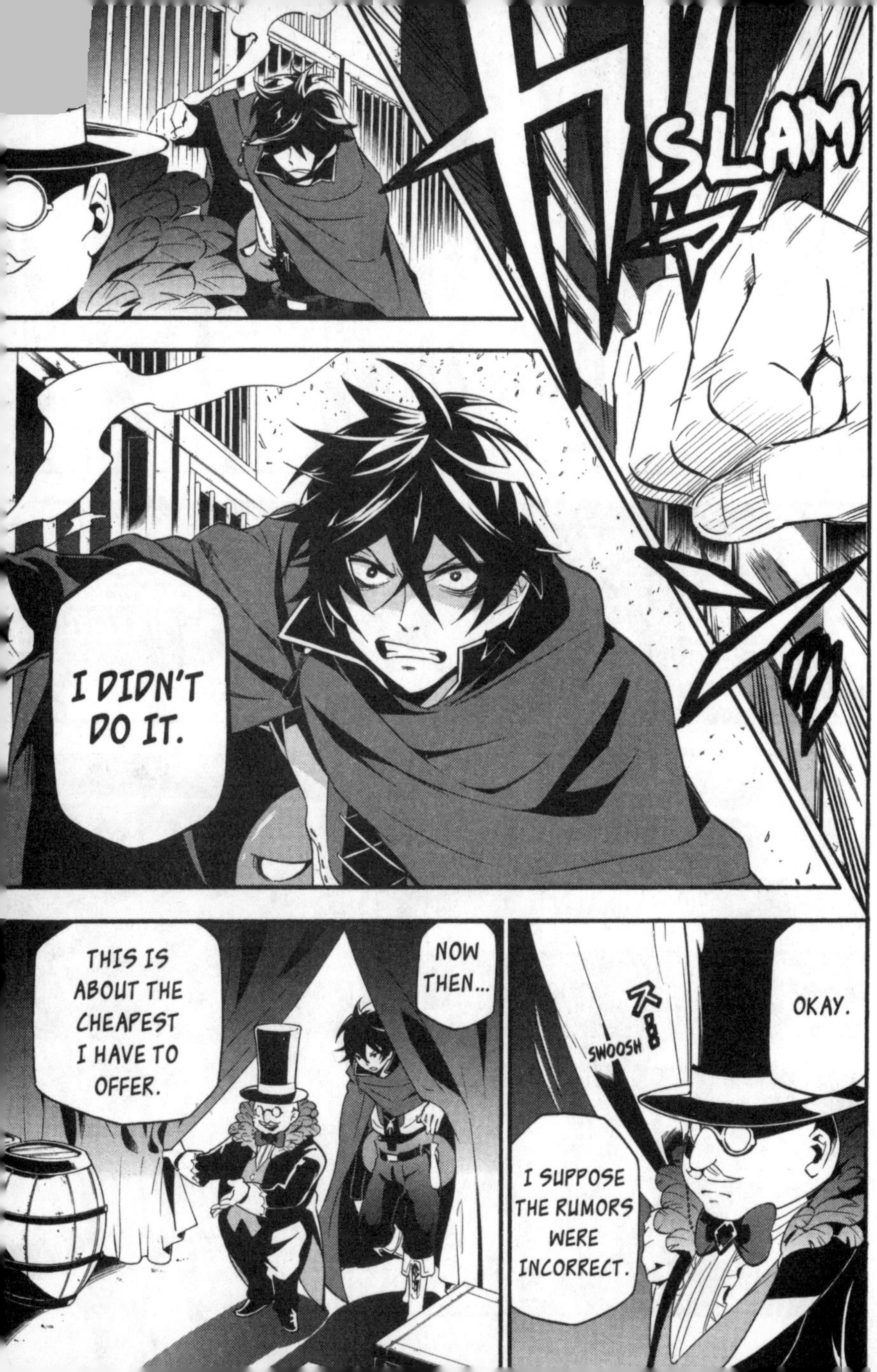
SLAM
I DIDN'T DO IT.
OKAY.
SWOOSH
I SUPPOSE THE RUMORS WERE INCORRECT.
NOW THEN...
THIS IS ABOUT THE CHEAPEST I HAVE TO OFFER.

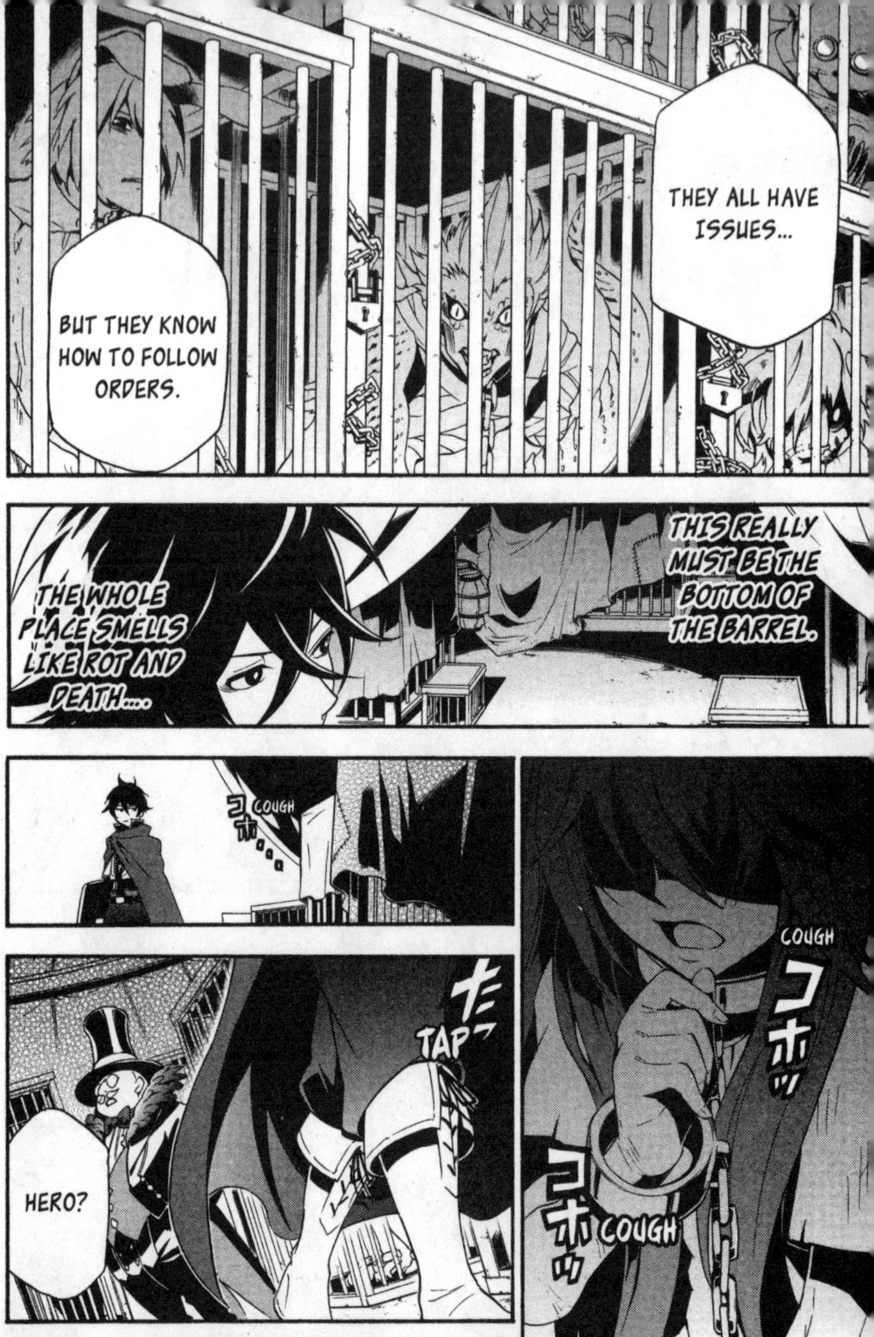
THEY ALL HAVE ISSUES...
BUT THEY KNOW HOW TO FOLLOW ORDERS.
THIS REALLY MUST BE THE BOTTOM OF THE BARREL.
THE WHOLE PLACE SMELLS LIKE ROT AND DEATH....
コホッ
COUGH
コホッ
COUGH
コホ...
COUGH
たっ
TAP
HERO?

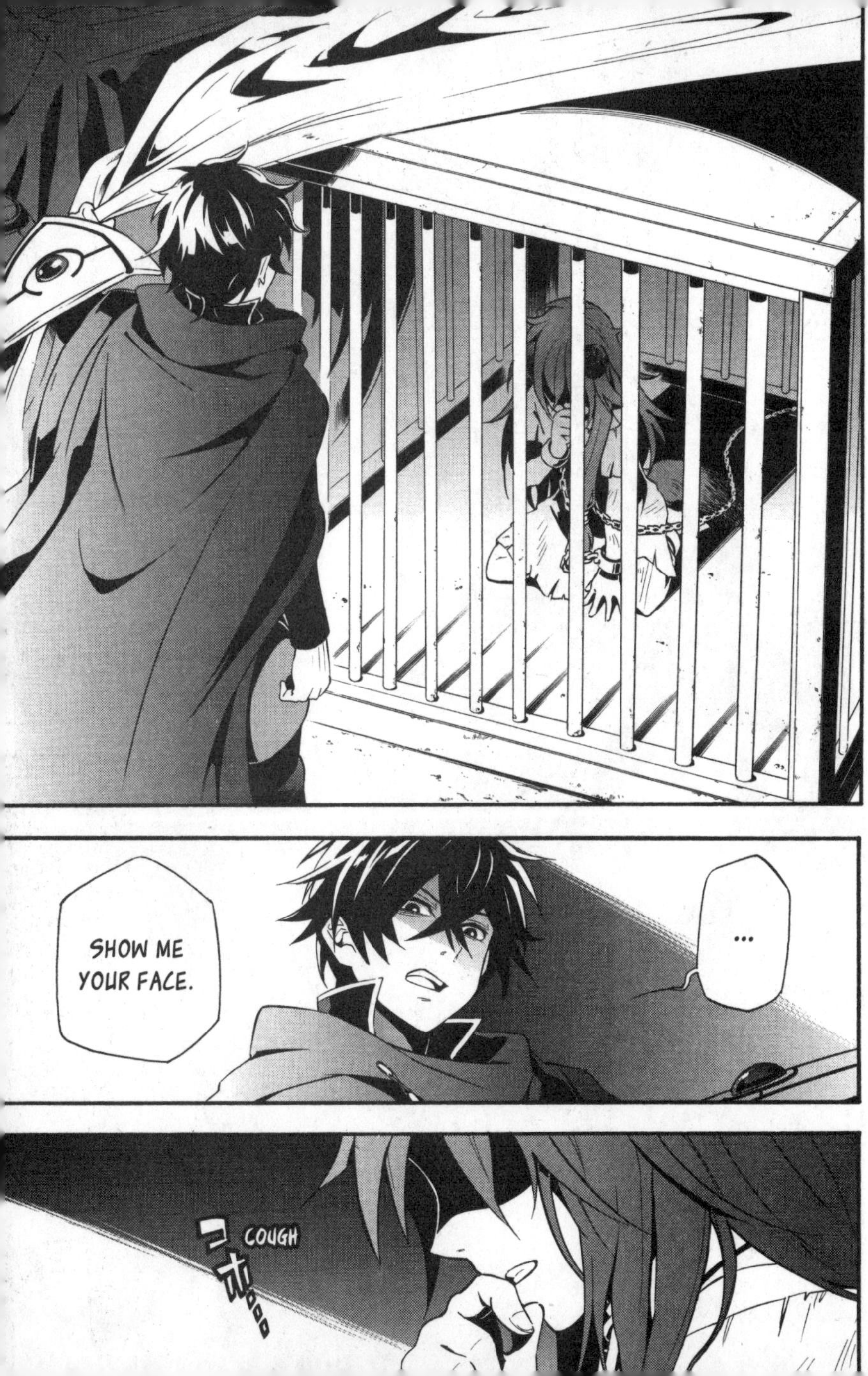
...
SHOW ME YOUR FACE.
COUGH

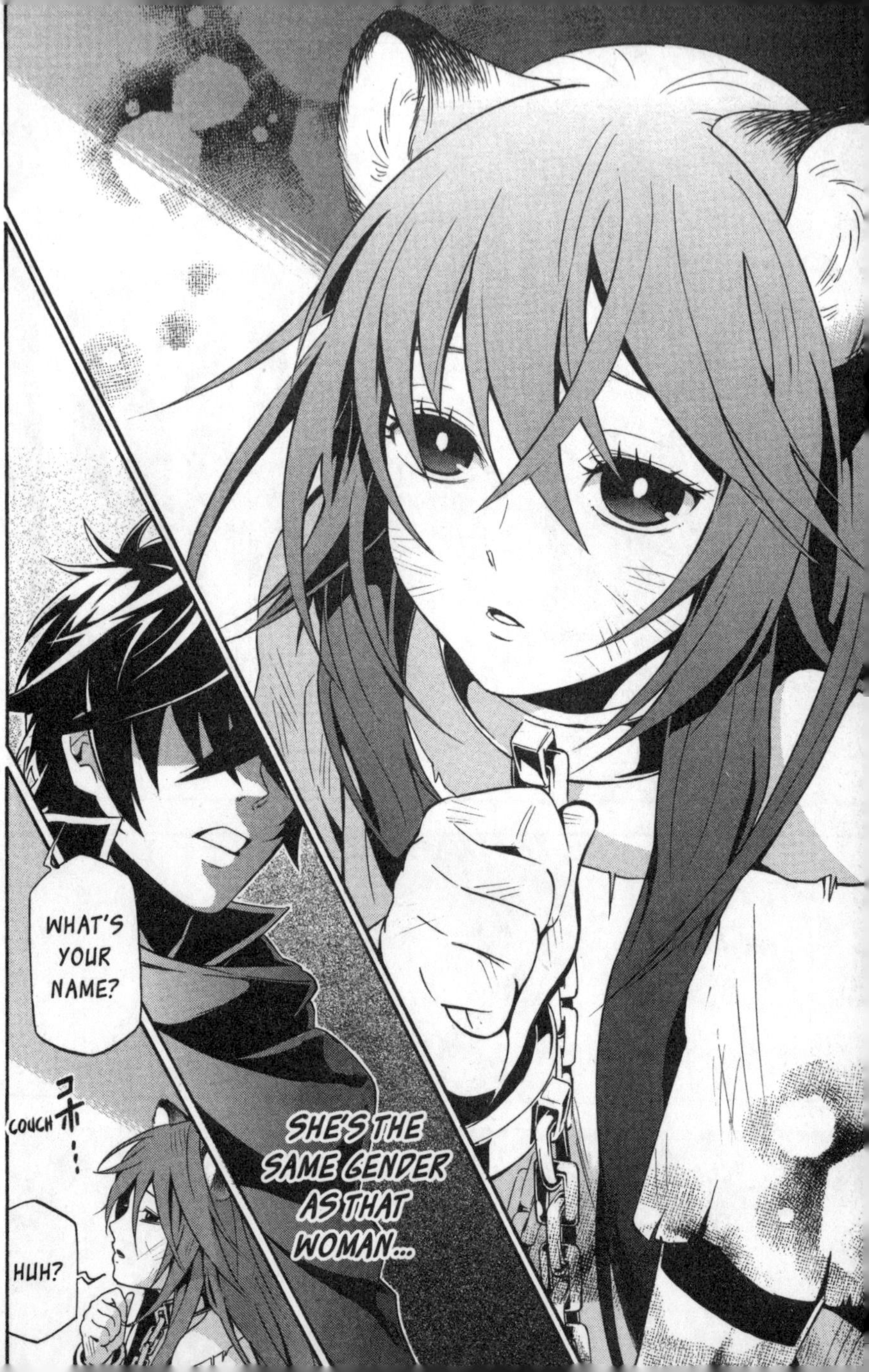
SHE'S THE SAME GENDER AS THAT WOMAN...
WHAT'S YOUR NAME?
コホ…
COUCH
HUH?

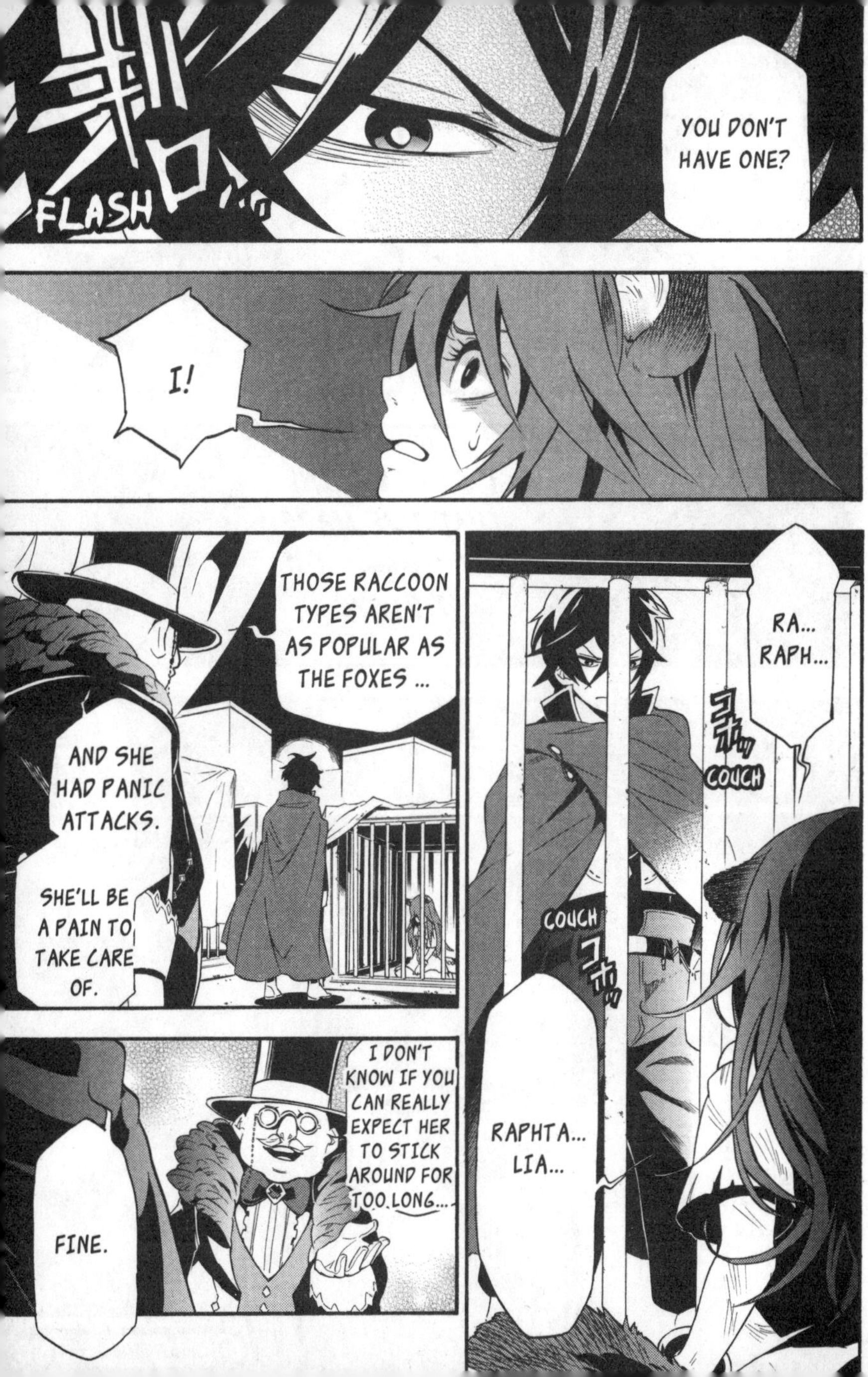
YOU DON'T HAVE ONE?
FLASH
I!
RA... RAPH...
COUCH
COUCH
RAPHTA... LIA...
THOSE RACCOON TYPES AREN'T AS POPULAR AS THE FOXES ...
AND SHE HAD PANIC ATTACKS.
SHE'LL BE A PAIN TO TAKE CARE OF.
I DON'T KNOW IF YOU CAN REALLY EXPECT HER TO STICK AROUND FOR TOO LONG...
FINE.

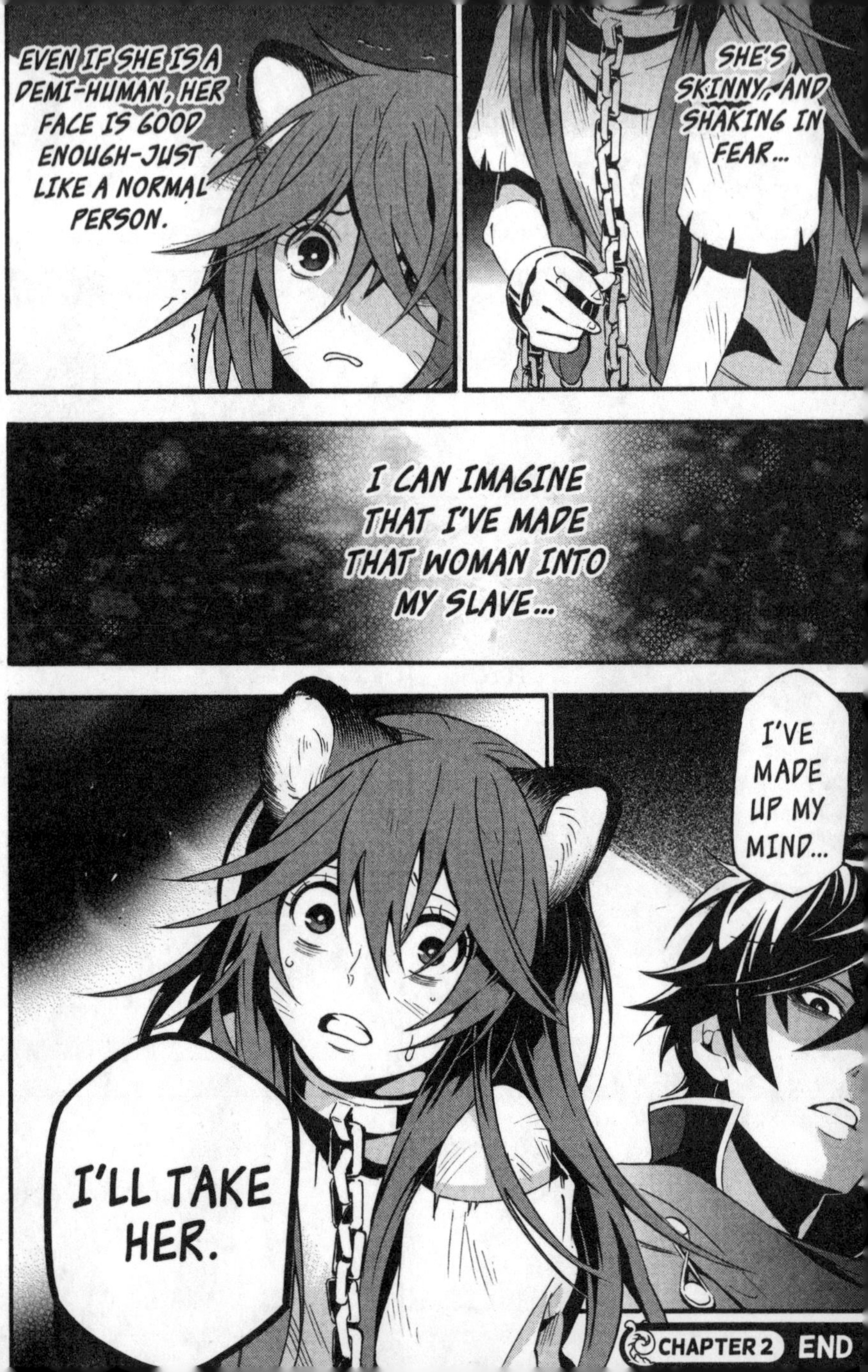
SHE'S SKINNY, AND SHAKING IN FEAR...
EVEN IF SHE IS A DEMI-HUMAN, HER FACE IS GOOD ENOUGH-JUST LIKE A NORMAL PERSON.
I CAN IMAGINE THAT I'VE MADE THAT WOMAN INTO MY SLAVE...
I'VE MADE UP MY MIND...
I'LL TAKE HER.
CHAPTER 2 END

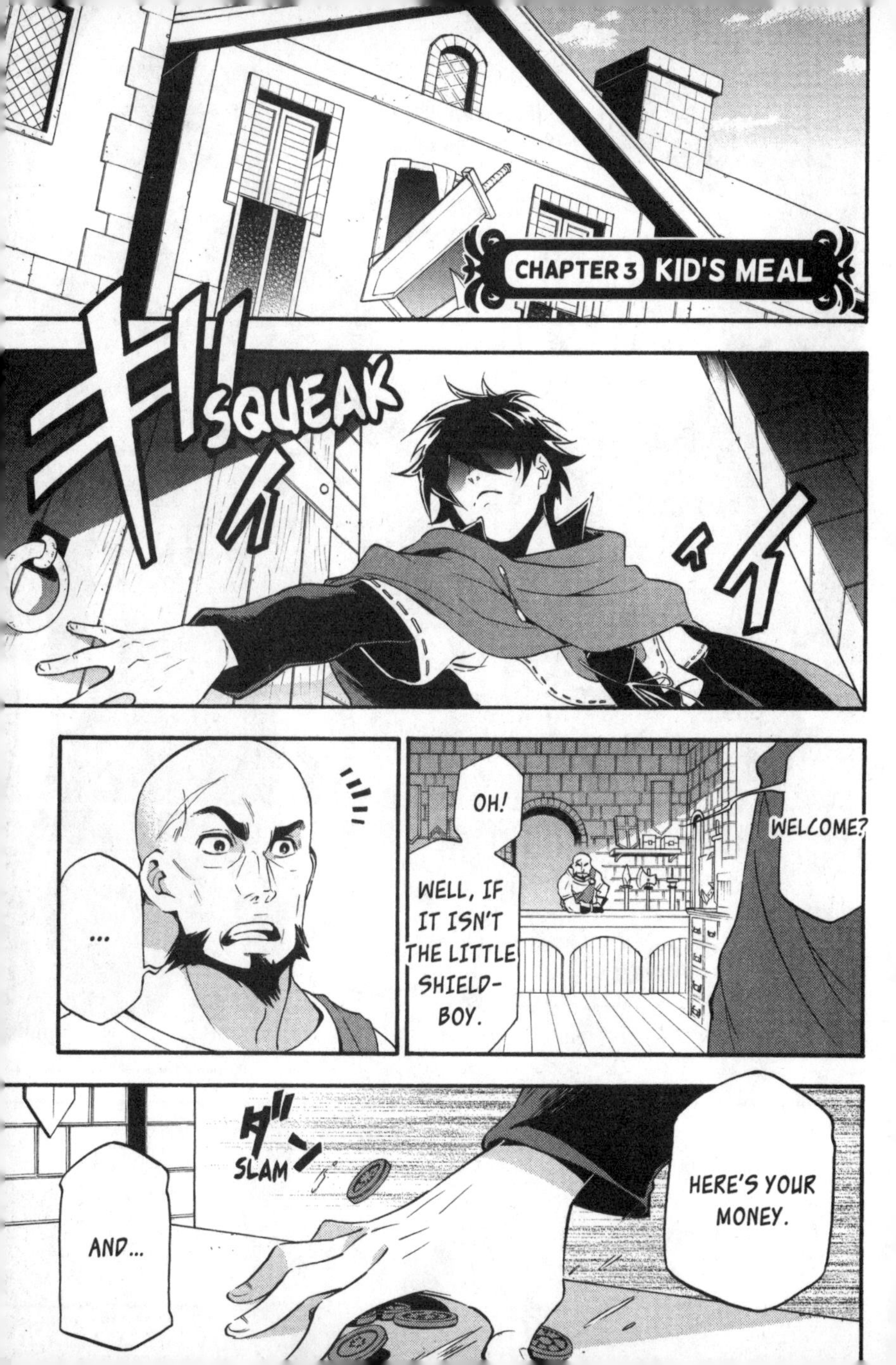
CHAPTER 3 KID'S MEAL
ギィ
SQUEAK
WELCOME?
OH!
WELL, IF IT ISN'T THE LITTLE SHIELD-BOY.
...
HERE'S YOUR MONEY.
ダン
SLAM
AND...

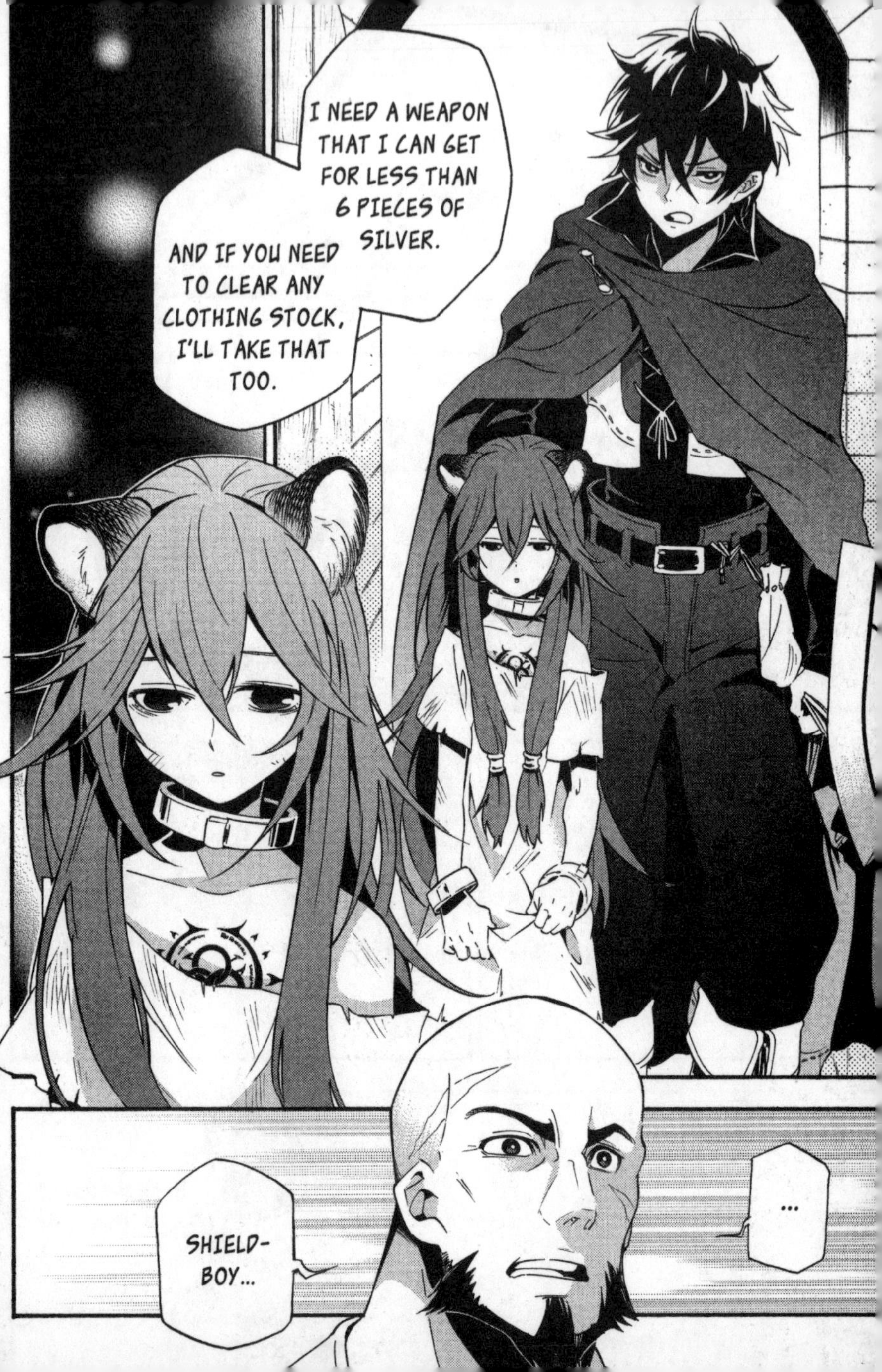
I NEED A WEAPON THAT I CAN GET FOR LESS THAN 6 PIECES OF SILVER.
AND IF YOU NEED TO CLEAR ANY CLOTHING STOCK, I'LL TAKE THAT TOO.
...
SHIELD-BOY...

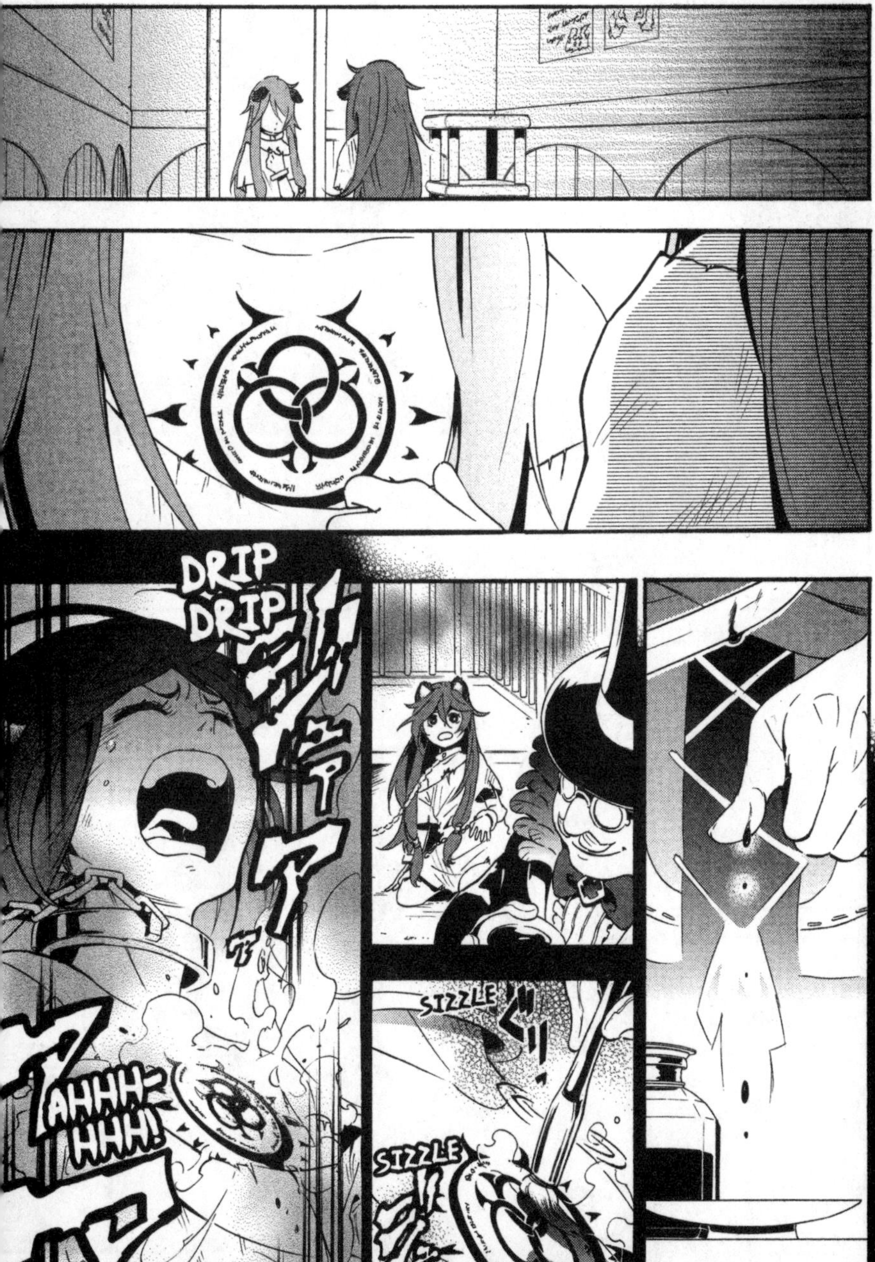
SIZZLE
SIZZLE
DRIP
DRIP
AHHH-
HHH!

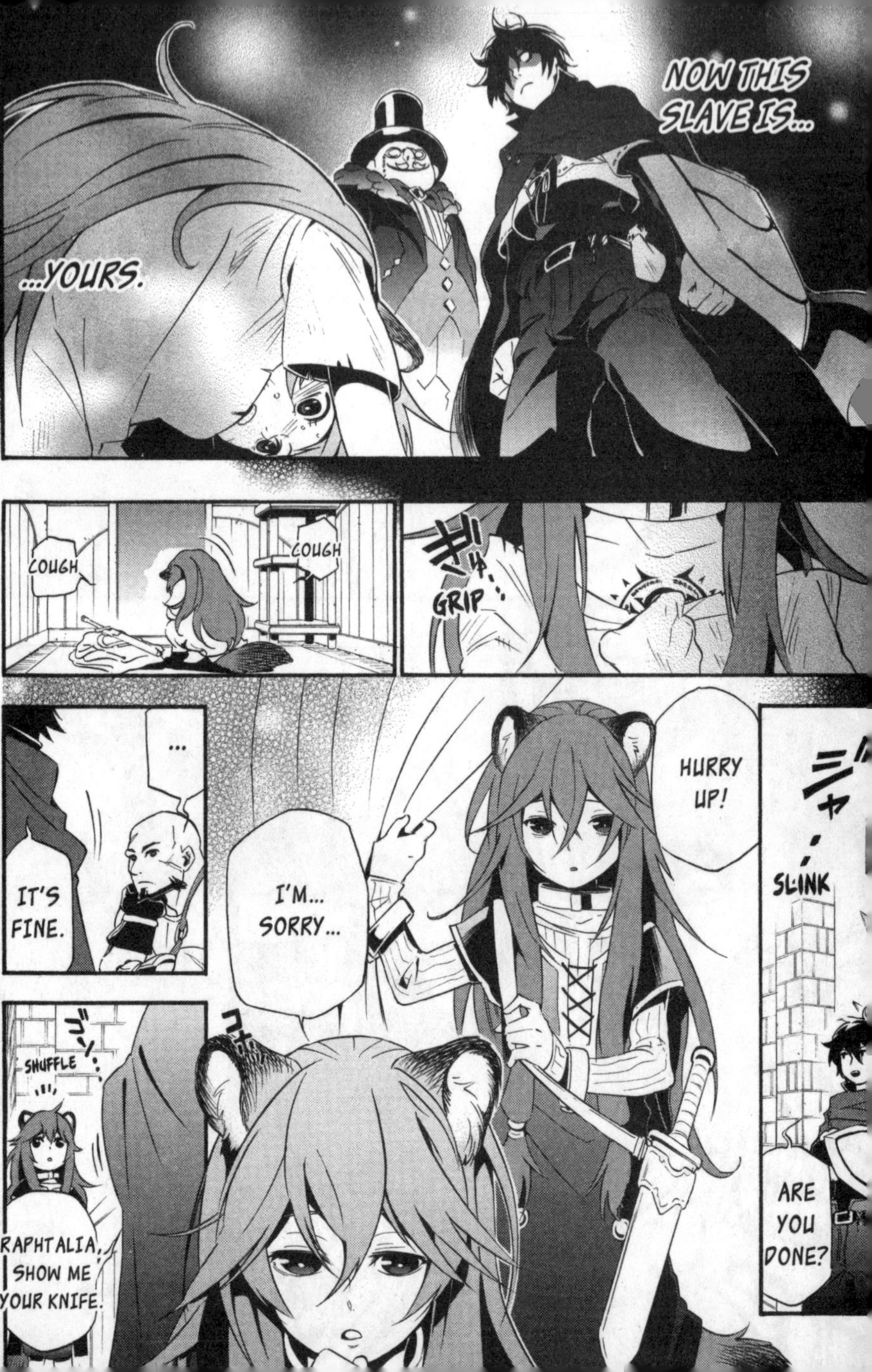

NOW THIS SLAVE IS...
...YOURS.
GRIP
COUGH
COUGH
SLINK
ARE YOU DONE?
HURRY UP!
I'M... SORRY...
...
IT'S FINE.
SHUFFLE
RAPHTALIA, SHOW ME YOUR KNIFE.

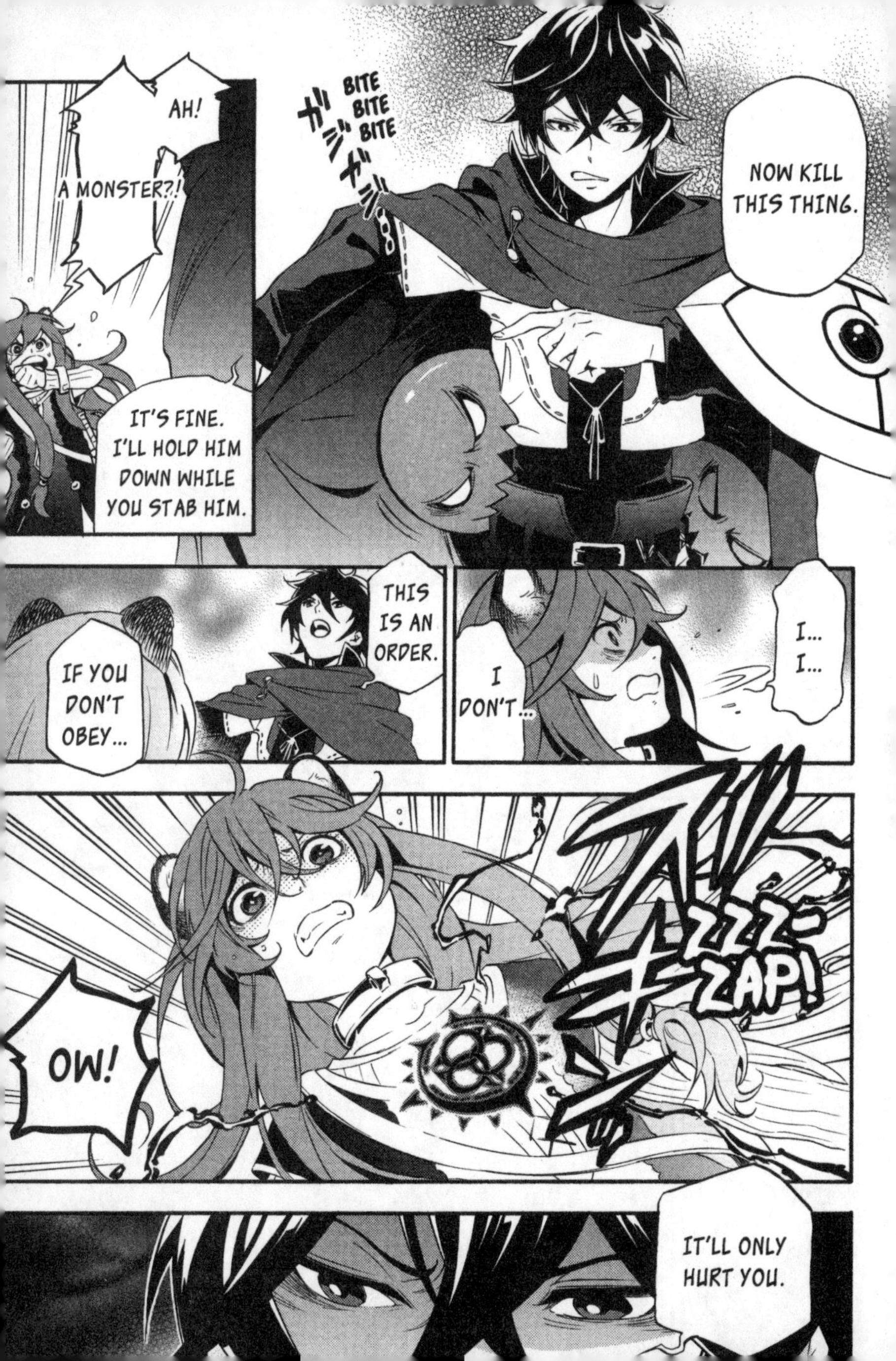
NOW KILL THIS THING.
ガジガジ
BITE BITE BITE
AH!
A MONSTER?!
IT'S FINE. I'LL HOLD HIM DOWN WHILE YOU STAB HIM.
I... I...
I DON'T...
THIS IS AN ORDER.
IF YOU DON'T OBEY...
ZZZZ-ZAP!
OW!
IT'LL ONLY HURT YOU.

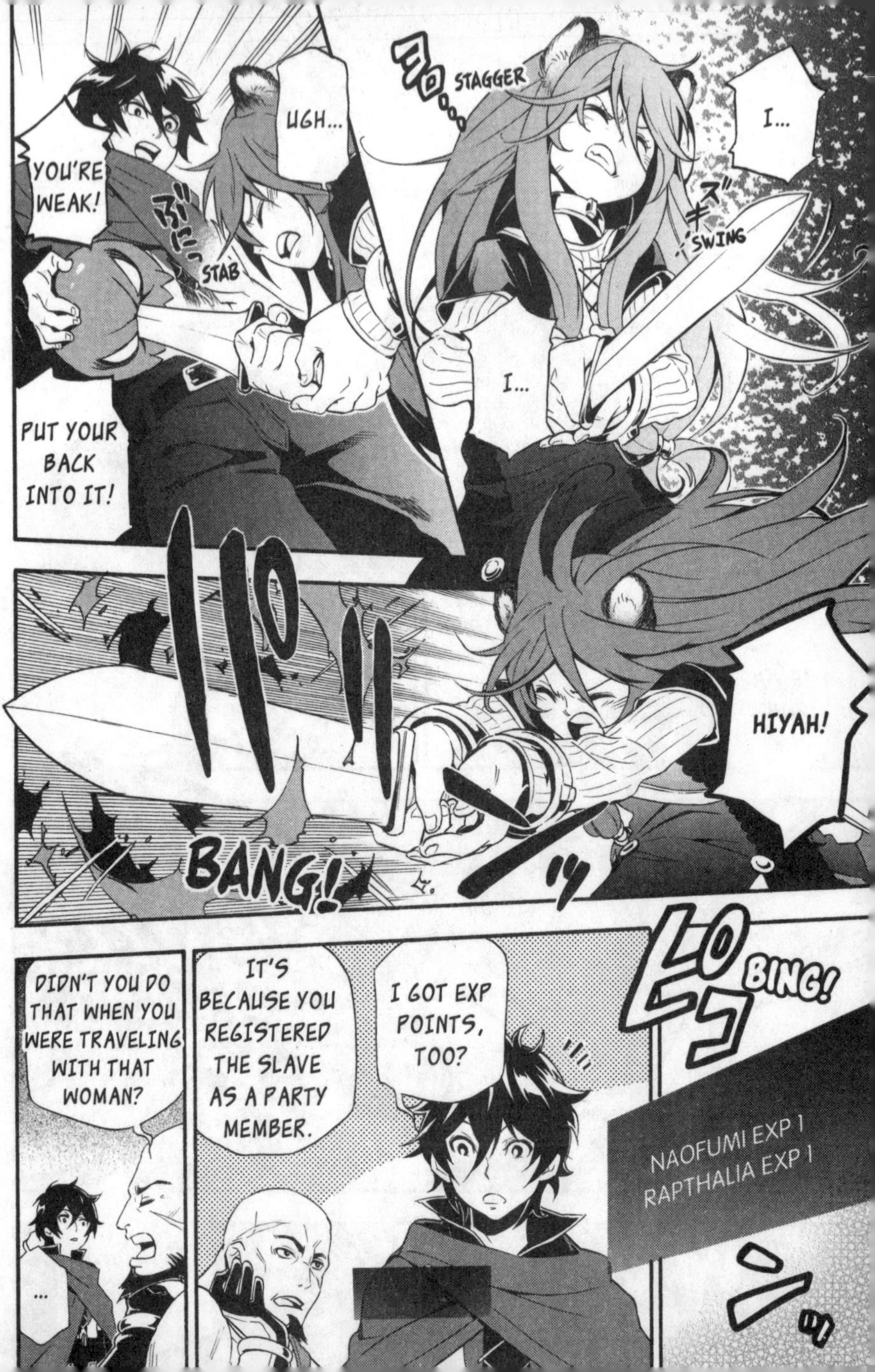
STAGGER
I...
SWING
I...
UGH...
YOU'RE WEAK!
STAB
PUT YOUR BACK INTO IT!
HIYAH!
BANG!
BING!
NAOFUMI EXP 1
RAPTHALIA EXP 1
I GOT EXP POINTS, TOO?
IT'S BECAUSE YOU REGISTERED THE SLAVE AS A PARTY MEMBER.
DIDN'T YOU DO THAT WHEN YOU WERE TRAVELING WITH THAT WOMAN?
...

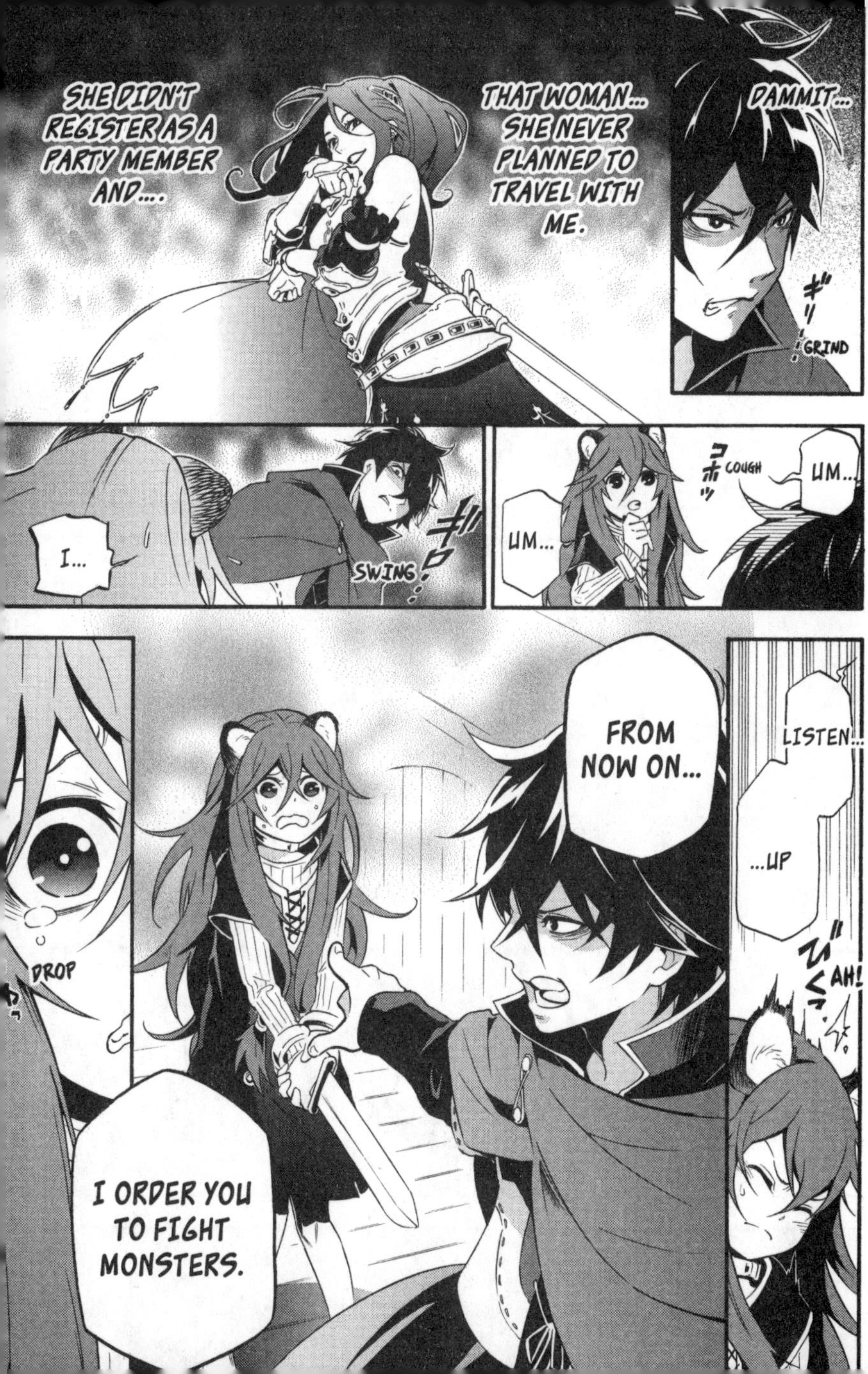
DAMMIT...
GRIND
THAT WOMAN... SHE NEVER PLANNED TO TRAVEL WITH ME.
SHE DIDN'T REGISTER AS A PARTY MEMBER AND....
UM...
COUGH
UM...
SWING
I...
LISTEN...
...UP
AH!
FROM NOW ON...
I ORDER YOU TO FIGHT MONSTERS.
DROP

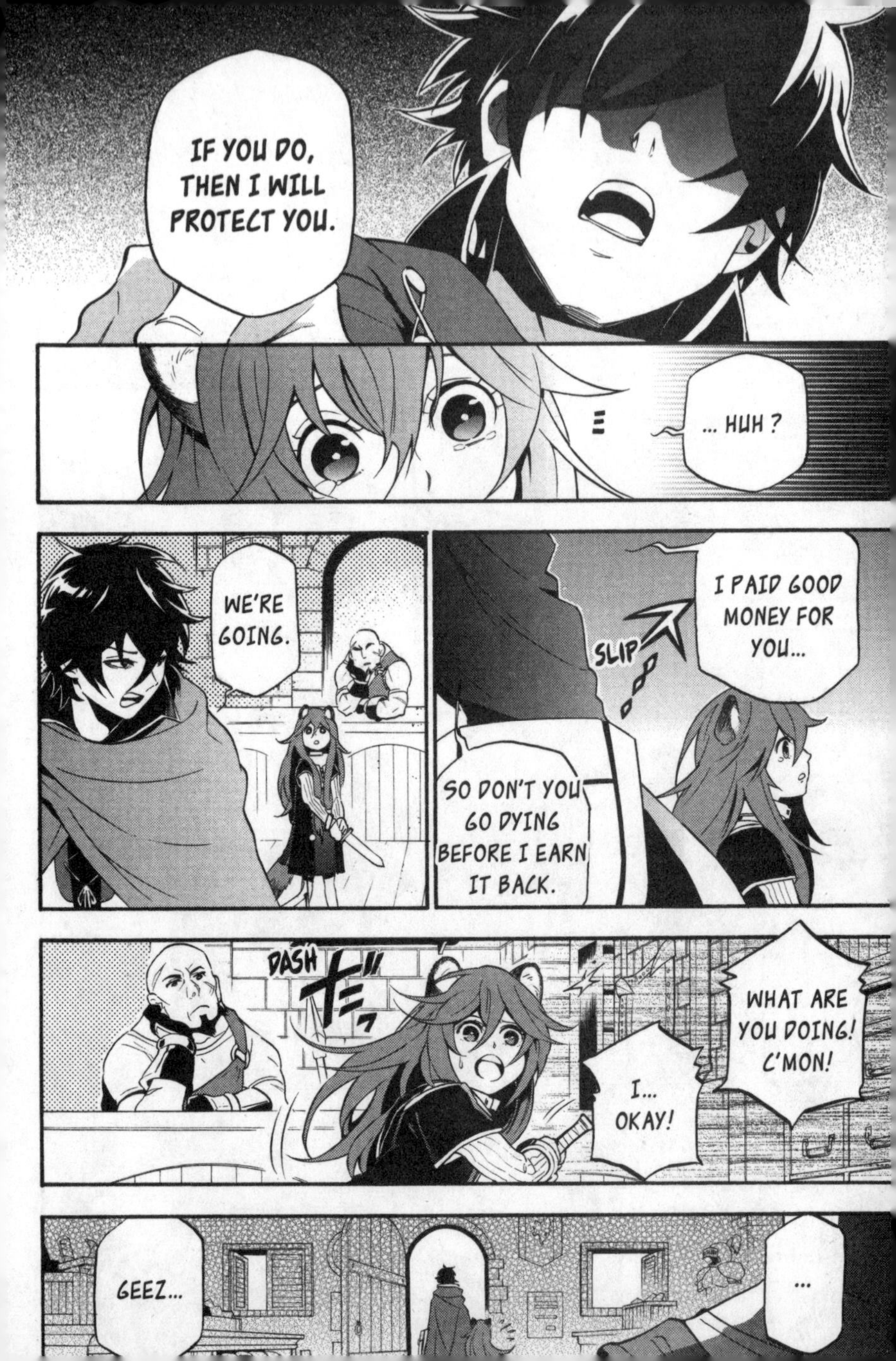
IF YOU DO, THEN I WILL PROTECT YOU.
... HUH ?
I PAID GOOD MONEY FOR YOU...
SLIP
SO DON'T YOU GO DYING BEFORE I EARN IT BACK.
WE'RE GOING.
WHAT ARE YOU DOING! C'MON!
I... OKAY!
DASH
...
GEEZ...

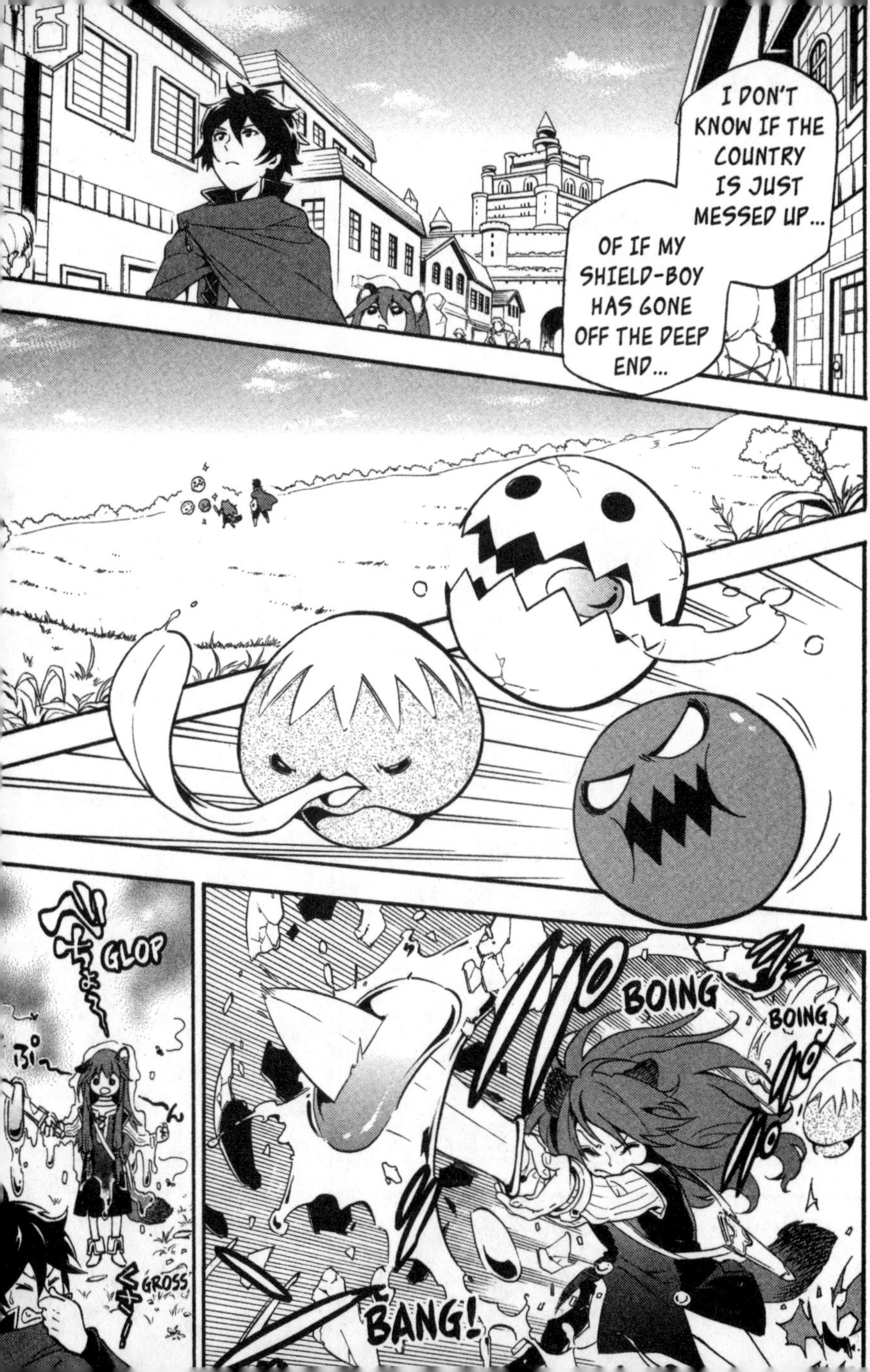
I DON'T KNOW IF THE COUNTRY IS JUST MESSED UP...
OF IF MY SHIELD-BOY HAS GONE OFF THE DEEP END...
BOING
BOING
BANG!
GLOP
GROSS

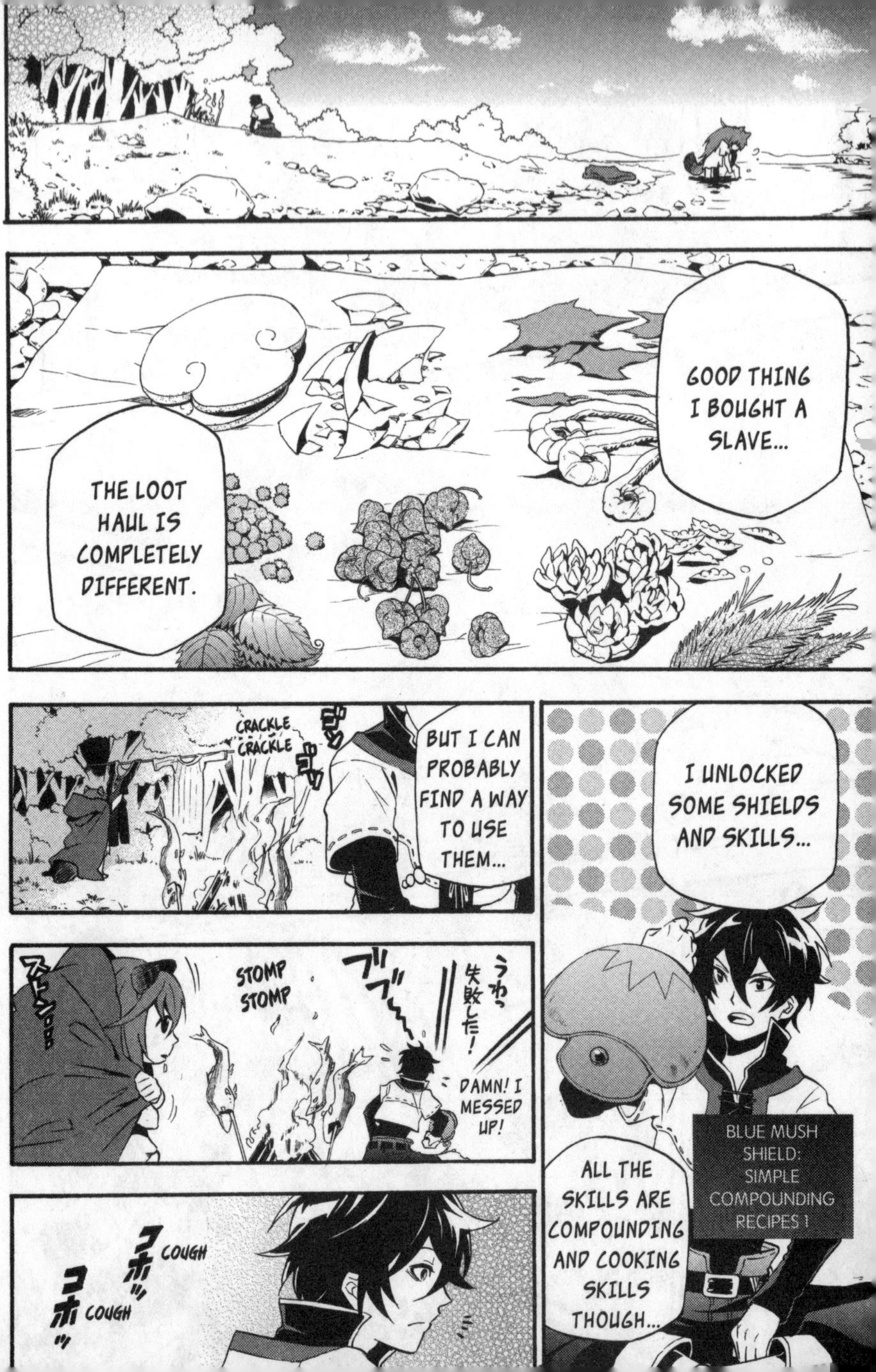
GOOD THING I BOUGHT A SLAVE...
THE LOOT HAUL IS COMPLETELY DIFFERENT.
I UNLOCKED SOME SHIELDS AND SKILLS...
BLUE MUSH SHIELD: SIMPLE COMPOUNDING RECIPES 1
ALL THE SKILLS ARE COMPOUNDING AND COOKING SKILLS THOUGH...
BUT I CAN PROBABLY FIND A WAY TO USE THEM...
CRACKLE CRACKLE
うわっ 失敗した！
DAMN! I MESSED UP!
STOMP STOMP
コホッ
COUGH
コホッ
COUGH

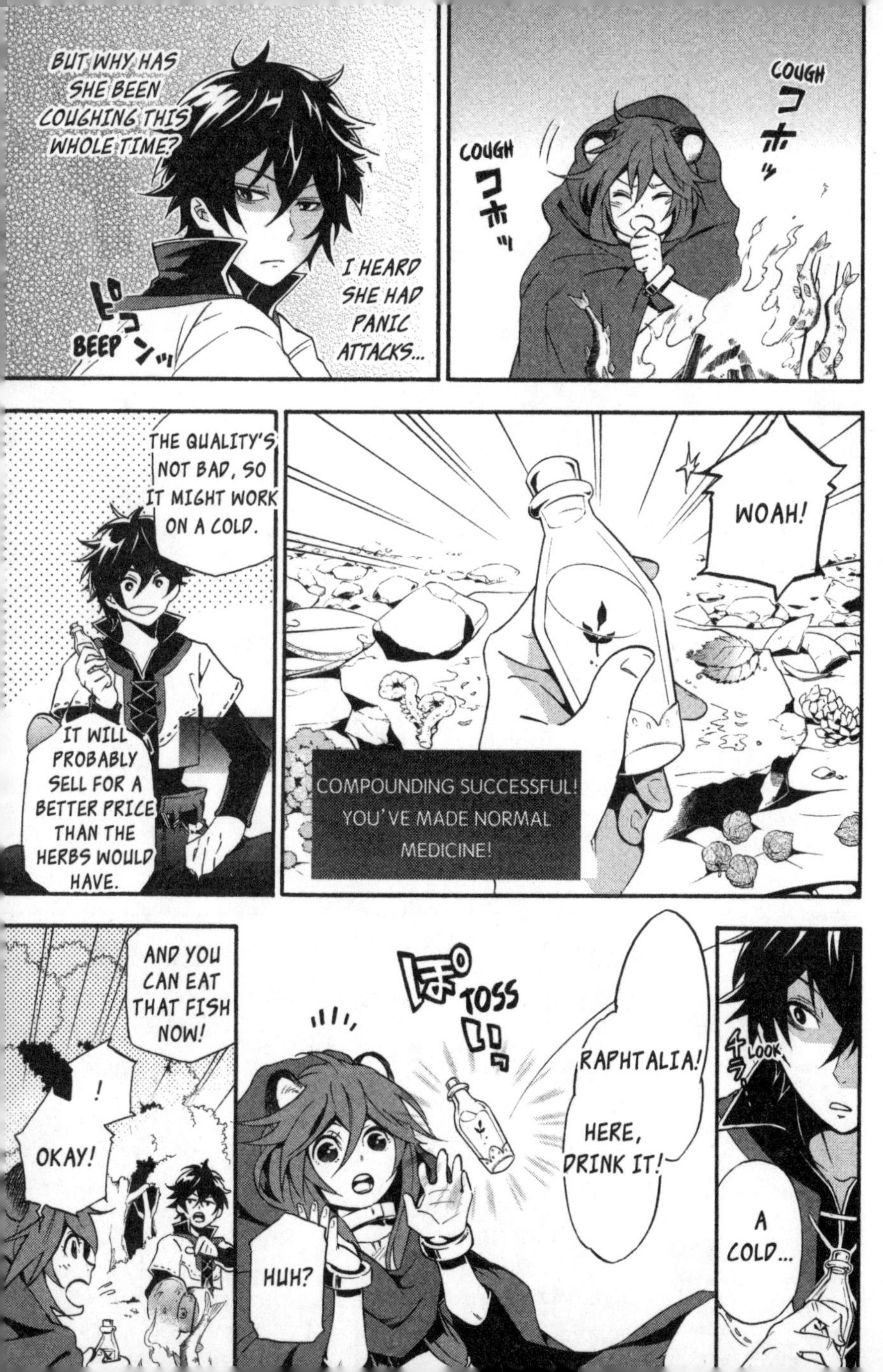
COUGH
コホッ
COUGH
コホッ
BUT WHY HAS SHE BEEN COUGHING THIS WHOLE TIME?
I HEARD SHE HAD PANIC ATTACKS...
BEEP
WOAH!
COMPOUNDING SUCCESSFUL! YOU'VE MADE NORMAL MEDICINE!
THE QUALITY'S NOT BAD, SO IT MIGHT WORK ON A COLD.
IT WILL PROBABLY SELL FOR A BETTER PRICE THAN THE HERBS WOULD HAVE.
LOOK
A COLD...
RAPHTALIA!
HERE, DRINK IT!
TOSS
HUH?
AND YOU CAN EAT THAT FISH NOW!
!
OKAY!

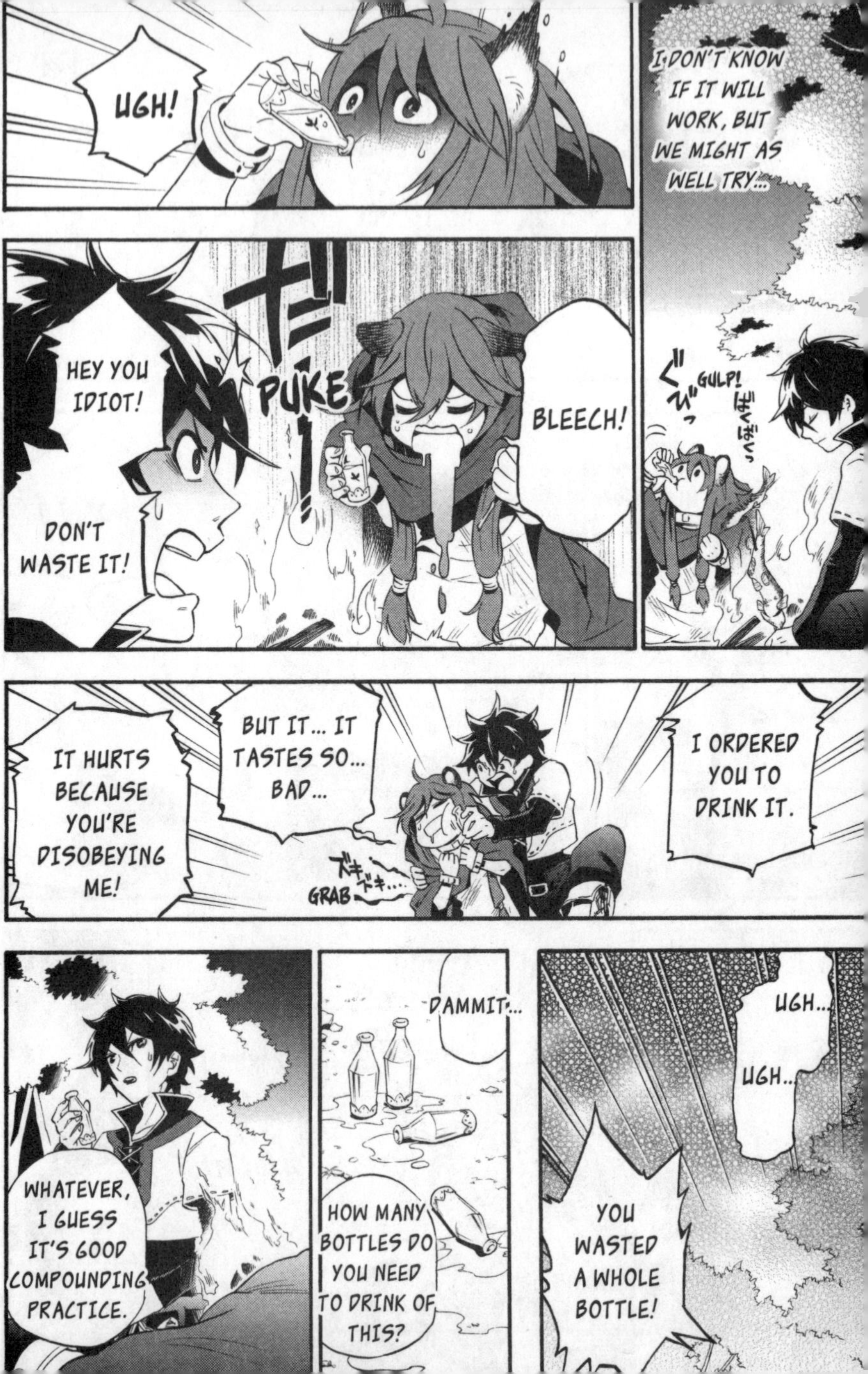
I DON'T KNOW IF IT WILL WORK, BUT WE MIGHT AS WELL TRY...
GULP!
UGH!
PUKE
BLEECH!
HEY YOU IDIOT!
DON'T WASTE IT!
I ORDERED YOU TO DRINK IT.
BUT IT... IT TASTES SO... BAD...
GRAB
IT HURTS BECAUSE YOU'RE DISOBEYING ME!
UGH...
UGH...
YOU WASTED A WHOLE BOTTLE!
DAMMIT...
HOW MANY BOTTLES DO YOU NEED TO DRINK OF THIS?
WHATEVER, I GUESS IT'S GOOD COMPOUNDING PRACTICE.

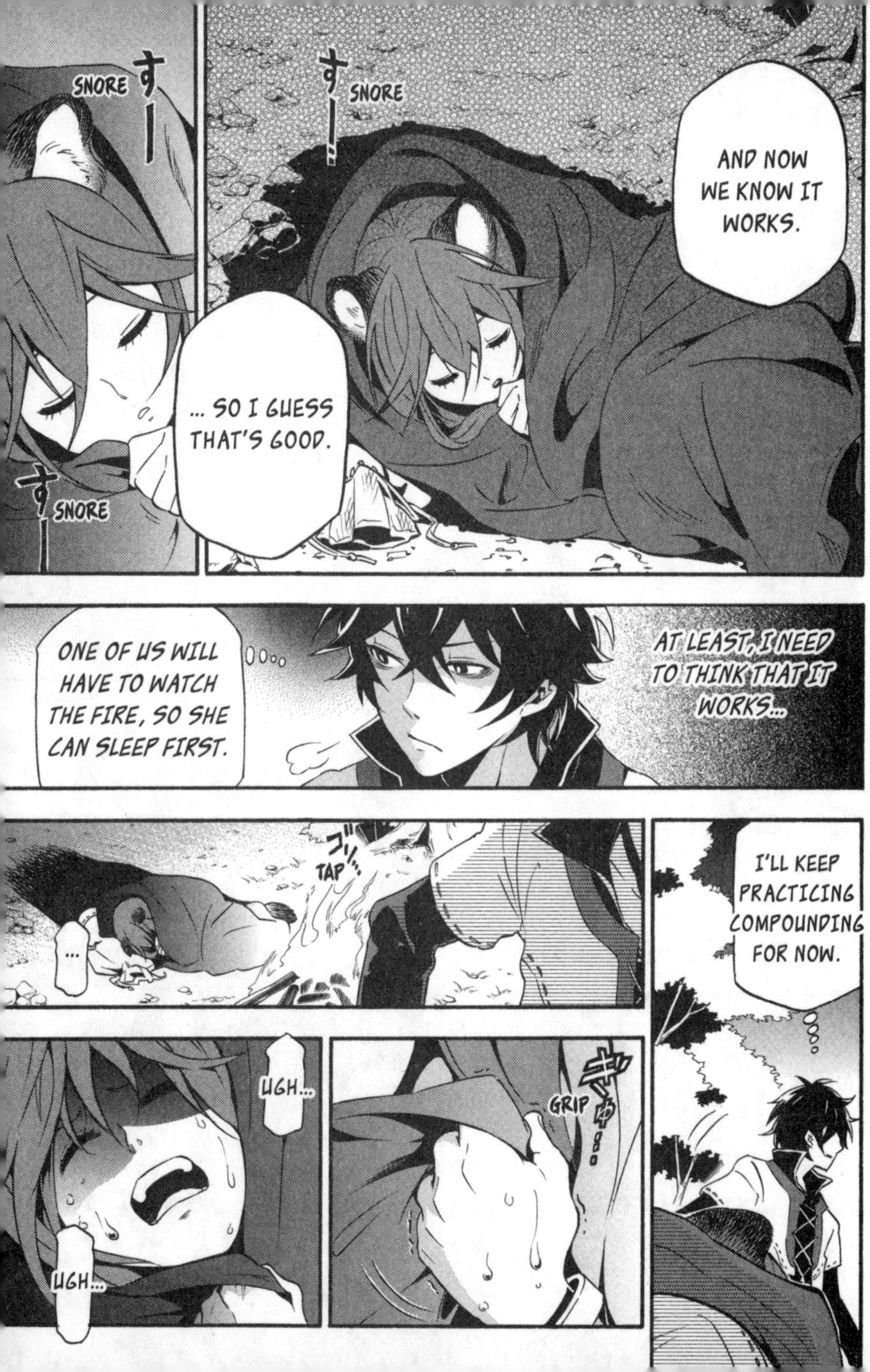
AND NOW WE KNOW IT WORKS.
SNORE
... SO I GUESS THAT'S GOOD.
SNORE
SNORE
AT LEAST, I NEED TO THINK THAT IT WORKS...
ONE OF US WILL HAVE TO WATCH THE FIRE, SO SHE CAN SLEEP FIRST.
I'LL KEEP PRACTICING COMPOUNDING FOR NOW.
TAP
...
GRIP
UGH...
UGH...

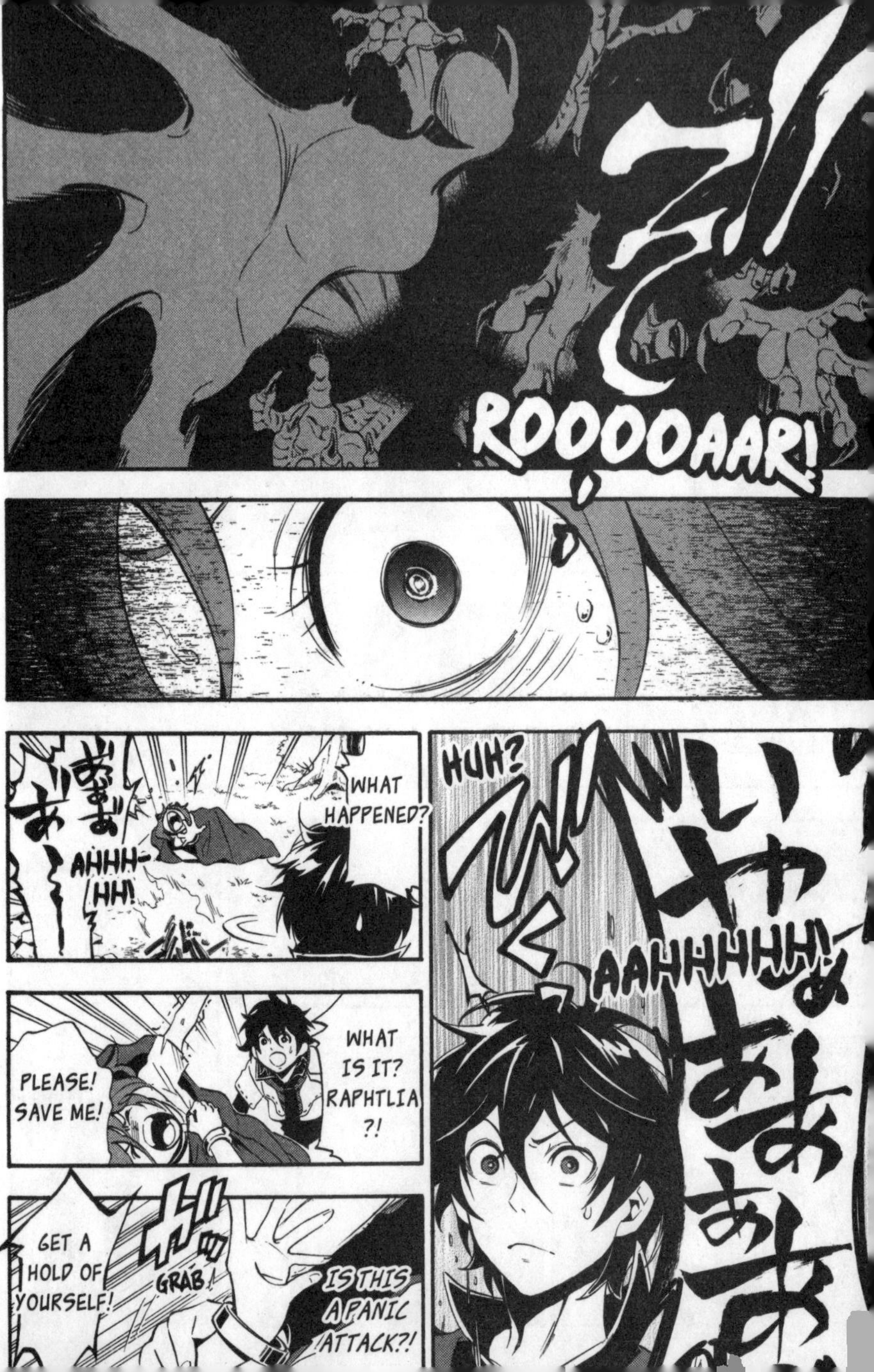
ROOOOAAR!
HUH?
AAHHHHH!
WHAT HAPPENED?
AHHH-HH!
WHAT IS IT? RAPHTLIA?!
PLEASE! SAVE ME!
IS THIS A PANIC ATTACK?!
GRAB
GET A HOLD OF YOURSELF!

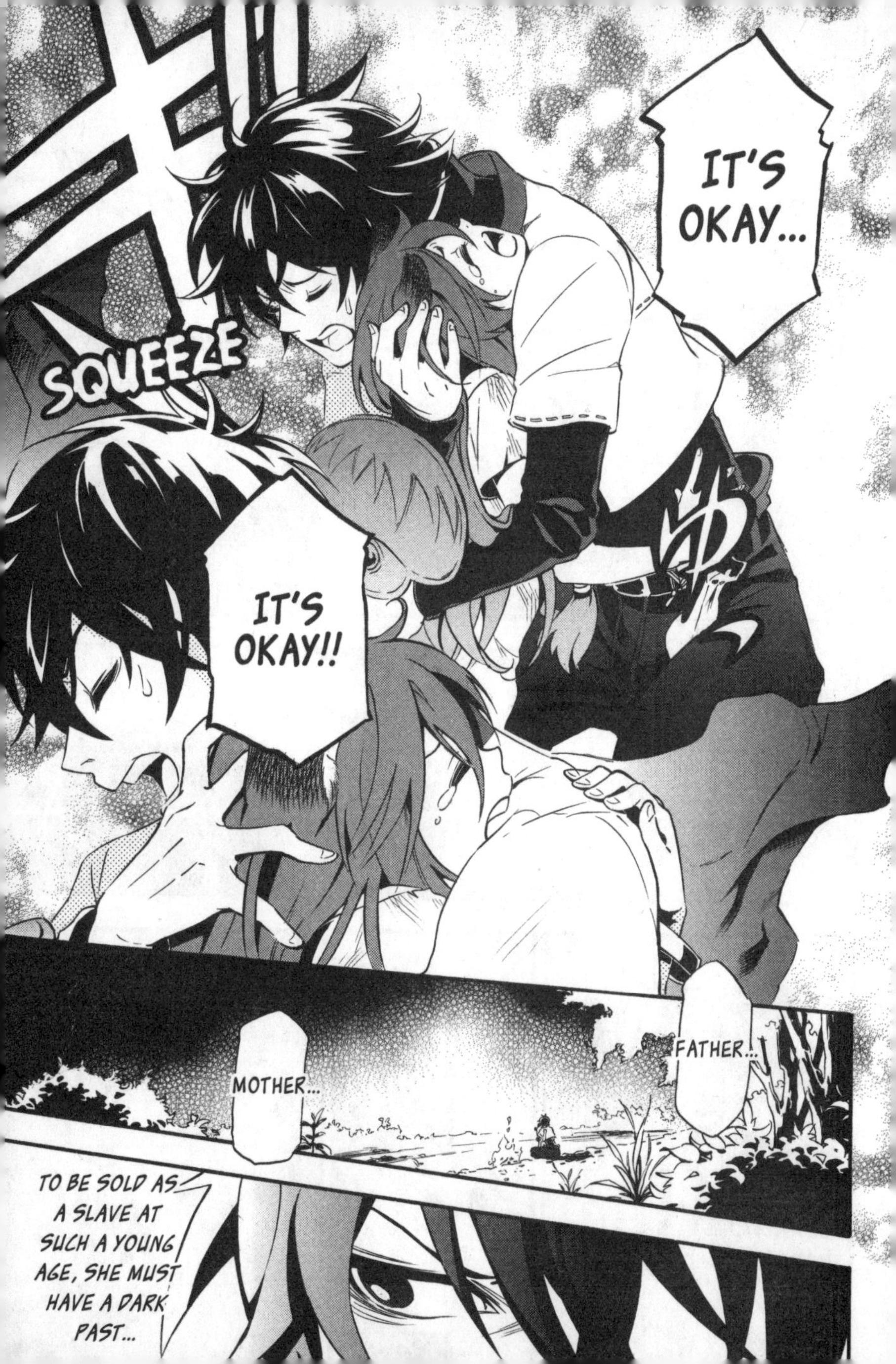
IT'S OKAY...
SQUEEZE
IT'S OKAY!!
FATHER...
MOTHER...
TO BE SOLD AS A SLAVE AT SUCH A YOUNG AGE, SHE MUST HAVE A DARK PAST...

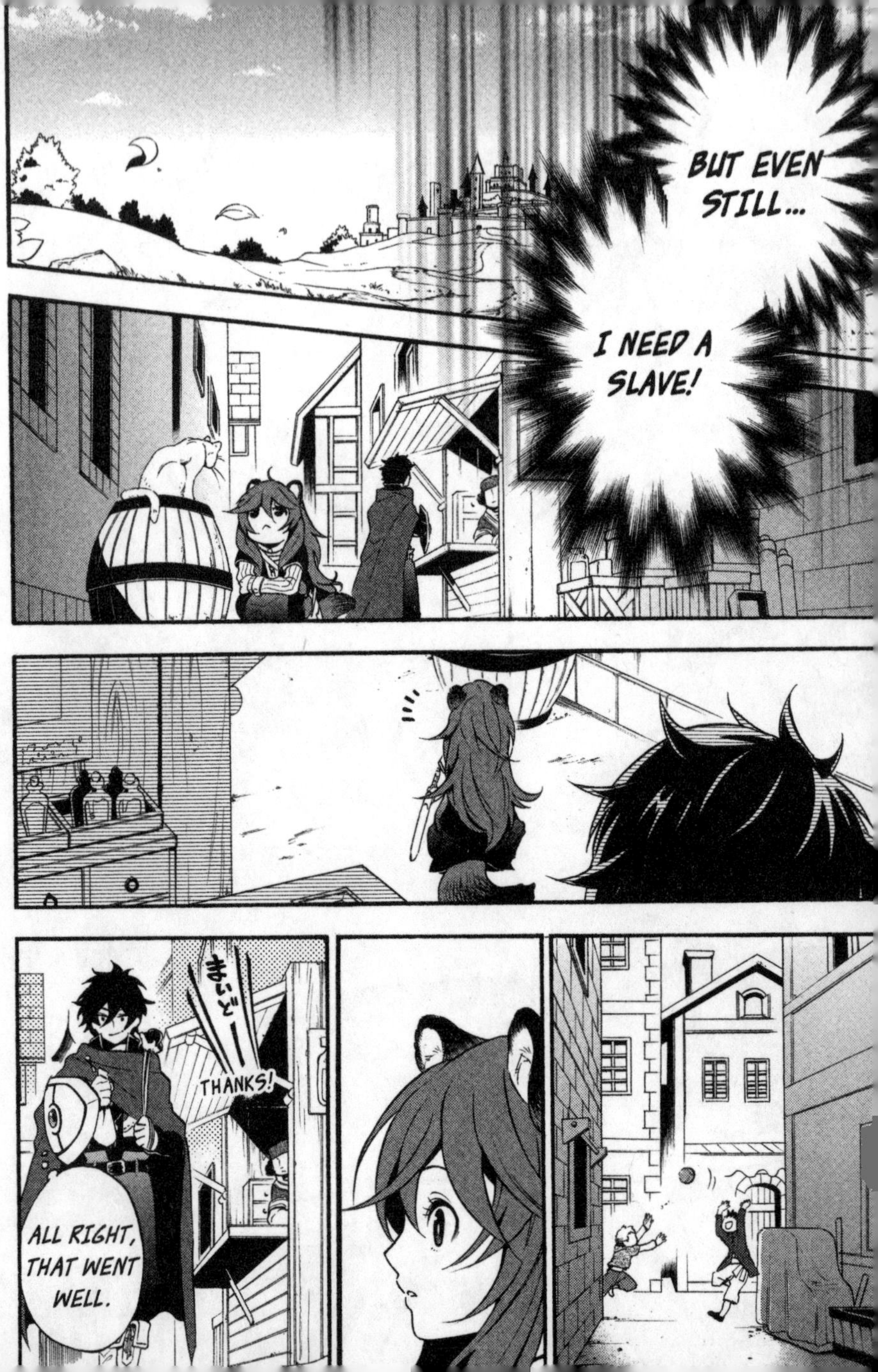
BUT EVEN STILL...
I NEED A SLAVE!
まいどー
THANKS!
ALL RIGHT, THAT WENT WELL.

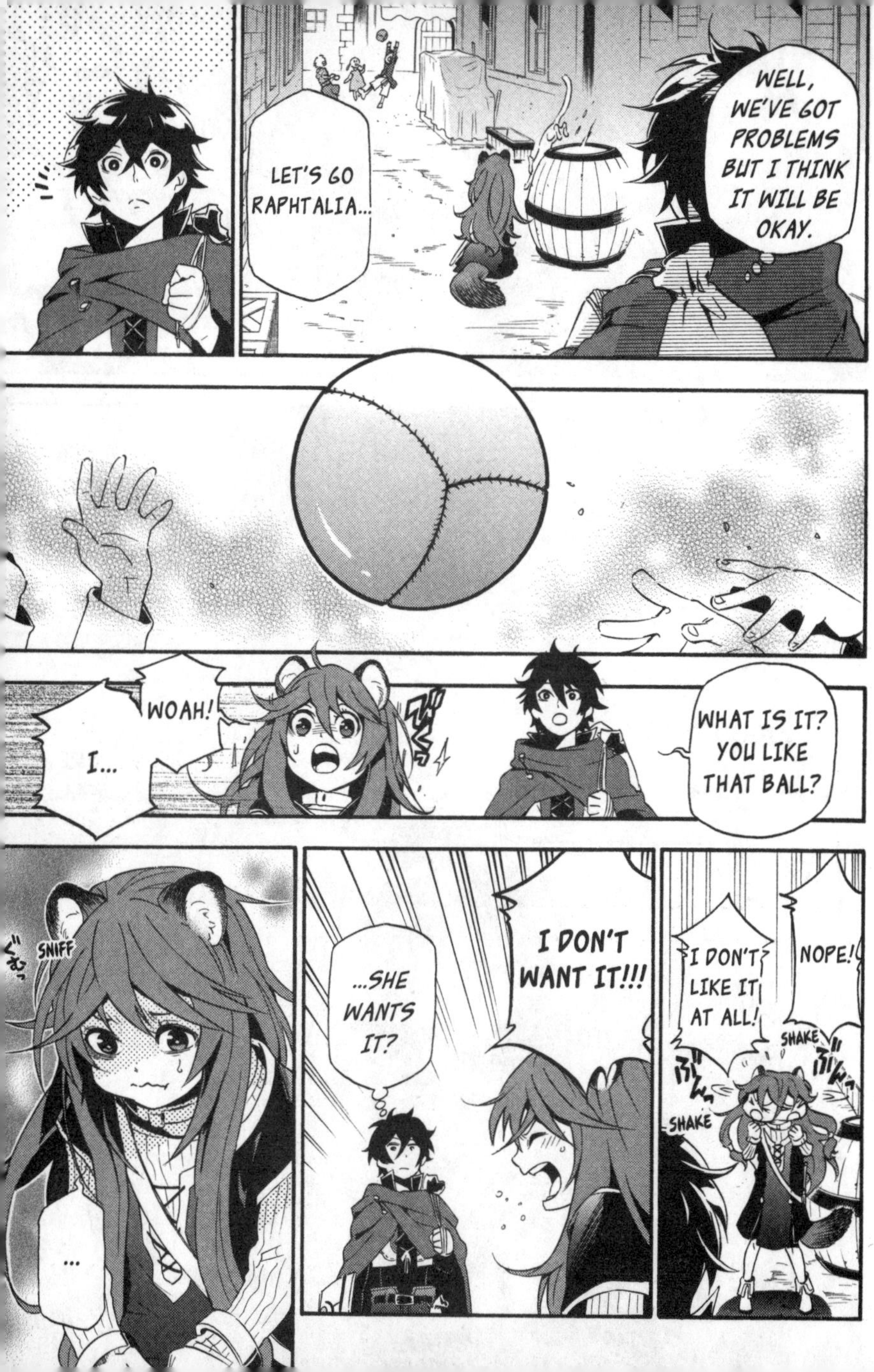
WELL, WE'VE GOT PROBLEMS BUT I THINK IT WILL BE OKAY.
LET'S GO RAPHTALIA...
WHAT IS IT? YOU LIKE THAT BALL?
WOAH!
I...
NOPE!
I DON'T LIKE IT AT ALL!
SHAKE
SHAKE
I DON'T WANT IT!!!
...SHE WANTS IT?
SNIFF
...

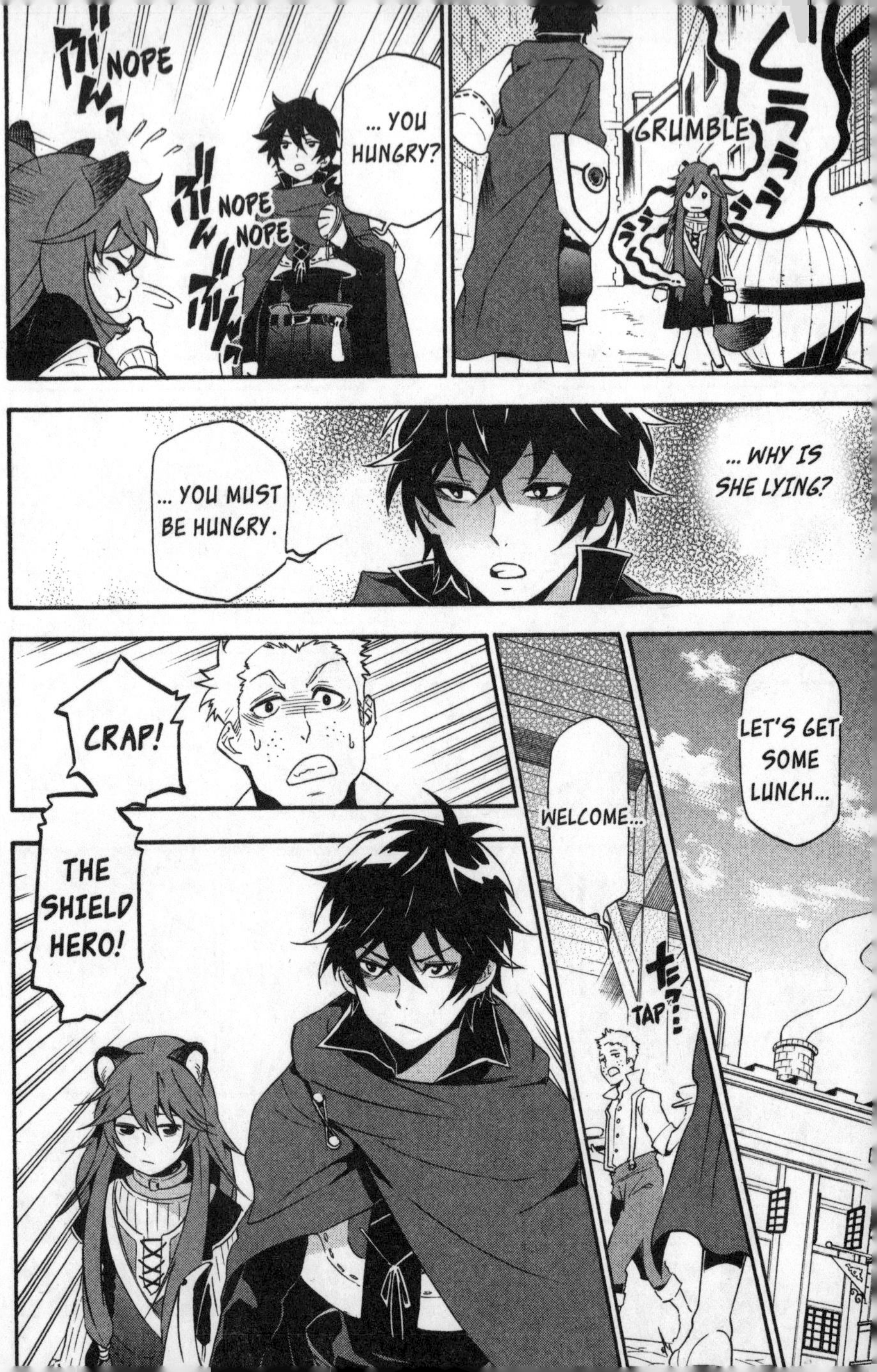
GRUMBLE
... YOU HUNGRY?
NOPE NOPE
NOPE
... WHY IS SHE LYING?
... YOU MUST BE HUNGRY.
LET'S GET SOME LUNCH...
WELCOME...
TAP
CRAP!
THE SHIELD HERO!

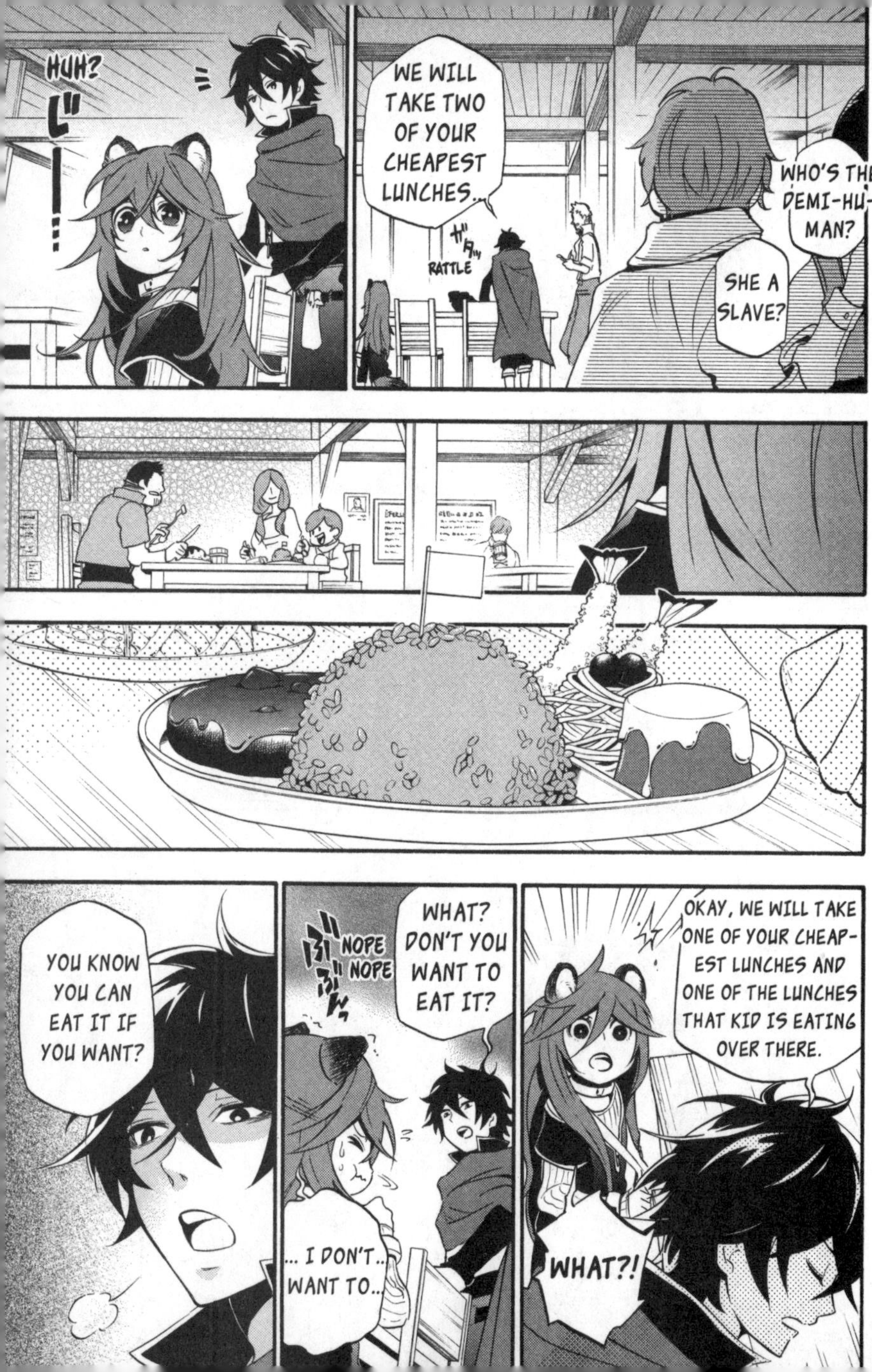
WE WILL TAKE TWO OF YOUR CHEAPEST LUNCHES...
RATTLE
WHO'S THE DEMI-HUMAN?
SHE A SLAVE?
HUH?
OKAY, WE WILL TAKE ONE OF YOUR CHEAPEST LUNCHES AND ONE OF THE LUNCHES THAT KID IS EATING OVER THERE.
WHAT?!
WHAT? DON'T YOU WANT TO EAT IT?
NOPE NOPE
... I DON'T.. WANT TO...
YOU KNOW YOU CAN EAT IT IF YOU WANT?

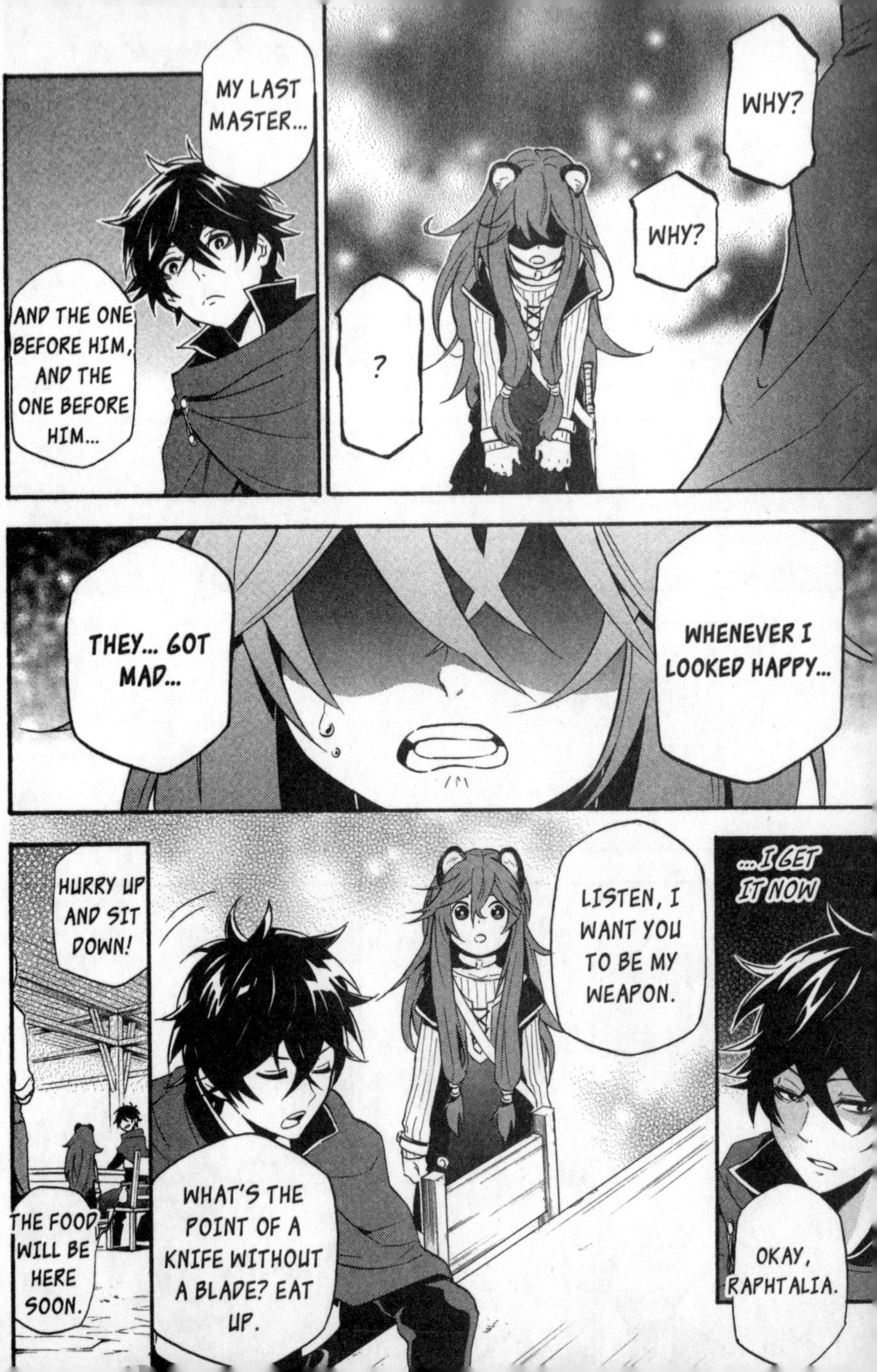
WHY?
WHY?
?
MY LAST MASTER...
AND THE ONE BEFORE HIM, AND THE ONE BEFORE HIM...
WHENEVER I LOOKED HAPPY...
THEY... GOT MAD...
...I GET IT NOW
OKAY, RAPHTALIA.
LISTEN, I WANT YOU TO BE MY WEAPON.
WHAT'S THE POINT OF A KNIFE WITHOUT A BLADE? EAT UP.
HURRY UP AND SIT DOWN!
THE FOOD WILL BE HERE SOON.

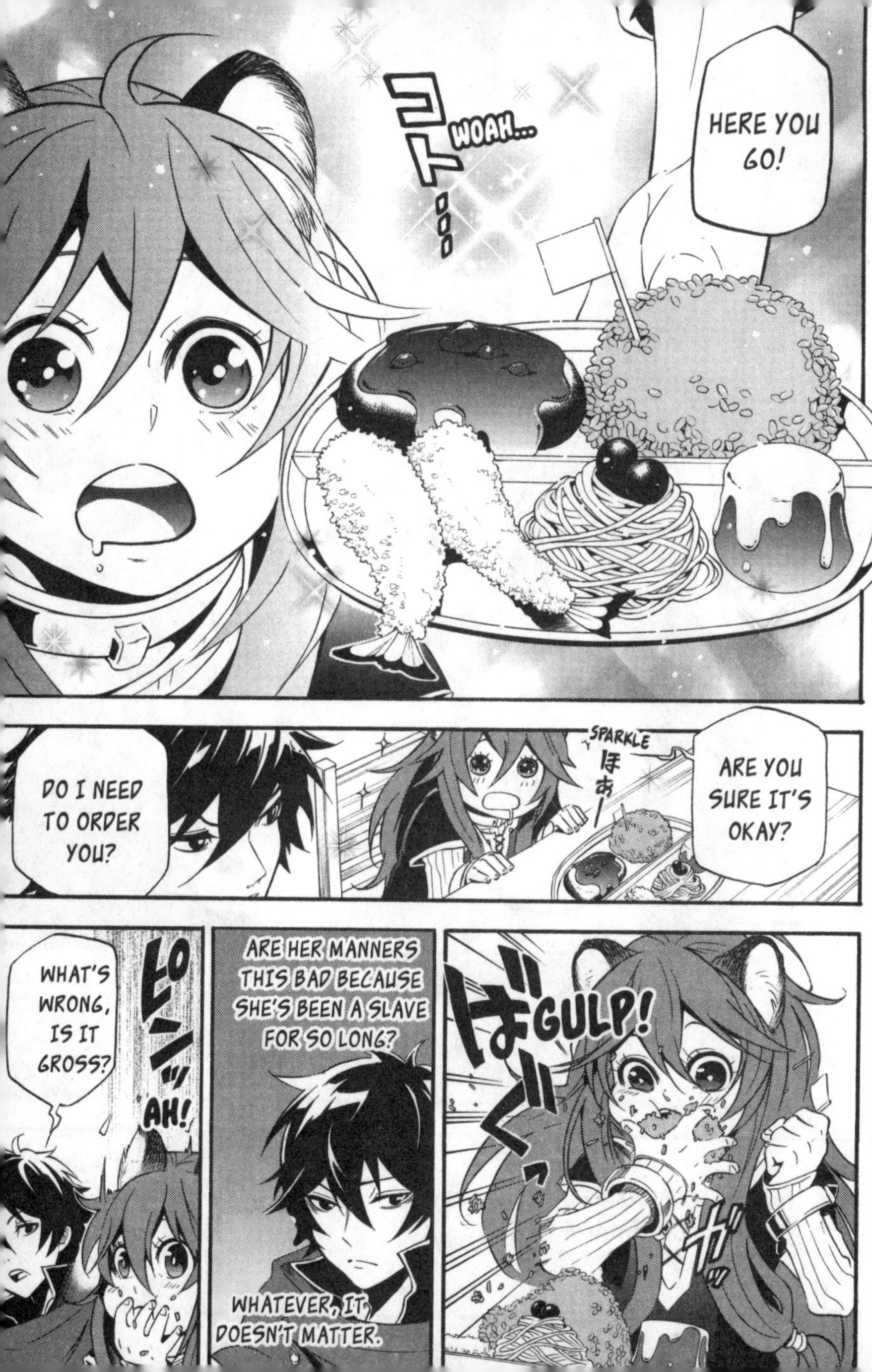
HERE YOU GO!
コト
WOAH...
ARE YOU SURE IT'S OKAY?
SPARKLE
ほあー
DO I NEED TO ORDER YOU?
GULP!
ARE HER MANNERS THIS BAD BECAUSE SHE'S BEEN A SLAVE FOR SO LONG?
WHATEVER, IT DOESN'T MATTER.
AH!
WHAT'S WRONG, IS IT GROSS?

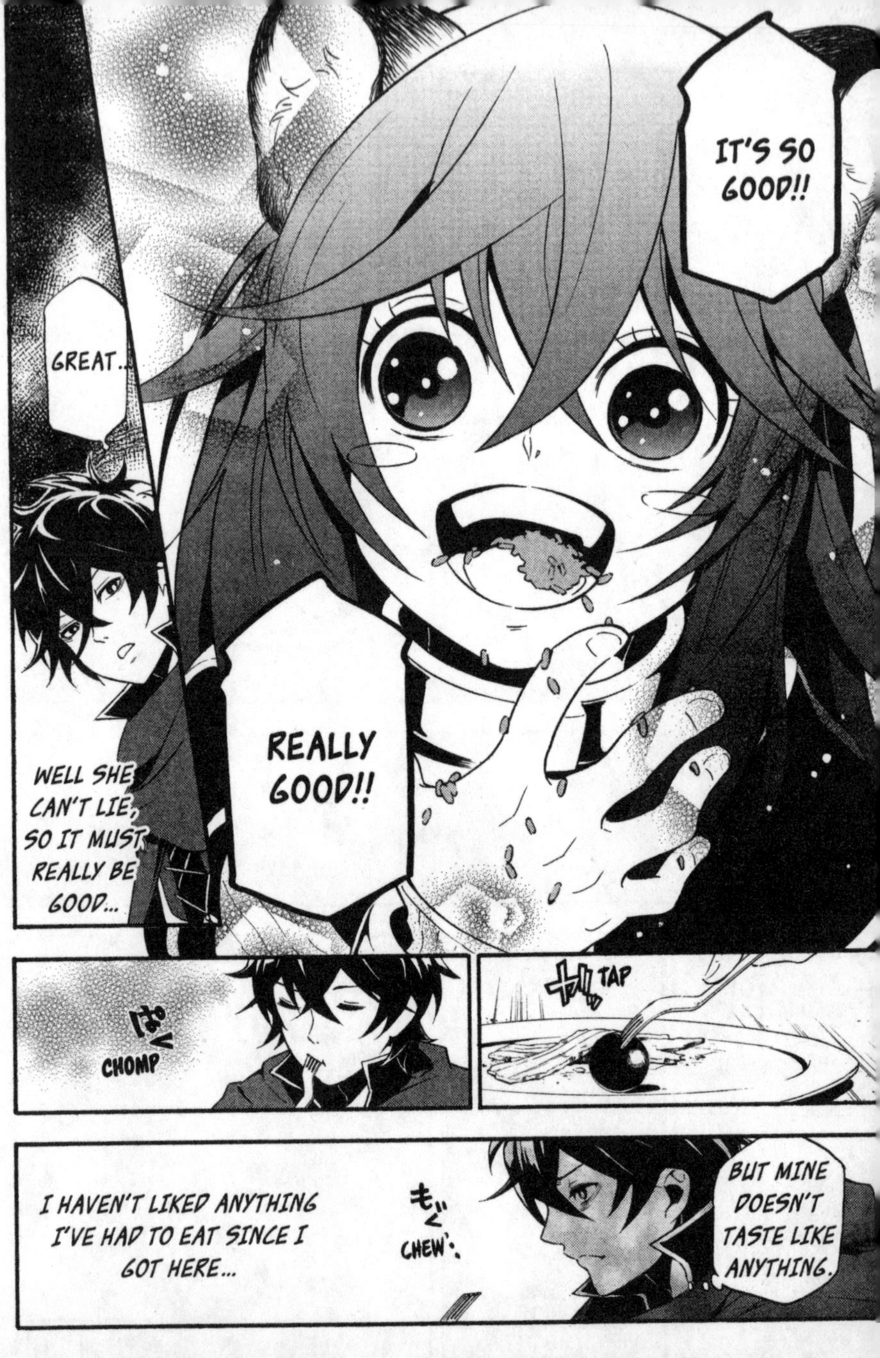
IT'S SO GOOD!!
REALLY GOOD!!
GREAT...
WELL SHE CAN'T LIE, SO IT MUST REALLY BE GOOD...
TAP
ぱく
CHOMP
BUT MINE DOESN'T TASTE LIKE ANYTHING.
もぐ
CHEW
I HAVEN'T LIKED ANYTHING I'VE HAD TO EAT SINCE I GOT HERE...

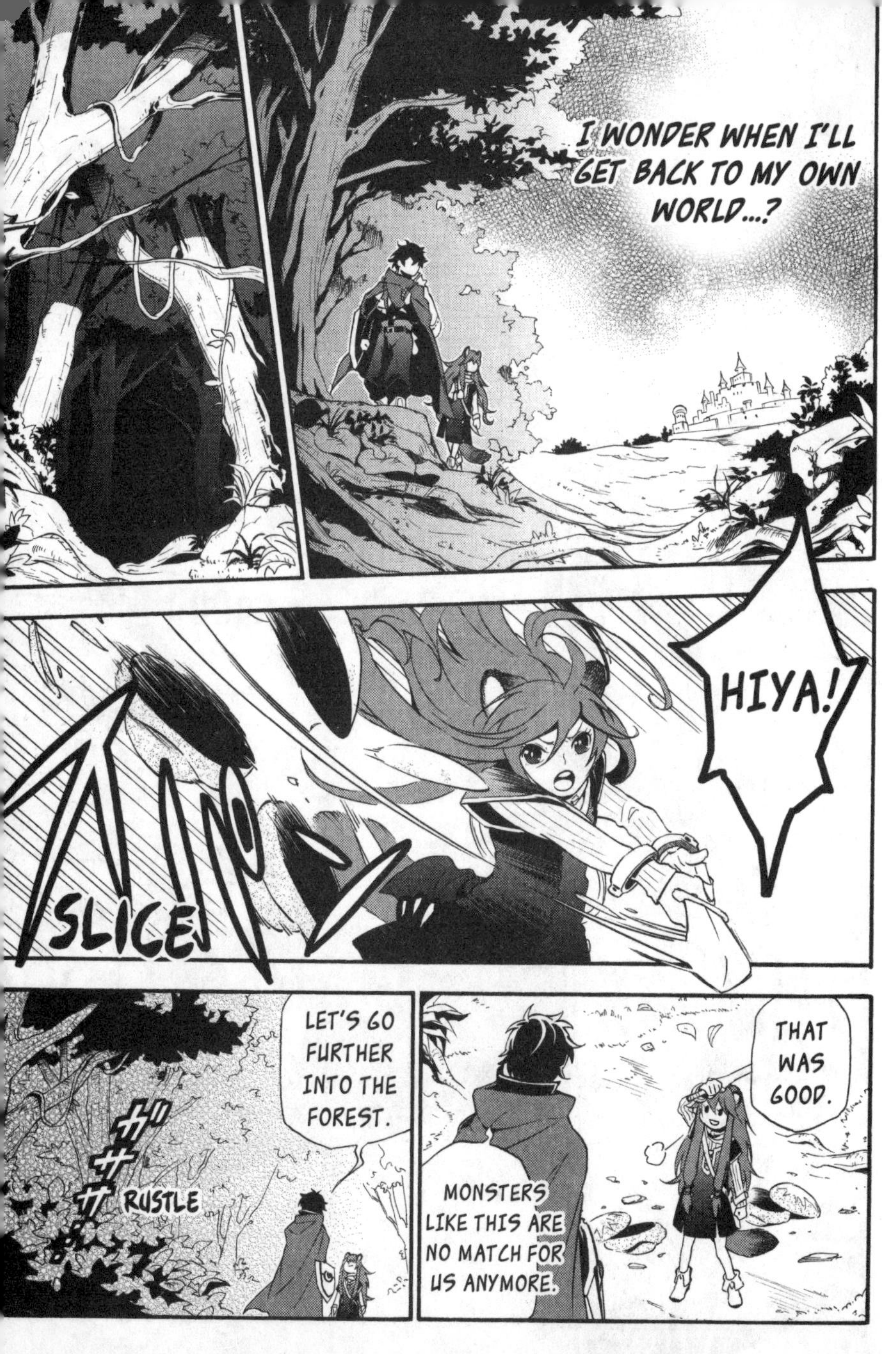
I WONDER WHEN I'LL GET BACK TO MY OWN WORLD...?
HIYA!
SLICE
THAT WAS GOOD.
MONSTERS LIKE THIS ARE NO MATCH FOR US ANYMORE.
LET'S GO FURTHER INTO THE FOREST.
RUSTLE

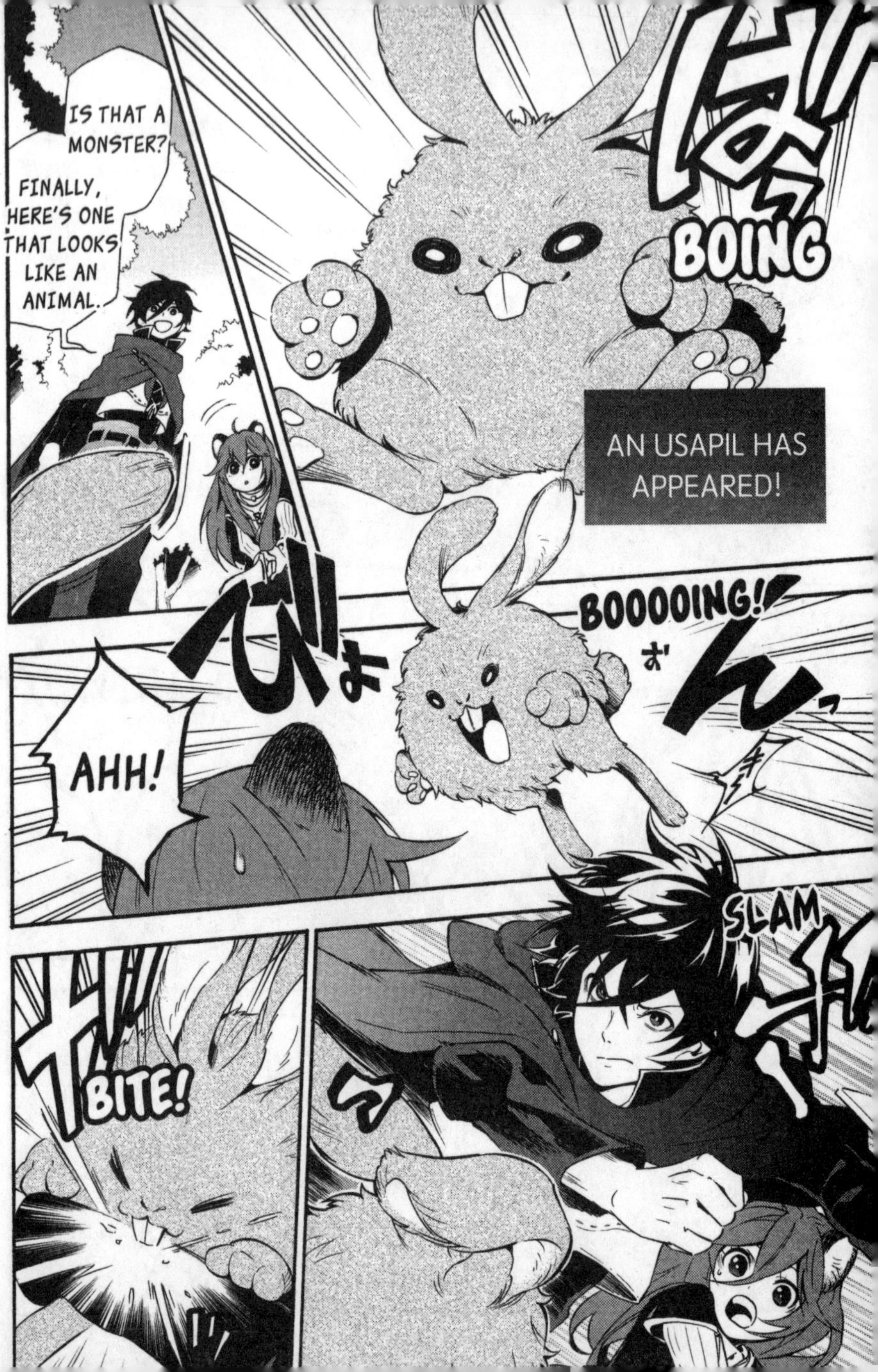

BOING
AN USAPIL HAS APPEARED!
IS THAT A MONSTER?
FINALLY, HERE'S ONE THAT LOOKS LIKE AN ANIMAL.
BOOOOING!
AHH!
SLAM
BITE!

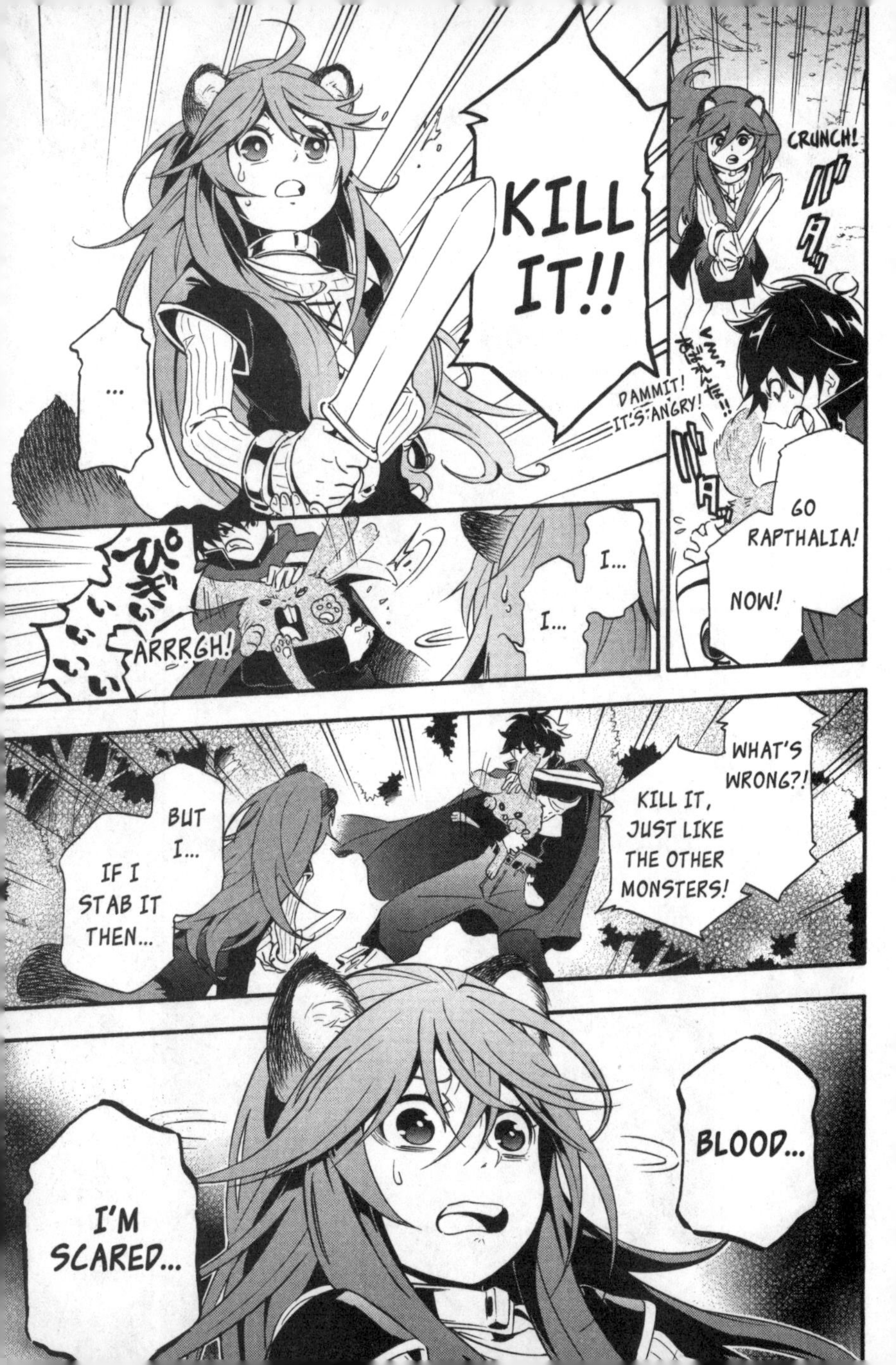
CRUNCH!
DAMMIT! IT'S ANGRY!
くそっ あばれんな!!
GO RAPTHALIA!
NOW!
KILL IT!!
...
I...
I...
ARRRGH!
WHAT'S WRONG?!
KILL IT, JUST LIKE THE OTHER MONSTERS!
BUT I...
IF I STAB IT THEN...
BLOOD...
I'M SCARED...

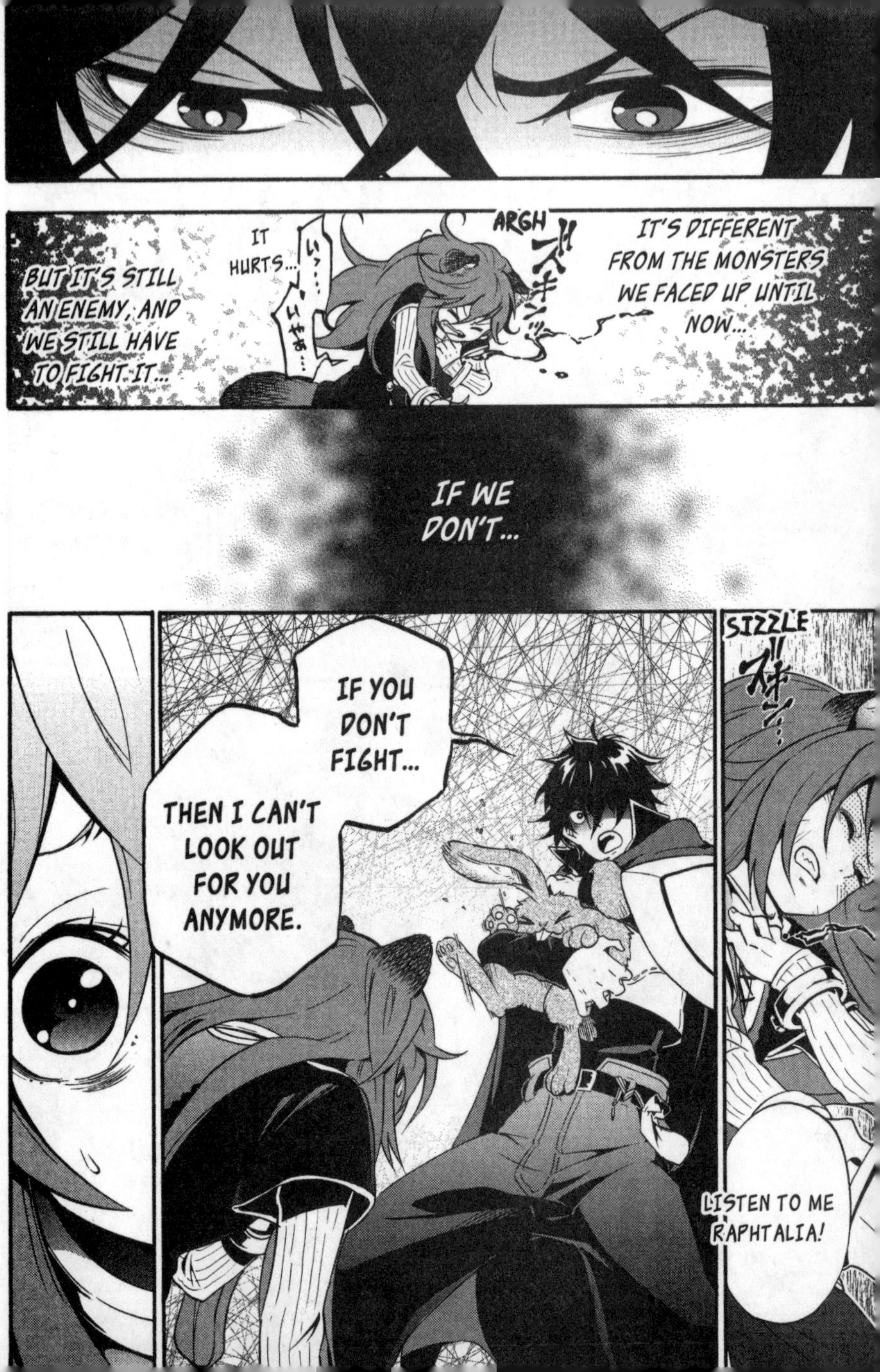
IT'S DIFFERENT FROM THE MONSTERS WE FACED UP UNTIL NOW...
ARGH
IT HURTS...
BUT IT'S STILL AN ENEMY, AND WE STILL HAVE TO FIGHT IT...
IF WE DON'T...
SIZZLE
LISTEN TO ME RAPHTALIA!
IF YOU DON'T FIGHT...
THEN I CAN'T LOOK OUT FOR YOU ANYMORE.

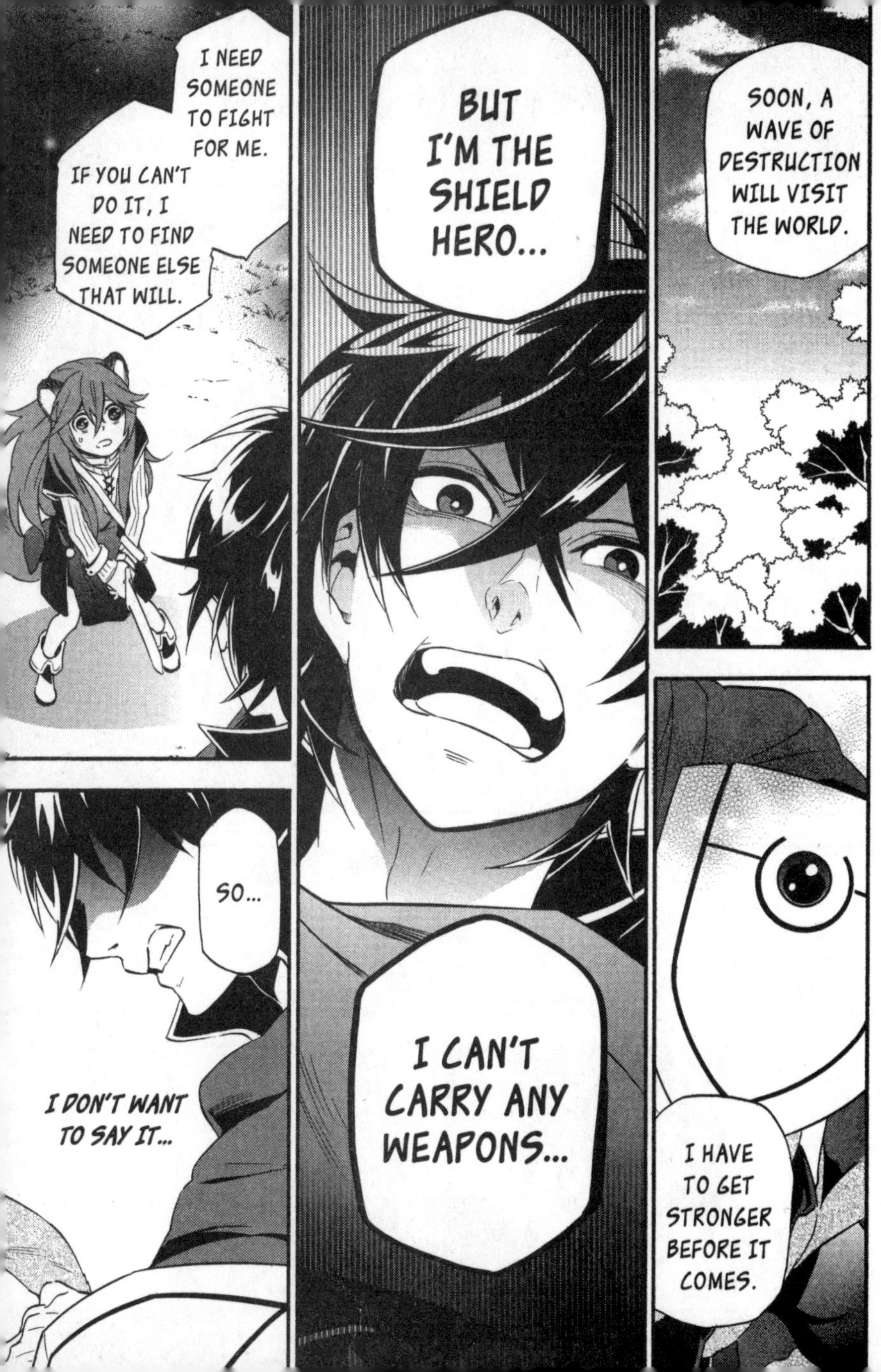
SOON, A WAVE OF DESTRUCTION WILL VISIT THE WORLD.
I HAVE TO GET STRONGER BEFORE IT COMES.
BUT I'M THE SHIELD HERO...
I CAN'T CARRY ANY WEAPONS...
I NEED SOMEONE TO FIGHT FOR ME.
IF YOU CAN'T DO IT, I NEED TO FIND SOMEONE ELSE THAT WILL.
SO...
I DON'T WANT TO SAY IT...

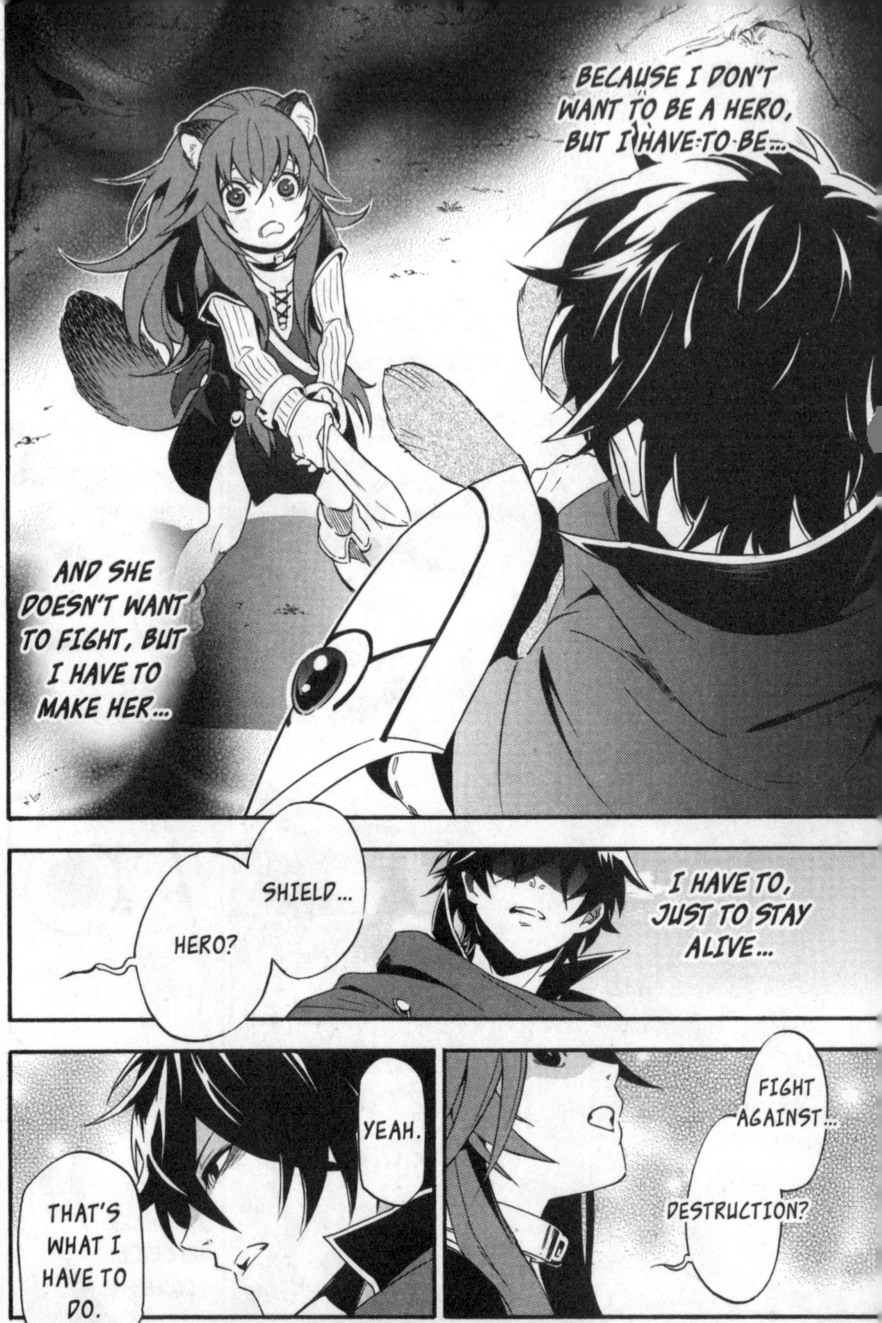
BECAUSE I DON'T WANT TO BE A HERO, BUT I HAVE TO BE...
AND SHE DOESN'T WANT TO FIGHT, BUT I HAVE TO MAKE HER...
I HAVE TO, JUST TO STAY ALIVE...
SHIELD... HERO?
FIGHT AGAINST... DESTRUCTION?
YEAH.
THAT'S WHAT I HAVE TO DO.

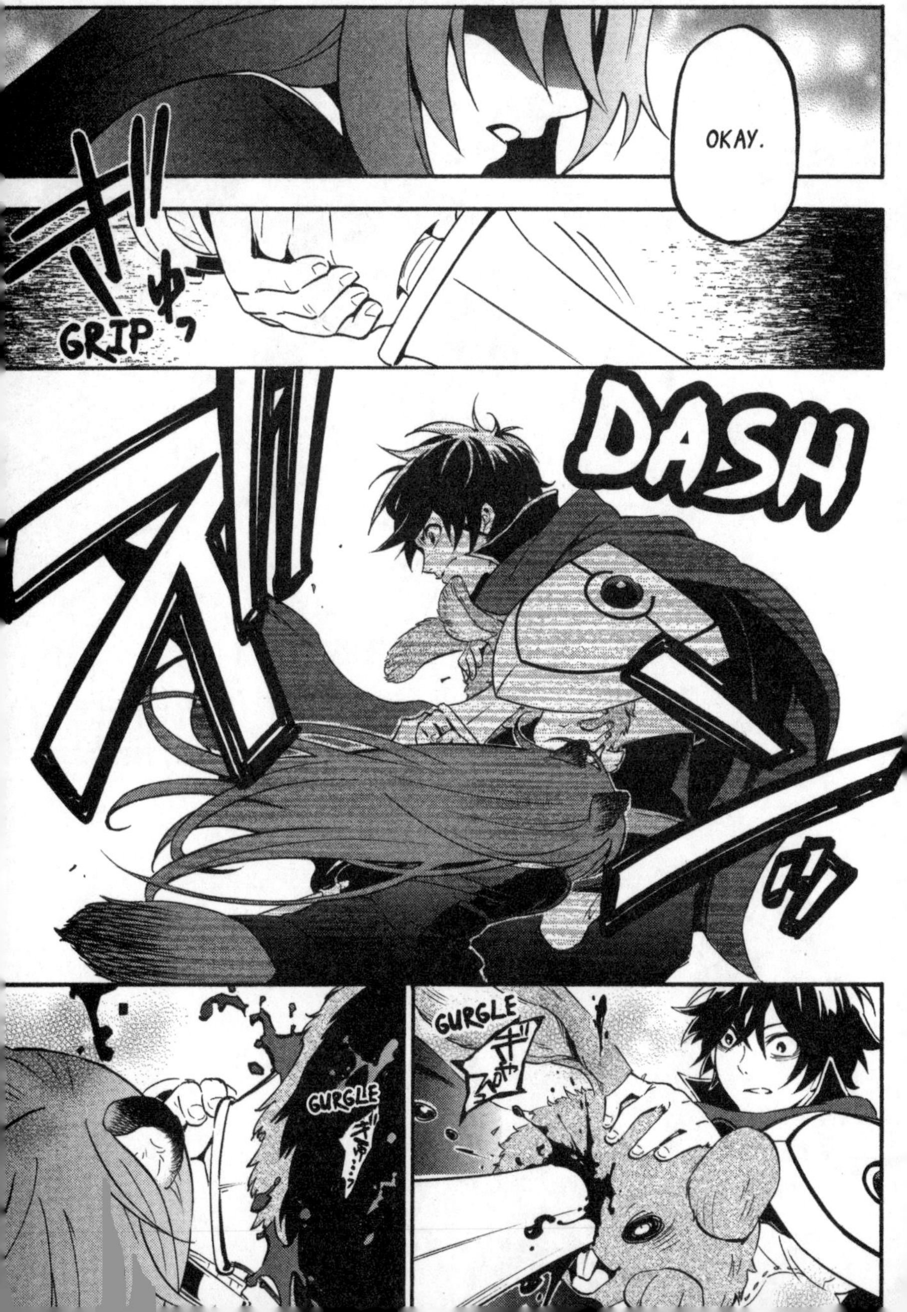
OKAY.
GRIP
DASH
GURGLE
GURGLE

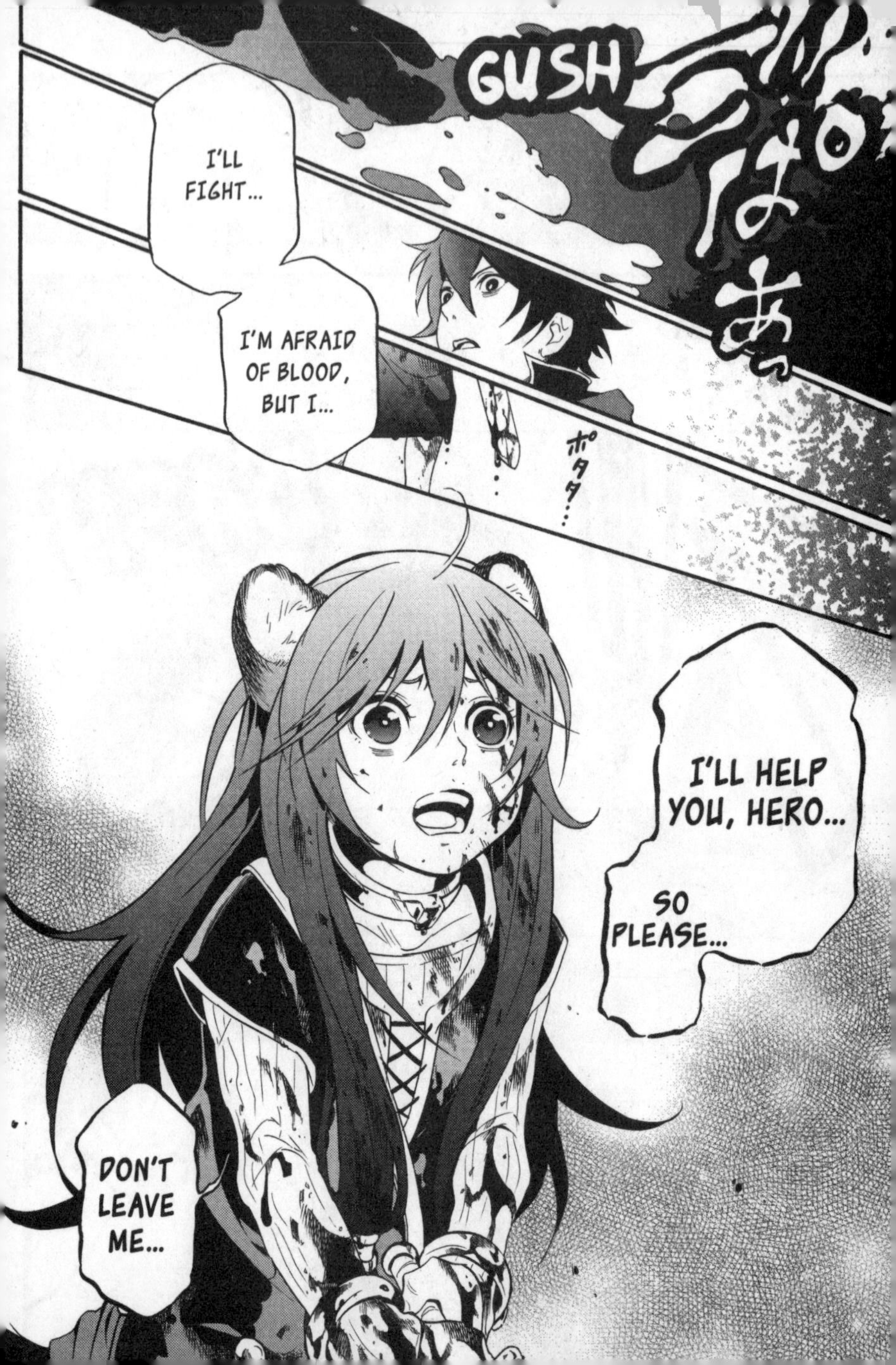
GUSH
ポタタ…
I'LL FIGHT...
I'M AFRAID OF BLOOD, BUT I...
I'LL HELP YOU, HERO...
SO PLEASE...
DON'T LEAVE ME...

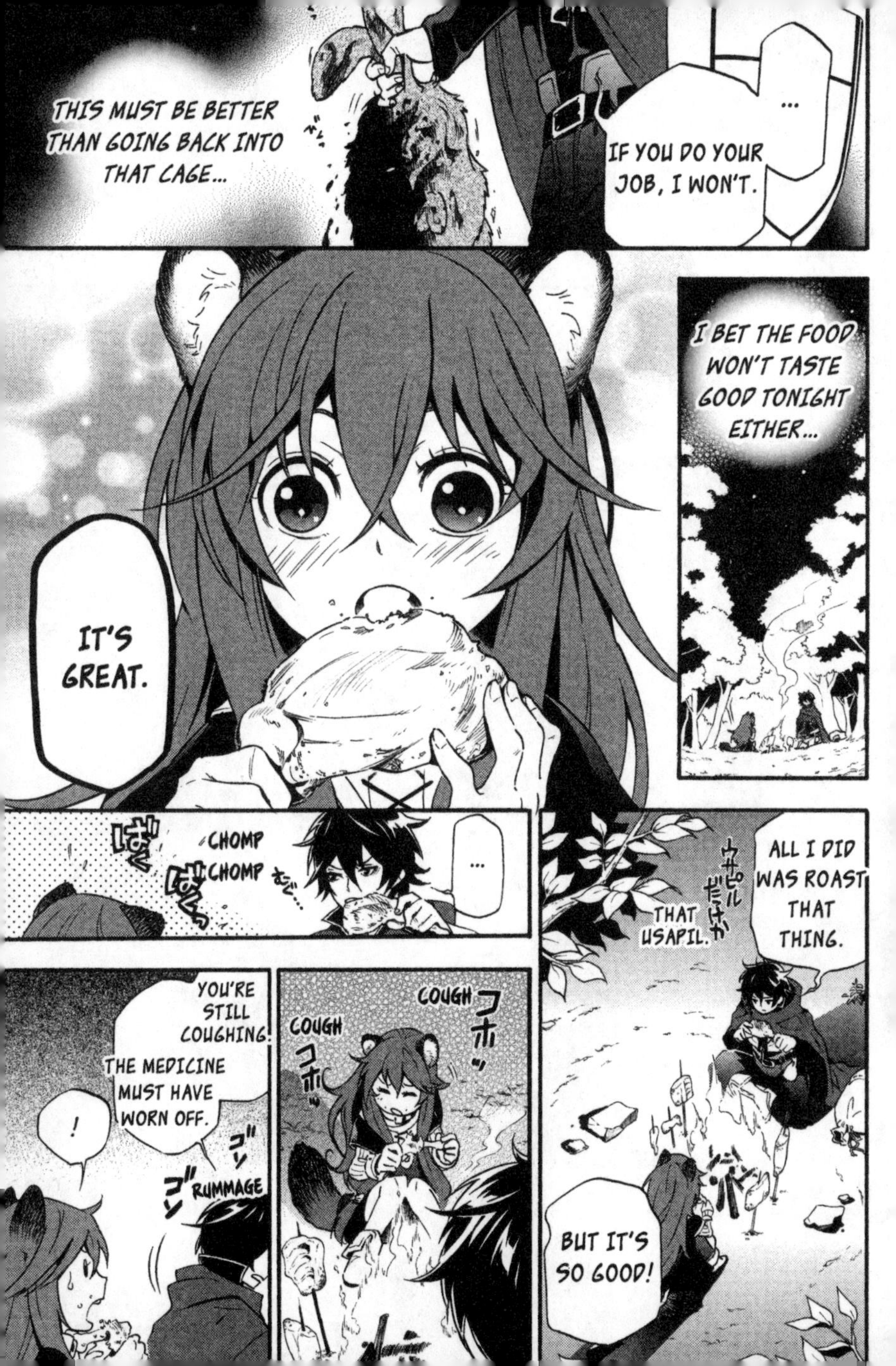
...
IF YOU DO YOUR JOB, I WON'T.
THIS MUST BE BETTER THAN GOING BACK INTO THAT CAGE...
I BET THE FOOD WON'T TASTE GOOD TONIGHT EITHER...
IT'S GREAT.
ALL I DID WAS ROAST THAT THING.
ウサピルだけか
THAT USAPIL.
BUT IT'S SO GOOD!
ばく
CHOMP
ぱくっ
CHOMP
むぐ…
...
COUGH
コホッ
COUGH
コホッ
YOU'RE STILL COUGHING.
THE MEDICINE MUST HAVE WORN OFF.
!
ゴソ
ゴソ
RUMMAGE

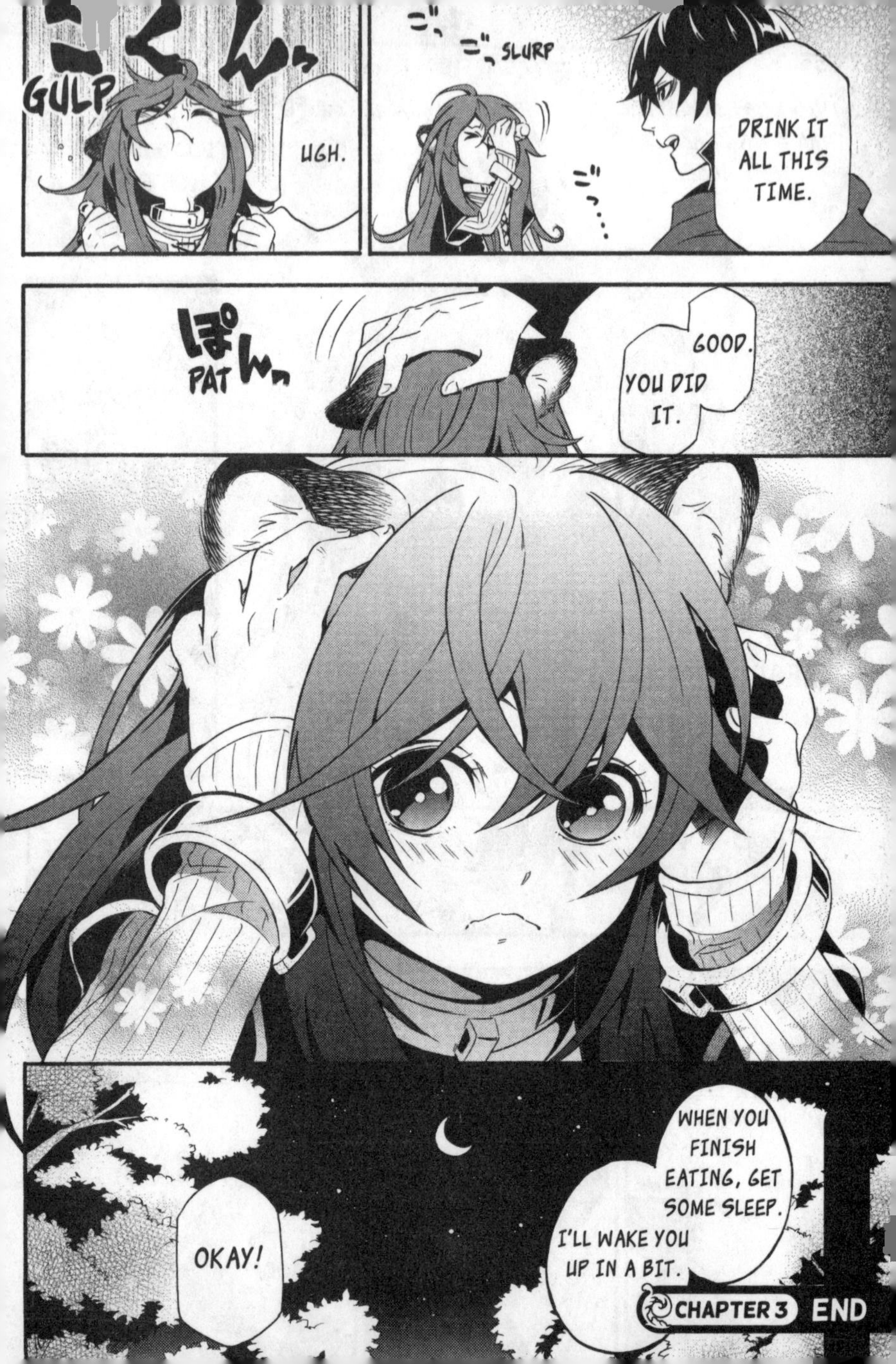
DRINK IT ALL THIS TIME.
SLURP
UGH.
GULP
GOOD.
YOU DID IT.
PAT
WHEN YOU FINISH EATING, GET SOME SLEEP.
I'LL WAKE YOU UP IN A BIT.
OKAY!
CHAPTER 3 END

CHAPTER 4 TWO-HEADED BLACK DOG

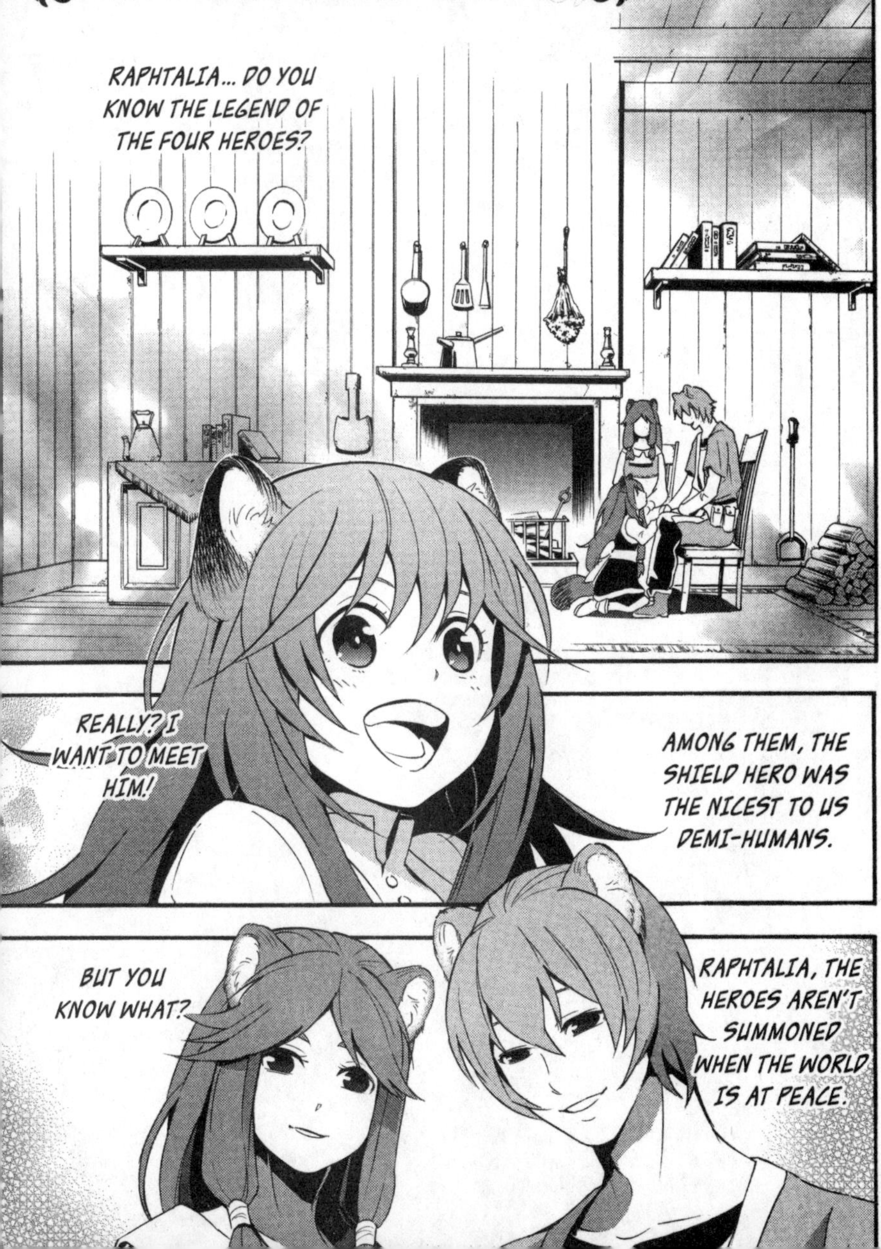
RAPHTALIA... DO YOU KNOW THE LEGEND OF THE FOUR HEROES?
AMONG THEM, THE SHIELD HERO WAS THE NICEST TO US DEMI-HUMANS.
REALLY? I WANT TO MEET HIM!
RAPHTALIA, THE HEROES AREN'T SUMMONED WHEN THE WORLD IS AT PEACE.
BUT YOU KNOW WHAT?

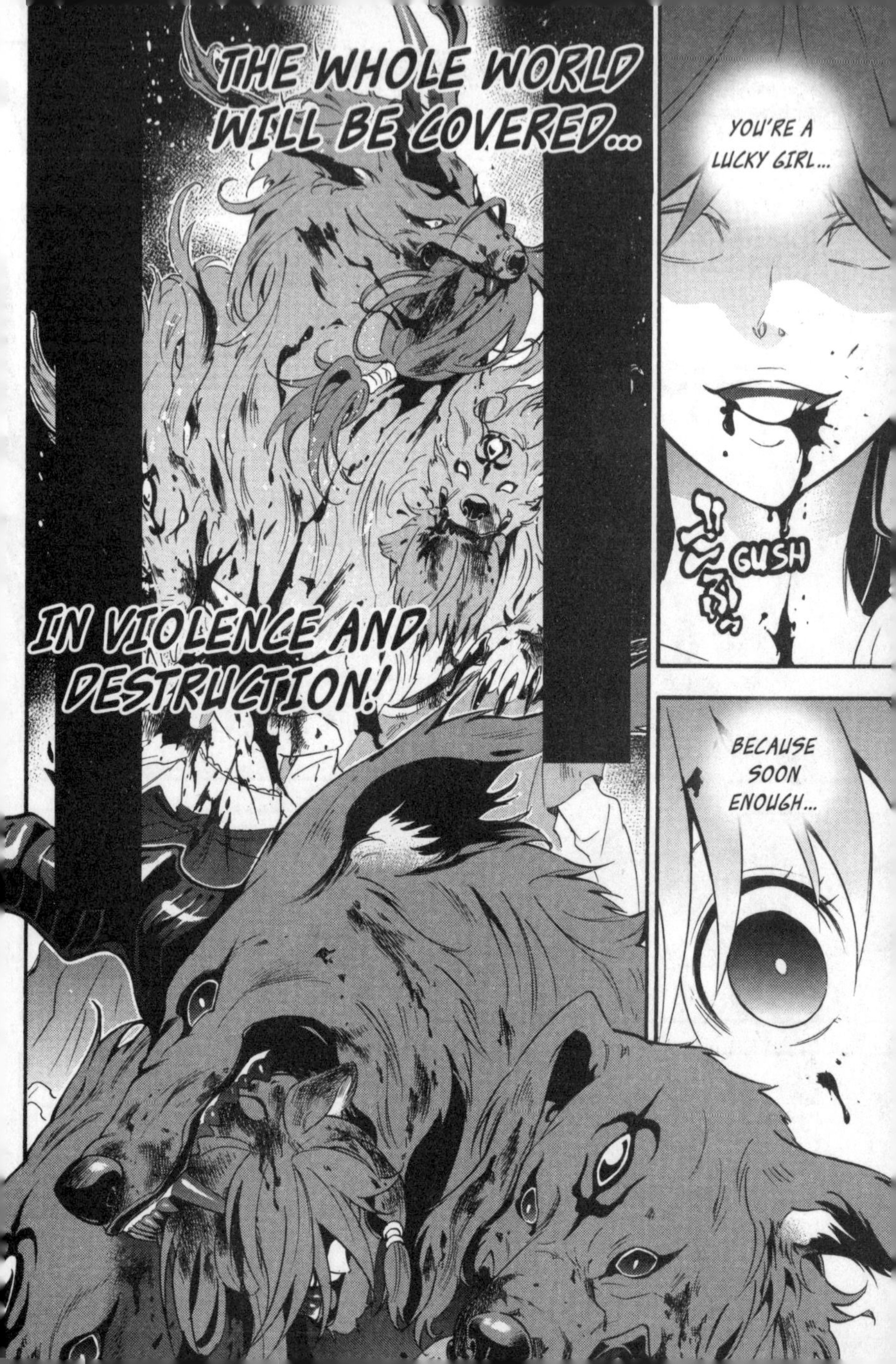
YOU'RE A LUCKY GIRL...
GUSH
BECAUSE SOON ENOUGH...
THE WHOLE WORLD WILL BE COVERED...
IN VIOLENCE AND DESTRUCTION!

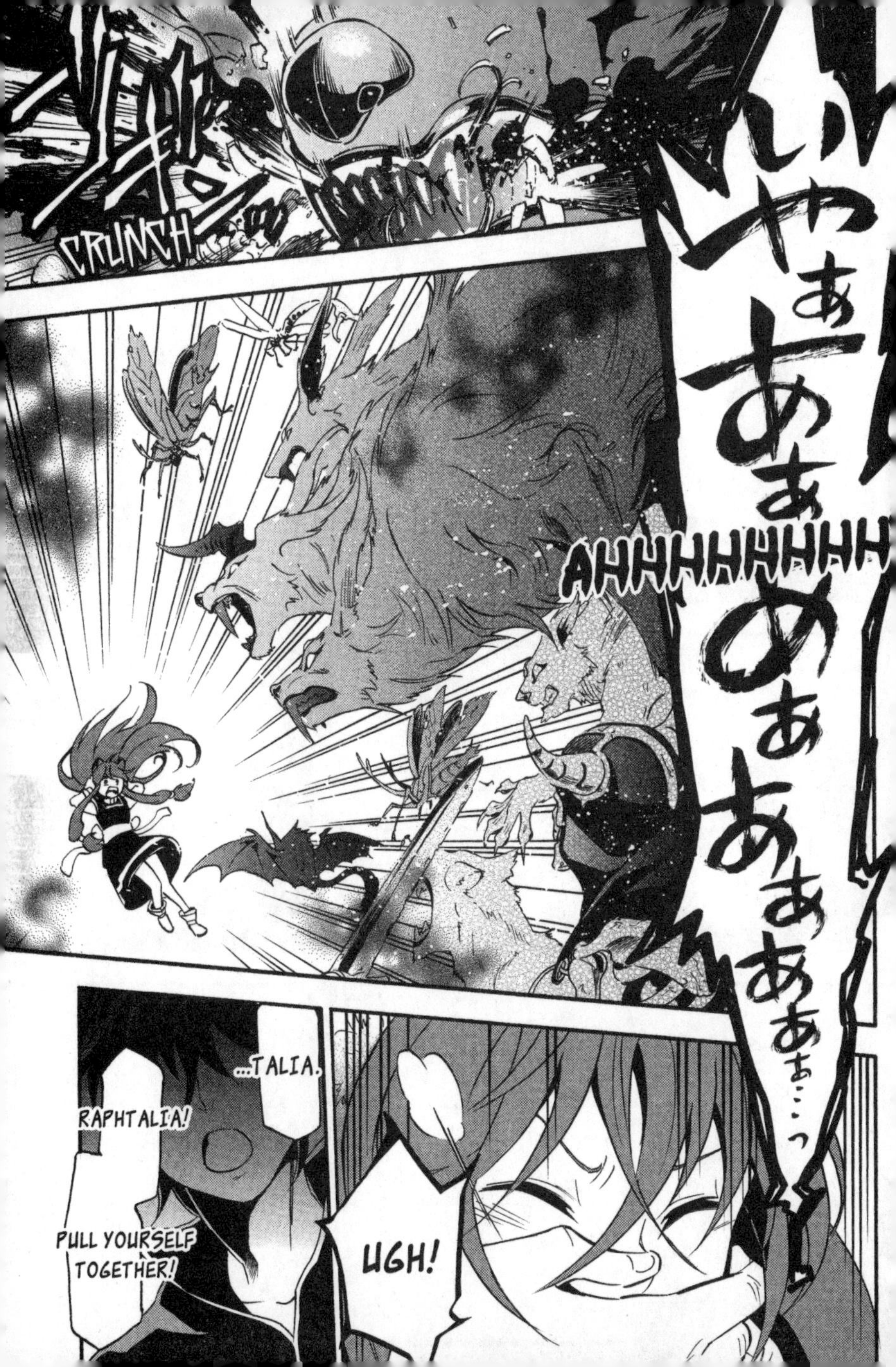

CRUNCH
AHHHHHHHH
UGH!
...TALIA.
RAPHTALIA!
PULL YOURSELF TOGETHER!

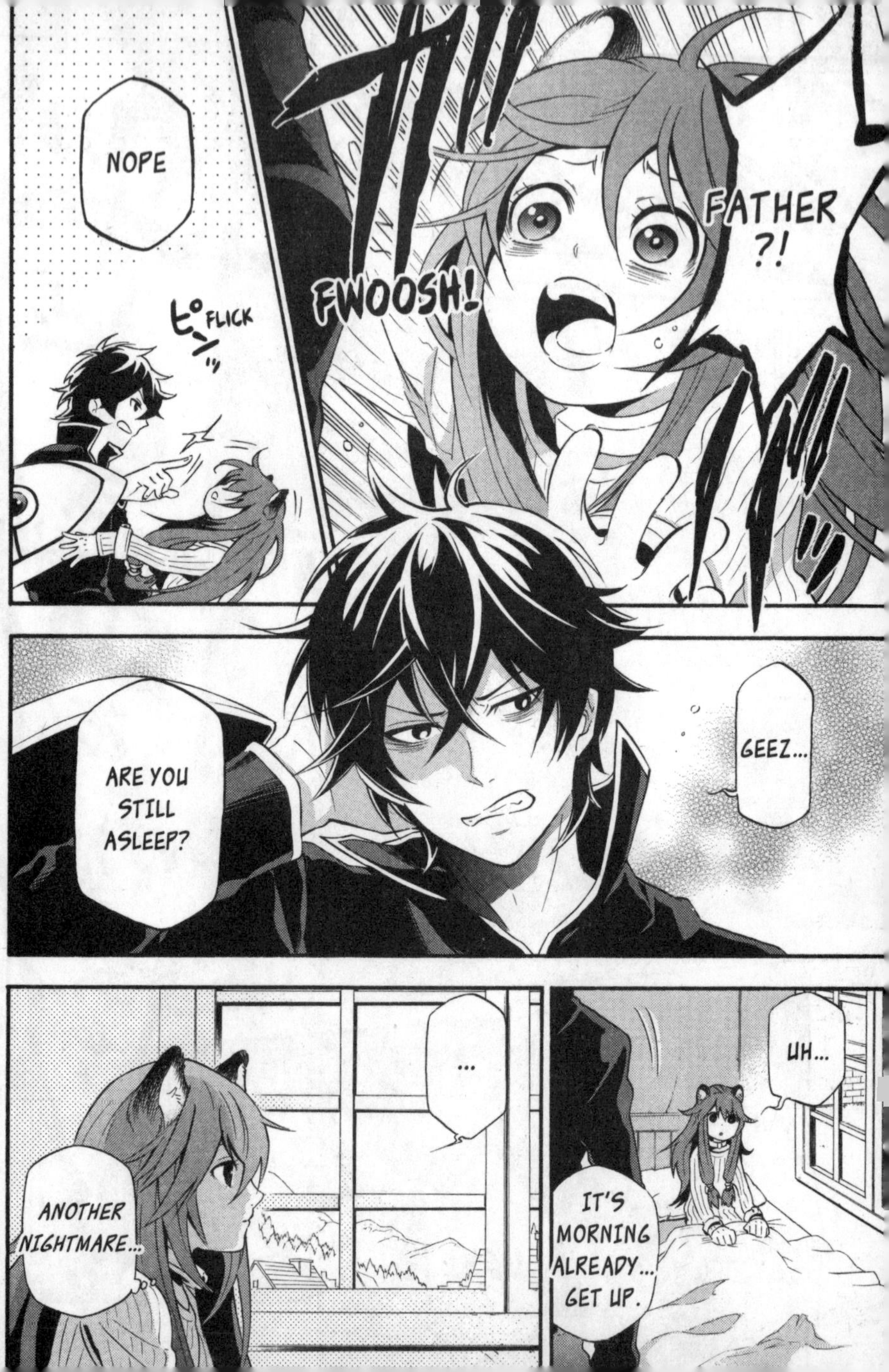
FATHER ?!
FWOOSH!
NOPE
FLICK
GEEZ...
ARE YOU STILL ASLEEP?
UH...
IT'S MORNING ALREADY... GET UP.
...
ANOTHER NIGHTMARE...

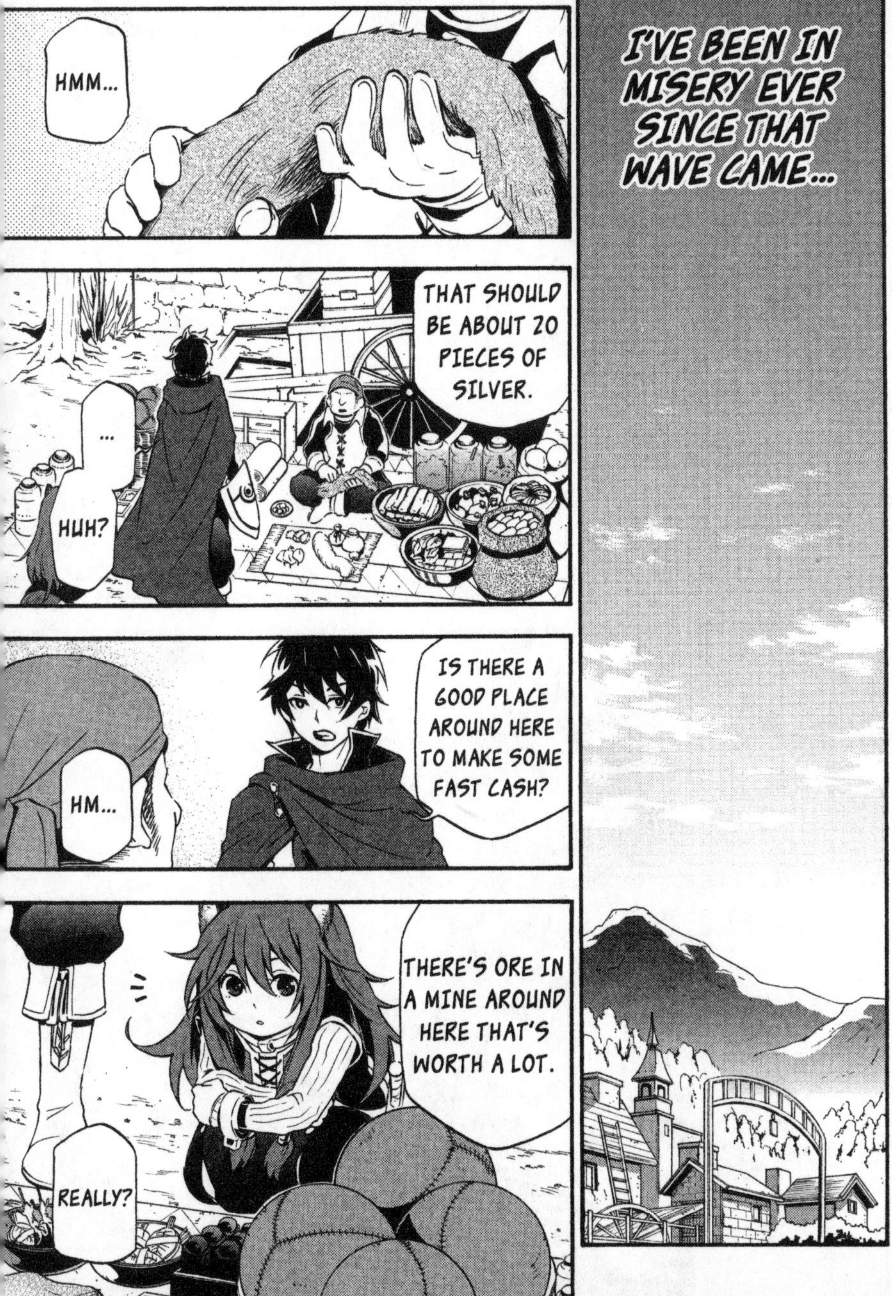
I'VE BEEN IN MISERY EVER SINCE THAT WAVE CAME...
HMM...
THAT SHOULD BE ABOUT 20 PIECES OF SILVER.
...
HUH?
IS THERE A GOOD PLACE AROUND HERE TO MAKE SOME FAST CASH?
HM...
THERE'S ORE IN A MINE AROUND HERE THAT'S WORTH A LOT.
REALLY?

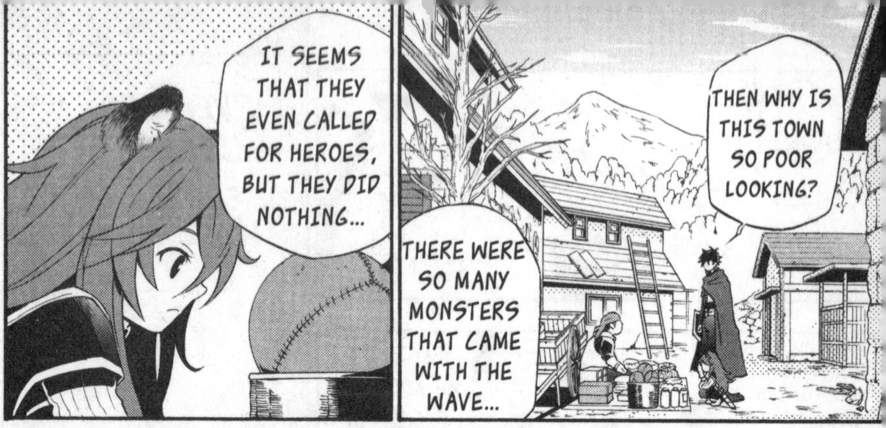
THEN WHY IS THIS TOWN SO POOR LOOKING?
THERE WERE SO MANY MONSTERS THAT CAME WITH THE WAVE...
IT SEEMS THAT THEY EVEN CALLED FOR HEROES, BUT THEY DID NOTHING...

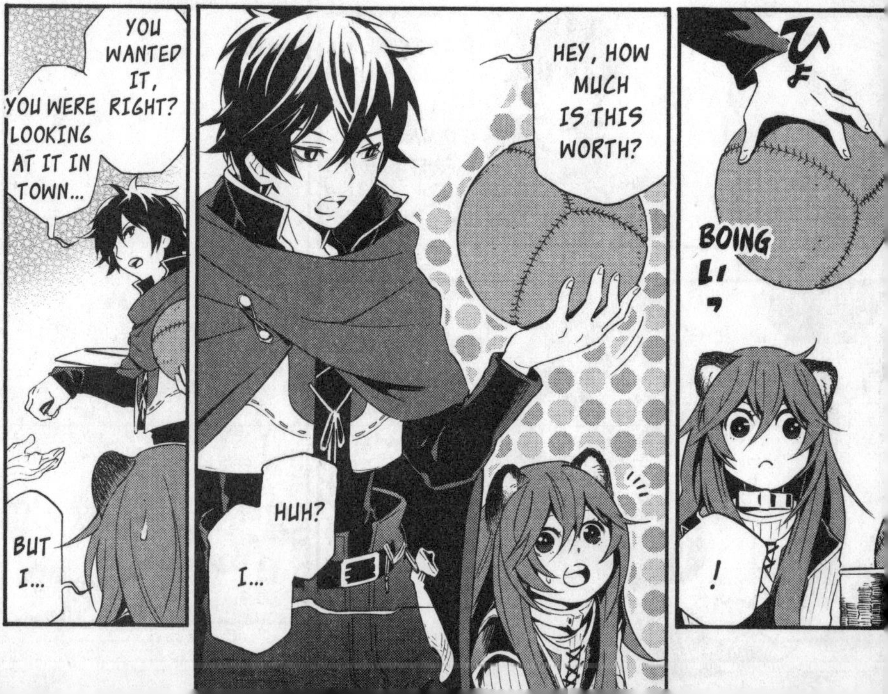
ひょ
BOING
!
HEY, HOW MUCH IS THIS WORTH?
HUH?
I...
YOU WANTED IT, RIGHT?
YOU WERE LOOKING AT IT IN TOWN...
BUT I...

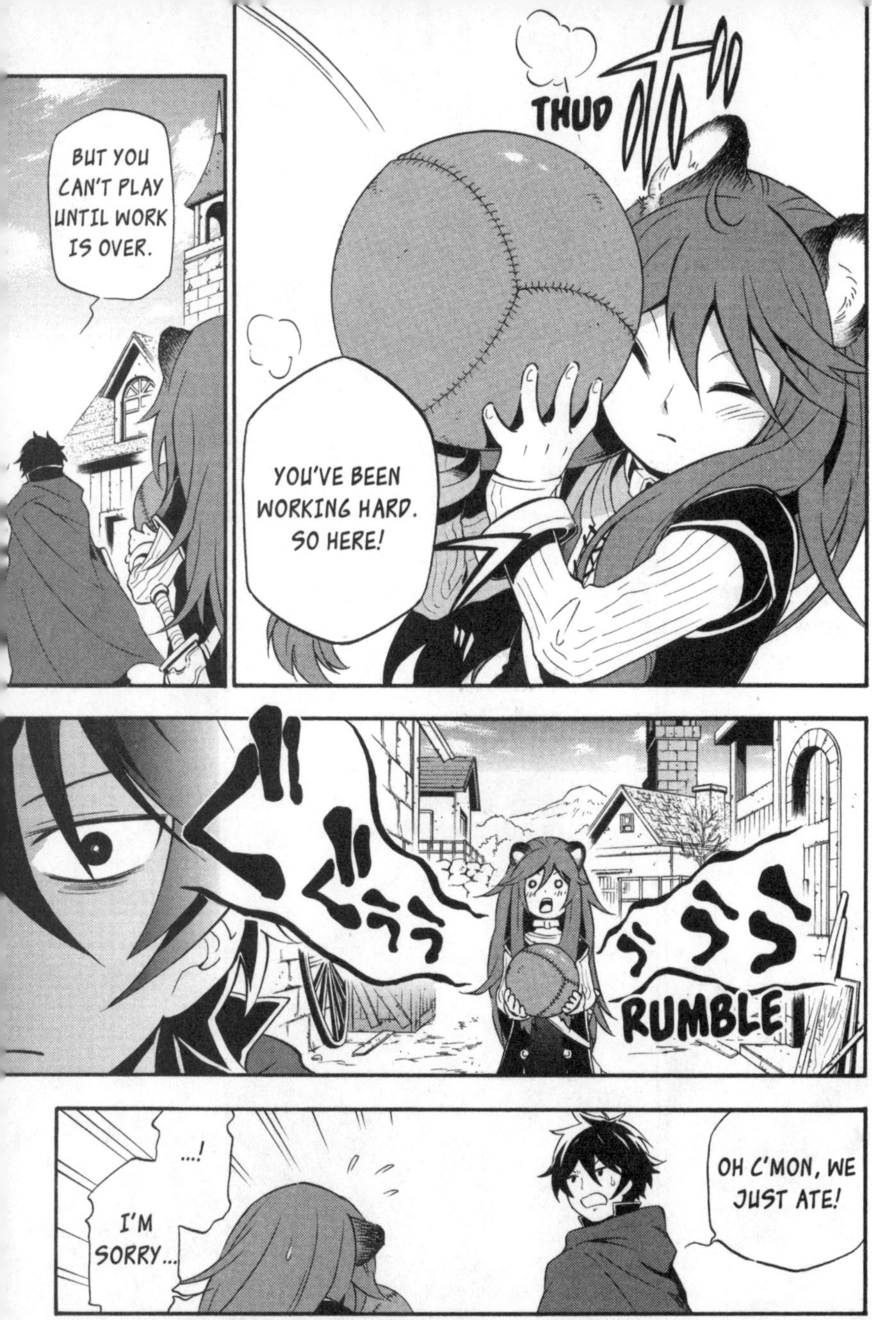

THUD
YOU'VE BEEN WORKING HARD. SO HERE!
BUT YOU CAN'T PLAY UNTIL WORK IS OVER.
RUMBLE
OH C'MON, WE JUST ATE!
...!
I'M SORRY...

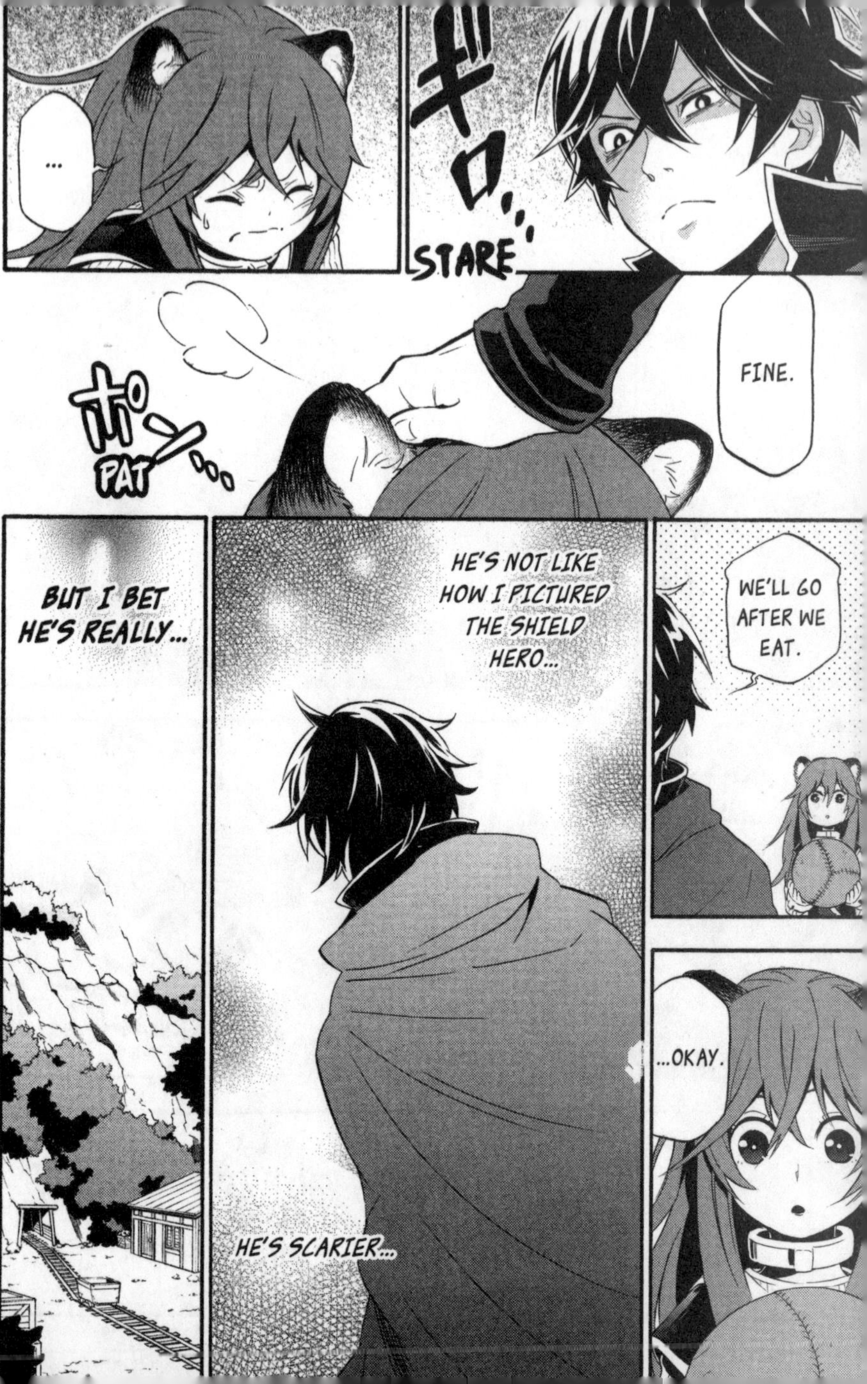

ギロ
STARE
...
FINE.
ポン
PAT
WE'LL GO AFTER WE EAT.
...OKAY.
HE'S NOT LIKE HOW I PICTURED THE SHIELD HERO...
HE'S SCARIER...
BUT I BET HE'S REALLY...

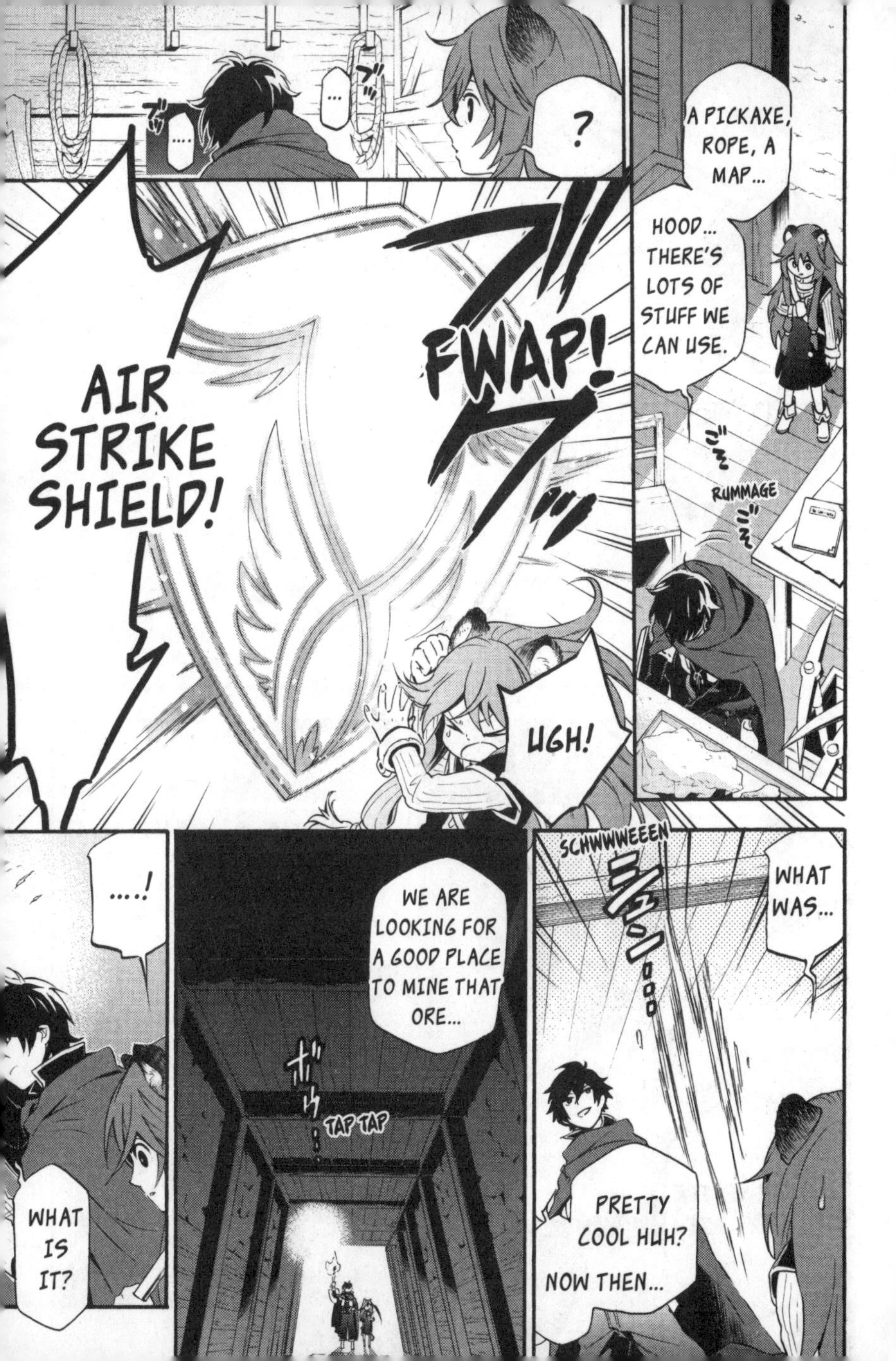
A PICKAXE, ROPE, A MAP...
HOOD... THERE'S LOTS OF STUFF WE CAN USE.
RUMMAGE
?
...
....
FWAP!
AIR STRIKE SHIELD!
UGH!
SCHWWWEEEN
WHAT WAS...
PRETTY COOL HUH?
NOW THEN...
WE ARE LOOKING FOR A GOOD PLACE TO MINE THAT ORE...
TAP TAP
....!
WHAT IS IT?

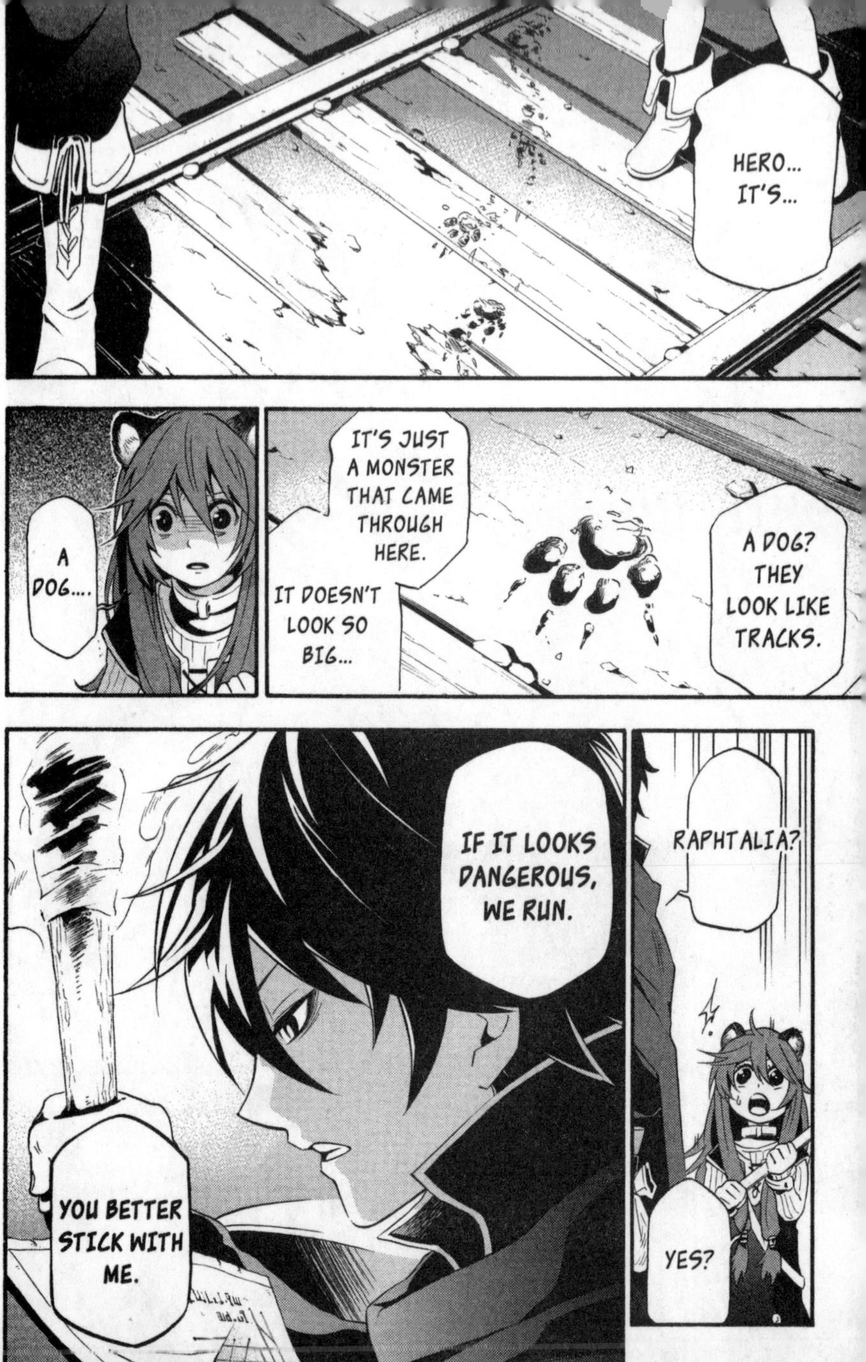
HERO... IT'S...
A DOG? THEY LOOK LIKE TRACKS.
IT'S JUST A MONSTER THAT CAME THROUGH HERE.
IT DOESN'T LOOK SO BIG...
A DOG....
RAPHTALIA?
YES?
IF IT LOOKS DANGEROUS, WE RUN.
YOU BETTER STICK WITH ME.

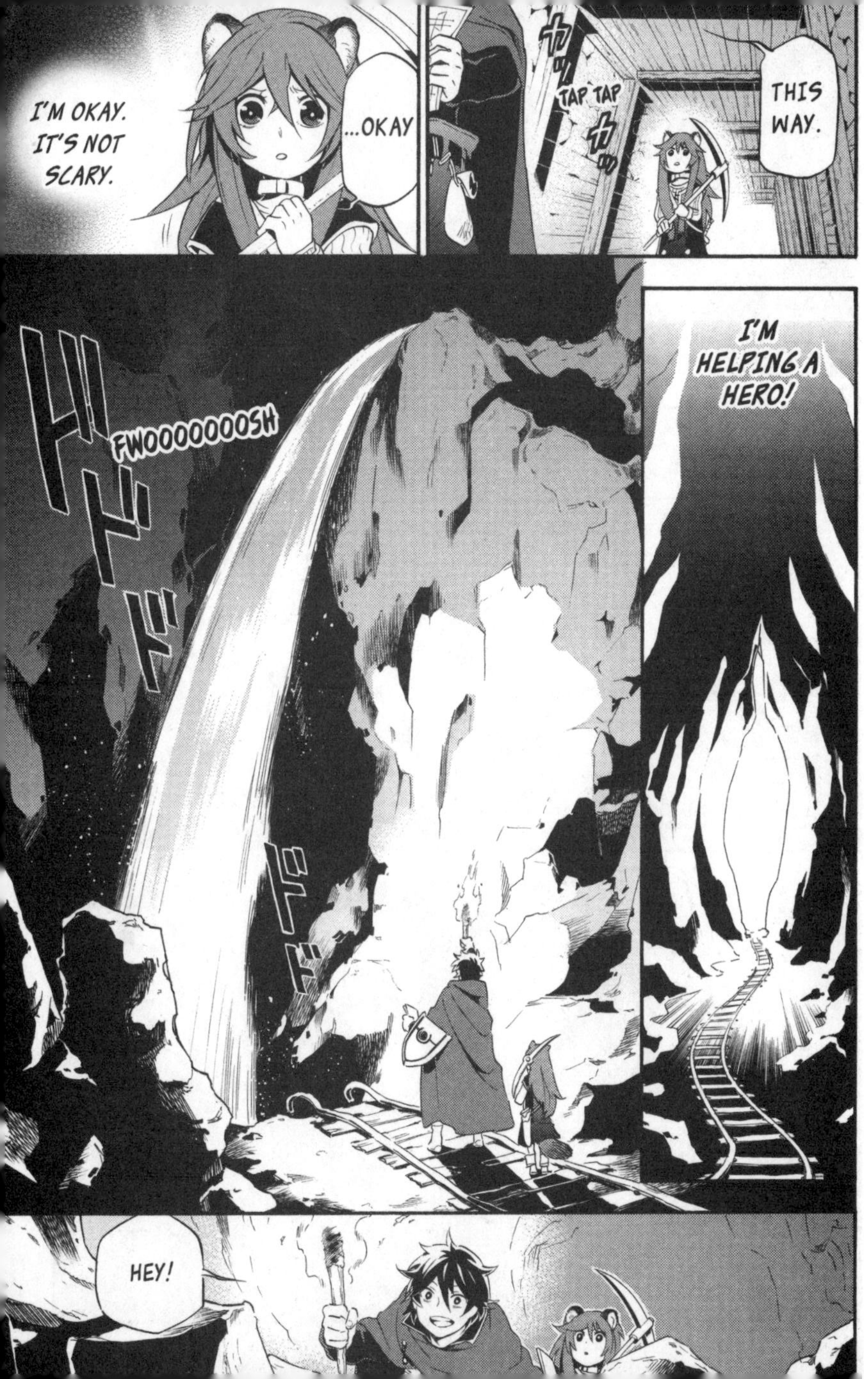
THIS WAY.
TAP TAP
...OKAY
I'M OKAY. IT'S NOT SCARY.
I'M HELPING A HERO!
FWOOOOOOOSH
HEY!

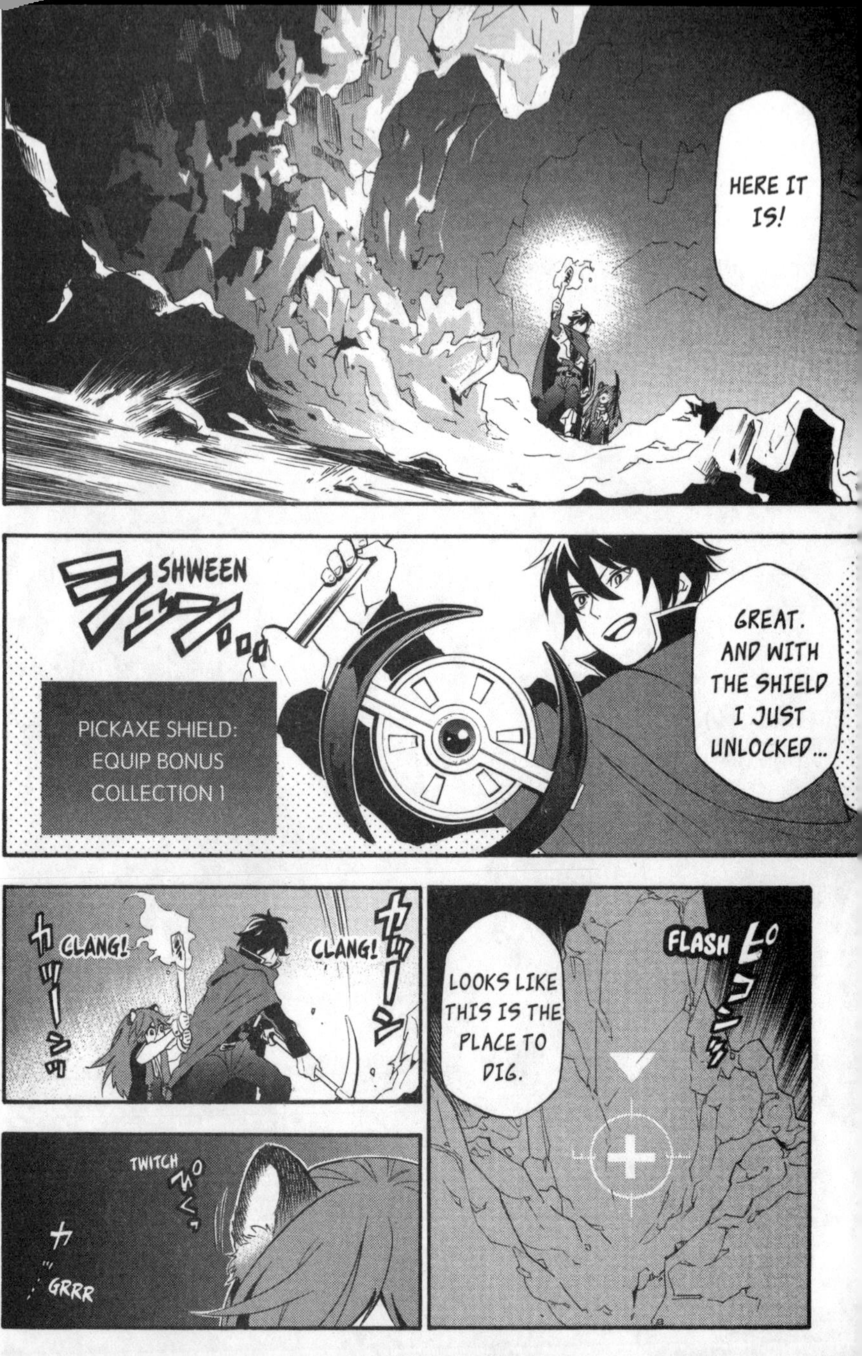
HERE IT IS!
GREAT. AND WITH THE SHIELD I JUST UNLOCKED...
SHWEEN
PICKAXE SHIELD: EQUIP BONUS COLLECTION 1
FLASH
LOOKS LIKE THIS IS THE PLACE TO DIG.
CLANG!
CLANG!
TWITCH
GRRR

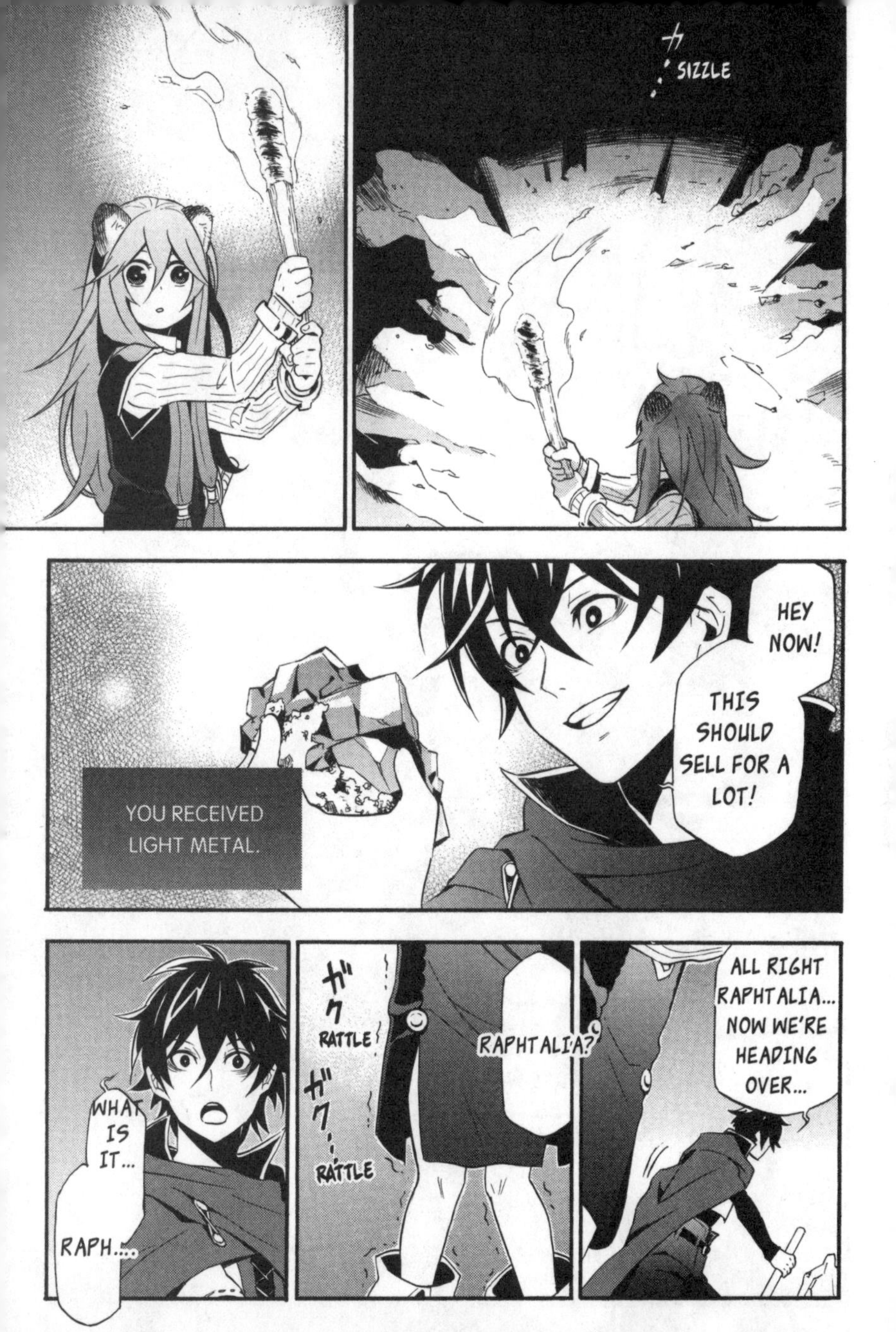
カ
SIZZLE
HEY NOW!
THIS SHOULD SELL FOR A LOT!
YOU RECEIVED LIGHT METAL.
ALL RIGHT RAPHTALIA... NOW WE'RE HEADING OVER...
RAPHTALIA?
ガク
RATTLE
ガク...
RATTLE
WHAT IS IT...
RAPH....

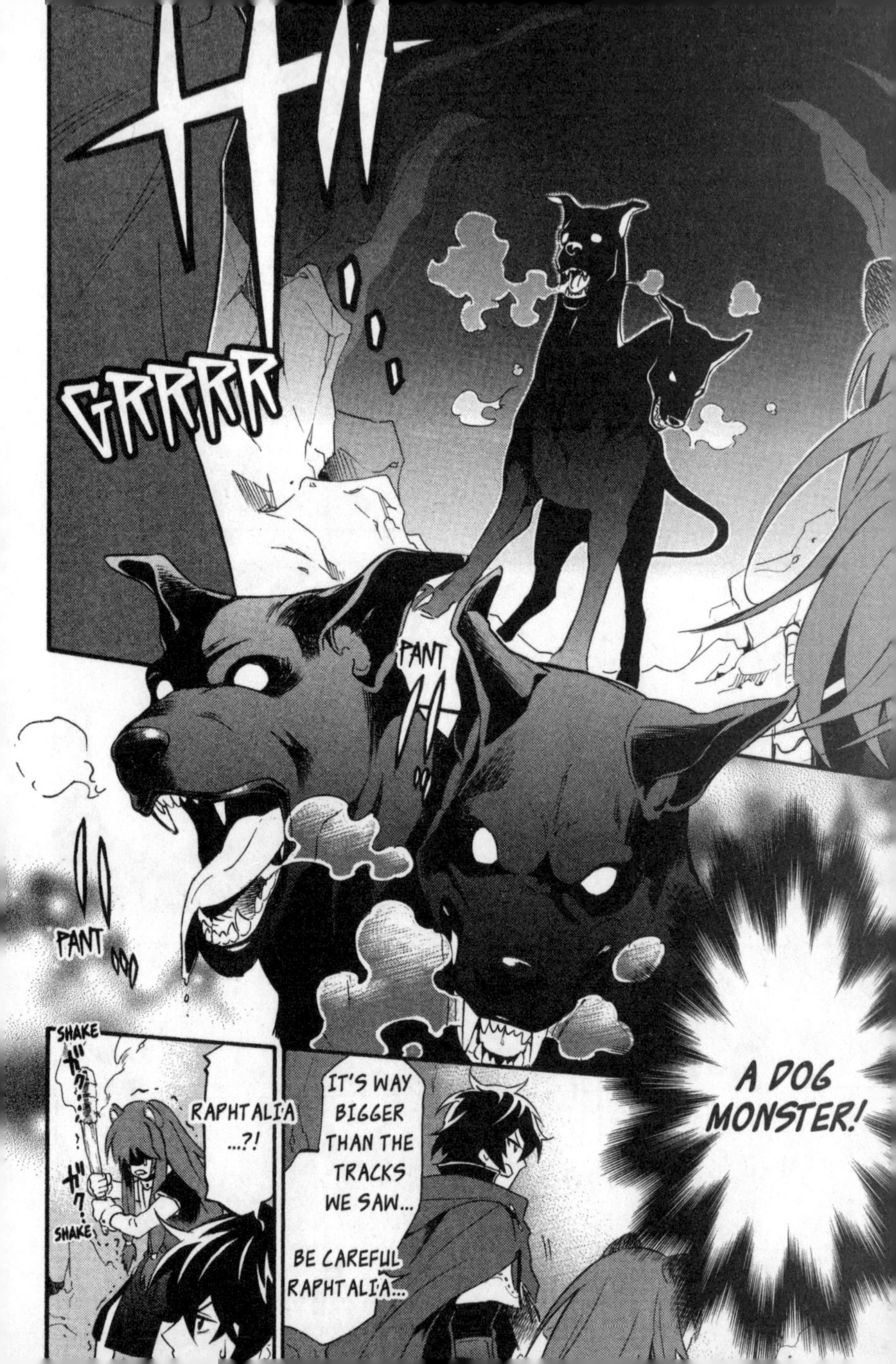
GRRRR
PANT
PANT
A DOG MONSTER!
IT'S WAY BIGGER THAN THE TRACKS WE SAW...
BE CAREFUL RAPHTALIA...
RAPHTALIA ...?!
SHAKE
SHAKE

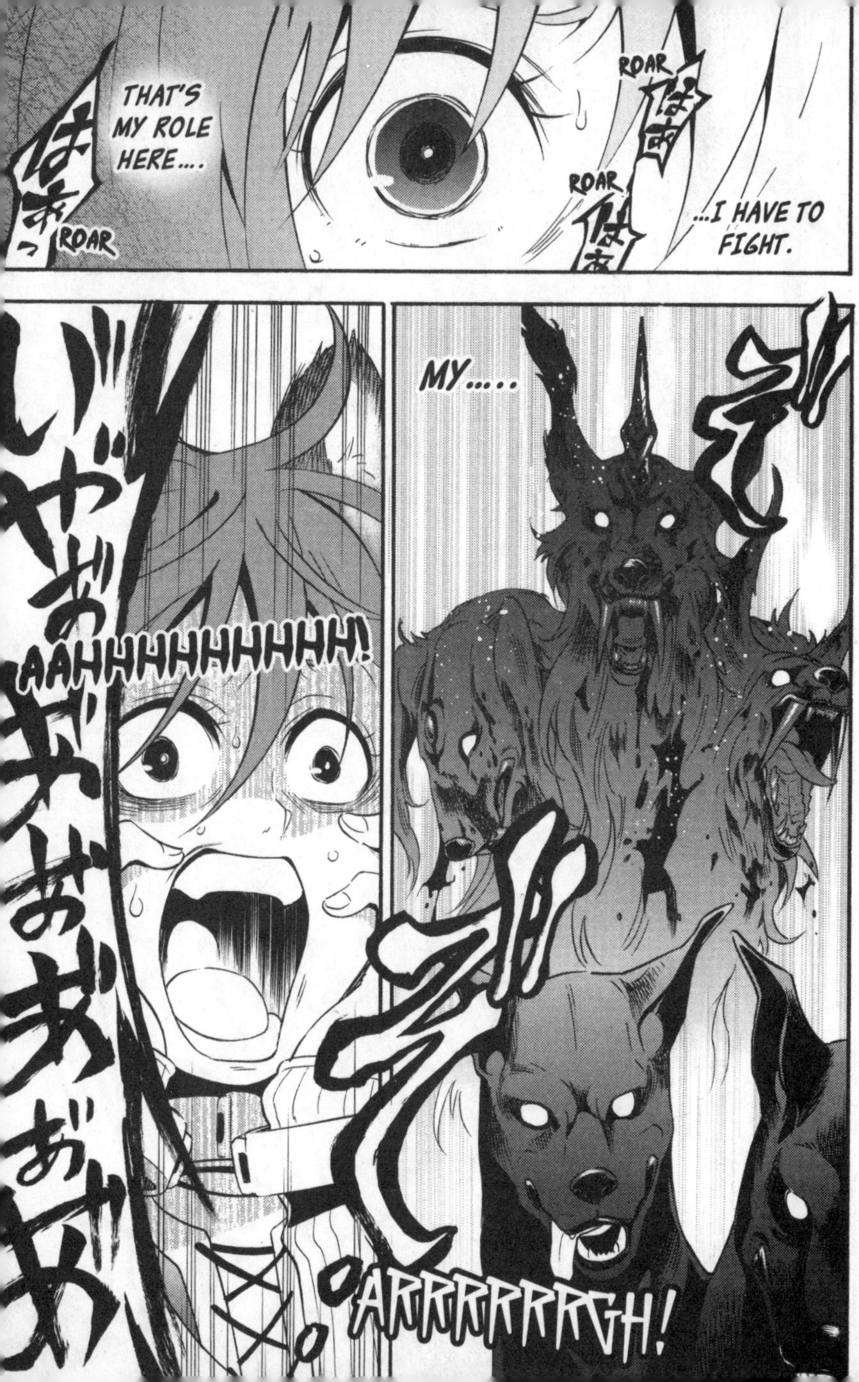
...I HAVE TO FIGHT.
ROAR
ROAR
THAT'S MY ROLE HERE....
ROAR
MY.....
ARRRRRRRGH!
AAHHHHHHHHHH!

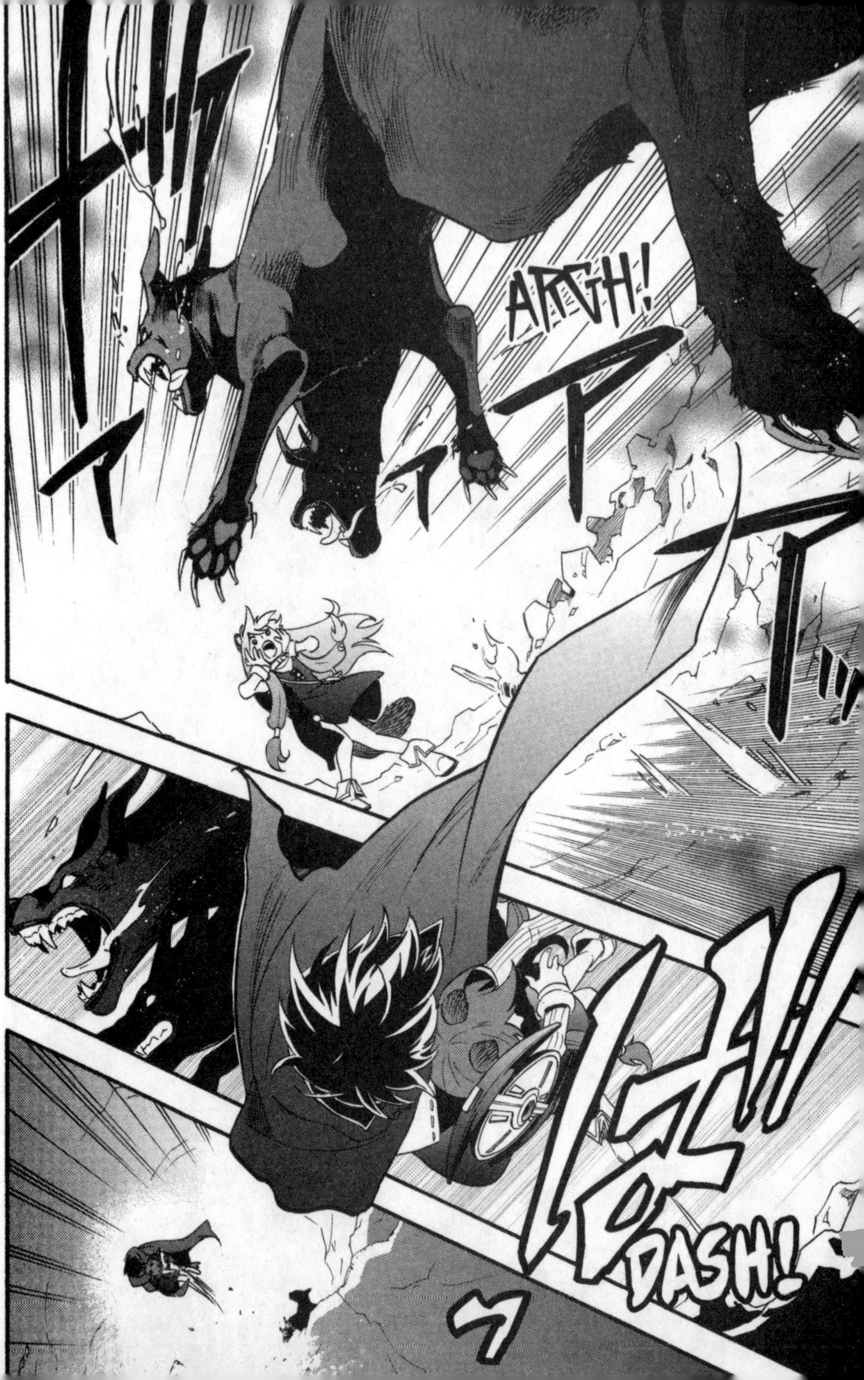
ARGH!
DASH!

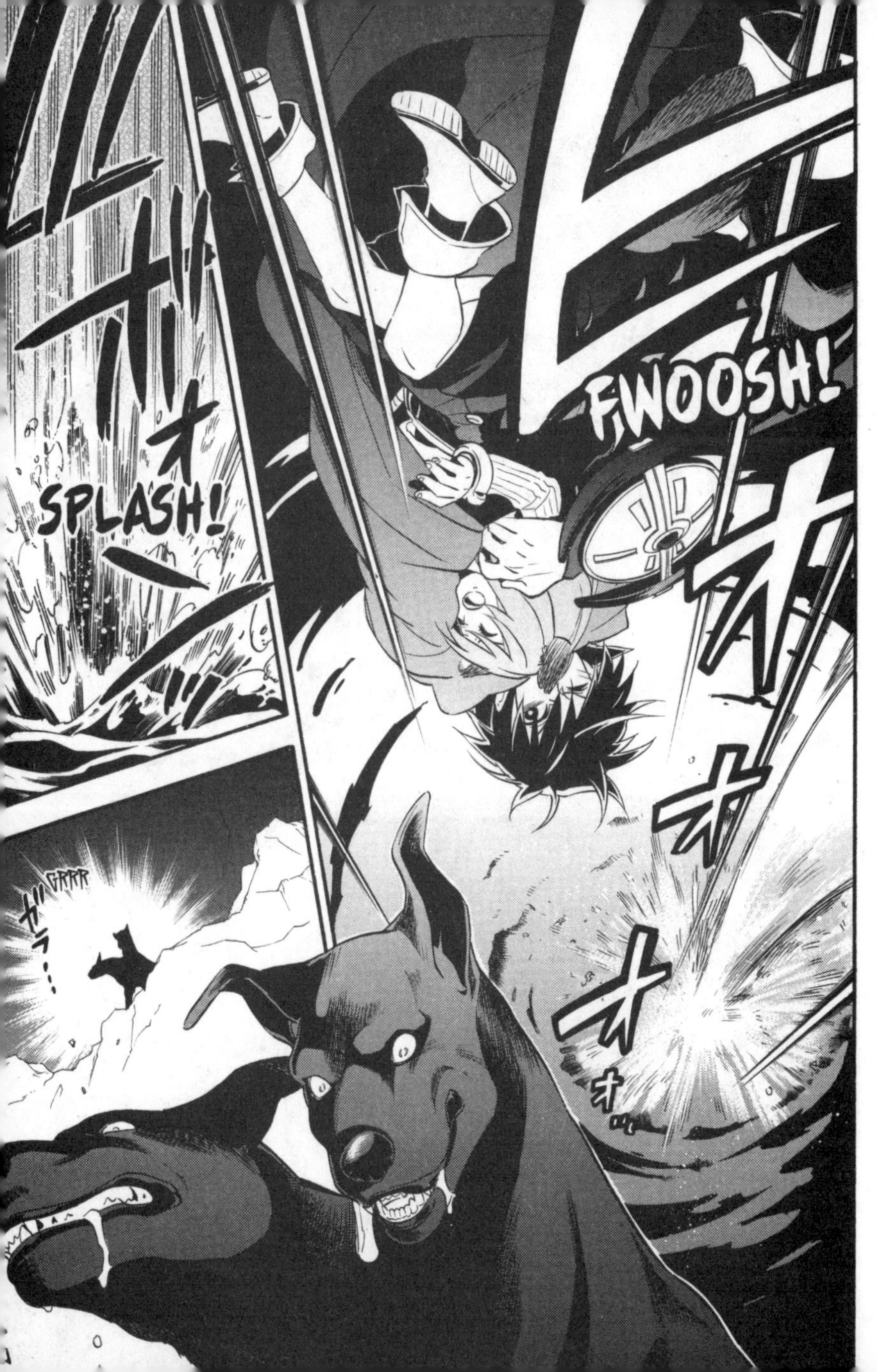
FWOOSH!
SPLASH!
GRRR

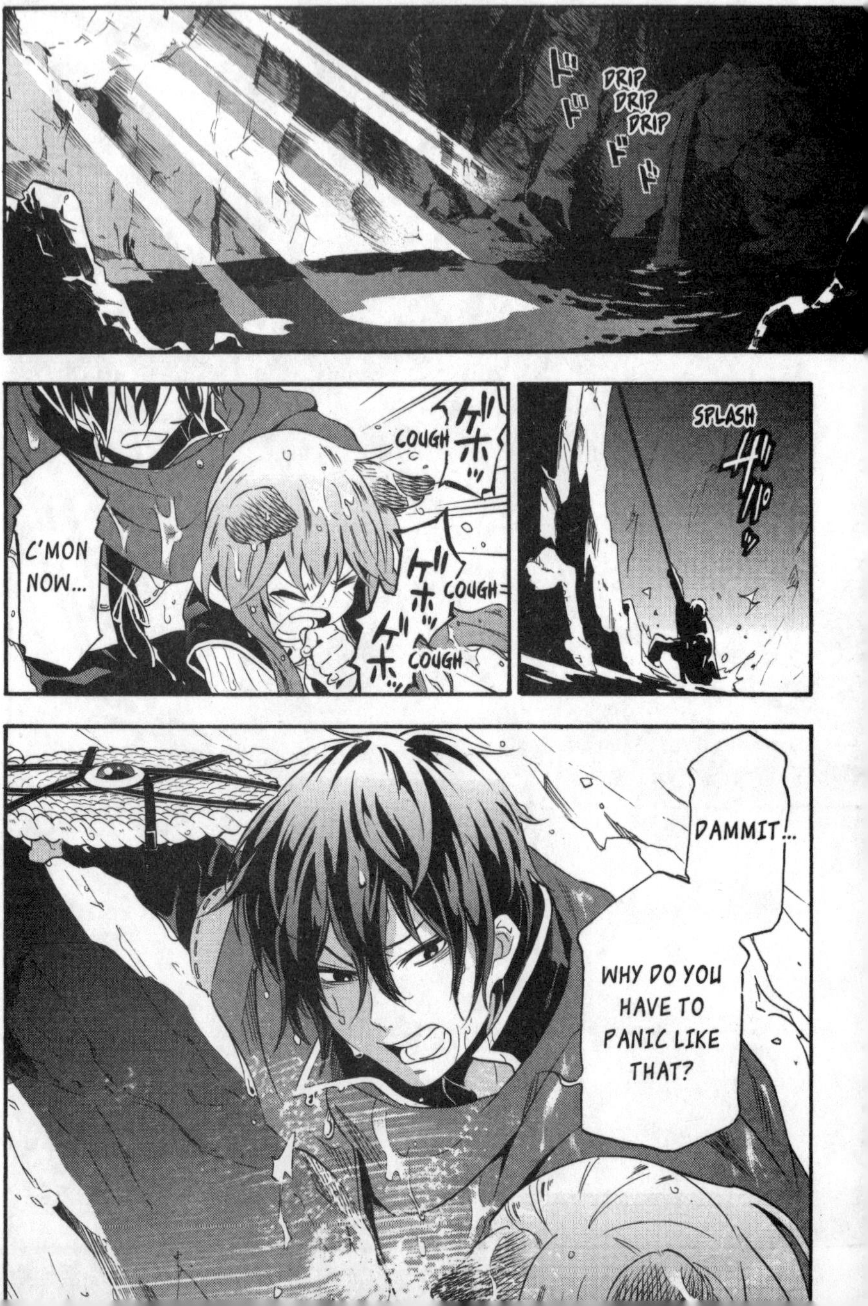
ドド
ドド
DRIP DRIP DRIP
SPLASH
ザパッ
COUGH
ゲホッ
C'MON NOW...
ゲホッ
COUGH
ゲホッ
COUGH
DAMMIT...
WHY DO YOU HAVE TO PANIC LIKE THAT?

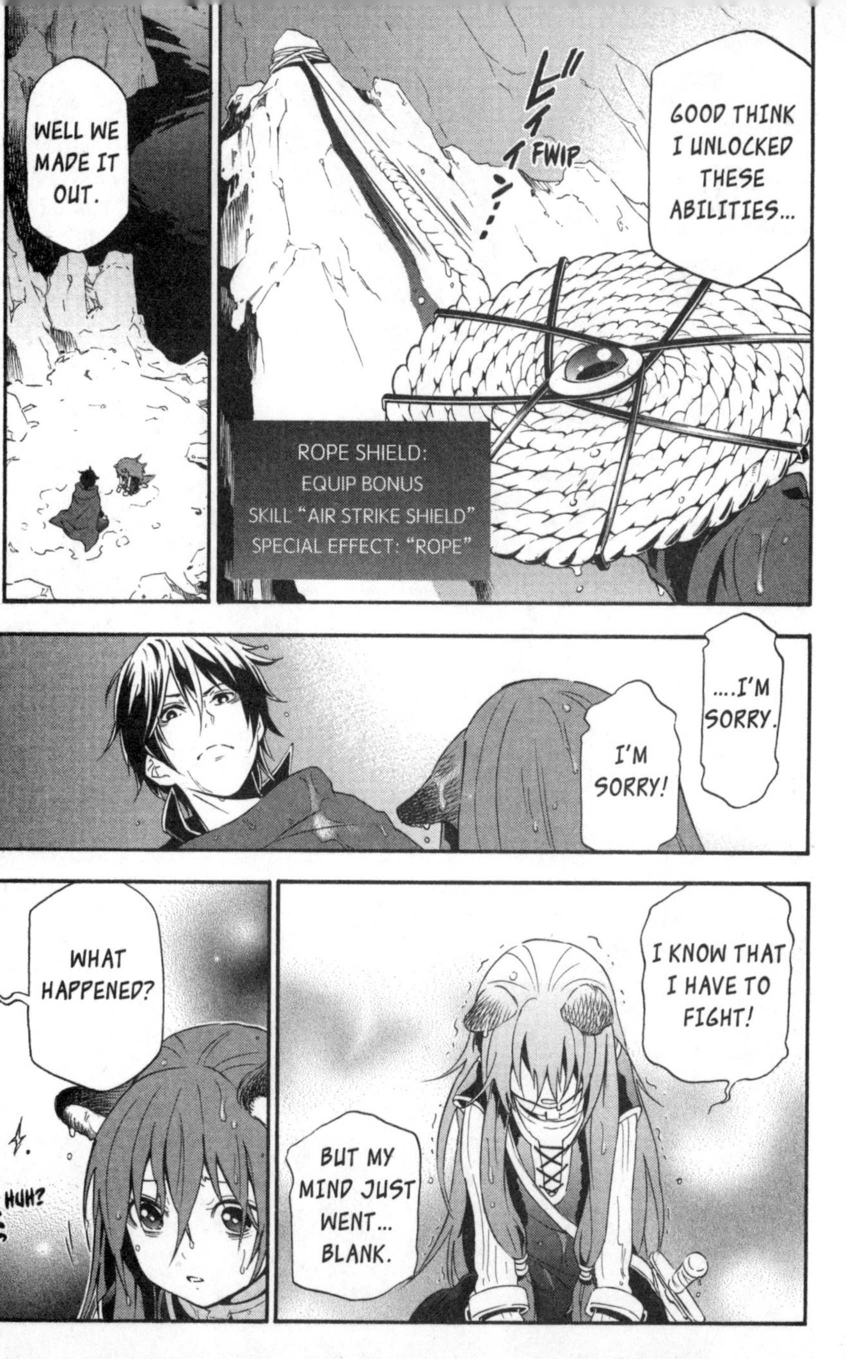
GOOD THINK I UNLOCKED THESE ABILITIES...
FWIP
ROPE SHIELD:
EQUIP BONUS
SKILL "AIR STRIKE SHIELD"
SPECIAL EFFECT: "ROPE"
WELL WE MADE IT OUT.
....I'M SORRY.
I'M SORRY!
I KNOW THAT I HAVE TO FIGHT!
BUT MY MIND JUST WENT... BLANK.
WHAT HAPPENED?
HUH?

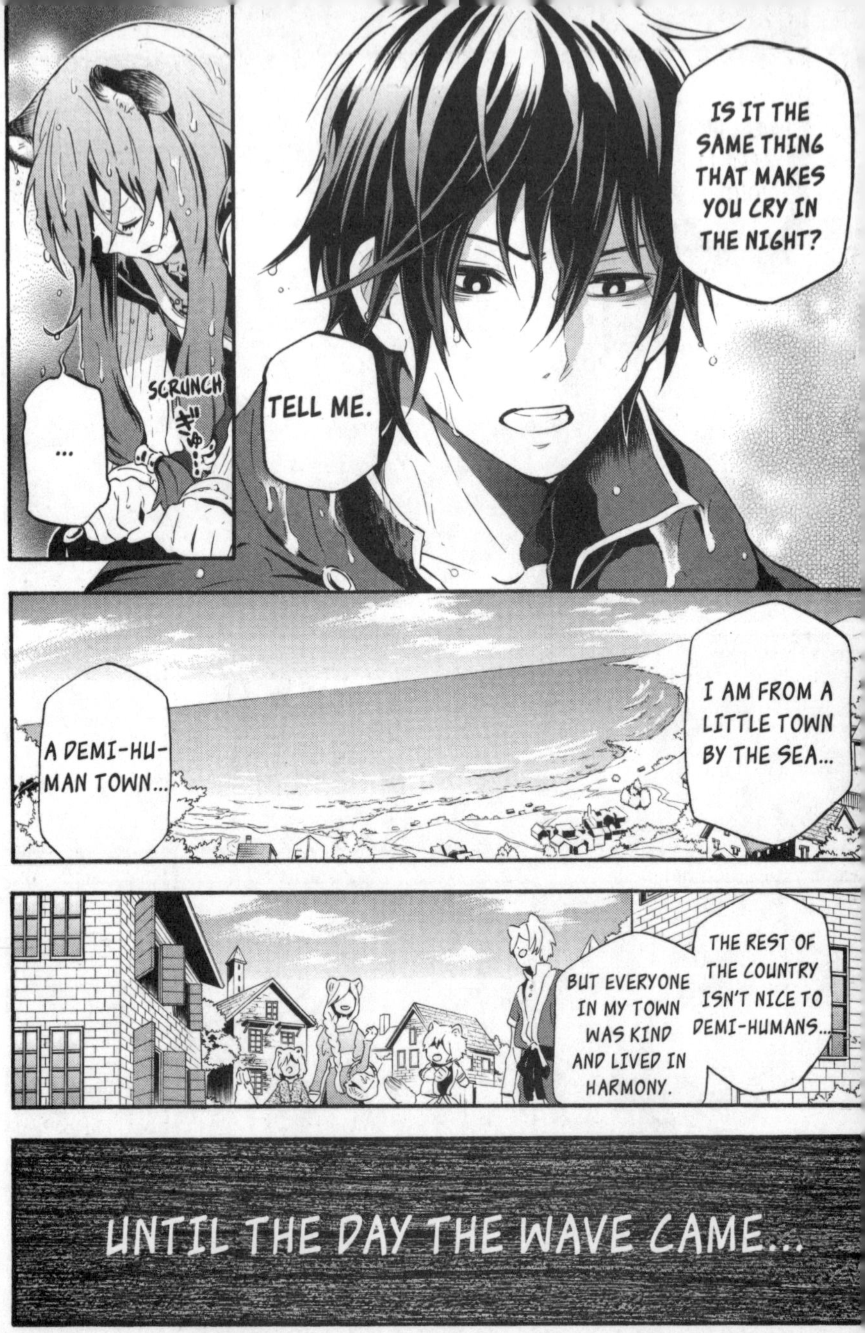
IS IT THE SAME THING THAT MAKES YOU CRY IN THE NIGHT?
TELL ME.
SCRUNCH
ぎゅ…
...
I AM FROM A LITTLE TOWN BY THE SEA...
A DEMI-HUMAN TOWN...
THE REST OF THE COUNTRY ISN'T NICE TO DEMI-HUMANS...
BUT EVERYONE IN MY TOWN WAS KIND AND LIVED IN HARMONY.
UNTIL THE DAY THE WAVE CAME...

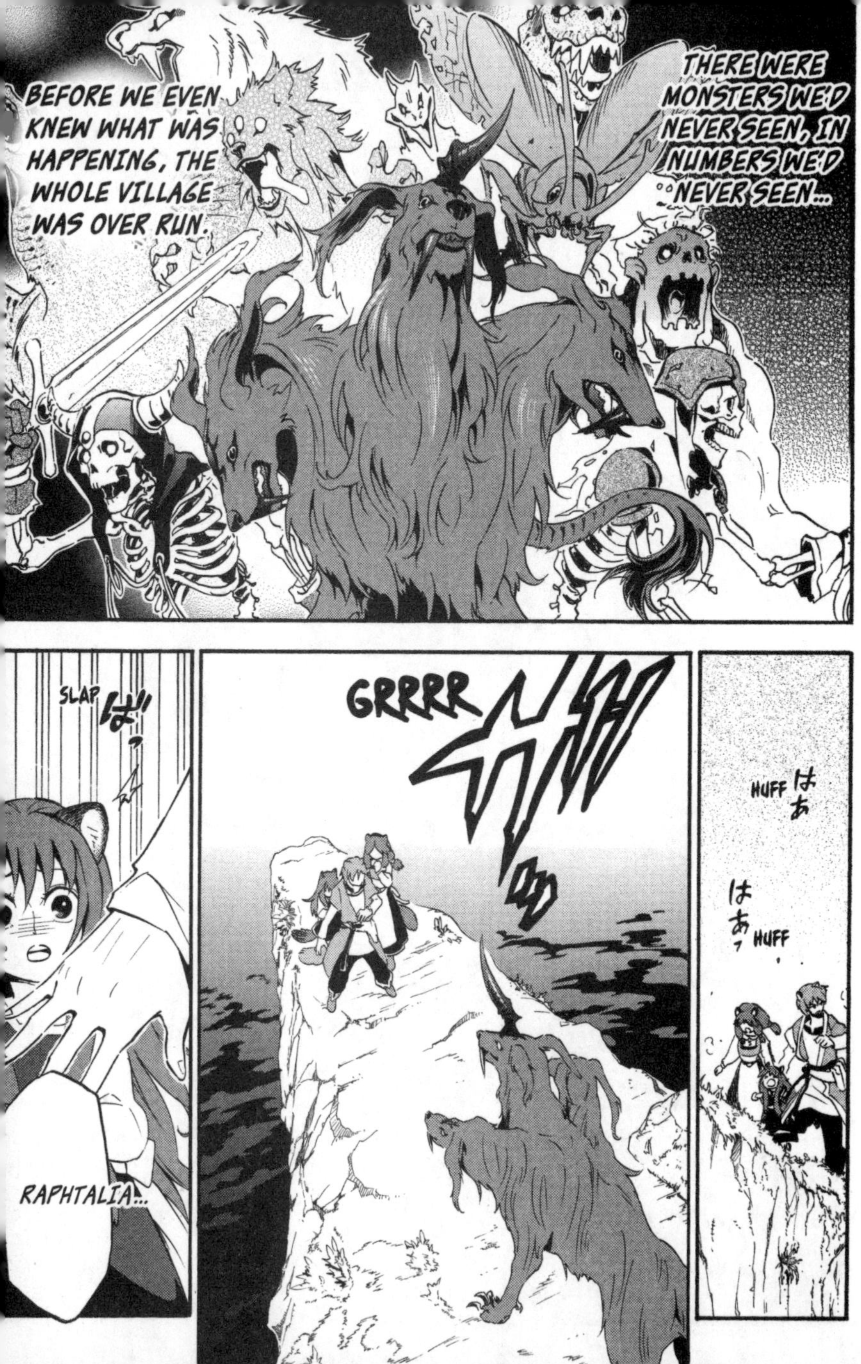
THERE WERE MONSTERS WE'D NEVER SEEN, IN NUMBERS WE'D NEVER SEEN...
BEFORE WE EVEN KNEW WHAT WAS HAPPENING, THE WHOLE VILLAGE WAS OVER RUN.
HUFF
はぁ
はぁっ
HUFF
GRRRR
SLAP
ばっ
RAPHTALIA...

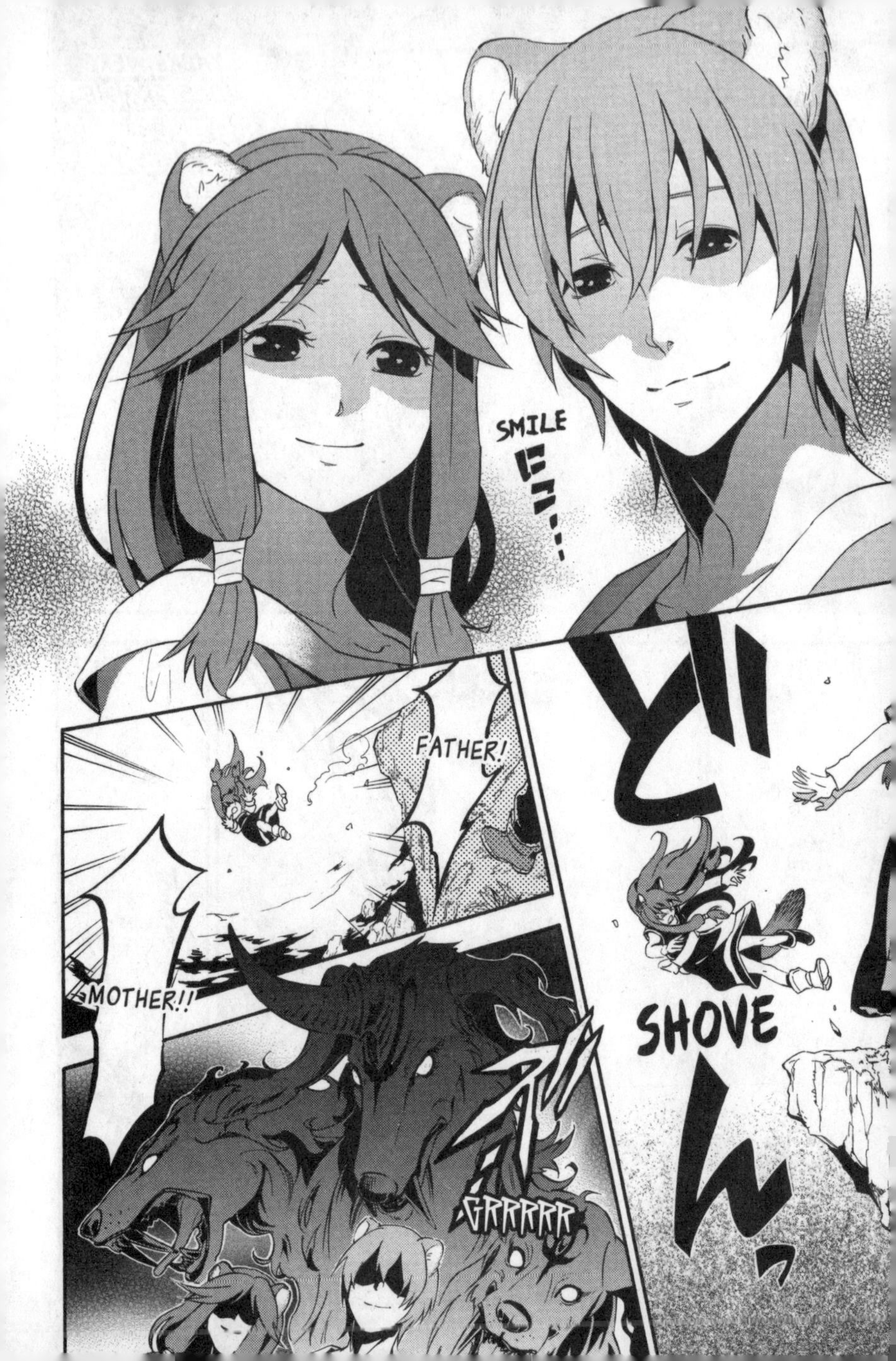
SMILE
ニコ…
SHOVE
どんっ
FATHER!
MOTHER!!
GRRRRR

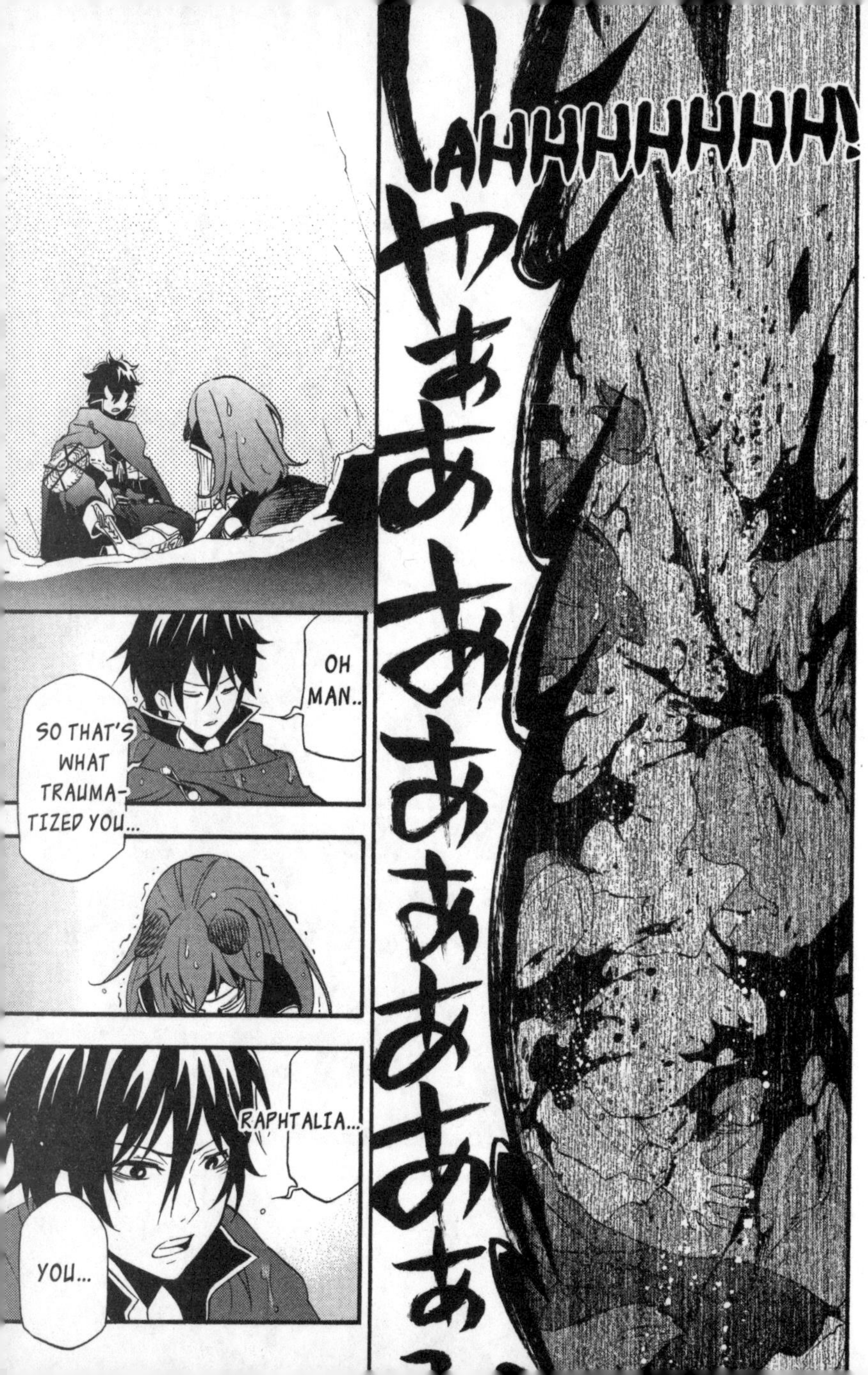
AHHHHHHH!
OH MAN..
SO THAT'S WHAT TRAUMA-TIZED YOU...
RAPHTALIA...
YOU...

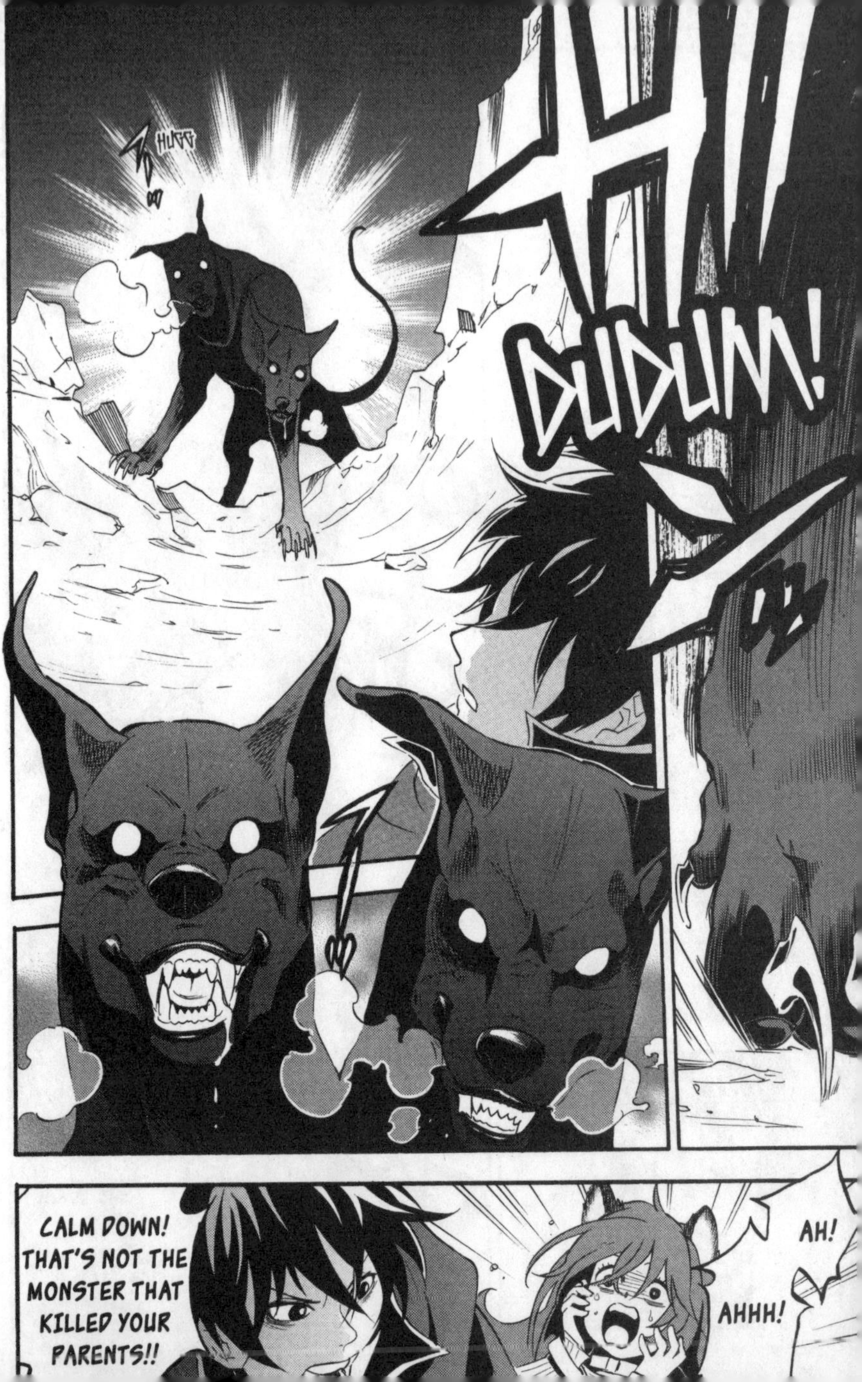
DUDUM!
HUGG
AH!
AHHH!
CALM DOWN! THAT'S NOT THE MONSTER THAT KILLED YOUR PARENTS!!

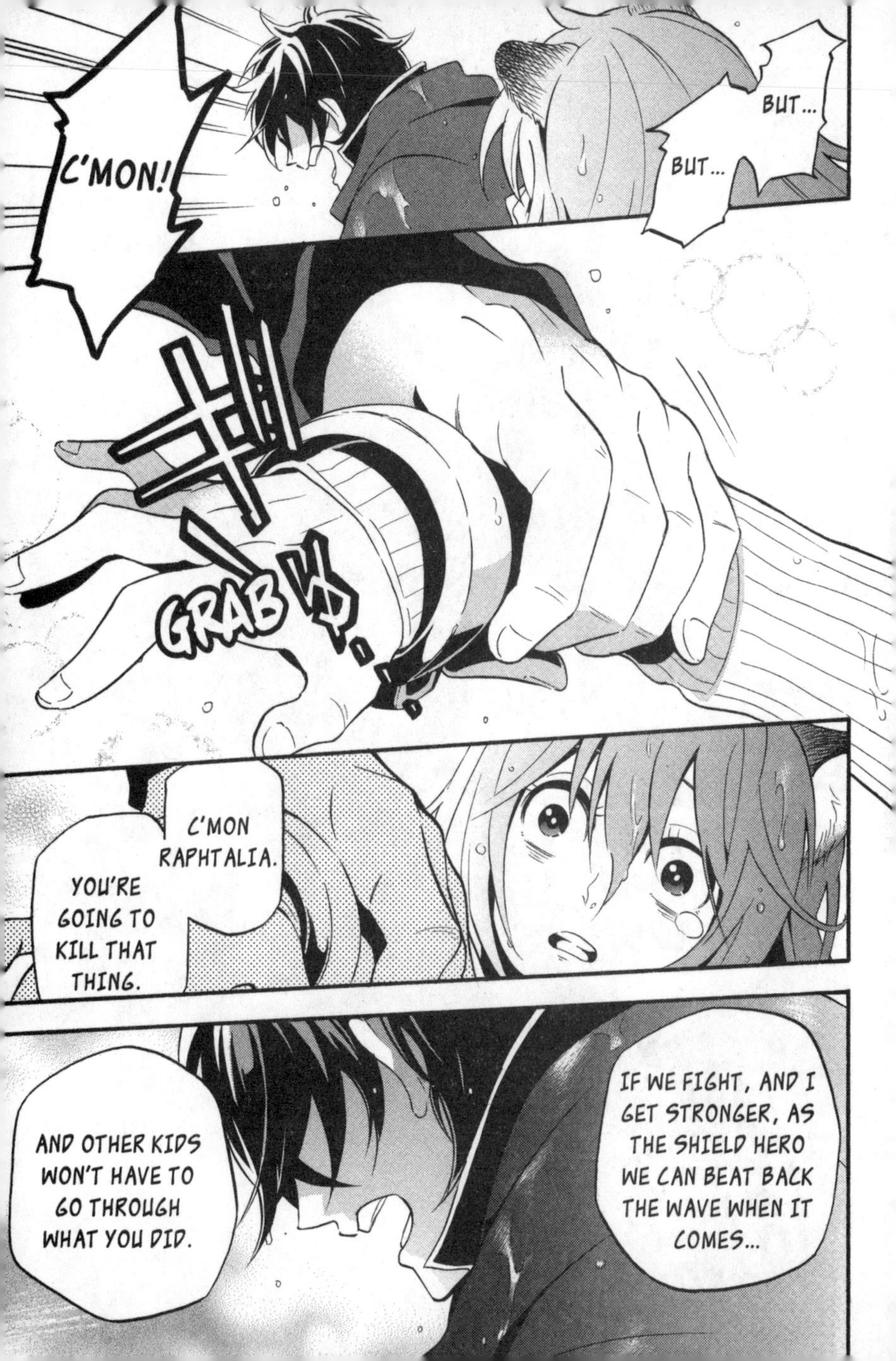
BUT...
BUT...
C'MON!
GRAB
C'MON RAPHTALIA.
YOU'RE GOING TO KILL THAT THING.
IF WE FIGHT, AND I GET STRONGER, AS THE SHIELD HERO WE CAN BEAT BACK THE WAVE WHEN IT COMES...
AND OTHER KIDS WON'T HAVE TO GO THROUGH WHAT YOU DID.

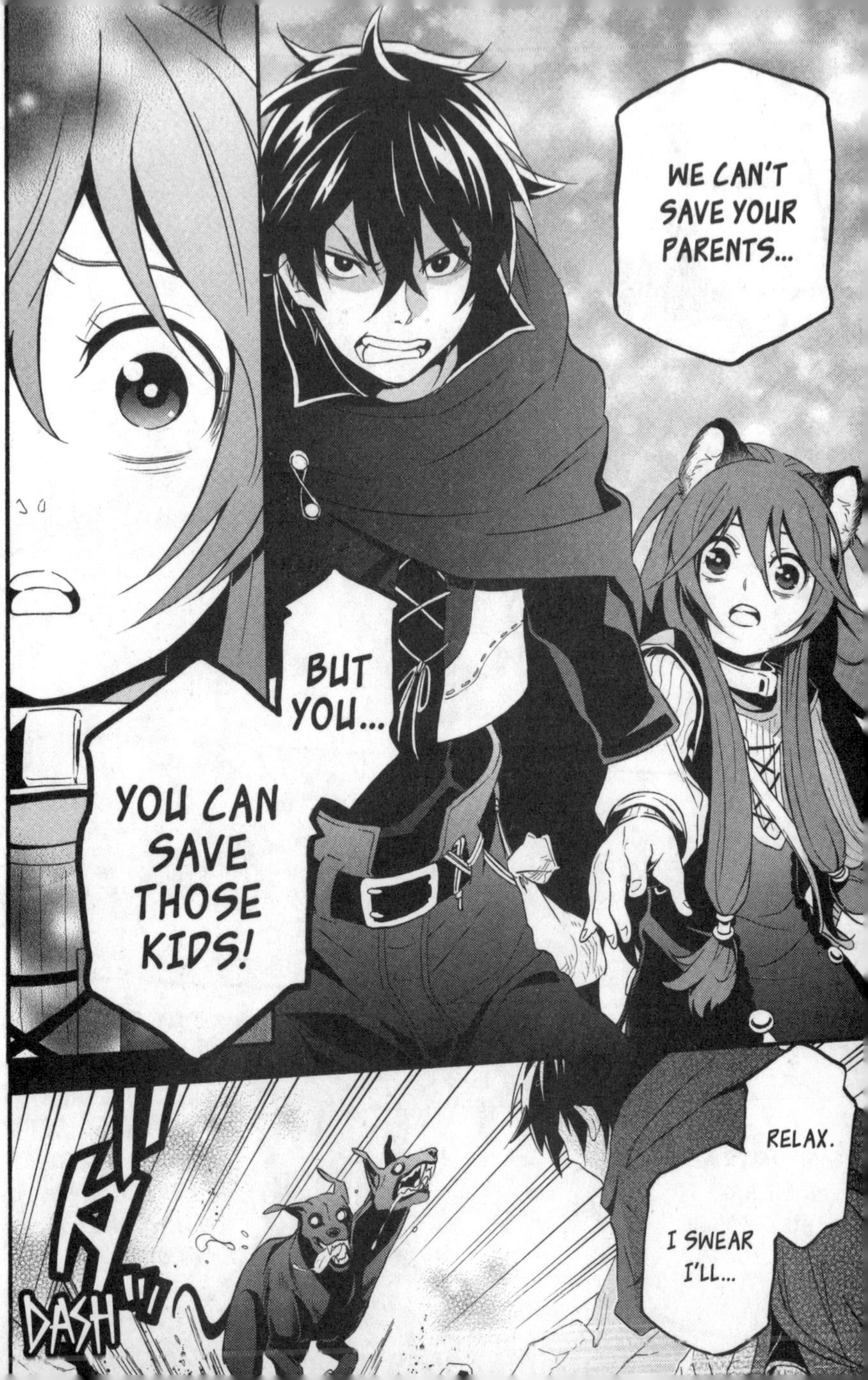
WE CAN'T SAVE YOUR PARENTS...
BUT YOU...
YOU CAN SAVE THOSE KIDS!
RELAX.
I SWEAR I'LL...
DASH

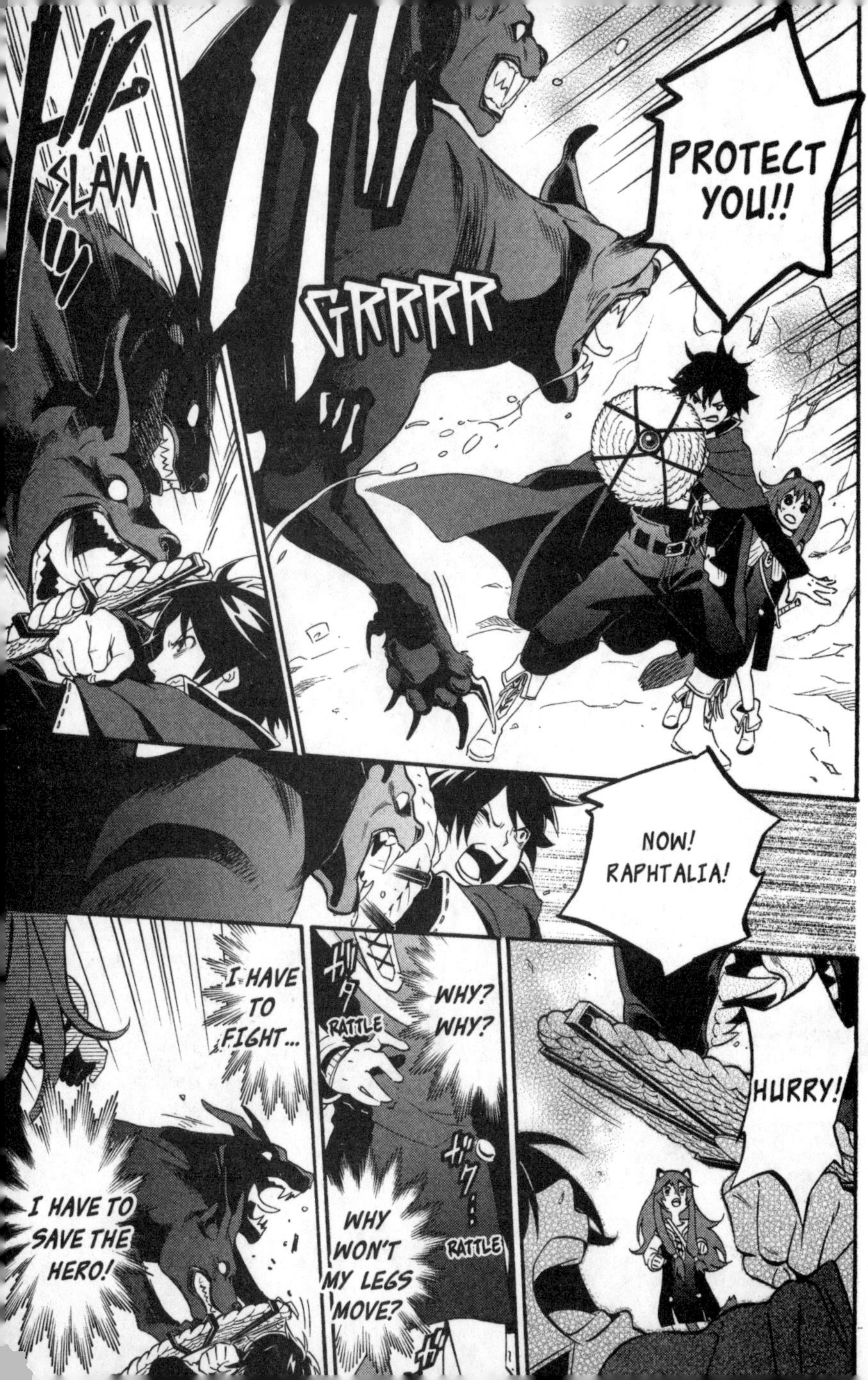
PROTECT YOU!!
GRRRR
SLAM
NOW! RAPHTALIA!
HURRY!
WHY? WHY?
RATTLE
WHY WON'T MY LEGS MOVE?
RATTLE
I HAVE TO FIGHT...
I HAVE TO SAVE THE HERO!

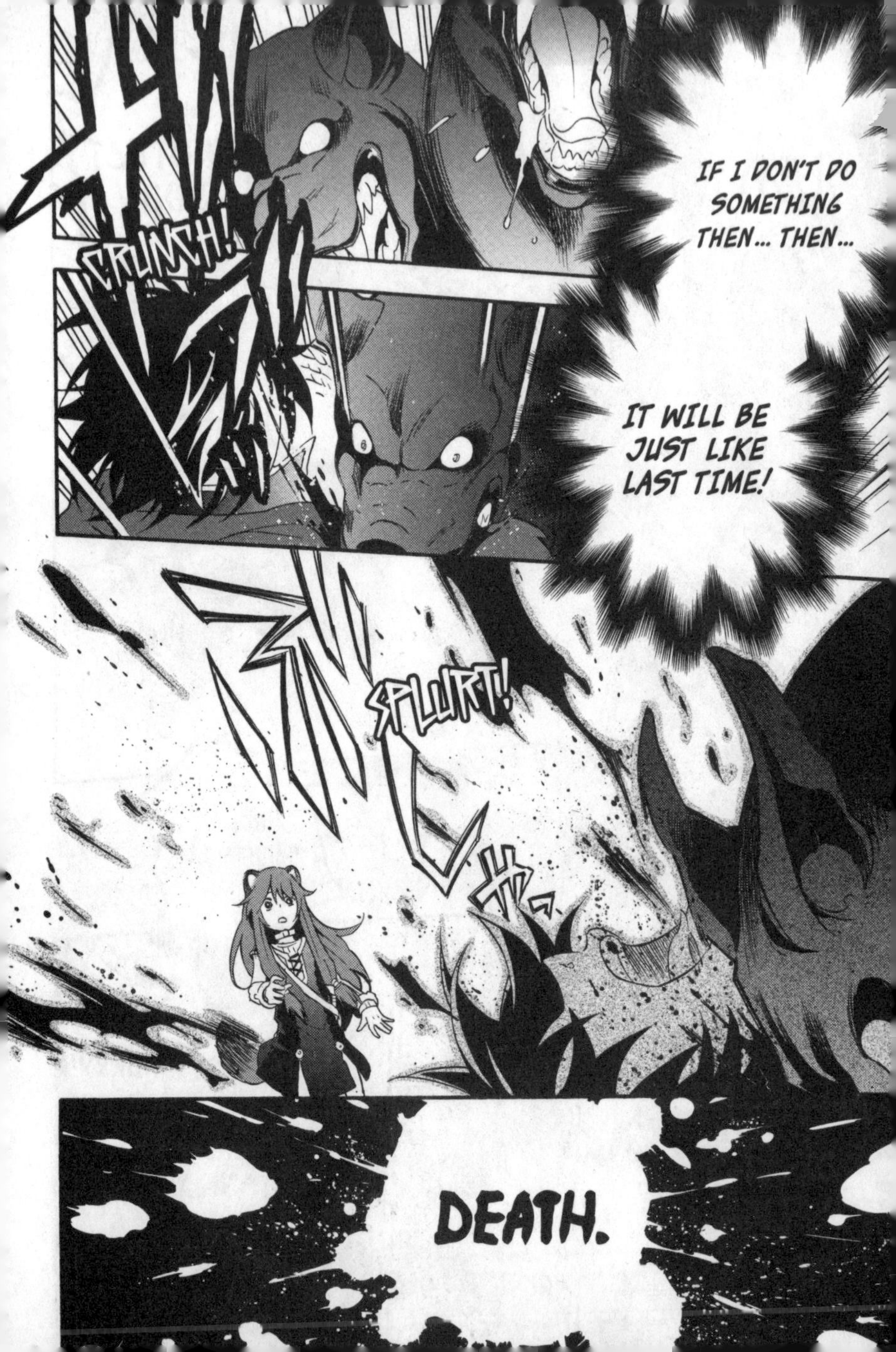
IF I DON'T DO SOMETHING THEN... THEN...
IT WILL BE JUST LIKE LAST TIME!
CRUNCH!
SPLURT!
DEATH.

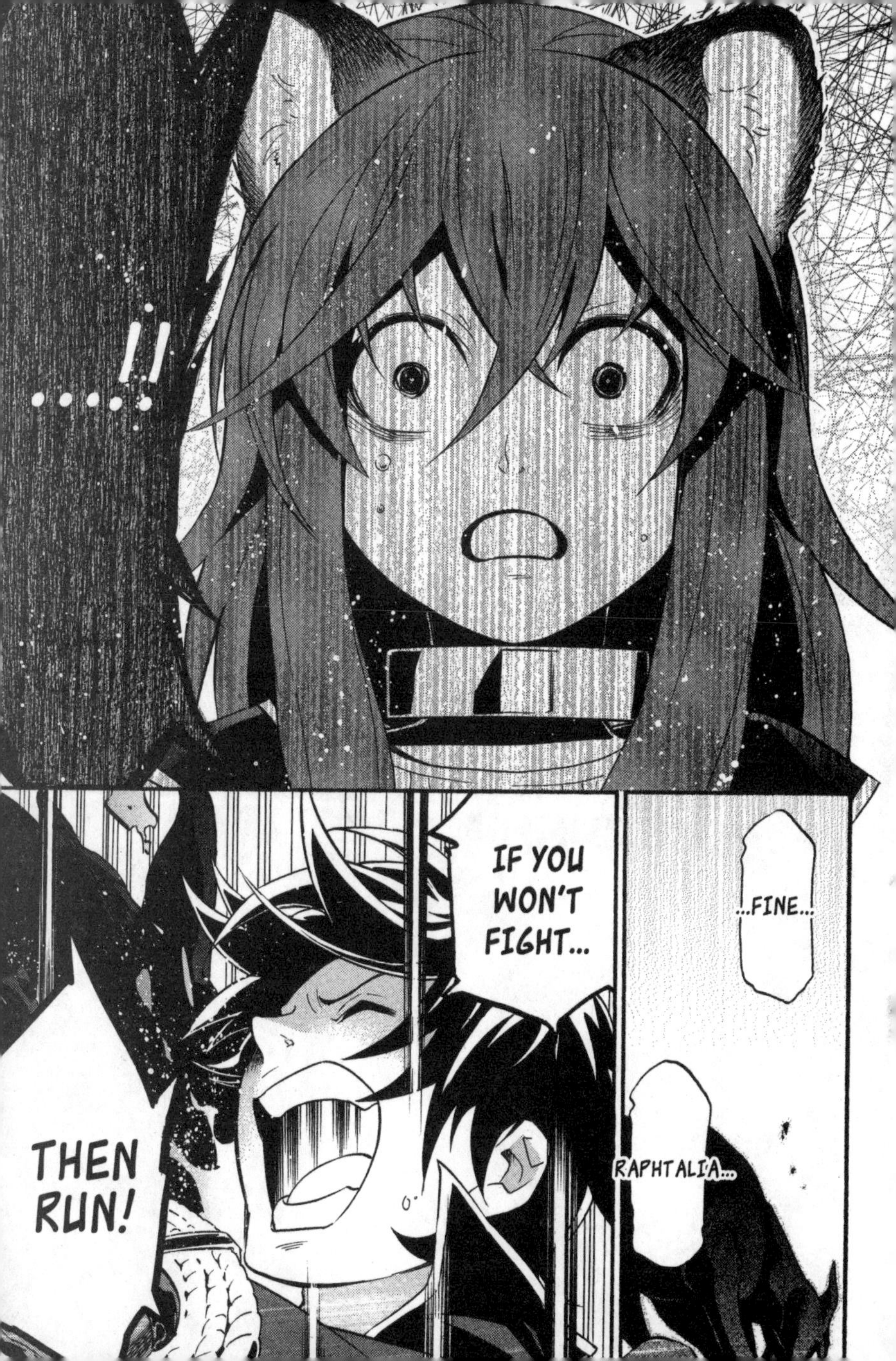
......!!
...FINE...
RAPHTALIA...
IF YOU WON'T FIGHT...
THEN RUN!

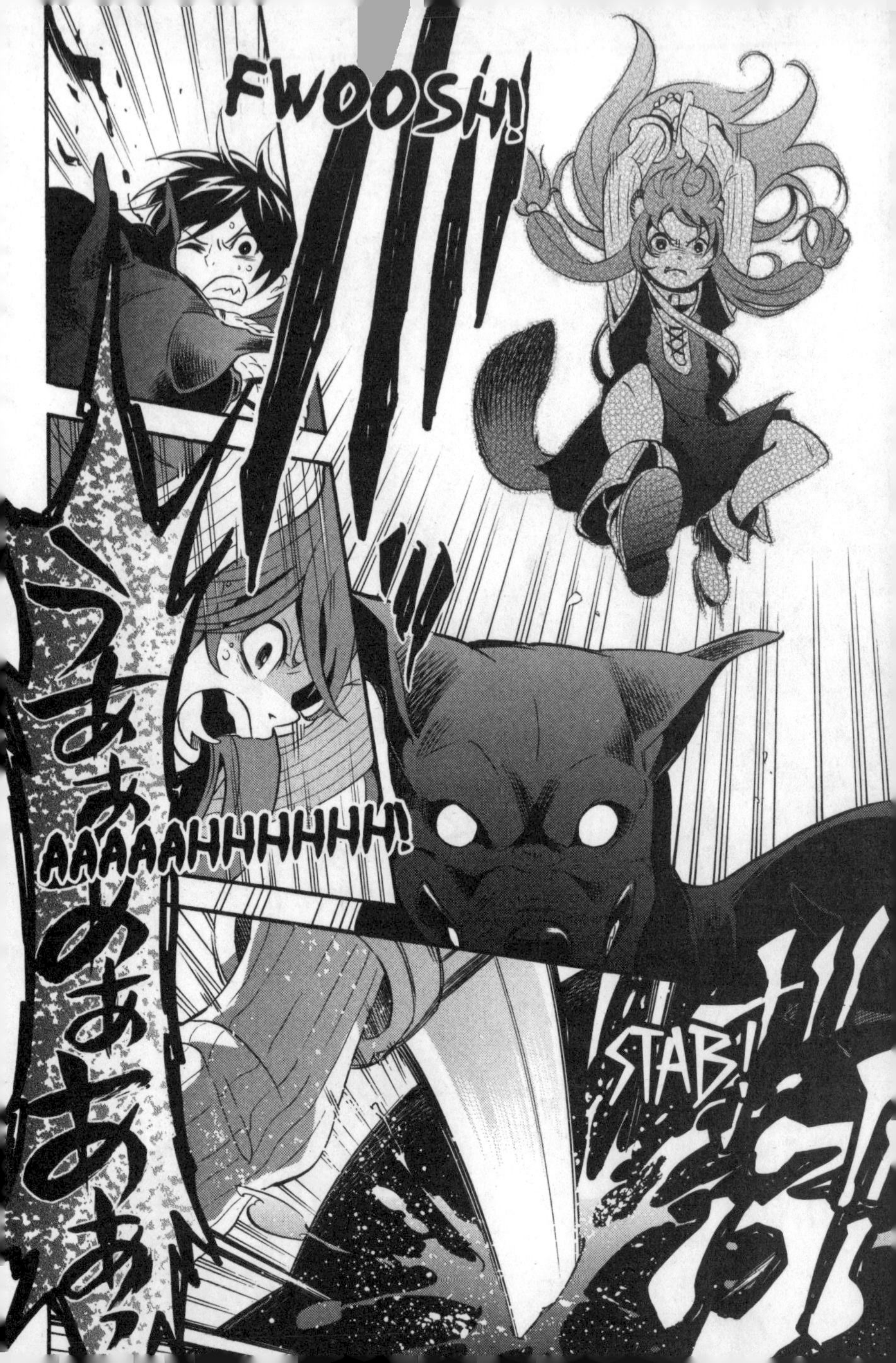
FWOOSH!
AAAAAHHHHHH!
STAB!

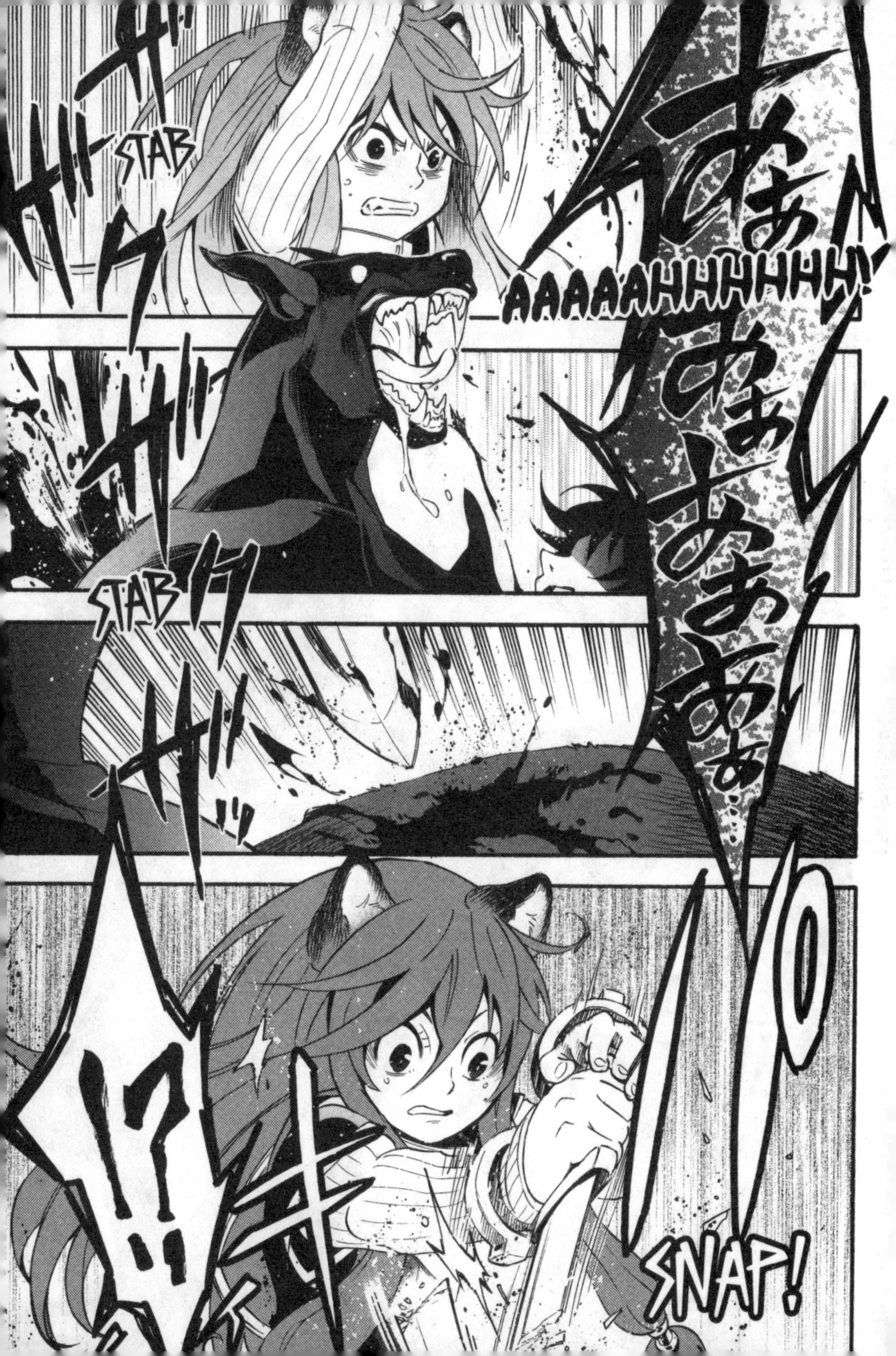
AAAAAHHHHHH!
STAB
STAB
SNAP!
!?

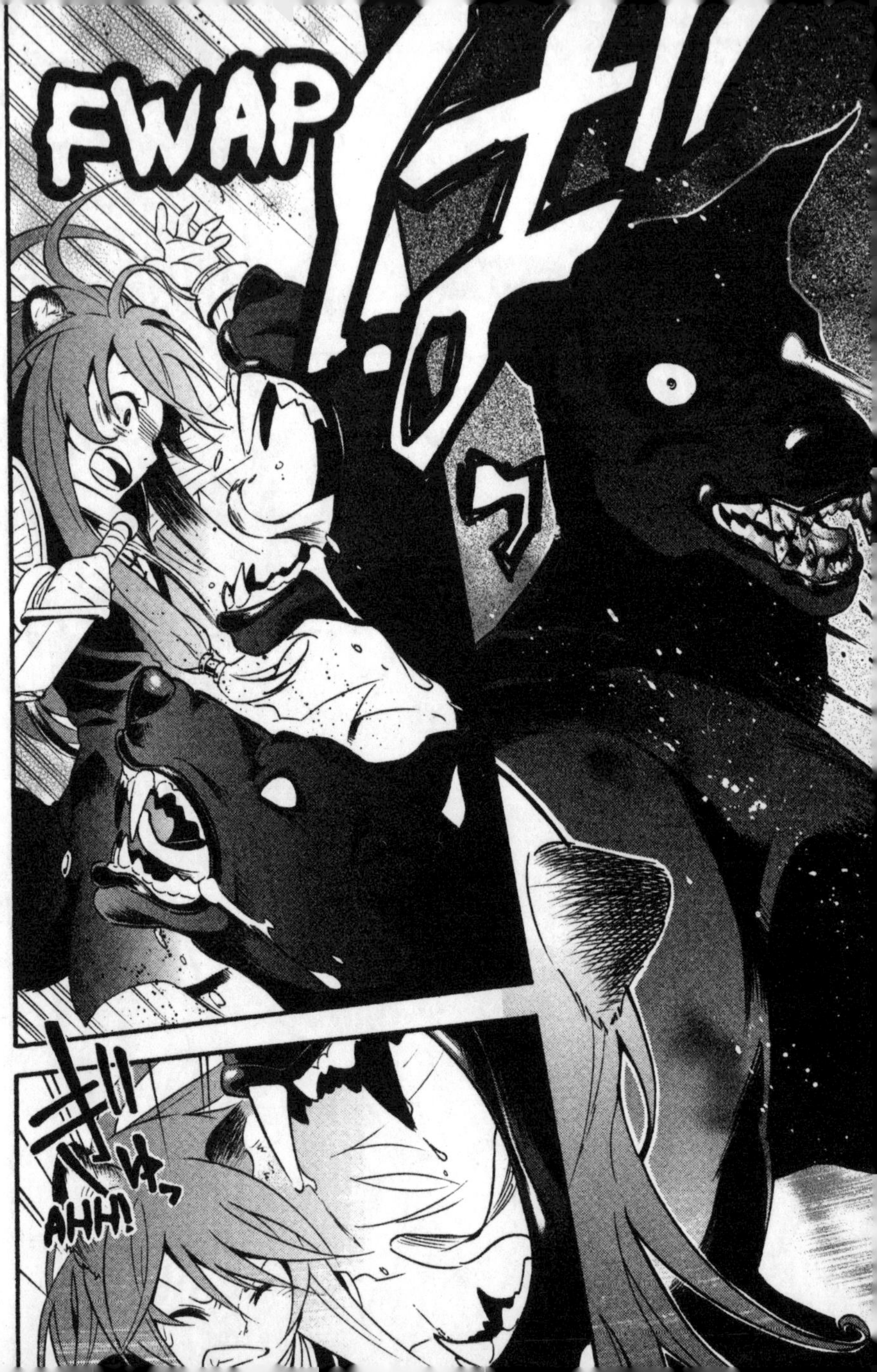
FWAP
AHH!

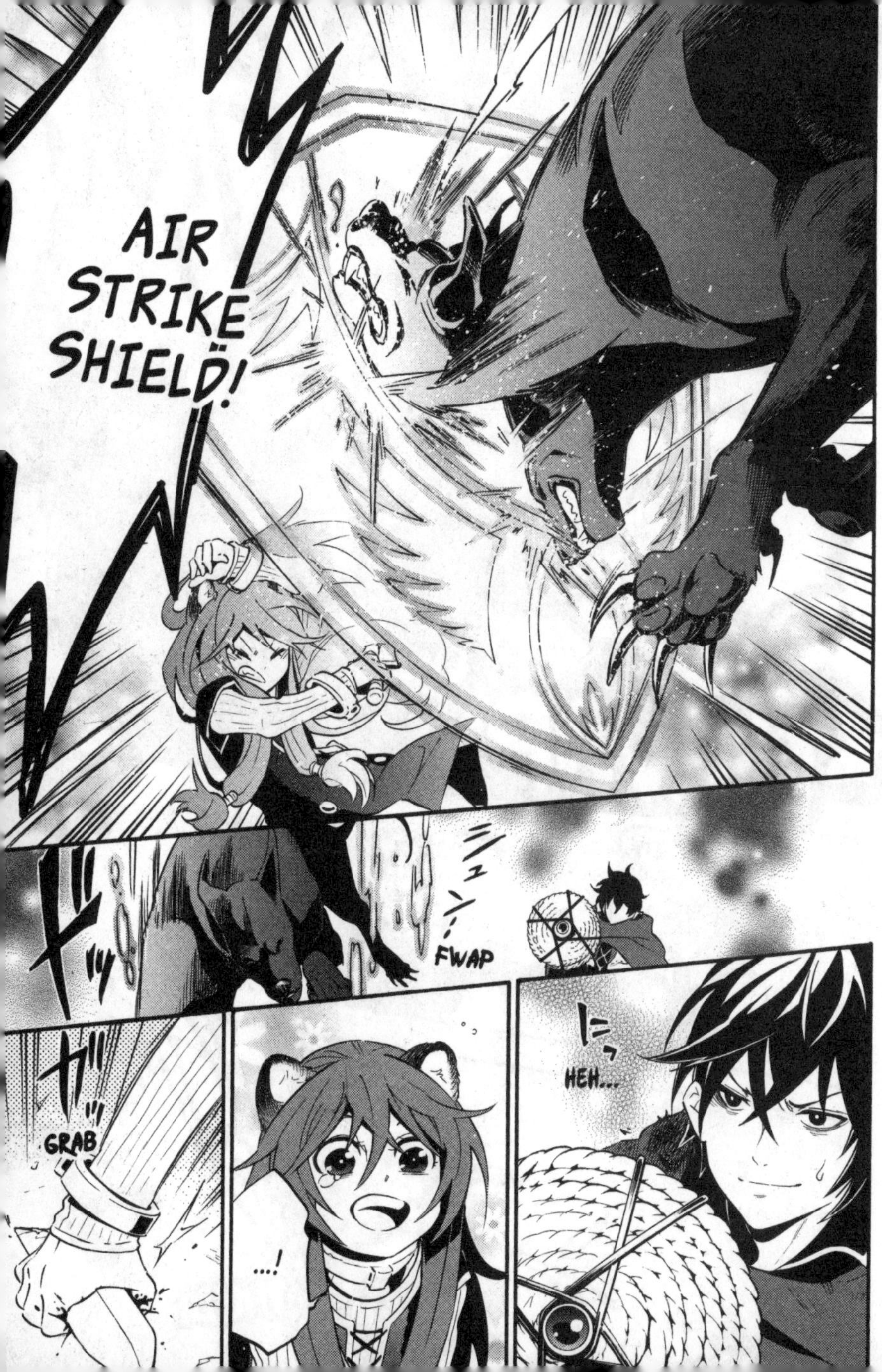
AIR STRIKE SHIELD!
FWAP
HEH...
...!
GRAB

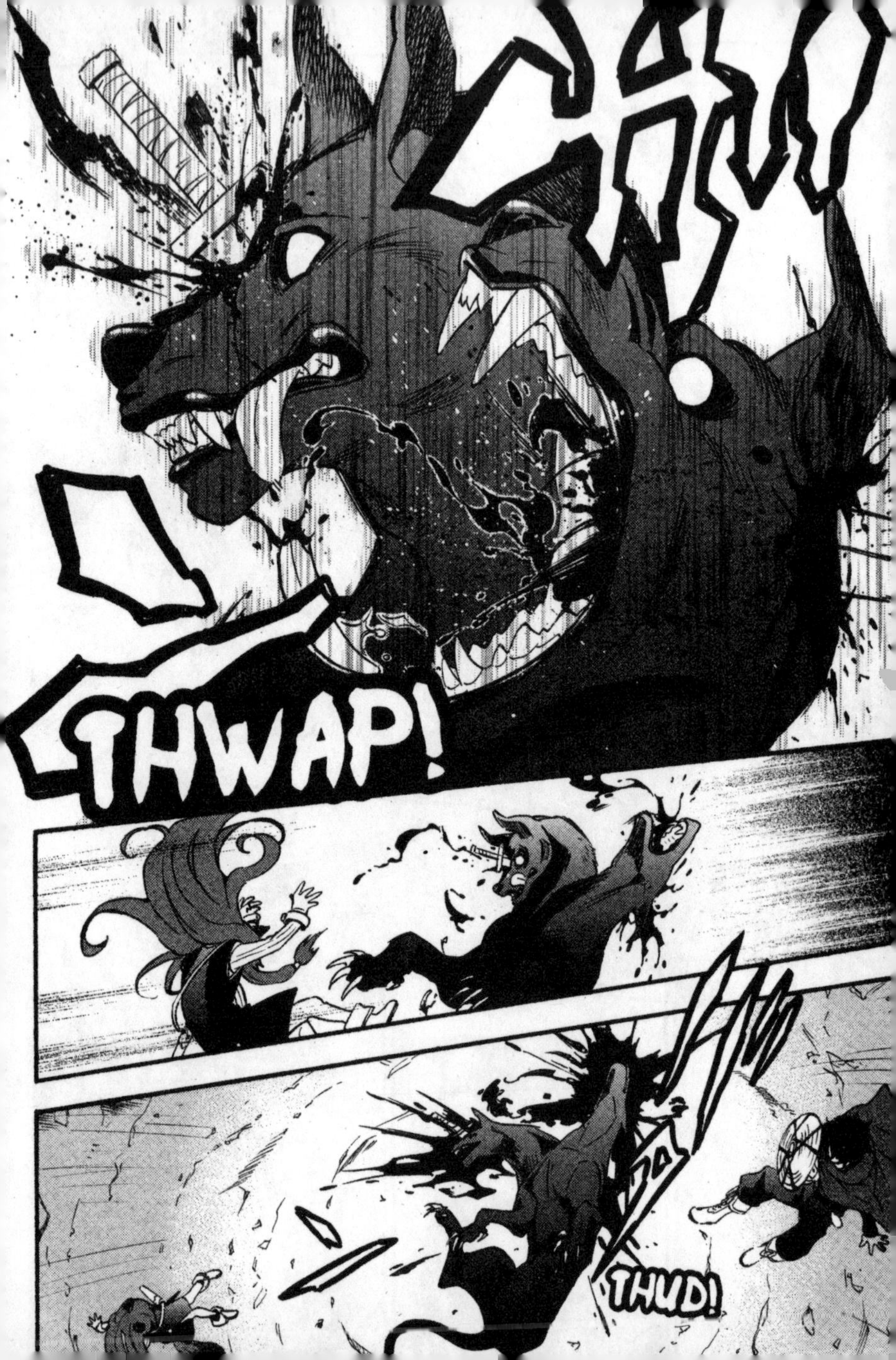
THWAP!
THUD!

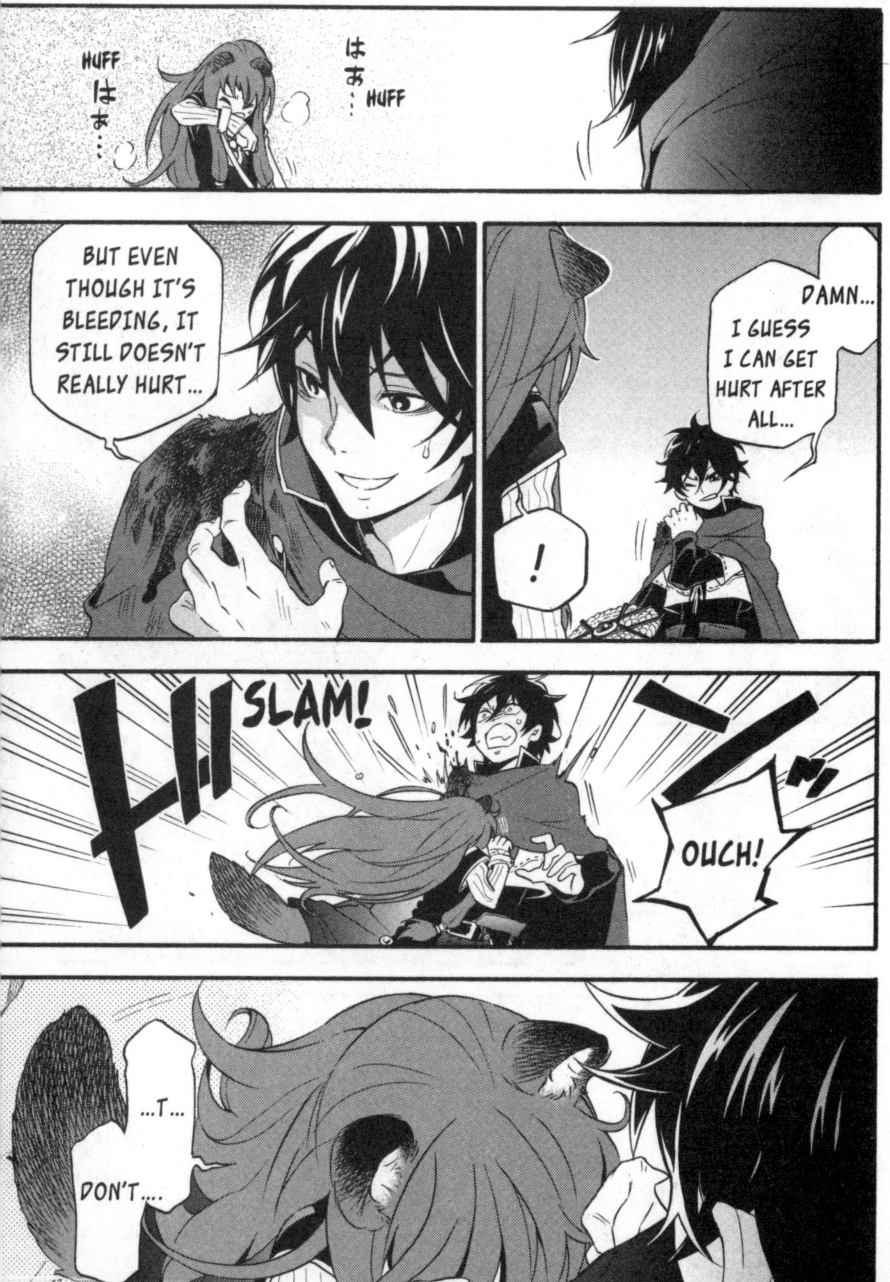
はあ…
HUFF
HUFF
はぁ…
DAMN... I GUESS I CAN GET HURT AFTER ALL...
!
BUT EVEN THOUGH IT'S BLEEDING, IT STILL DOESN'T REALLY HURT...
SLAM!
OUCH!
...T...
DON'T....

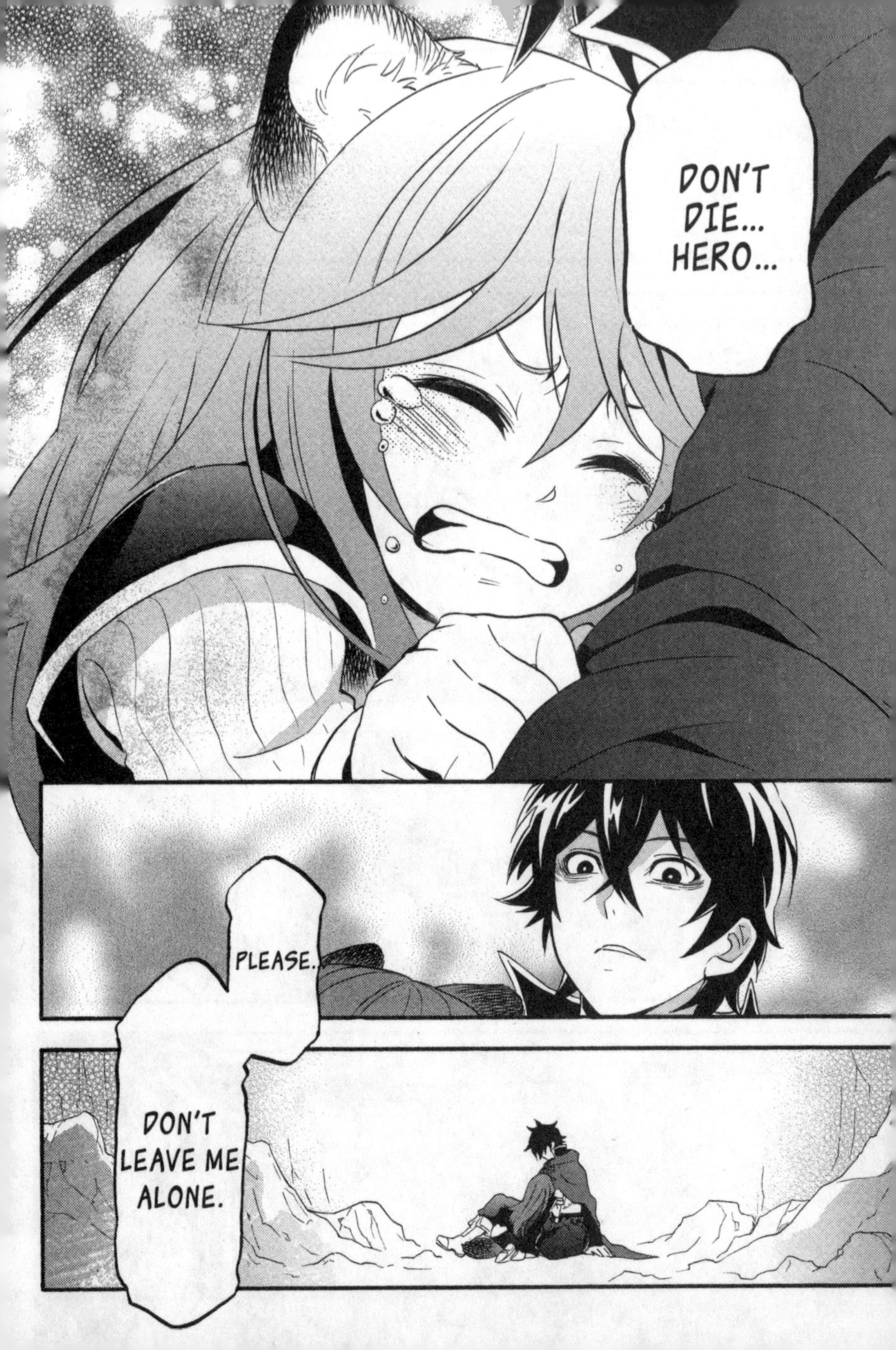
DON'T DIE... HERO...
PLEASE...
DON'T LEAVE ME ALONE.

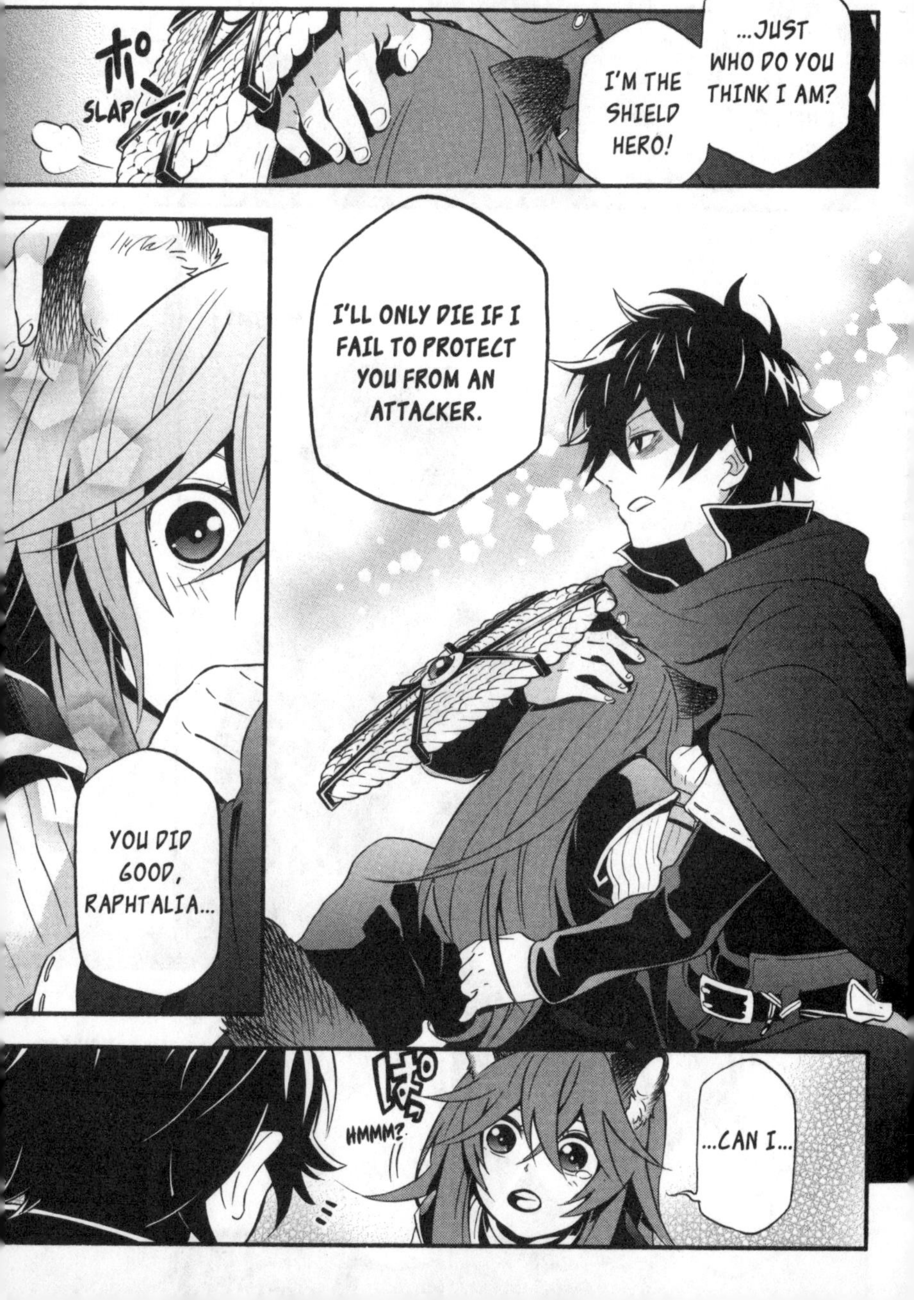
...JUST WHO DO YOU THINK I AM?
I'M THE SHIELD HERO!
ポ
SLAP
I'LL ONLY DIE IF I FAIL TO PROTECT YOU FROM AN ATTACKER.
YOU DID GOOD, RAPHTALIA...
...CAN I...
HMMM?

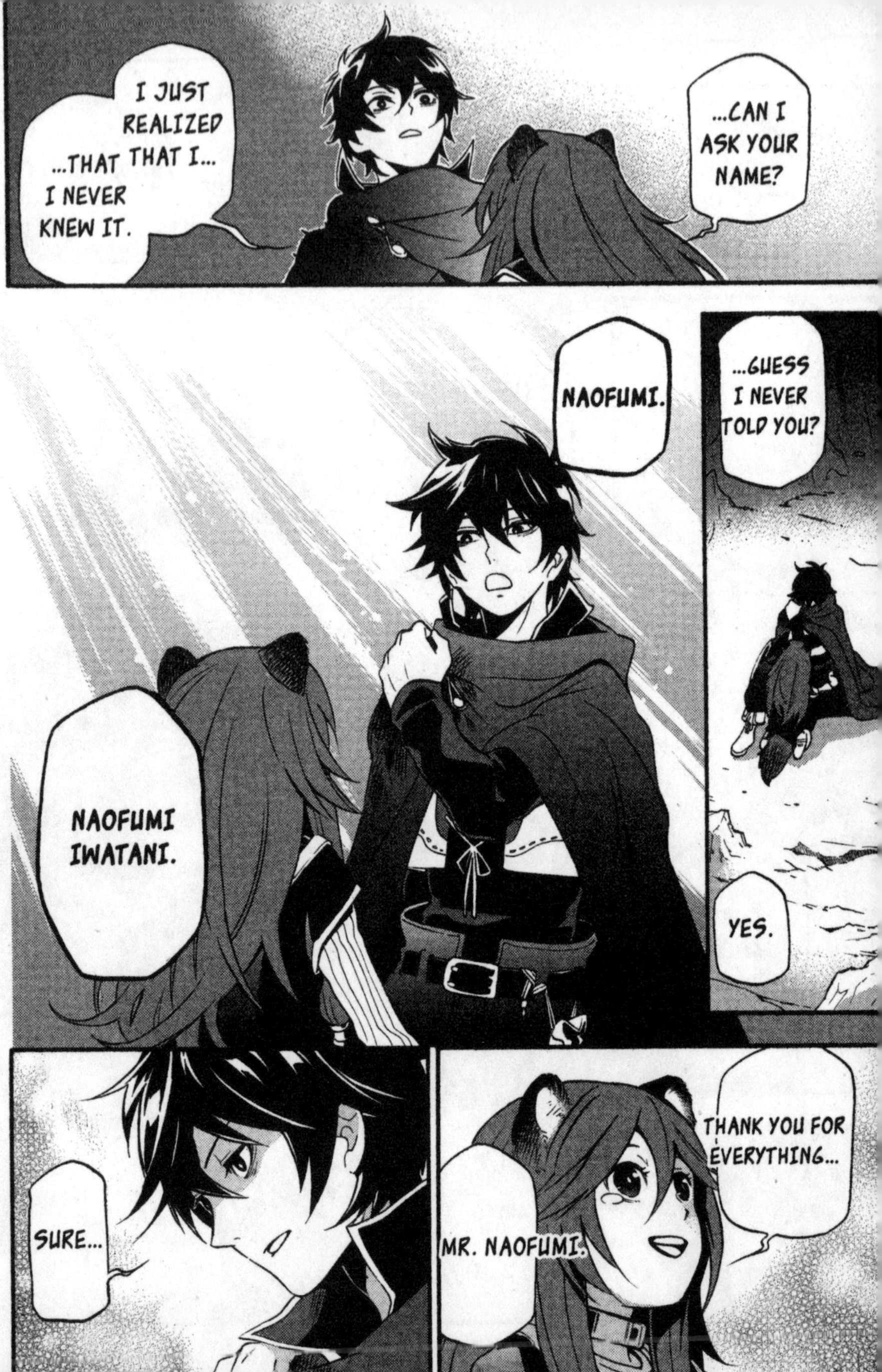
...CAN I ASK YOUR NAME?
I JUST REALIZED THAT I...
...THAT I NEVER KNEW IT.
...GUESS I NEVER TOLD YOU?
YES.
NAOFUMI.
NAOFUMI IWATANI.
THANK YOU FOR EVERYTHING...
MR. NAOFUMI.
SURE...

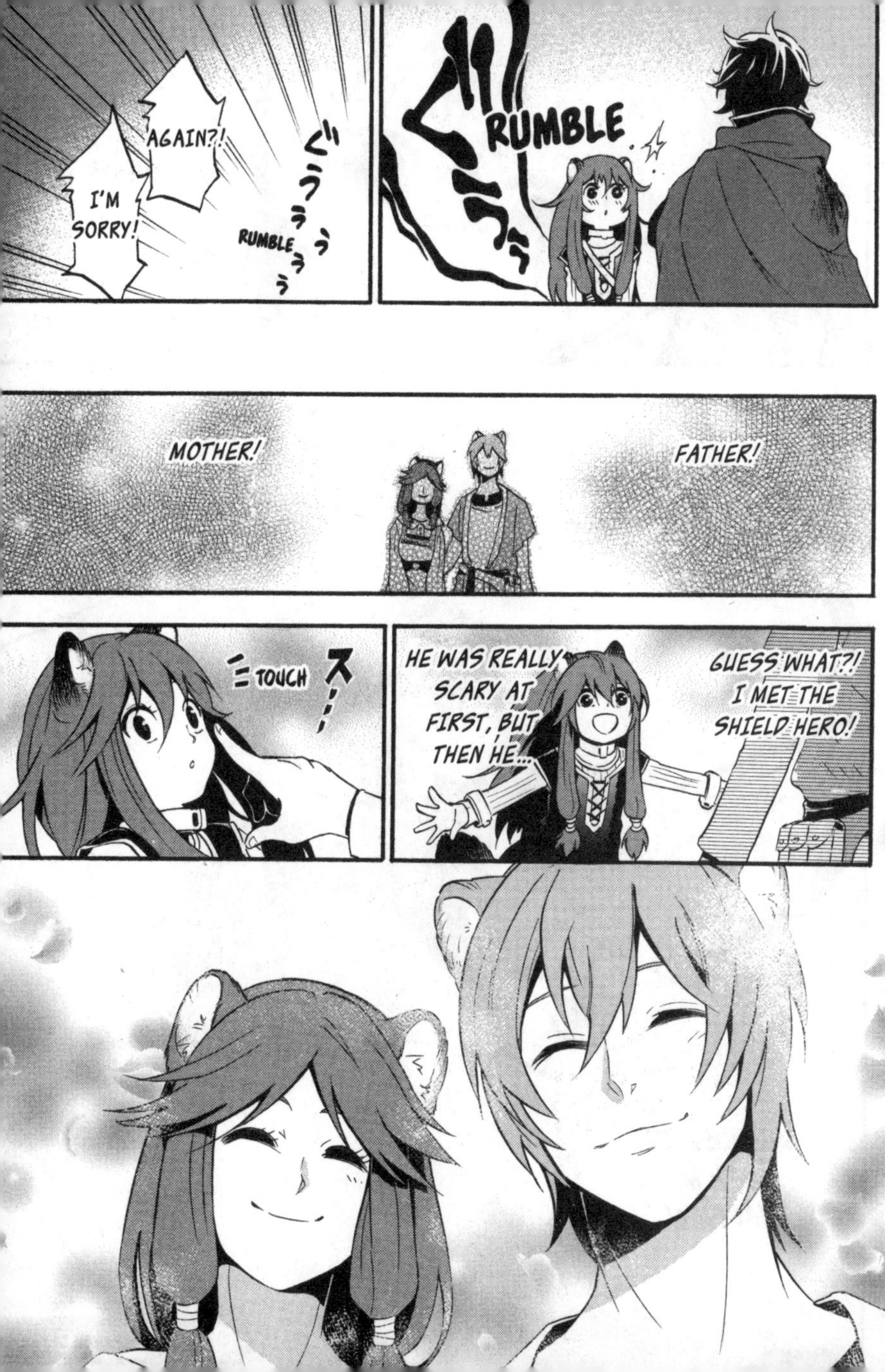
RUMBLE
RUMBLE
AGAIN?!
I'M SORRY!
FATHER!
MOTHER!
GUESS WHAT?! I MET THE SHIELD HERO!
HE WAS REALLY SCARY AT FIRST, BUT THEN HE...
TOUCH

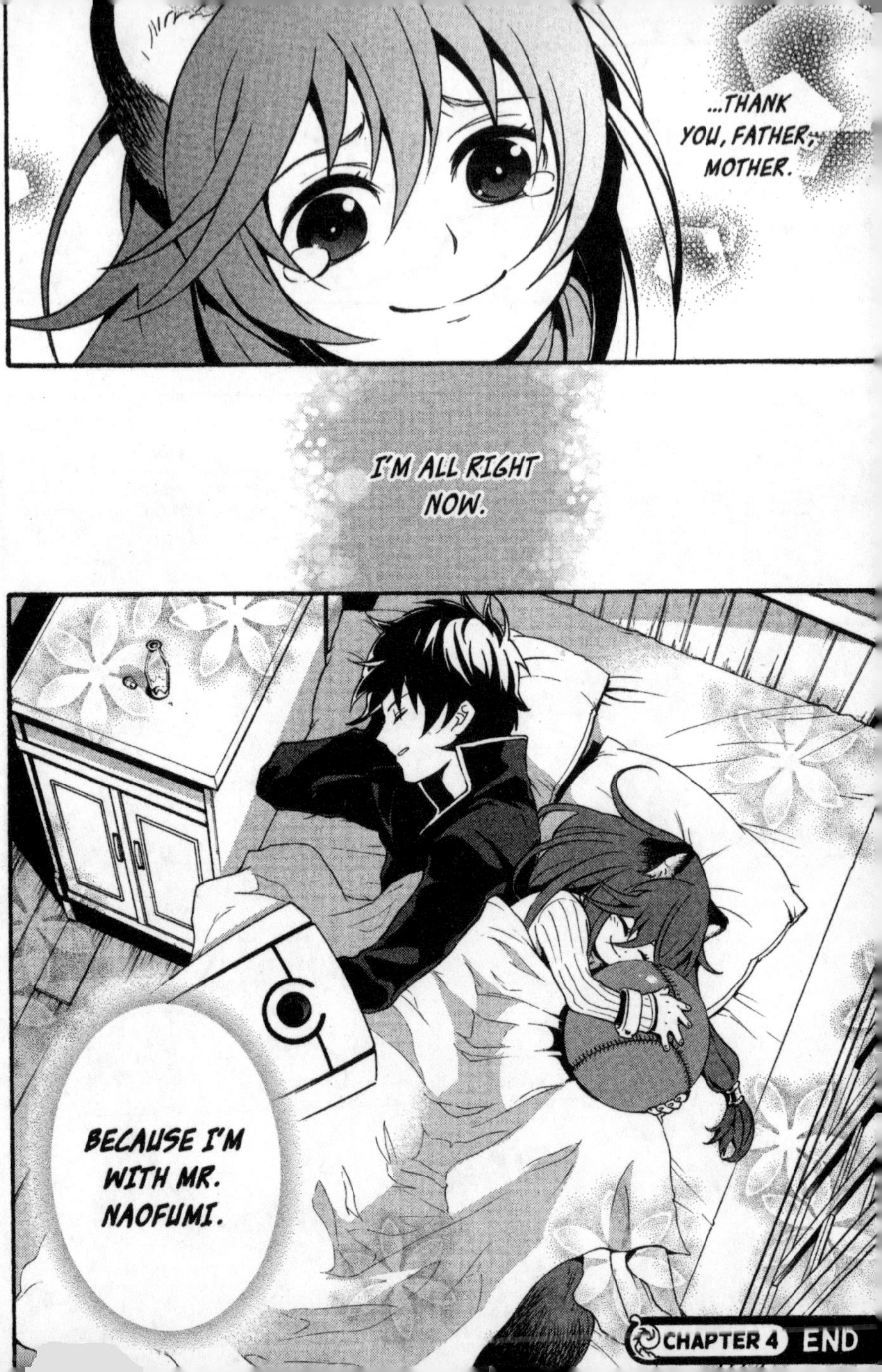
...THANK YOU, FATHER, MOTHER.
I'M ALL RIGHT NOW.
BECAUSE I'M WITH MR. NAOFUMI.
CHAPTER 4 END

THE DAY BEFORE BY ANEKO YUSAGI

"Master, yesterday was crazy www."

My name is Naofumi Iwatani. I'm twenty years old, and I'm just an average college student. I was just chatting with a friend from an online game. We'd had an "off party" the previous day. An "off party" is when you meet with people you know from an online game, but in real life.

I've honestly always found it a little strange—meeting online friends in the real world. We'd usually meet up and hang out for the night, and then when we saw each other again online the next time it was that much more fun. By the way, they were calling me master because we had an alliance in the game, and I was in charge of it.

"Sorry, sorry…I mean, can you blame me for letting loose a bit? If not then, when?"

"wwwwwwwwsMaster, you're so seriouswwwwwwwwww."

By the way "w" means that you're laughing online. This guy overused it a little, but he didn't mean any harm, so I didn't let it bother me.

"Master, you're the funniest! Everyone loves that about you. Your limbo dance was hilarious yo!"

Last night really had been a lot of fun.

We all me up in Tokyo, and there had even been some girls! I was pretty surprised by that. The girl characters in our alliance… I'd always assumed that they were actually guys just pretending to be girls. Whatever, who cares about what gender they are, anyway?

We went to Akihabara and ate at a maid cafe, and the girls LOVED it. They must really be guys on the inside. After that, we went to Karaoke, and I ended up doing a limbo dance there, right in the middle of it! The whole room was electric—it was weird. Why did I dance the limbo? I even moonwalked. I must have really been in a good mood.

"So where are we going today?"

We were standing in a town square talking it over. We were all going to go out and try to level up.

"Sorry, but I can only play in the morning. So let's level up somewhere with strong monsters."

"Yeah, me too. My parents are so annoying. You know a good place we could go, even for just a couple hours?"

"Hm…"

We stood in the square chatting, and I thought about where we could go. Our alliance was the third biggest on the server, and I was one of the leaders. I had a pretty good idea of where everyone wanted to go. There was a dungeon that you could only enter if you'd been victorious in a guild war—when the guilds fight one another.

Fine, if it's only for a little while…

"Ok, let's head to the guild dungeon!"

"Awesome! Master, you sure know what's up!"

"You better make it up to me later. I know you don't think you get into the guild dungeon for free."

"Master, will you go out with me then? I'm hoping it will lead to marriage. I mean this in real life."

"What are you talking about? Jokes need to be funny. Let me switch to a character who is good for that dungeon. Hold on."

I had a few characters on that server, so I chose one that would best compliment the party's strengths. A defender form… yeah, the Shield Warrior that gets to protect everyone else.

The character didn't have much of an attack rating. The damage it dealt was entirely dependent on the weapon's attach power, so it wasn't so efficient. The upside was that the defense rating was really high, so he could take a lot of damage without going down.

"I'm back! Let's get going!"

"Yeah!"

I stood at the front of the party and defended the others from attacks. That left them free to focus on bringing down the enemy. I led everyone into the dungeon, and stirred up some enemies. My party members took care of them.

"Huh? Hey, it's a boss. Can we win, Master?"

In the game there was typically a powerful boss at the end of each dungeon. Depending on the game, sometimes these bosses are so powerful that normal players have no hope of defeating them. The game we were playing just happened to be that kind of game.

"If we take it slow and stick to the strategy, we can win this one. Let's do it!"

My character took a hit from the boss.

The fight ended up taking around five minutes. The thing fell over with a satisfying crash, and it left a number of rare item drops. Then a screen appeared that calculated and displayed each party member's contributions to the battle. Huh? Looks like I was the MVP this time, and I got an extra bonus item as a result.

"You get a rare item?"

"I did. And it was an event item drop too."

"Nice! You're going to be rich!"

That item could only be procured by winning this fight, so it would sell for a huge profit. If I sold it, everyone would be happy.

"We're almost out of time. Should we head out?"

"Yeah!"

"With Master around, there's nothing we can't do."

"Yeah, master really likes using that character."

"I know, but why don't you level it up to its max level? This would be so much easier if you did!"

When you raised a character to its maximum level, it was called a counter-stop. I didn't have any characters that I had counter-stopped. So within our alliance, I really wasn't the most powerful, when you looked at it that way.

"Because I like making money in these games. All I can think about is how much this item is going to sell for!"

"There it is! Master's entrepreneurial spirit!"

It was true, I loved making money. I knew how useful money was on the server, how it would translate into success in battle. I loved items in games. I collected them all.

"Speaking of which… I'm about to go sell this. You all could only hang out in the morning right? This is good timing. I'll give you all your share of the profits the next time I see you, so look forward to that."

"Roger!"

"I hope you get good money for it YO!"

"Now we can buy that other thing!"

"We're going to be so strong!"

I switched to a merchant character and put my new item out for sale in a spot that people would be sure to see it. I could sell off some other items at the same time.

…Until a customer stopped by though, I didn't have all that much to do. I could leave the computer on and just head out for the day…

Hmmm…

I leaned back, stretched, and got out of my chair.

"I guess I shouldn't play games all day anyway. I should get out of the house."

…But where should I go?

I could have gone over to a friend's house, but I wasn't really in the mood. School was out too…. Yeah, and the "off party" had been expensive, so I didn't have a lot of money to play with.

"I guess I'll go to the library and hang out for a while."

Of course I only really read manga and light novels.

I hummed a song to myself as I walked down the street towards the library.

Thinking over how I spend my free time these days, I had to admit that I'd become a pretty hardcore Otaku. Each individual day was fun, but I didn't feel like I was making full use of my time. I was a university student now, so I felt a little silly thinking it, but I still kind of wished that I could have an adventure like the protagonists of games and manga do.

It's a little cliché by now, but I really like those old stories of heroes defeating monsters with magic. The sort of story you'd have to blow the dust off of. Not that something like that would ever happen to me. So, I made up my mind to read some fantasy, and I hurried on toward the library.

At the time, I had no way of knowing how foolish I was being, or the terrible horrors that lay in wait for me. I'd find out soon, but that's another story.

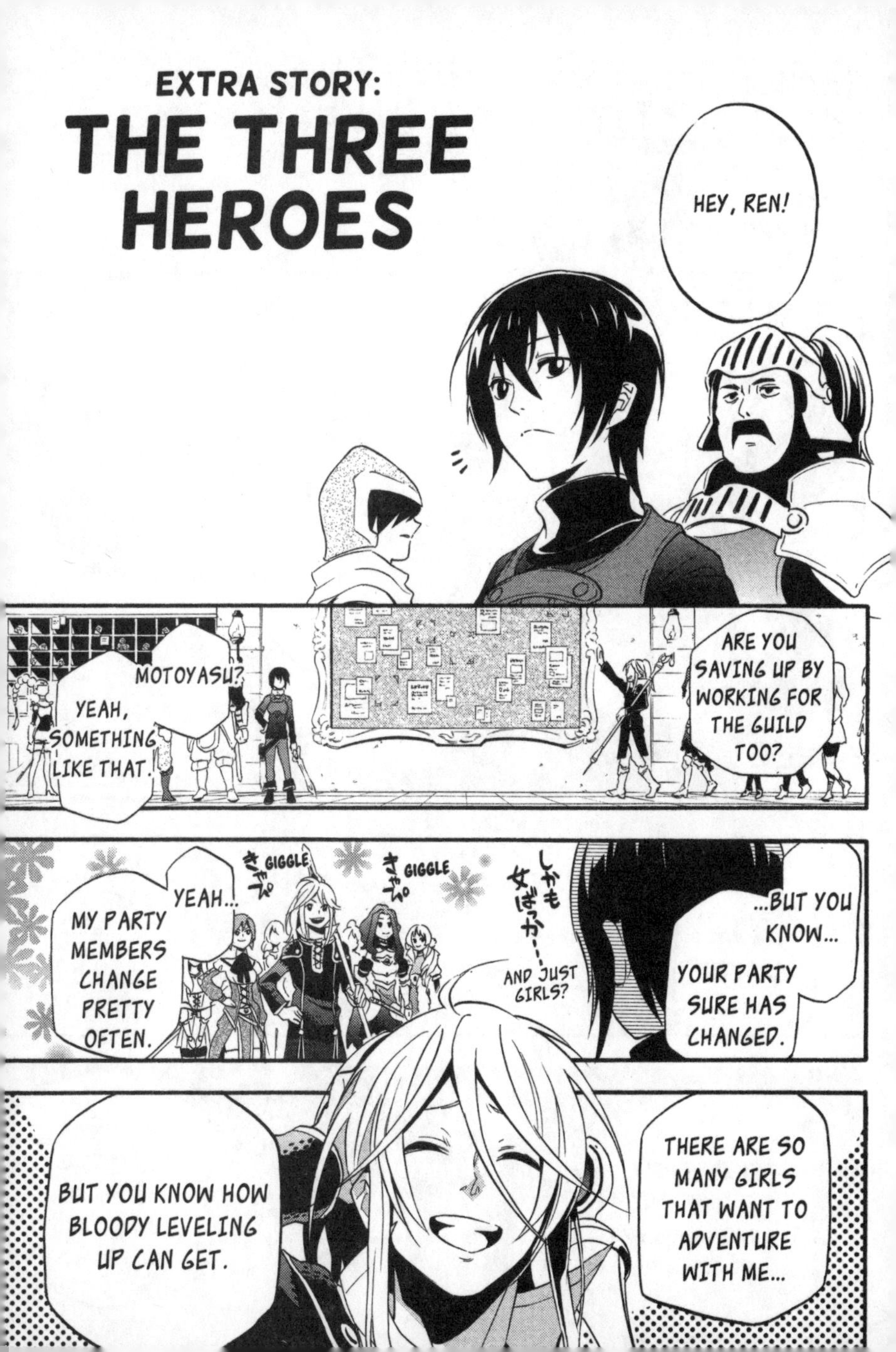
EXTRA STORY:
THE THREE HEROES
HEY, REN!
ARE YOU SAVING UP BY WORKING FOR THE GUILD TOO?
MOTOYASU?
YEAH, SOMETHING LIKE THAT.
...BUT YOU KNOW...
YOUR PARTY SURE HAS CHANGED.
しかも女ばっか・・・
AND JUST GIRLS?
きゃぴ GIGGLE
きゃぴ GIGGLE
YEAH...
MY PARTY MEMBERS CHANGE PRETTY OFTEN.
THERE ARE SO MANY GIRLS THAT WANT TO ADVENTURE WITH ME...
BUT YOU KNOW HOW BLOODY LEVELING UP CAN GET.

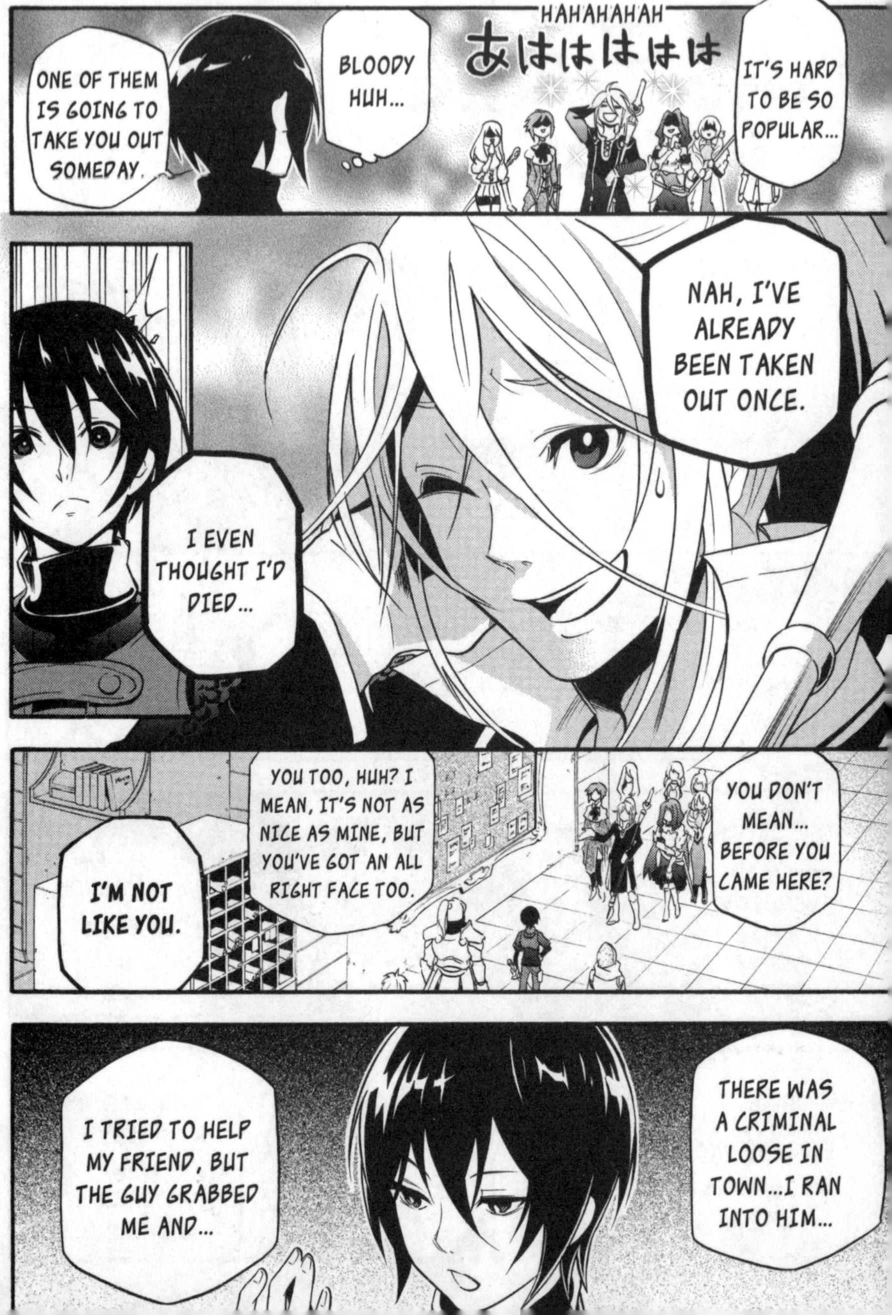
IT'S HARD TO BE SO POPULAR...
HAHAHAHAH
あははははは
BLOODY HUH...
ONE OF THEM IS GOING TO TAKE YOU OUT SOMEDAY.
NAH, I'VE ALREADY BEEN TAKEN OUT ONCE.
I EVEN THOUGHT I'D DIED...
YOU DON'T MEAN... BEFORE YOU CAME HERE?
YOU TOO, HUH? I MEAN, IT'S NOT AS NICE AS MINE, BUT YOU'VE GOT AN ALL RIGHT FACE TOO.
I'M NOT LIKE YOU.
THERE WAS A CRIMINAL LOOSE IN TOWN...I RAN INTO HIM...
I TRIED TO HELP MY FRIEND, BUT THE GUY GRABBED ME AND...

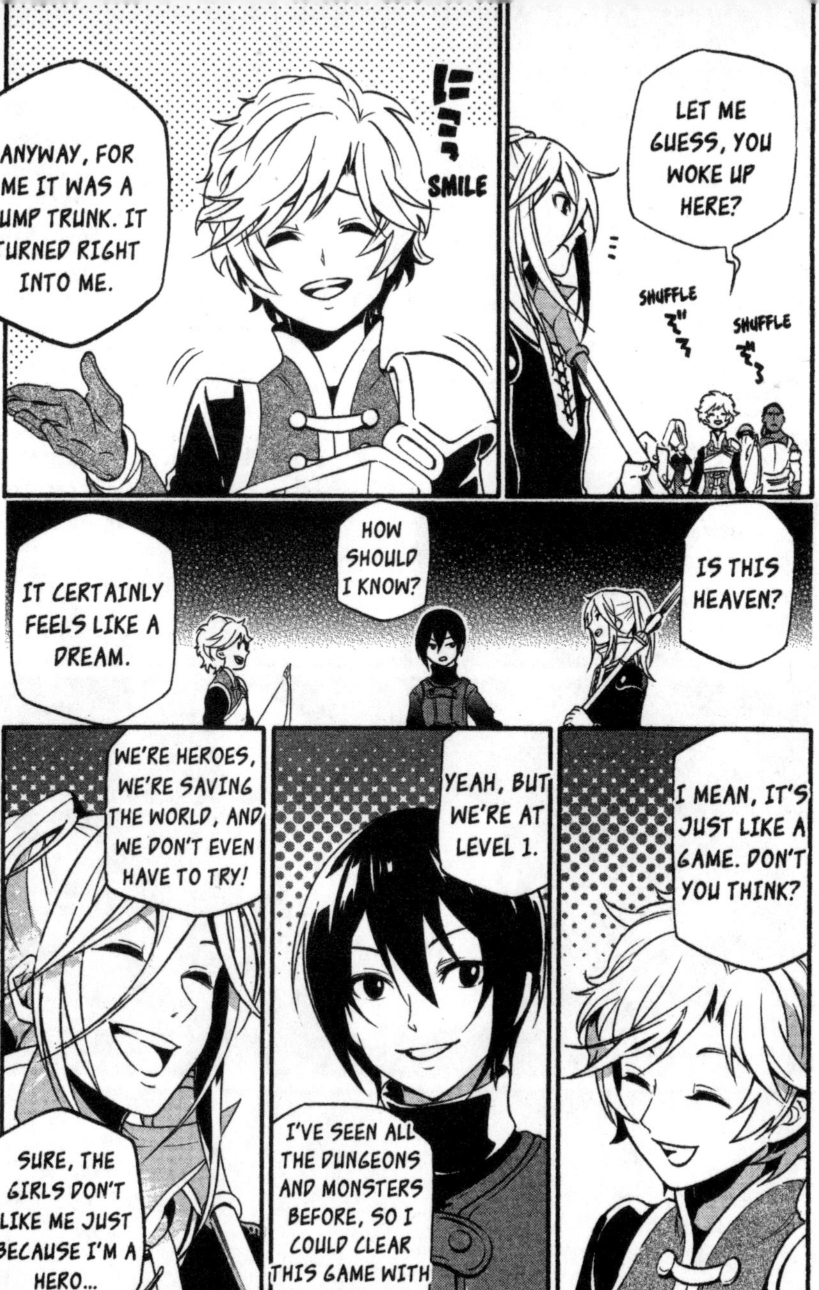
LET ME GUESS, YOU WOKE UP HERE?
SHUFFLE
SHUFFLE
SMILE
ANYWAY, FOR ME IT WAS A DUMP TRUNK. IT TURNED RIGHT INTO ME.
IS THIS HEAVEN?
HOW SHOULD I KNOW?
IT CERTAINLY FEELS LIKE A DREAM.
I MEAN, IT'S JUST LIKE A GAME. DON'T YOU THINK?
YEAH, BUT WE'RE AT LEVEL 1.
I'VE SEEN ALL THE DUNGEONS AND MONSTERS BEFORE, SO I COULD CLEAR THIS GAME WITH MY EYES SHUT.
WE'RE HEROES, WE'RE SAVING THE WORLD, AND WE DON'T EVEN HAVE TO TRY!
SURE, THE GIRLS DON'T LIKE ME JUST BECAUSE I'M A HERO...

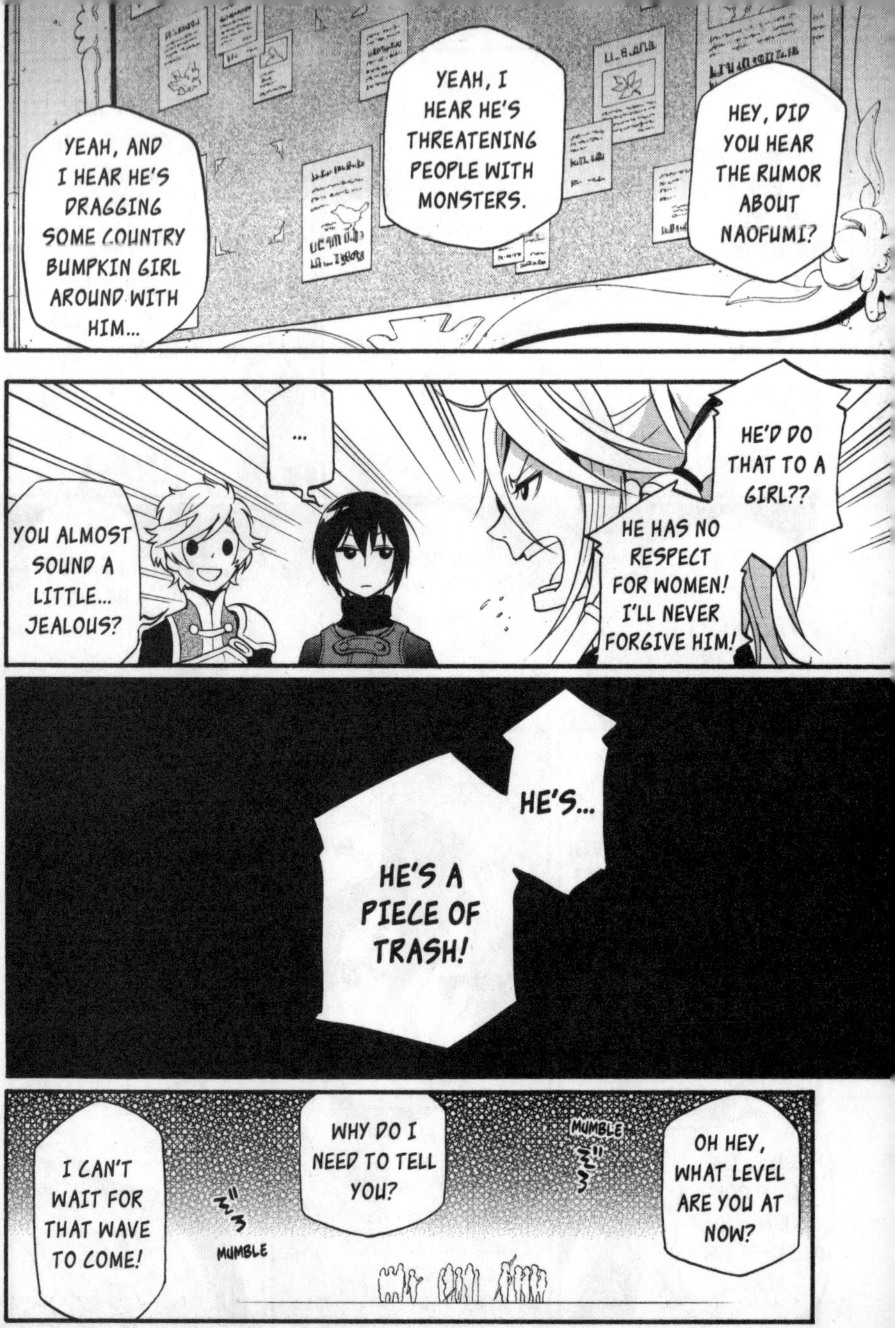
HEY, DID YOU HEAR THE RUMOR ABOUT NAOFUMI?
YEAH, I HEAR HE'S THREATENING PEOPLE WITH MONSTERS.
YEAH, AND I HEAR HE'S DRAGGING SOME COUNTRY BUMPKIN GIRL AROUND WITH HIM...
HE'D DO THAT TO A GIRL??
HE HAS NO RESPECT FOR WOMEN! I'LL NEVER FORGIVE HIM!
...
YOU ALMOST SOUND A LITTLE... JEALOUS?
HE'S...
HE'S A PIECE OF TRASH!
OH HEY, WHAT LEVEL ARE YOU AT NOW?
MUMBLE
WHY DO I NEED TO TELL YOU?
MUMBLE
I CAN'T WAIT FOR THAT WAVE TO COME!

VERY NICE TO MEET YOU, I AM ANEKO YUSAGI, THE AUTHOR OF THE
ORIGINAL LIGHT NOVEL.
SEEING MY OWN WORK TURNED INTO A MANGA HAS BEEN AN AMAZING
EXPERIENCE. TO SEE IT REWORKED AS A MANGA, TO SEE THE WORLD
COME TO LIFE IN A WAY THAT IS IMPOSSIBLE WITH JUST WORDS,
HAS MADE ME VERY HAPPY INDEED.
MINAMI SEIRA SENSEI, AIYA KYU SENSEI, THE EDITORIAL TEAM,
AND EVERYONE AT MEDIA FACTORY, AND YES, TO YOU, MY READERS:
THANK YOU VERY MUCH!
PLEASE CONTINUE READING!

❖

AUTHOR: ANEKO YUSAGI

 COMMENTARY FROM THE AUTHOR AND CHARACTER DESIGNER

CONGRATULATIONS ON THE SALE OF YOUR FIRST MANGA VOLUME!
WHILE I AM ALREADY VERY FAMILIAR WITH THE STORY, IT'S
STILL VERY INTERESTING TO SEE IT COME TO LIFE AS A MANGA. THERE
ARE MANY WAYS TO TELL A STORY THAT ONLY WORK IN THE MANGA MEDI-
UM. I CAN'T WAIT TO FOLLOW THIS MANGA WITH EACH MONTH'S ISSUE.
THERE ARE SO MANY SCENES I WASN'T ABLE TO PORTRAY IN MY ILLUS-
TRATIONS, AND TO SEE THEM DONE HERE IS EVEN BETTER AND MORE
SATISFYING THAN I COULD HAVE HOPED.
I'M VERY HAPPY.
MY FAVORITE PART OF THIS VOLUME WAS SEEING RAPHTALIA SEATED,
BUT FROM BEHIND.
HER TAIL IS SO FLUFFY (LAUGHS)!

❖

CHARACTER DESIGNER: MINAMI SEIRA

The Rising of the Shield Hero: The Manga Companion Volume 01
© Aiya Kyu 2014
© Aneko Yusagi 2014
First published by KADOKAWA in 2014 in Japan.
English translation rights arranged by One Peace Books
under the license from KADOKAWA CORPORATION, Japan.

ISBN: 978-1-935548-70-6

Written by Aiya Kyu
Original Story by Aneko Yusagi
Character Design by Minami Seira
English Edition Published by One Peace Books 2015

Printed in Canada
10 11 12 13 14 15

One Peace Books
43-32 22nd Street STE 204 Long Island City New York 11101
www.onepeacebooks.com